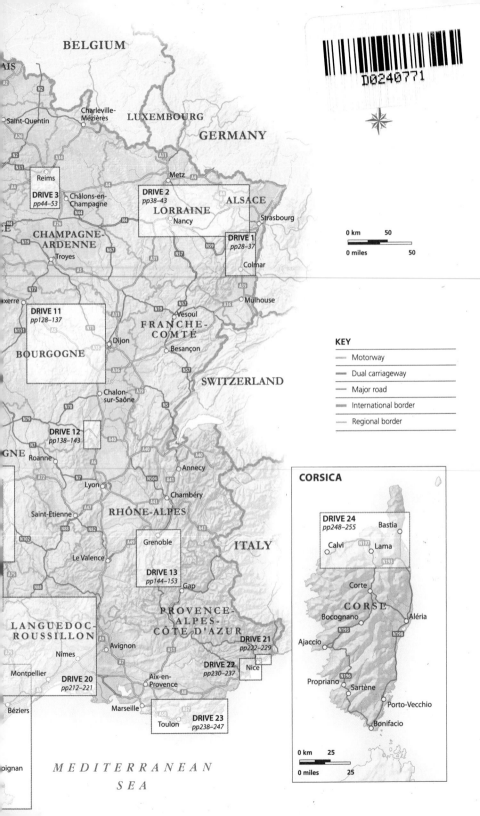

BELGIUM

AIS

Saint-Quentin

Charleville-
Mézières

LUXEMBOURG

GERMANY

Metz

DRIVE 3
pp44–53

Reims

Châlons-en-
Champagne

DRIVE 2
pp38–43

LORRAINE

Nancy

ALSACE

Strasbourg

DRIVE 1
pp28–37

Colmar

CHAMPAGNE-
ARDENNE

Troyes

Mulhouse

Vesoul

DRIVE 11
pp128–137

FRANCHE-
COMTÉ

Dijon

Besançon

BOURGOGNE

SWITZERLAND

Chalon-
sur-Saône

DRIVE 12
pp138–143

Roanne

GNE

Annecy

Lyon

Chambéry

Saint-Étienne

RHÔNE-ALPES

Le Valence

Grenoble

ITALY

DRIVE 13
pp144–153

Gap

PROVENCE-
ALPES-
CÔTE D'AZUR

DRIVE 21
pp222–229

LANGUEDOC-
ROUSSILLON

Avignon

Nîmes

DRIVE 22
pp230–237

Nice

Montpellier

DRIVE 20
pp212–221

Aix-en-
Provence

Béziers

Marseille

DRIVE 23
pp238–247

Toulon

pignan

MEDITERRANEAN
SEA

D0240771

0 km   50

0 miles   50

KEY

— Motorway

— Dual carriageway

— Major road

— International border

— Regional border

CORSICA

DRIVE 24
pp248–255

Bastia

Calvi

Lama

Corte

CORSE

Bocognano

Aléria

Ajaccio

Propriano

Sartène

Porto-Vecchio

Bonifacio

0 km   25

0 miles   25

EYEWITNESS TRAVEL

BACK ROADS
FRANCE

EYEWITNESS TRAVEL

BACK ROADS
FRANCE

CONTRIBUTORS:

Rosemary Bailey, Fay Franklin,

Nick Inman, Nick Rider,

Tristan Rutherford, Tamara Thiessen,

Kathryn Tomasetti

DK

LONDON, NEW YORK,
MELBOURNE, MUNICH AND DELHI
www.dk.com

MANAGING EDITOR Aruna Ghose

EDITORIAL MANAGER Ankita Awasthi

DESIGN MANAGER Kavita Saha

PROJECT EDITOR Souvik Mukherjee

EDITORS Trisha Bora,
Parvati M. Krishnan

PROJECT DESIGNER Shruti Singhi

DESIGNER Neha Sethi

PICTURE RESEARCH Sumita Khatwani

DTP DESIGNER Azeem Siddiqui

CARTOGRAPHY
Uma Bhattacharya,
Mohammad Hassan, Suresh Kumar,
Lovell Johns Ltd

ILLUSTRATIONS
Arun Pottirayil

Printed and bound in China by
South China Printing Company (Ltd)

First published in Great Britain in 2010 by Dorling
Kindersley Limited, 80 Strand, London
WC2R 0RL, UK, A Penguin Company

12 13 14 15 10 9 8 7 6 5 4 3 2 1

Reprinted with revisions 2013

Copyright 2010, 2013 © Dorling
Kindersley Limited, London

A CIP catalogue record is available from the
British Library.

ISBN 978-1-4093-8768-8

Jacket: Lavender field, Provence-Alpes-Côte d'Azur

MIX
Paper from
responsible sources
FSC™ C018179
www.fsc.org

CONTENTS

Above View over the beach and old town of
Villefranche-sur-Mer, Provence-Alpes-Côte d'Azur

Below Avenue-du-Viaduc, Die, Rhône-Alpes   **Below** Poppies along the route in the Médoc region

Above Château de Bazoches, Côte d'Or

Above Spectacular view of the mountains from the Belvédère de l'Obiou, Rhône-Alpes.

Below Town hall, Arreau, Hautes-Pyrénées   **Below** Sign for St-Palais-sur-Mer, Charente-Maritime

Title page Panaromic view of the vineyards in Alsace
Half-title page Renaissance buildings in Quercy-Perigord in the Dordogne valley

About this Book

The 24 driving tours in this guide reflect the fantastic diversity of France. One of the largest countries in Europe, its landscape ranges from rugged mountain plateaux to lush, rolling farmland, from tranquil river valleys to wild, rocky coastlines. This landscape has influenced each region's unique cultural identity: its architecture, cuisine, customs and festivals.

By guiding readers away from the most commonly explored tourist routes (although not missing out on any must-see places en route), the insider knowledge of each tour rewards visitors with the sights, sounds and flavours of the real France – the one that other visitors speed through on the *autoroutes* – and delightful discoveries at every turn.

Getting Started

The guide begins with all the practical information you need to plan a driving holiday in France. This includes an overview of ways to get there; tips on bringing your own vehicle or hiring one; details of documentation necessary and in-depth motoring advice, including the rules of the road; where and when you can buy petrol; and what to do if your car breaks down. There is also information on health, money and communications, as well as a guide to the lodging and dining options available, from luxury hotels to camping, and from gourmet restaurants to riverside picnics. A language section at the back lists essential words and phrases, including key driving-related vocabulary.

The Drives

The main touring section of the guide is divided into leisurely drives, ranging in duration from one to seven days. All the tours are on paved roads and can be undertaken in a standard vehicle. No special driving skills are required.

The drives have been chosen to encompass every region of France, from the lush orchards of Normandy and the rugged cliffs and coves of Brittany to the breathtaking passes of the Pyrenees and the sun-soaked Provençal coast. There are drives to

appeal to lovers of culture, history and architecture; outdoor types and beach-bound families; gastronomes and wine buffs; and those who enjoy taking the road less travelled.

To help visitors choose and plan the trip, each drive begins with a list of highlights and a clearly mapped itinerary. There is advice on the best time of year to do the drive, road conditions, market days and major festival dates. The tour pages contain detailed descriptions of each sight and activity, linked by clear driving instructions. Side panels offer information on the most authentic places to stay and eat. Tinted boxes feature background information, fascinating anecdotes or suggestions for extra activities. These might include details of a local festival or regional speciality; tips for a wine-tasting tour; or information on the least-known beach. Each drive also features at least one mapped town or countryside walking tour, designed to take a maximum of two hours at a gentle pace with stops along the way.

Using the Sheet Map

A pull-out road map of the entire country is supplied. This map contains all the information you need to drive around the country and to navigate between the tours. All motorways, major roads, airports, both domestic and international, plus all the ferry ports are also clearly identified. This makes the pull-out map an excellent addition to the drive itinerary maps within the book. There is a map index for quick and easy location of sights. The map is further supplemented by a clear distance chart so you can gauge the distances between the major cities.

The flexible nature of the tours means that some can be linked to create a longer driving holiday; conversely, they can be dipped into to plan day trips while based in one particular region.

Top left Imposing Château Guillaume-le-Conquérant, Falaise, Basse-Normandie **Top right** Magnificent Viaduc de Millau **Middle left** Restaurants in the old town of Nice **Middle right** Terrace café in Bordeaux **Below left** Rolling vineyards of the Montagne de Reims **Below right** Grand Château de Chambord **Right** Cars passing by the peaks of the Pyrénéan mountains

Introducing France

France is a land of contrasts that cannot be discovered from its network of *autoroutes*. It is the back roads – often tree-lined, perhaps with a river running alongside – that lead to the heart of France. By driving the back roads you can enjoy sea-fresh oysters at a Breton shack or sip Chablis from the winemaker's tasting glass; watch eagles circling below from an Alpine road or flamingos drifting over a Mediterranean lake; browse market stalls for home-grown asparagus or hand-crafted olivewood bowls. On the back roads, the France that some say no longer exists is still alive and well and waiting to be discovered.

When to Go

Each of the drives suggests ideal times to do the trip, either because the scenery is especially attractive at a particular time of year, a festival is taking place, a seasonal local product is available, or for any of countless other reasons unique to a particular region. The weather is, of course, a key factor in choosing the right time. In mid-western, northwest, and north-ern France, it is generally rare to have extremes of temperature. Atlantic winds tend to bring warm summers, with rainfall possible at any time, and cool, wet winters, especially in coastal areas. In the southwest, summers are hotter, sunnier and more settled than further north, with short but heavy periods of rain; winters are pleasantly mild, with occasional brief cold spells. The east experiences continental extremes of cold, frosty winters, and hot summer weather with moderate, often thundery rainfall. The Pyrénées, Alps, Vosges and Jura mountains are the coldest parts of France, with heavy snow in winter; summer and autumn can also be quite wet. The higher parts of the Massif Central can also be cold and wet or snowy in winter. The southern Alps, Pyrénées and the Massif Central can be pleas-antly warm in summer, but low cloud and rain can arrive quite suddenly. The Mediterranean region has long, hot, dry summers punctuated by short, dramatic thunderstorms, and generally sunny, mild winters except when fierce, bitter winds, such as the Mistral, blow beneath deceptively clear blue skies.

Times to Avoid

The tours also advise on times to avoid, perhaps because the weather is inhospitable or the roads are impassable. Despite the relative emptiness of French roads, there are certain times when it is best to avoid travelling if possible. At the start of the holiday season (the *Grand Départ*), main routes to the south are busiest; towards the end, the situation reverses. By checking with traffic organizations such as **Bison Futé** *(see p18)* visitors should be able to avoid the worst traffic jams. Conversely, while it is pleasant to take a holiday out of season, check that hotels and sights on the proposed trip are open. Some popular southern destinations do not reopen in full until after Easter.

Festivals

In spring, **Easter** is marked by concerts of sacred music and processions, while **Carnaval** is celebrated with dancing and street festivals. Flower festivals take place in the south, and small villages host charming and very traditional celebrations when they move their animals from winter to summer pastures. Summer is the season for local *fêtes*, and dates such as the summer solstice and **Bastille Day** are marked with fireworks and parades. Fishing villages often host *fêtes de la mer*. Open-air music and drama festivals, such as those at Avignon and Nice, also abound.

Autumn sees festivals dedicated to local produce; wine is, of course, the most important, and the grape harvest is marked by celebrations in every wine village and town. Winter celebrations revolve around Advent, **Christmas** and the **New Year**, and lively Christmas markets and fairs are held across the country.

Public Holidays

New Year's Day (1 Jan)
Easter Sunday & Monday (varies)
Ascension (6th Thu after Easter)
Whitsun (2nd Mon after Ascension)
Labour Day (1 May)
Victory in Europe Day (8 May)
Bastille Day (14 Jul)
Assumption (15 Aug)
All Saints' Day (1 Nov)
Remembrance Day (11 Nov)
Christmas Day (25 Dec)

Left Glorious view from Roquebrune towards Nice **Right** Flowers on sale at the country market of St-Pierre-sur-Dives, Pays d'Auge

Getting to France

France benefits from excellent air, road and rail networks, both internal and international. Direct flights from all over the world serve Paris and regional airports. Paris is the hub of Europe's high-speed rail network, including Eurostar to London, Thalys to Brussels and high-speed TGVs to Geneva, Frankfurt and Munich, as well as France's vast and efficient internal state railway system, SNCF. Motorways cross over into all neighbouring countries including, via the Channel Tunnel, the UK. France can also be reached by frequent Channel and Mediterranean ferry services.

Above A 1960s souvenir glass ashtray from Air France, the national airline

Arriving by Air

France is served by nearly all international airlines. **Air France** has direct flights from over 100 cities worldwide. Full-service and budget carriers, such as **British Airways** and **Ryanair** fly direct from London and other UK and Irish airports to Paris and a number of regional destinations. From North America there are direct flights to Paris on several major carriers, such as **American Airlines** and **Delta Airlines**, with internal links to regional airports such as Nice and Lyon. Connecting flights operate to Paris from Australia and New Zealand. There are direct flights to Corsica from several UK airports as well as from Orly, Nice, Montpellier and Lyon.

The two main Paris airports are Roissy-Charles-de-Gaulle (CDG) and Orly. CDG is 23 km (14 miles) northeast of the city centre and Orly is 14 km (9 miles) south of the city.

Arriving by Sea

There are numerous ship and catamaran crossings between the UK and continental ports. **P&O Ferries** run frequent services between Dover and Calais. Freight carrier **Norfolkline** and **DFDS Seaways** also take cars on their crossings from Dover to Dunkerque, while **P&O North Sea Ferries** runs an overnight service from Hull to Zeebrugge in Belgium, which has good road links to the whole of northeast France.

Transmanche Ferries/LD Lines sail to Dieppe from Newhaven and to Le Havre from Portsmouth, Newhaven and Rosslare, Ireland. **Condor Ferries** have a summer-only fast ferry from Poole to St-Malo. They also run a service between St Malo, Jersey and Guernsey and a summer Sunday timetable from Portsmouth to Cherbourg.

Brittany Ferries runs a fast ferry from Portsmouth to St-Malo, Cherbourg (summer only) and Caen. They also sail from Poole to Cherbourg. There is also a service from Plymouth to Roscoff and to Santander and Bilbao in Spain (convenient for southwest France), and a weekly overnight sailing from Cork, Ireland, to Roscoff.

Corsica is accessible by **SNCM Ferryterranée** ferries from Nice, Marseille and Toulon. **Corsica Ferries** also runs from Toulon and Nice to Corsica and to Corsica from Italy, with sailings from Savona, Livorno and Piombino. **La Meridionale** serves Bastia from Marseille. SNCM Ferryterranée also runs ferries from Marseille to several destinations in North Africa.

The Channel Tunnel

The Channel Tunnel is a 52-km (31-mile) rail link beneath the English Channel. There are two ways to use it. **Eurotunnel** rail shuttles carry vehicles and their passengers (who remain with their car) on specially constructed trains between Folkestone in Kent and Sangatte near Calais. The terminals link directly to motorways – the M20 in England, the A16 in France. LPG-powered vehicles are not permitted on Eurotunnel. Rail passengers without transport can board **Eurostar** trains in London or Kent, and disembark at Paris, Disneyland Paris, Calais-Fréthun or Lille. In summer a direct service runs to Avignon on Saturdays, and in winter there are direct trains from London to the ski resorts of the French Alps.

Arriving by Rail

For travellers from Britain, Eurostar gives access to **SNCF**, the French rail network. From Lille, passengers can board TGVs bypassing Paris and continuing southeast to Lyon, the Rhône Valley and the Mediterranean, or southwest to Brittany, the Loire Valley and southwest France. Eurostar's Paris destination is the Gard du Nord; Thalys trains from Brussels, Cologne and Amsterdam arrive here too. Artesia runs trains from Rome, Milan, Turin, Florence and Venice to Paris and Lyon. Riviera trains link Italian and French cities along the Mediterranean coast. A TGV route connects several west German cities to eastern France and Paris. From Barcelona, Alicante and Valencia in Spain, high-speed Talgo trains run to Montpellier during the day, while their overnight sleeper, the Joan Miró, links Barcelona and Paris. **Rail Europe** sells a wide range of passes for European train travel, including Motorail, a summer-only service to transport travellers with their cars from Calais to southern France. From Paris's six stations, routes fan out to about 6,000 French destinations. The main TGV stations are Gare du Nord, Gare de l'Est for Champagne and Alsace, Gare de Lyon for Burgundy and southeastern France and Gare Montparnasse for Brittany, west and southwest France.

Arriving by Road

France's *autoroutes* are fully integrated into the European road network, and travellers are rarely stopped at border controls. From Belgium, there are four major links: between Veurne and Dunkerque (E40–A16); between Kortrijk and

Tournai and Lille (E17–A22 and E429–A27); and between Mons and Valenciennes (E19–A2). From Luxembourg the E25–A31 runs via Thionville to Metz. From Germany major border crossings include Saarbrucken (E50–A6) and numerous links between the E35 and the A35, notably at Strasbourg and Mulhouse. From Switzerland, the two most important crossings are at Basel in the north (E60–A35) and Geneva (E62/E25–A40/A41) in the south. Note that many Alpine passes are closed in winter. The Mont Blanc tunnel connects Courmayeur in Italy with Chamonix in France (E40–A25). Further south, the Fréjus tunnel runs between Bardonecchia and Modane (E70–A43). For visitors to the south of France, the spectacular Riviera *corniche* roads link San Remo with Menton, Monaco, Nice and beyond (E74–A8 and others). The two main crossings from Spain into France are at either end of the Pyrénées, and can get congested in summer. On the Atlantic coast, the A8–A63 runs from Spain to France near St-Jean-de-Luz; on the Mediterranean side, the A7–A9 crosses the border between La Jonquera and Le Perthus. As with the other mountain ranges, mountain passes make for an attractive, more leisurely alternative, but are often closed in winter. For advice on road conditions and possible delays, consult **Bison Futé** or **CNIR** (see p19).

Below far left Roissy-Charles-de-Gaulle Airport, Paris **Below left** Ferry of SNCM Ferryterranée **Below middle** Ticket validating machine at a French station **Below right** High-speed TGV train pulling out of Montparnasse station, Paris

DIRECTORY

AIRLINES

Air France
36 54 (within France); www.airfrance.fr

American Airlines
1-800-433-7300 (US/Canada), 01 55 17 43 41 (France); www.aa.com

British Airways
0844 493 0 787 (UK), 08 25 82 54 00 (France); www.britishairways.com

Delta Airlines
800-241-4141 (US/Canada), 08 11 64 00 05 (France); www.delta.com

Ryanair
0871 246 0000 (UK), 0818 30 30 30 (Ireland), 08 92 23 23 75 (France); www.ryanair.com

FERRY SERVICES

Brittany Ferries
0871 244 0744 (UK), 0845 828 828 (France); www.brittany-ferries.com

Condor Ferries
0845 609 1024 (UK), 02 33 88 44 88 (France); www.condorferries.com

Corsica Ferries
0845 609 1024 (UK), 04 95 32 95 95 (France); www.corsica-ferries.co.uk

La Meridionale
810 20 13 20 (France); www.lameridionale.com

Norfolkline/ DFDS Seaways
0208 127 8305 (UK), 03 28 59 01 01 (France); www.norfolkline.com

P&O Ferries
08716 642 121 (UK), 08 25 12 01 56 (France); www.poferries.com

SNCM Ferryterranée
08 25 88 80 88 (France), 32 60 (within France); www.sncm.fr

Transmanche Ferries/LD Lines
0800 917 1201 (UK), 08 25 30 43 04 (France); www.transmancheferries.com

CHANNEL TUNNEL

Eurostar
08455 191523 (UK), 0892 353 539 (France); www.eurostar.com

Eurotunnel
08705 35 35 35 (UK), 08 10 63 63 04 (France); www.eurotunnel.com

RAIL TRAVEL

Rail Europe
08448 484 064 (UK), 1-622-8600 (US); www.raileurope.co.uk

SNCF
36 35 (within France); www.sncf.com

Practical Information

France's excellent health system, emergency infrastructure and other public services operate smoothly and efficiently, although it pays to have the right documentation in advance. Broadband and mobile phone accessibility is almost universal, and, while banks in smaller towns may keep seemingly erratic hours, most have an ATM outside. The traditional French lunch break still holds sway almost everywhere, with all but the largest shops closing for around two hours and all day on Monday. Many museums are closed on Tuesdays.

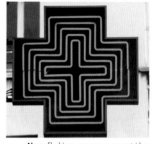

Above Flashing green neon cross outside a French pharmacy

Passports and Visas

EU nationals may enter France with a current valid identity card, but a passport is obligatory for all other visitors. Citizens of the UK will be required to show their passport at UK passport control on leaving and re-entering the UK. Currently there are no visa requirements for EU citizens or visitors from the US, Canada, Australia or New Zealand who plan to stay in France for under three months. For stays longer than this, a visa should be applied for well in advance of your departure (allow at least four weeks) from your local French consulate. Visitors from most other countries require a tourist visa. When applying for a visa, you should be aware that you may be asked to provide details of your travel arrangements, accommodation address and travel insurance. Your consulate will also keep your passport for the duration of your application.

Travel Insurance

All travellers should consider getting travel insurance, and non-EU citizens are obliged to carry medical insurance. A policy will normally cover you for loss or theft of luggage and other belongings such as passports and money, personal accident, delayed or cancelled flights and even abandonment of the holiday by you in certain cases, such as the illness of a family member or business partner. Most also cover you for damage you may cause to a third party.

In general a standard policy will not cover you for hazardous or extreme sports, so if you decide on a day's canoeing, or plan to ski or go rock climbing, make sure that you are covered. Nearly all policies cover legal costs up to a certain level, as do comprehensive motor policies (see p16) in the event of any legal advice or action being needed, for example after an accident.

Health

All EU nationals are entitled to French social security coverage. However, treatment must be paid for and reclaimed, and hospital rates vary widely. For EU visitors, partial reimbursement can be obtained if you have a European Health Insurance Card (EHIC, which British citizens can order online from the Department of Health before travel). You should be given a signed statement regarding your treatment (a *feuille de soins*) to be sent to the nearest Sickness Insurance Office while you are still in France. The refund process takes about a couple of months.

In case of a medical emergency, you can call **SAMU** (*Service d'Aide Médicale Urgence*). However, it is often faster to call the **Sapeurs Pompiers** (the fire service), who offer a first aid and ambulance service. This is especially true in rural areas where the local fire station is likely to be much closer than the ambulance service based in town. Paramedics are called *secouristes*.

Casualty departments (*service des urgences*) in public hospitals can deal with most medical problems. Your consulate should be able to recommend an English-speaking doctor in the area.

In France, pharmacists can diagnose health problems and suggest appropriate treatments. Pharmacies have a green cross outside (often flashing green neon). If closed, a card in the window will

Above left French fire engine **Above right** Signboard of the French *gendarmerie*, the military police force

give details of the nearest *pharmacie de garde*; these will be open on Sundays and at night.

If you suffer from a medical condition such as diabetes or epilepsy, or have a serious allergy, an international medical ID bracelet or other alert can warn paramedics or hospital staff to your condition and provide a multilingual phone service that holds details of your condition. If any condition requires you to carry a syringe when travelling by air, ask your doctor for a letter of notification of your condition and keep it with your medical equipment.

Personal Security

Violent crime is not a major problem in France. Take the same precautions that you would at home. If you are involved in an argument or accident, avoid confrontation. In potentially difficult situations you should stay calm, be polite and speak French if you can; this may help to defuse the situation.

Beware of pickpockets in bustling town centres, and if leaving your car, put belongings in the boot. Keep valuables concealed and, if carrying a bag or case, never let it out of your sight. Keep an especially close eye

on your mobile phone and camera. Only carry as much cash as you think you will need. Having said all that, in villages and small towns off the beaten track in France, you are more likely to have someone run after you to give you back an item you have dropped or mistakenly left behind.

Telephone or visit the **police** to report a crime that takes place in a town, missing persons or stolen property, robbery or assault. The *commissariat de police* is the police headquarters. In a small town or village, go to the town hall (*mairie*), which will only be open during office hours, or the nearest **gendarmerie**. The Gendarmerie Nationale is the part of the police body that deals with all crimes outside urban areas. If your passport is lost or stolen, call your embassy or consulate.

Hunting with shotguns is an integral part of French rural life. If you are walking in the countryside during hunting season (August–February and especially Sunday) dress in highly visible colours and make sure you avoid any place which has signs relating to *la chasse* – these indicate that the area concerned is being used for hunting.

DIRECTORY

PASSPORTS AND VISAS

Australia
4 rue Jean Ray, Paris, 75015; 01 40 59 33 00; www.france.embassy.gov.au

United Kingdom
35 rue du Faubourg St-Honoré, Paris, 75008; 01 44 51 31 00; http://ukinfrance.fco.gov.uk/en

United States
2 avenue Gabriel, Paris, 75008; 01 43 12 22 22; www.france.usembassy.gov

HEALTH

Department of Health
www.dh.gov.uk

SAMU (ambulance)
15

Sapeurs Pompiers (fire and ambulance)
18 or 112

PERSONAL SECURITY

Police or Gendarmerie
17

Below far left Emergency heart defibrillator kit **Below left** Pharmacy housed in a half-timbered building **Below middle** Passport and boarding pass **Below right** Fire hazard sign **Below far right** Soap on sale in St-Tropez

Communications

All French telephone numbers have ten digits. The first two indicate the region: 01 for Paris and the Île de France; 02 for the northwest; 03, the northeast; 04, the southeast and Corsica; and 05, the southwest. A 06 number indicates a mobile phone.

Most mobile phones from European or Mediterranean countries function normally in France. US cell phones need to be at least "triple band" to work in France. Coverage by the three main networks is good, and improving all the time. Making and receiving calls while "roaming" (not in your phone's home country) can be very expensive, but users do not pay to receive a text message.

In rural areas, where mobile reception can be weak or even non-existent, there will always be a payphone *(cabine téléphonique)*. Many accept credit cards (with a PIN), otherwise you will need to buy a phone card *(télécarte)*. Very few payphones take coins. Sold in tobacconists *(tabacs)*, post offices and some newsagents, phone cards are available in 50 or 120 units and are simple to use. For local calls, a unit lasts up to 6 minutes.

The Internet is readily accessible everywhere in France, with broadband (called ADSL) now widely available. Many tourist offices and some libraries provide Internet access for a small fee. In-room Wi-Fi *(wee-fee)* access is often complimentary in hotels that cater to business travellers, and free hotspots can increasingly be found in cafés and bars aimed at the younger market, and in branches of a well-known international burger chain. With Wi-Fi,

the Internet café is becoming a thing of the past in France.

The French postal system is called La Poste, and you will see this name on a distinctive yellow background outside post offices and on post boxes. All international mail is sent by air, so sending parcels home can be costly. Stamps *(timbres)* are sold at La Poste and at *tabacs*. Allow up to two days for delivery of a letter within France, and up to five days for international delivery.

Above Sign advertising a regional newspaper in Mittelbergheim, Alsace

Money and Banks

France is one of the European nations using the Euro (€). You may bring any amount of cash into France, but anything over €7,500 must be declared on arrival and departure. Traveller's cheques are the safest way to carry money; **American Express** cheques are accepted. Cash Passports, prepaid currency cards that are loaded before travelling and can be used in shops and ATMs abroad, are also gaining popularity. They are available from **Thomas Cook**, **Travelex** and various banks. However, credit or debit cards, which can be used to withdraw local currency, are most convenient. Bureaux de change are located at airports, large stations, and in some hotels and shops, but banks usually offer the best rates.

Most banks have an ATM (automatic teller machine) open 24 hours a day, which accepts credit cards in the **Visa/Carte Bleu** or **Mastercard** groups and debit cards (Switch, Maestro, Cirrus) enabling you to withdraw money in local currency from your own bank account. If there is no ATM you can withdraw up to €300 per day on Visa at the foreign counter of

any bank that has the Visa sign. Banking hours vary greatly, and ATMs may run out of notes at peak times. The most commonly accepted credit cards are MasterCard/Eurocard and Visa/Carte Bleu. Many businesses do not accept American Express credit cards. Cards issued in France are "chip-and-PIN". Most retailers have machines designed to read both a chip and a magnetic strip. You will be asked to key in your PIN code and press the green key on the keypad. If the microchip cannot be read, have the card swiped through the magnetic reader *(bande magnetique)*.

Tourist Information

All major French cities and large towns have *offices de tourisme*. Small towns and even villages have *syndicats d'initiative*. Both can provide town plans, advice on accommodation, and information on regional recreational and cultural activities. In small rural villages, the town hall often provides local information.

Before you leave for France, you can get information from French Government Tourist Offices, called **Maisons de la France**.

Above left Tourist Information office in Hautvillers **Above middle** Post office in Espelette **Above right** Sign for a tourist office

Opening Hours

Most sights are open 10am–noon and 2–5pm with one late evening per week. Most are closed on public holidays and on either Monday or Tuesday. There is usually an admission charge, which may be lowered or waived on Sundays or for concession card holders (students and those over 60 years of age).

Shops (even some supermarkets) usually close for at least 2 hours at lunchtime, although department stores and hypermarkets remain open all day. In the south, the lunch break may be longer but shops tend to stay open later. Virtually everything is closed on Sunday afternoon; bakers, newsagents and some supermarkets are often open on Sunday morning.

Disabled Facilities

While most museums and larger sites, as well as restaurants, now provide at least partial wheelchair access, the very nature of some historic buildings implies inaccessibility. The number of hotels with adapted rooms is increasing steadily. More information can be found on the website of the **GIHP**. For information on driving in France, *see p19*. If you are travelling to France from the UK with an assistance dog or guide dog, the animal will have to comply with the terms of the Pet Passport scheme. However, it is down to the individual airline or ferry company to decide whether or not your dog can accompany you onto the passenger deck or into the cabin, so be sure to check before you book. On the Channel Tunnel, your dog will travel in your vehicle with you.

Time

France uses Central European Time (CET), which is one hour ahead of Greenwich Mean Time (GMT). Summer (Daylight Saving) Time comes into effect from 2am on the last Sunday of March, and ceases at 2am on the last Sunday in October. The French use the 24-hour clock.

Electricity

The voltage in France is 220 volts. Plugs have two round pins, or three round pins for appliances that need to be earthed. Some hotels offer built-in adaptors for shavers only and many now offer hairdryers.

Below far left Banque de France in Bastia, Corsica **Below left** Tourist office in Grimaud, Provence **Below middle** Old church clock **Below right** Bright yellow French post box **Below far right** Sign for an Internet café

DIRECTORY

COMMUNICATIONS
International directory enquiries
11 87 00

Reverse charge calls
30 06

To call France from abroad
UK and US: 00 33; Australia: 00 11 33; omit the first 0 of the French number

To call home from France
Dial 00 then the country code; omit the first 0 of the number being called

Country codes
Australia: 61; Ireland: 353; New Zealand: 64; UK: 44; US and Canada: 1

MONEY AND BANKS
American Express
08 00 83 28 20 (card and cheques)

MasterCard
08 00 90 13 87

Thomas Cook
www.thomascook.com

Travelex
www.travelex.com

Visa/Carte Bleu
08 00 90 11 79

MAISONS DE LA FRANCE
Australia
Level 13, 25 Bligh Street, 2000 NSW, Sydney; (2) 9231 5244; http://au.franceguide.com

United Kingdom
Lincoln House, 330 High Holborn, London WC1V 7JH; 09068 244 123; http://uk.franceguide.com

United States
825 3rd Ave, 29th floor (entrance on 50th St), New York, NY 10022; (514) 288 1904; http://us.franceguide.com

DISABLED FACILITIES
GIHP
www.gihpnational.org

Pet Passport
www.defra.gov.uk/wildlife-pets/pets/travel

Driving in France

France has one of the densest road networks in Europe, with modern motorways allowing quick and easy access to all parts of the country. However, it is only by driving the back roads that you will discover the real France. This will, of course, mean tackling anything from roundabouts and road signs to herds of sheep in your path. To get the most from your travels, and to do so safely, it is essential to familiarize yourself with the rules and requirements for driving in France before you set out.

Above No entry road sign

Insurance and Breakdown Cover

Car insurance is a legal requirement in France. If your normal car insurance policy is fully comprehensive, most insurers automatically cover you for up to 90 days' driving in EU countries, so it is not necessary to obtain a "Green Card and Bail Bond", although you may wish to have this as well. Breakdown and accident cover is also recommended, with an English-speaking helpline that can liaise on your behalf with local breakdown assistance (there is currently no nationwide service in France).

What to Take

You should carry your vehicle insurance policy with you, ideally with a statement of cover in French (usually provided by the insurer). It is also compulsory to take the original registration document for the car, as well as a valid driving licence. If you are not the registered owner of the vehicle, carry a letter from the owner giving you permission to drive it. You must also have your passport or national ID card. Any of these documents should be produced upon demand by the police or

gendarmerie. A badge showing the country of registration must be displayed near the rear number plate. The headlights of right-hand-drive cars must be adjusted for left-hand driving or be fitted with deflectors (available at most ports). You must carry a red warning triangle, even if your car is fitted with hazard lights, and also a reflective yellow waistcoat for any person stepping out of the car at the scene of an accident *(see p19)*. Neither a spare bulb kit nor a first aid kit are compulsory but both are recommended. In mountain areas in winter, snow chains *(chaînes)* are often essential.

Road Systems

Most motorways (marked A for *autoroute*) in France have a toll *(péage)* system. Usually, upon joining the system, you collect a ticket showing your point of entry. You do not pay until you reach an exit toll, where you are charged by distance traveled and type of vehicle used. Sections in or around major towns are usually free. Tolls can be paid with cash or credit cards. Motorways are usually in excellent condition and

traffic is normally very light. RNs *(route nationale)* are the main alternative, but can be busy with freight traffic. D *(départementale)* roads are the small, quiet country roads on which you will usually be travelling.

Speed Limits and Fines

Speed limits in France are strictly enforced, with radar traps increasingly common. Fines are payable on the spot and drivers caught exceeding the limit by 25 km/h (15 mph) can have their licence confiscated on the spot. It is illegal to carry a radar detector, even one that is not switched on. If cars coming in the opposite direction flash their headlamps, slow down as they are warning you of a trap ahead.

Speed limits are as follows:
• On *autoroutes*: 130 km/h (80 mph); 110 km/h (68 mph) in wet weather.
• On dual carriageways: 110 km/h (68 mph); 90–100 km/h (55–62 mph) in wet weather.
• On other roads: 90 km/h (55 mph); 80 km/h (50 mph) in wet weather.
• In towns: 50 km/h (30 mph). This applies anywhere in a village, hamlet or city, unless marked otherwise. In some places it may be lower.

Limits are lower if you are towing, if you have held a licence for less than two years, or if there is fog.

Do not drink and drive. The blood-alcohol content limit in France is very low (0.05 per cent) and the penalties extremely high.

Rules of the Road

Take care always to drive on the right in France. Pay extra attention at round-abouts and at crossroads, where it is easy (and dangerous) to forget or get confused. Unless road signs indicate otherwise, *priorité à droite* means that you must give way to any vehicle joining your road from the right, except on roundabouts or from private property. Most major roads outside of built-up areas have the right of way indicated by *passage protégé* signs. Contrary to the UK convention, if there is only room for one car to pass, flashing headlights means the driver doing so is claiming the right of way. Other French motor-ing rules include the compulsory wearing of seatbelts, front and back. For more information, consult the websites of the **UK Foreign Office** and **Opteven** *(see p19)*.

Driving with Children

Children under ten years of age are not allowed in the front seats, other than babies or infants in an official rear-facing child seat (and then only when no airbag is fitted). In the back you must use a restraint system suited to the child's height and weight. This means a child seat is required if the child weighs between 9 and 15 kg (20 and 33 lb). Above this, a seat belt and booster cushion can be used. Motorway rest areas *(aires)* are ideal places for kids to let off steam during long journeys as there are often play facilities *(see p18)*.

Buying Petrol

Diesel *(gazole* or *gas-oil)* and unleaded petrol *(sans plomb)* are sold everywhere in France. LPG *(PLG)* is increasingly available, leaded petrol *(super)* decreasingly so. Large super-markets and hypermarkets are the cheapest places to buy, *autoroute* services the most costly. Most petrol stations are self-service. Out of normal hours, many stations have a credit-card pump but very few accept anything other than French cards. Village and supermarket stations usually close at lunchtime, and rural stations are often closed on Sundays. Petrol prices can vary from region to region. A French Government website *(www.prix-carburants.gouv.fr)* gives frequent updates on lowest prices in each region.

(see p19). *(see p18)*.

INSTRUCTIONS FOR DRIVERS

Allumez vos feux
Switch on headlamps

Attention travaux
Road works

Cedez le passage
Give way

Chaussée deformée
Bumpy or damaged road

Ralentissez
Slow down

Rappel
Restriction continues

Route barrée
Road closed

Sauf riverains
Except for residents/local access
(after a no entry sign)

Sens unique
One way

Vous n'avez pas la priorité
Give way

Above left Road sign for the Route Touristique du Champagne **Above right** Cars on a French motorway **Below far left** Mountain pass altitude sign near Col de Jau, Aude **Below left** Quiet French village road **Below middle** *Autoroute* toll booth **Below right** Petrol pump **Below far right** Road sign cautioning motorists about wildlife crossing

Road Conditions

French roads, *autoroutes* in particular, usually flow freely, but there are exceptions. Try to avoid travelling at French holiday rush periods (*grands départs*). The worst times are at weekends in mid-July, and at the beginning and end of August, when holidays begin and end. Sunday is usually a good day for long journeys as there are very few trucks on the road. If you are bypassing Paris it is best to take motorways on either side of the city rather than tackling the busy inner ring-road (*boulevard péripherique*).

Bison Futé is a government-run initiative to give travellers tips and alternative routes to avoid congestion or heavy traffic. Look out for their green signs, sometimes shortened to "Bis". A map of all their recommended routes can be obtained from **Maisons de la France** (*see p14*) or from one of around 60 Bis offices all over France, and live traffic information is given in English on the *Bison Futé* website. **CNIR** (*Centre National d'Information Routière*) also gives general information on road conditions in English. Local radio stations do the same in French – look out for motorway signs listing their frequencies. For advance weather warnings and forecasts in English for France, contact the **Met Office**. For an online weather forecast, consult **La Chaîne Météo**.

Mountain Roads

Getting to some of France's most spectacular locations and viewpoints will inevitably involve tackling some steep, narrow roads with hairpin bends and sheer drops. In spring, road surfaces may have suffered from the effects of a hard winter, but most are usually in good condition with crash barriers on the sharpest bends and passing points where the road is narrow. Drive slowly, approach blind bends with caution; remember that it is accepted practice to sound your horn and listen for others doing so. Ascending trucks may be very slow, but remain patient and do not try to overtake unless you can see a considerable way ahead. Only stop to admire a view when there is a designated viewpoint.

Driving in Winter

Local municipalities and the *autoroute* organizations are remarkably efficient in keeping roads free from snow and ice, preparing well in advance and sending gritters and snowploughs out day and night to keep arterial roads clear. However, minor roads and alpine passes may be closed completely, or only open to vehicles fitted with snow chains (*chaînes*). A blue sign (*see back endpaper*) indicates where, in snowy conditions, their use is obligatory. Practice fitting them before you go, and keep an old pair of gloves in the

Above Tourist map of the Department of Aude

car to use when doing so in icy conditions. When diversions occur in the mountains they can be lengthy, so make sure your tank is topped up with fuel before setting off. In snowy conditions drive slowly, use a high gear to prevent wheel spin, and try to keep moving, even if very slowly, to avoid loss of traction. If you have to park on a slope, do so facing downhill (an uphill start in icy conditions is not advisable) and put the car into reverse gear once the engine in switched off.

Taking a Break

French motorways have good rest areas (*aires*) every 10–20 km (6–12 miles). At the very least these have toilets and picnic tables; many have play areas, nature walks, fine views, or displays on local themes. In the south, some even have watermist sprays to cool you down. Petrol stations are located every 40 km (25 miles), with shops, restaurants (often very good) and other facilities.

Breakdown or Accident

If your vehicle breaks down, try to get it to as safe a place as possible. Use your hazard warning lights. Put

on a yellow safety vest before getting out of the car, then place the red warning triangle 30 m (100 ft) down the road to alert oncoming traffic *(see p16)*. On motorways, there are orange emergency phones every 2 km (1 mile), or call your breakdown service on the number provided by them. They should be able to take over and contact a local breakdown *(dépannage)* garage.

If your vehicle is involved in a minor traffic accident with a French car, the driver will produce a form called a *constat à l'amiable* (if you have a Green Card you will have an English version called a **European Accident Statement**, or it can be downloaded from the Internet). This is an agreed statement of events. One copy of such a form (there are carbon layers) should be filled in with personal, insurance and vehicle details, a plan of the accident, and indications of damage. Both drivers sign this and keep a copy. You must send a copy to your insurers within five days. Only call the **police** or **gendarmerie** *(see p13)* if someone is hurt or there is a dispute as to what happened. If you do not understand what is going on, you may need to accompany the other driver to the nearest *gendarmerie* to make a statement *(procès-verbal* or PV*)*. In

case of a serious accident, call the police immediately. If you need an **ambulance**, use the emergency phones or dial 15 or 18 *(see p13)*.

Parking

Parking regulations vary from place to place. Most towns operate pay-and-display systems *(horodateurs)*. Some machines accept a parking payment card, as well as cash, that can be purchased from a tobacconist *(tabac)*. Parking bays for which you have to pay are usually indicated with a blue *payant* sign. Parking is normally limited to 2 hours. If you are in a town where parking discs are used, the local tourist office will supply you with one. Temporary discs are also sometimes sold at *tabacs*. Provincial towns often offer free parking from noon to 2pm. In small towns with narrow streets, parking is confined to one side of the street only, alternating at different times of the month. In larger cities, finding a space can be difficult. Cars are often "bumped" along to create more room.

Disabled drivers holding a blue badge can park in marked disabled spaces. However, parking on roads is not automatically free. In some time-restricted car parks, no time limit applies to blue-badge-holders.

DIRECTORY

RULES OF THE ROAD
Opteven
www.opteven.com

UK Foreign Office
www.fco.gov.uk/en/travelling-and-living-overseas/staying-safe/driving-abroad

ROAD CONDITIONS
Bison Futé
www.bison-fute.equipement.gouv.fr

La Chaîne Meteo
www.lachainemeteo.com

CNIR
www.autoroutes.fr

Met Office
0870 900 0100, 00 44 1392 885 680 (UK); www.metoffice.gov.uk

BREAKDOWN OR ACCIDENT
European Accident Statement
http://european-accident-statement.
accidentsketch.com

Above left Parking in front of Cathédrale Notre-Dame de Bayeux **Above right** Busy parking lot near Mont St-Michel **Below far left** Three-lane French motorway **Below left** Road sign for a cycling route **Below middle** Road sign near the Pyrenees **Below right** Road winding through snowcapped peaks in the Rhône-Alpes region

Caravans and Motorhomes/RVs

When crossing to France by ferry, you will need to ensure that your LPG supply, meant for cooking, has been turned off correctly. On Eurotunnel the valves must be sealed and your roof vents opened for safety.

Rules of the road and speed limits are the same for caravans and RVs/motorhomes as they are for cars (*see pp16–17*). Outside of built-up areas, outfits longer than 7 m (25 ft) or heavier than 3.5 tonnes (4 US tons) must leave more than 50 m (165 ft) between them and the vehicle in front. They must also use only the inner two lanes of roads with three or more lanes.

France has a great many well-equipped official campsites, both privately and municipally owned, fully geared up for mobile homes. Good sites in holiday regions fill up quickly at peak times so it is advisable to book ahead or arrive early. Voltage on most sites is 220 volts but can be less. Reverse polarity can occur (when the site's live line is connected to a mobile home's neutral one) so check with a polarity tester before you connect and report any problem.

Sites called **aires de service** (or *aires de stationement*) also offer limited facilities for mobile homes, such as fresh water and waste water disposal, electrical hook-ups *(bournes)* and overnight spaces. There may be a small charge for using these facilities. Caravan organizations, such as **RV Club** and **Caravan Club**, advise against using on-motorway *aires* for overnight stops, especially in the south, as these are a target for thieves.

Above Motorhome parked in a campsite

Calor gas is unavailable in France, but Campingaz is easy to find. Popular brands include Primagaz, Butagaz and Totalgaz. A deposit is required for cylinders and you will need a regulator as pressure varies widely.

Motorbikes

French rules of the road apply to bikers too, but there are extra things to remember. Your headlamp must be on at all times, and helmets must be worn by both driver and pillion. Filtering or lane splitting (riding between lanes) is tolerated, but if you have an accident as a result, it will be considered your fault.

Almost all public parking garages are free for motorbikes (you can tell if the barrier is only three-quarter width). However, do not park in a car space. On a toll *autoroute* you will need to go through a manned (as opposed to credit card) lane to get the motorcycle discount.

There is a great deal of biker camaraderie in France, up to and including the motorcycle *gendarmes*, but do not take liberties and always be courteous to fellow motorcyclists. A greeting or a thank you is often marked by an outstretched foot.

Car and Motorhome/RV Hire

All the major vehicle-hire companies operate in France. It is worth doing an Internet search or ringing around before you leave home, as there are numerous special deals for rentals booked and prepaid in the UK and USA and you can save as much as 50 per cent. **Autos Abroad** is a very competitive broker for other companies such as Europcar, Budget and Alamo.

For car hire booked in combination with flights, your travel company can usually offer a good price. SNCF, the French national railway, offers combined train and car-hire fares with convenient collection points at over 200 stations. **Rail Europe** *(see p11)* can provide details.

For non-EU residents planning to drive in France for a minimum of three weeks, the best option is the short-term tax-free purchase-and-buy-back scheme (sometimes called TT leasing) offered by Citroën, Peugeot and Renault. **Drivetravel** has details and offers. They also offer a range of mobile home/RV and motorcycle hire. For the ultimate convenience in luxury travel hire a Mercedes-Benz CLS Coupes, a Jaguar

XF Saloon or a Range Rover Vogue from **Europcar**.

To hire a vehicle in France, you must be over 20 years old and (usually) under 70, and have held a full licence for more than a year. Your hire policy should include Collision Damage Waiver and Theft Protection, as well as unlimited mileage. Any extras, such as child seats, SatNav (GPS) or snow chains, should be booked in advance. If you are uneasy about left-hand driving you may wish to consider hiring a vehicle with automatic transmission.

You will need to produce your passport, driver's licence and a credit card (an impression will be taken as a security deposit) when you collect the vehicle. It will normally be supplied with a full tank of petrol, and it is cheapest for you to return it refilled, or you will be charged at a high rate. When you collect the vehicle, check it against the paperwork supplied for dents, scratches or other damage.

If you are renting a motorhome/RV you may well be shown a video on its operation and facilities while your paperwork is being completed. You should also be shown around inside and out. Take time to check that interior facilities are in good condition, and working, before you set out. If you return the vehicle less clean than you found it, you may be charged up to €100 for cleaning.

Maps

In this guide, each drive has a detailed itineray map with the drive route and the sights clearly marked. Each suggested walk has a map as well. There is also a pull-out sheet map covering the entire country.

It is advisable to carry a road atlas. The two most useful series of maps are **Michelin** and **IGN**. The Michelin map, covering the whole of France at a scale of 1:1,000,000, is good for planning your trip – look for the distinctive red cover. The excellent Michelin road atlas has generously overlapping maps at a scale of 1:200,000 and is the best map for driving currently available. Individual regional maps, with yellow covers, are available at the same scale. IGN (*Institut Géographique National*) has its own set of maps, with scales varying from 1:250,000 down to invaluable, detailed maps for walkers at 1:25,000, recognizable by their turquoise blue covers.

Espace IGN, just off the Champs-Elysées in Paris, is a haven for map lovers. All newsagents and petrol stations in France stock the more commonly used maps.

Above left Road sign for camping and caravans **Above right** Motorcyclist in Le Faou, Bretagne **Below far left** Camper-jeep in Corsica **Below left** Caravan in Pourville, Haute-Normandie **Below middle** Parking sign for caravans **Below right** Caravans in a campsite, Basse-Normandie

Where to Stay

The accommodation in this guide has been specially selected to reflect the undiscovered France. On the back roads you will find charming, family-run *chambres d'hôtes*, offering comfortable rooms in anything from cottage to château; small, welcoming hotels where the *patron* cooks local specialities and whose little bar is the focus of village life; and rare delights like luxury campsites, set amid vines or under shady pines by the lapping Mediterranean.

Above Hotel in Dabo in the region of Lorraine

Chambres d'Hôtes

These are the French equivalent of bed-and-breakfast – and yet somehow so much more than the term implies. They come in all shapes and sizes, from tiny cottages and rustic farmhouses to historic châteaux and manor houses. Once offering very simple accommodation, and seen as the budget option, they now offer a chance to experience real French hospitality and local flavour, often with stylish or country-chic decor, *en suite* facilities, Internet access and other comforts, yet at a very reasonable price. Breakfast is, of course, included in the room price and may well include local produce and home-made preserves. Many offer dinner – *table d'hôte* – on advance request. Your host will almost certainly serve local food and wine specialities, but there is unlikely to be a choice of menu. If you have dietary requirements you are advised to notify the owners in advance.

For most owners the *chambres d'hôtes* are as much a labour of love as a business. In all cases, due to the small, family-run nature of these enterprises, you should reserve well in advance, online or by phone. Over 25,000 of these establishments are registered and inspected by **Gîtes de France**. Their reliable grading system is in "ears of wheat" *(épis)*: one signifies basic rooms; two means comfortable rooms, at least one with private shower or bath; three guarantees well-appointed rooms, each with its own private bathroom; and four means luxury rooms or suites, each with its own private, fully-fitted bathroom, housed in a residence of character, in a beautiful setting.

To be sure of an exceptional experience, it is worth seeking out a *chambre d'hôte de charme*; 750 of those listed by Gîtes de France fall into this "charming" category. To qualify, the establishment must merit at least three *épis*, be in a building noted for its architecture or setting, and be in a peaceful environment away from road or other noise. It must offer warm and attentive service, and its owners are expected to have extensive knowledge of their region and its places of interest. Of these superior establishments, 100 are classed as *gîtes de chateaux*, set in castles, manors, former monasteries and similar, often with lavish suites and always furnished in luxury style. Set in idyllic grounds, many offer facilities such as a pool or horse-riding.

Chambres d'hôtes are also offered by **Clévances**, including some in towns. Interesting features of their range include *chambres d'hôtes de Bacchus*, on vineyards, and the "Offbeat" selection, which includes a house-boat in Paris and Mongolian yurts (tents) on the banks of the Loire. Their grading system is from one to four keys *(clés)*. **Fleurs de Soleil** offers only *chambres d'hôtes de charme*, in both the countryside and towns. Both Clévances and Gîtes de France have a huge range of self-catering accommodation as well, which can often be rented for a weekend, especially out of season.

Hotels

Almost every French town and village has a small, welcoming, family-run hotel, often with its own restaurant or bar. The annual **Logis de France** guide and website details over 4,000 of the best, which have to meet its standards of accommodation and cuisine. Although independently run, they are inspected regularly and awarded one, two or three "fireplace" symbols according to standard. Menus often feature a *menu de terroir*, a set meal of local dishes at a bargain price, to encourage you to

Above left Hotel in Basse-Normandie **Above middle** Sign for a *chambres d'hôtes* **Above right** Façade of a hotel in Barr, Alsace

sample regional cuisine. At the top end of the scale, château-hotels feature grand rooms, period furnishings and fine dining. The grounds may boast amenities such as a pool, golf course or riding stables. Hotels in the **Relais et Châteaux** collection are among the *crème de la crème*.

Always book hotel accommodation well in advance if you are travelling in July or August or over public holidays (see p9). In "holiday regions" such as Provence, many hotels shut down from October to Easter, so check before travelling out of season. Reservations can normally be made by phone with a credit card, and even small hotels can usually be booked online. If you arrive somewhere without a reservation, the tourist office often has a list of vacancies in busy periods.

French hotel rooms usually have a double bed (grand lit); twin beds (lits jumeaux) must be requested when booking. There are very few single rooms. Bathroom facilities range from an en suite bathroom (salle de bain) with bath (baignoire) or shower (douche) to a cabinet de toilette with just a basin and bidet. In the cheapest hotels a visit to the bathroom may mean a short walk down the corridor to shared facilities.

Hotels are graded from zero to five stars according to things like room size and percentage of *en suite* rooms. Rates, inclusive of tax and service, are quoted per room. Breakfast is charged separately and can be expensive for what you get.

Camping

France has over 11,000 campsites. The **Fédération Française de Camping et de Caravaning (FFCC)** publishes a comprehensive annual listing. Gîtes de France's *Camping à la Ferme* guide covers simple sites on farms. Some sites only accept visitors with a camping *carnet*. These are available from motoring organizations and camping clubs (see p20).

Campsites are graded from one to four stars. Three- and four-star sites are usually spacious, with plenty of amenities for tents and caravans or mobile homes/RVs. One- and two-star sites always have a toilet, a public phone and running water.

Stylish camping and caravanning is developing rather slowly in France. One-off enterprises may offer tipis or treehouses, retro Airstream or Romany caravans, but for camping that is out of the ordinary, there is currently no single website or organization that rounds up everything on offer.

DIRECTORY

CHAMBRES D'HÔTES

Clévances
05 61 13 55 66; www.clevacances.com

Fleurs de Soleil
www.fleursdesoleil.fr

Gîtes de France
01 49 70 75 75;
www.gites-de-france.com

HOTELS

Logis de France
01 45 84 83 84;
www.logis-de-france.fr/uk

Relais et Châteaux
www.relaischateaux.com

CAMPING

FFCC
www.ffcc.fr

PRICE BANDS

The following price ranges are for a standard double room in high season including tax and service:

inexpensive: under €70;
moderate: €70–€150;
expensive: over €150

Below far left Hotel room in Côtes de Beaune, Bourgogne **Below left** Hôtel Restaurant de Bourgogne, Cluny, see p141 **Below middle** Hotel-restaurant sign in Barr **Below right** La Maison d'Hôtes, Arras, see p60 **Below far right** Hostellerie La Tour d'Auxois, Saulieu, see p136

Where to Eat

One of the greatest pleasures of travelling in France is sampling the country's regional dishes. Menus will nearly always feature local specialities that showcase the best and most typical produce of the area. Seasonality also prevails strongly in France, on menus as well as in markets. There is also a range of enticing shops where you can stock up with delicious items for an outdoor feast – the French take their *pique-niques* as seriously as any other meal.

Above Basket filled with various kinds of Normandy cheese

French Regional Cuisine

Each region takes great pride in its own cuisine. In the north and west, the seafood – mussels, oysters, sole, lobster – is superb. Northern dishes, especially those of Normandy and Brittany, feature butter and cream, orchard fruits in autumn and fine early-season vegetables in spring. Cheeses are rich with cow's milk, and often pungent. The cuisine of north-east France reflects its centuries of Germanic rule and influence, with cabbage, ham and sausages (notably combined as *choucroute garnie*) on the menu. Alpine food is warming and sociable, typified by the classic *fondue*. Duck and goose rule in the southwest, featuring most famously in the hearty bean and meat stew, *cassoulet*. The south is the land of olive oil, where little butter or cream features, dryish goat's cheeses predominate, and dishes are perfumed with wild herbs, ripe tomatoes, and spices. *Bouillabaisse*, the fish soup-stew of Marseille, is an iconic dish.

Dining in France

The traditional large meal at noon survives mainly in rural France. Elsewhere, dinner is the main meal of the day. Usually, lunch is served from noon to 2pm and dinner from 7pm to 10.30pm, with last orders taken 30 minutes before closing time. Most restaurants are closed at least one day per week and, off the beaten track and in resort towns, they are often closed out of season. It is always best to phone ahead.

Credit cards are widely accepted but small country restaurants may take cash only. Tax and service charge are included in the bill by law, but most people leave some small change in cafés, 5 per cent elsewhere, and up to 10 per cent for outstanding service.

The dress code in restaurants is generally very relaxed, except in high-end places, but the French are generally well turned-out and you may feel more comfortable if you are too. French children are typically very well behaved in restaurants, so children are usually made welcome but are expected to be similarly civilized. Smoking is now banned from any indoor area, including cafés and bars. Wheelchair access may be restricted, so check in advance.

Most eating places offer a choice of set-price (*prix fixe*) menus as well as à la carte. These are usually very good value. Many offer a dish of the day (*plat du jour*), often a good choice. Bread and tap water are usually provided free. Cheese is served as a separate course, before or instead of dessert. Coffee is served black unless you specify *café crème*. Lunch menus can be very good value, offering the chance to dine affordably at a top restaurant. Menus must, by law, be displayed outside, giving you the chance to make an informed choice before you enter.

Restaurants

This term encompasses everything from tiny rural places with rush-bottomed chairs to stately dining rooms lit by chandeliers, and the cutting-edge kitchens of world-famous chefs, but it generally implies something a little more formal than a bistro or brasserie. Prices at restaurants of the same rating are more or less consistent throughout France, except in large cities where they are usually more expensive and can be stratospheric. As well as restaurants serving French food ranging from classical *haute cuisine* to fashionable *cuisine moderne*, there is a growing number of foreign dining options in France, from African to Japanese. Except in university towns, strictly vegetarian restaurants are limited or

Above left Glass bar sign in Bordeaux **Above middle** Crêperie in Le Faou, Bretagne **Above right** Restaurant sign in Hautvillers, Champagne-Ardenne

non-existent, with crêperies (serving savoury and sweet pancakes) and pizzerias the best option.

Bistros and Brasseries

Bistros are the quintessential French dining choice – small, relatively informal, and generally offering good, home-cooked, moderately priced meals. They vary enormously, from simple places with paper cloths and napkins, where you may be expected to keep your knife and fork between courses, to fashionable "annexes" of upscale restaurants.

Brasseries originated in Alsace as brewery alehouses, but are now found all over France. Usually large and bustling, they typically serve shellfish platters, grills and Alsatian specialities like *choucroute garnie* (sauerkraut with sausage and ham). They offer beer on tap as well as wine and are normally open and serving all day and evening.

Cafés and Bars

These are the very soul of France, ranging from celebrated literary and artists' haunts to the local *café-tabac*. Everywhere but the tiniest hamlet can be counted upon to have a variation on this theme, serving simple meals, snacks and drinks throughout the day. As well as serving refreshments, they are a good source of local information and provide the traveller with endless opportunities to observe the French at their most relaxed.

Wine bars *(bars à vin)* are less common in France than you might imagine, except in wine regions and larger towns. They offer wines by the glass as well as the bottle, and usually a choice of light dishes.

Picnics

Picnicking is a great way to enjoy regional produce – local cheeses and cured meats, fresh-baked baguettes and pastries, and ripe seasonal fruit. Picnic areas are common and are furnished with tables and chairs. You will see entire French families dining here, complete with linen and glassware. Every village in France has either a *boulangerie* or a bread van that visits at least once a day. For hams and pâtés, visit a *charcuterie*. A *traiteur* sells cooked items like quiches as well as a range of prepared salads such as *celeri remoulade* (grated celeriac in a mustardy mayonnaise). Of course, if you are lucky enough to arrive somewhere on market day, all of your picnic needs will be satisfied.

DIRECTORY

PRICE BANDS

The following price bands are based on a three-course meal for one, including half-bottle of house wine, cover charge, tax and service:

inexpensive: under €20;
moderate: €20–€40;
expensive: over €40

Below far left People sitting under umbrellas at an open-air café in Alsace **Below left** Tomatoes on sale in the Antibes market **Below middle left** Olives on sale in the Antibes market **Below middle right** Bottle of cassis, a blackcurrant liqueur **Below right** Sign for vineyards in Côtes de Beaune, Bourgogne **Below far right** Interior of a bar in the Champagne region

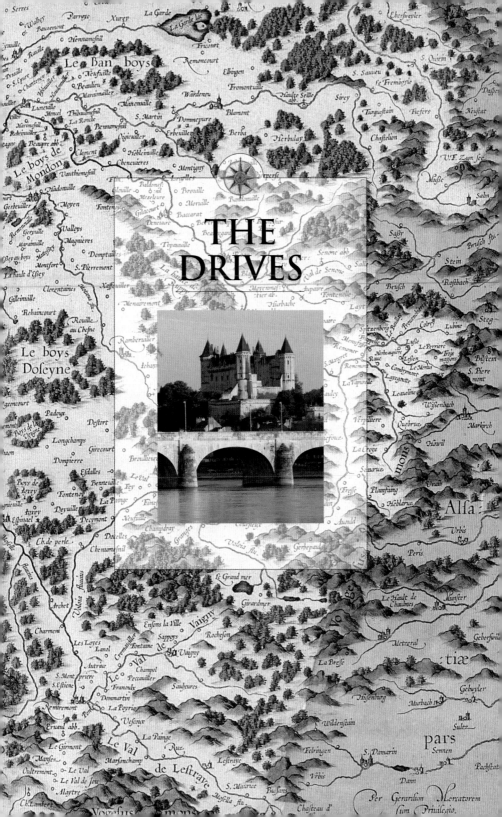

THE
DRIVES

Alsace Wine Route

Obernai to Eguisheim

Highlights

- *Colombage* **villages**
  Admire the intense paintwork, flowers and decorative details in Alsace's half-timbered houses

- **Delicious tarts**
  Savour the region's famous mirabelle, blueberry and red plum tarts, *tarte à l'oignon* and *tarte flambée* with crème fraîche and diced bacon

- **Châteaux-forts**
  Explore Haut-Koenigsbourg's medieval château as well as castles and ruins in the hills above Andlau, Ribeauvillé, Kaysersberg and Eguisheim

- **Mont Sainte-Odile**
  Experience mountain magic, megalithic mystery and forest walks in the mid-Vosges forest

Beautiful and charming Auberge Le Brochet on Grand Rue in Barr

Alsace Wine Route

According to French writer Victor Hugo (1802–85), Europe's history ran down the Rhine. The river is the only thing separating Germany's Black Forest from the Plaine d'Alsace, and between 1871 and 1945 Alsace changed nationality five times. This is reflected in the Alsatian dialect, which is a unique hybrid of German and French. The region's roots, however, go back beyond the wars to deep Roman and Frankish influences. France's smallest region has a penchant for the pastoral: between the vines, Vosges mountains and hilltop castles, Alsace's villages appear as colourful clusters of wood, stone and spires, fountains and flower boxes.

Above Vineyards surrounding the Château de Haut-Koenigsbourg, *see p34*

ACTIVITIES

Visit ten medieval châteaux-forts in a 5-km (3-mile) radius of Mont Sainte-Odile

Walk from Mont Sainte-Odile to the *mur païen* megalithic wall built by Celtic tribes

Dine on *choucroute* (sauerkraut) in a village *winstub* (wine cellar)

Hike the Sentier des Espiègles in the vines near the Château d'Andlau

Sip gluhwein and eat *pain d'epices* (gingerbread) at a Christmas market

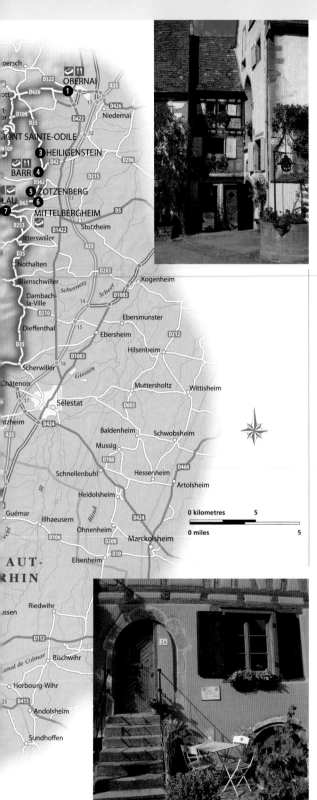

Left Typical *colombage* houses in Riquewihr, see p36 **Below** Bright façade of a building in Kaysersberg, see p36

PLAN YOUR DRIVE

Start/finish: Obernai to Eguisheim.

Number of days: 4–5, allowing at least a day between Mont Sainte-Odile and Haut-Koenigsbourg and two days between the villages and other sights along the wine route.

Distances: 110 km (70 miles).

Road conditions: Alsace is a very wealthy, efficient region – both facts are reflected even on well-signed and sealed minor roads.

When to go: The region has a gorgeous summer, with lots of blue skies. While winter can be very cold, it is the time of festivities and skiing.

Opening times: Many wineries have tasting rooms and cellar-doors on site which are generally open daily from Easter to Christmas, from 10am to 12.30pm and from 2 to 6pm, though check ahead on individual winery hours. Outside these months contact the winery for visiting information.

Main market days: Obernai: Thu; Barr: Sat; Andlau: Wed; Ribeauvillé: Sat; Kaysersberg: Mon, Fri; Eguisheim: Thu.

Shopping: Buy fine wines and wine-related produce, accessories, wooden cases and gift packs from the *caves vinicoles* (wine-cellars).

Major festivals: Obernai: Les Estivales d'Obernai, Jul–Aug; **Barr:** Foire aux Vins, Jul; **Andlau:** Fête du Vin, Aug; **Riquewihr:** Marché de Noël, Nov–Dec; **Kaysersberg:** Marché de Noël, Nov–Dec; **Eguisheim:** Fête des Vignerons, Aug.

DAY TRIP OPTIONS

Mont Sainte-Odile is a wonderful day out for both the **spiritually-inclined** and **nature lovers**; the château of Haut-Koenigsbourg is a fun **family** outing; while the wine route in the Haut-Rhin area offers joys to **epicureans**. For details, see p37.

Above Oriel windows of the Hôtel de Ville in Obernai **Below left** Panoramic view of the countryside around Mont Sainte-Odile **Below right** Mural on Mont Sainte-Odile **Bottom** Wine cellar sign in Heiligenstein

WHERE TO STAY

OBERNAI

Hôtel Le Colombier *moderate*
Cosy and friendly, this hotel is known for its smart service and modern style.
6 rue Dietrich, 67210; 03 88 47 63 33; www.hotel-colombier.com

Le Parc *moderate–expensive*
This stylish and sumptuous family-run hostelry has 62 rooms and suites decorated with works of Alsatian artists. It has a restaurant and a spa.
169 route d'Ottrott, 67210; 03 88 95 50 08; www.hotel-du-parc.com

BARR

Hôtel Château Landsberg *moderate*
In the Vosges foothills, just 2 km (1 mile) from the town, this romantic, rustic château has rooms with Jacuzzis, salons and fireplaces.
133 rue de la Vallée, 67140; 03 88 08 52 22; www.chateaulandsberg.fr

① Obernai
Bas-Rhin, Alsace; 67210
A map from the tourist office lists the various sights along the "historic route" of Obernai. The **Kapellturm**, a 12th-century belfry, the **Hôtel de Ville** and houses with lacquered roof tiles are on the Place du Beffroi. Opposite is the crowded **Place du Marché** with its large half-timbered houses, Gothic gables and **Halle aux Blés**, a 1553 wheat market-hall, now a brasserie. On the Rue du Chanoine Gyss stands the Neo-Gothic **Église Saints Pierre-et-Paul**. The **Chapelle du Mont des Oliviers** and beautiful ramparts of the **Jardin du Selhof** are also worth visiting.

Signage of the Halle aux Blés

🚗 *From Obernai follow the D426 to Ottrott, then turn left on the D103 towards St-Nabor. Follow the signs to Mont Sainte-Odile.*

② Mont Sainte-Odile
Bas-Rhin, Alsace; 67530
Mont Sainte-Odile draws a huge number of Christian pilgrims every year. It is also a place of interest for nature lovers and archaeologists. Celtic tribes, who occupied the region from 1000 BC, built a 10-km (6-mile) *mur païen* (pagan wall) of stones, grottos and megalithic fences which extends to Klingenthal and Ottrott. The monastery *(open daily)* has stunning views from the cloister's cliff-faced outer wall. The look-out sweeps over the entire corridor of Alsace from a height of 765 m (2,500 ft). A series of marked trails in the surrounding forest make for glorious rambling, including a 5-minute return walk to the **Grotte de Lourdes** or a 20-minute return walk to the **Source Sainte-Odile** *(open daily)*.

🚗 *From Mont Sainte-Odile take the same road back to St-Nabor then turn onto the D109. Go through St-Nabor. Turn right onto the D35 towards Heiligenstein.*

③ Heiligenstein
Bas-Rhin, Alsace; 67140
The brightly coloured wine cellars along the main street are as much a reason to stop as the vision of the Roman church rubbing shoulders with the **Restaurant Raisin d'Or** and its ornate golden grape sign. The town is known for its unique white aperitif and dessert wine, Klevener. A dozen winemakers are found along Rue Principale, Rue de la Montagne and Rue de l'Ours; the latter is home to the beautiful **Fontaine de l'Ours**.

🚗 *Continue on the D35 to Barr.*

④ Barr
Bas-Rhin, Alsace; 67140
Widely considered the capital of the wine route, Barr is the archetypal scenic Alsatian town nestled between the mountain foothills and the Vallée Saint-Ulrich. The main hub, along Grand Rue, is set around two intensely coloured, flower-decked *colombage* (half-timbered) houses. One of them is a hotel, the **Auberge Le Brochet**, with a pink stone fountain opposite it. Dominating the town square is the other *colombage* building, the **Hôtel de Ville**, its façade covered in projecting oriel windows and allegoric statues. Walking paths crisscross the Altenberg and Kirchberg hills above – the latter is where the grapes of Barr's *grands crus* wine are grown.

🚗 *Take the D362 to Mittelbergheim. The Zotzenberg car park is on the right hand side of the road just after the village sign for Mittelbergheim.*

⑤ Zotzenberg
Bas-Rhin, Alsace; 67140

The wine trail through the Zotzenberg hillsides traverses the grape-growing territory of Mittelbergheim village below. The trail is one of 38 wine trails – *sentiers viticoles* – along the Alsace wine route.

A two-hour walking tour
The walk is most pleasant in the afternoon amid spring flowers or the thick vines of summer and autumn. The trail starts from the Zotzenberg car park on the D362. The walking area is rippled with hills, culminating in the foothills of the Vosges mountains and silhouette of Mont Sainte-Odile.

Leave the car park and take the path on the left through the vineyards. Turn left at the intersection towards the forest, and then left again at the fork through the pine forest to the **Colline du Crax** ①. On the southern hillside of the Colline du Crax, part of the sub-Vosges mountain slopes, Zotzenberg lies within a hilly basin between the valley of Andlau and the plane of the

Rhine. It is a prized grape-growing terrain which produces top grade *grands crus* wines. At the top of the hill is a forest road. Take the left hand path towards the rocky platform, **Rocher Sainte-Richarde** ② which takes in the views of the Château du Spesbourg. Return to the fork and turn left to walk up the gentle hills and the bottle-green forested pleats to reach the ruins of the14th-century **Château d'Andlau** ③.

Continue on the forest road until the first crossing. Here turn right towards the Trois Chennes crossroads. On reaching the crossroads, take the path towards Mittelbergheim. After getting back at the fork that led to the "Espiègles", turn left and take the path through the vineyards. Move straight on and take the Rippelholz path to reach the Zotzenberg car park.

Along the well-marked Rippelholz path there are 17 information panels dedicated to Alsace's seven different grape varieties. Nine other panels illustrate the work of the winemaker, from the vineyard to the bottle. For much of the walk visitors will be viewing crops of Sylvaner – the "queen" grape of the region accounting for about 40 per cent of the growing area.

🚗 *Continue on the D362 and turn left onto the Rue Principale of Mittelbergheim.*

Above Zotzenberg *grand cru* grapes above the village of Mittelbergheim **Below** Brasserie on the Grand Rue in Barr

VISITING ZOTZENBERG

Tourist Information
1 place Hôtel de Ville, Barr, 67140; 03 88 08 66 65

EAT AND DRINK

OBERNAI

La Cloche *inexpensive*
Alsatian specialities include *choucroute* and potato pancakes.
90 rue Général Gouraud, 67310; 03 88 40 90 43; closed Wed out of season

Le Bistro des Saveurs *expensive*
Housed in a 400-year-old building, this place serves fine regional dishes.
35 rue de Sélestat, 67210; 03 88 49 90 41; closed Mon and Tue

BARR

Au Potin *inexpensive*
This Parisian-style genial café-brasserie serves Alsatian dishes.
11 rue du Général Vandenberg, 67140; 03 88 08 88 84; closed Mon and Tue

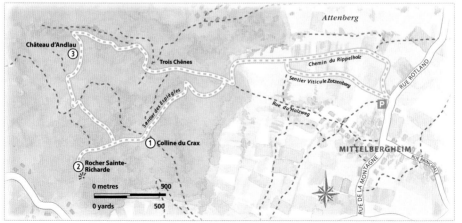

Eat and Drink: inexpensive, under €20; moderate, €20–€40; expensive, over €40

Top Parish church of Mittelbergheim **Above** *Colombage* house in Ribeauvillé

WHERE TO STAY

MITTELBERGHEIM

Winstub Gilg Hôtel Restaurant
inexpensive–moderate
The rooms of this small inn have a country elegance to them.
1 route du Vin, 67140; 03 88 08 91 37; www.hotel-gilg.com

ANDLAU

Zinck Hotel *inexpensive–moderate*
Housed in a former corn mill, the rooms here are based on three themes – the English, the Empire and the Fifties.
13 rue de la Marne, 67140; 03 88 08 27 30; www.zinckhotel.com

RIBEAUVILLÉ

L'Hôtel de la Tour
inexpensive–moderate
This intimate hotel has a salon, a cosy wine cellar and a restaurant.
1 rue de la Mairie, 68150; 03 89 73 72 73; www.hotel-la-tour.com

Le Clos Saint-Vincent
moderate–expensive
An elegant hotel among the vines, this has refined furnishings.
Osterbergweg, 68150; 03 89 73 67 65; www.leclossaintvincent.com

⑥ Mittelbergheim
Bas-Rhin, Alsace; 67140

Frankish king and Holy Roman Emperor Charles le Gros gifted this winemaking fiefdom to his wife Richarde at the end of the 9th century. Visitors can wander down the steep Rue Principale past a couple of small public squares, Gothic churches and geranium-covered water wells. Marvel at the beautiful ornate façades of old winemaker houses, and peep into their inner courtyards, surrounded by hefty wooden beams. Enthusiasts of wine history may like to see the antique oak grape crusher – the *pressoir* – in the **Cour d'imière** on Rue de la Montagne, while the Renaissance town hall, **Hôtel de Ville**, has a display on winemaking since 1510.

🚗 *Continue down Rue Principale, then, at the end, turn right onto the D62 towards Andlau.*

⑦ Andlau
Bas-Rhin, Alsace; 67140

Bears and wines are clearly the sacred things here – the bear on the town hall square, Place de la Mairie, is clutching a cluster of grapes. Every village baker who came to sell bread here was once required to bring a loaf a week for the bears. Andlau is home to three of Alsace's Grand Cru Rieslings, which local winemakers attribute to the purity invested by the mineral-rich soils – the schist of Kastelberg, the sandstone of Wiebelsberg and the fossilized limestone of Moenchberg. Guided visits to the **Abbatial d'Andlau** (Abbey of Andlau) can be organized through the **tourist office** (*open Mon–Sat except public holidays*). Andlau is also known for its parish church, **Saints-Pierre-et-Paul**, which is a fine example of Romanesque architecture. The ruins of the nearby castles of **Haut-Andlau** and **Spesbourg** are worth exploring. Both were built during the 13th century.

🚗 *From Andlau take the D253 towards Itterswiller, then turn right and take the D35 through Itterswiller, Dambach-la-Ville, Scherwiller, Châtenois to Kintzheim. Turn right into the D159 to Haut-Koenigsbourg. Parking along the road to the château is free, but the queue can be long.*

⑧ Château de Haut-Koenigsbourg
Orschwiller, Bas-Rhin, Alsace; 67600

The château is mostly a medieval-style reconstruction of the castle as it was in 1600 (*open daily*). The spectacular pink sandstone goliath towers 800 m (2,625 ft) above the Alsace plain from its forest realm. It was built to watch over the wine and wheat routes to the north, and silver and salt routes from west to east. The château-fort was demolished by the Swedish army during the Thirty Years War in the 17th century. It was rebuilt in 1899 by German Emperor Guillaume II as a symbol of the regaining of Alsace from France. Inside there are murals, antediluvian furniture, cast-iron stoves and medieval weaponry and furniture. The views from the top of the tower reach as far as Germany's Black Forest and the Alps.

🚗 *Take the D1bis1 to Saint-Hippolyte, turn right into the D1bis Route du Vin*

Wine Elites

The *grand cru* vintages represent just 4 per cent of Alsace wines. The French National Appellations Institute classifies two other special wine styles: the intensely sweet and aromatic *Vendages Tardives* made from late-harvested, overripe grapes; and the complex, honey- and apricot-scented botrytis wines, *Selection de Grains Nobles*. Some of these are considered masterpieces as their high prices reflect.

⑨ Bergheim
Haut-Rhin, Alsace; 68750

The surrounding walls of this flowery fortressed town sweep in eight medieval towers from the main gateway – the *Obertor* or upper tower. Its *colombage* tower is topped by an ornate tiled roof. The main village square, the **Place du Marché**, with its sandstone fountain, sundial and vine growers' houses in Gothic and Renaissance styles, is the town's highlight. In the late 16th and early 17th centuries dozens of women were accused of witchcraft and burnt to death in this town. The **Maison des Sorcières** (*open May–Nov, closed Mon, Tue*) holds exhibitions

Where to Stay: inexpensive, under €70; moderate, €70–€150; expensive, over €150

focusing on Alsace and the history of the trials. Children will enjoy the stories of spells and sorcery. This is mostly an audiovisual experience and although the information panels in the museum are only in French and German, others can still enjoy the visit. Also see the **Jardin d'Annette**, a medieval garden with medicinal plants.

🚗 *Continue on the D1bis. Cars can be parked at the bottom of the pedestrianized town. Those who want to avoid walking uphill can take the tourist train.*

⑩ Ribeauvillé

Haut-Rhin, Alsace; 68150

The town is named after the Ribeaupierre family of seigneurs who owned much of the land in the area during the Middle Ages. The Grand'Rue of Ribeauvillé rings true to its name: from the medieval upper town, *Ville Haute*, to the lower *Ville Basse*, it extends through the old ramparts past the **Place de l'Hôtel de Ville**. The square is graced by the sumptuously furnished town hall, the Gothic **Église Saint-Grégoire**, known for its organ, and drinking fountains and towers topped with stork's nests. In side streets visitors will find wine cellars fronted by alembics and carts full of geraniums. The flower boxes perfectly match the paintwork of the gorgeously coloured *colombage* houses, from purple to tangerine. The town, in fact, is nationally honoured for its floral façades. A walking trail links the ruins of three châteaux-forts in the vine-covered foothills of the Taennchel mountain above.

🚗 *Continue on the D1bis and turn right onto D1bis3 to Hunawihr.*

⑪ Hunawihr

Haut-Rhin, Alsace; 68150

In the distance Hunawihr appears as a cluster of witch-hat roofs among hills of vines. From the base of Rue de l'Église alongside the village fountain and the Winstub Suzel restaurant, walk up to the church and its fortified cemetery for the best views along the wine route and forest castle ruins. On the way, admire the wood-beamed houses and courtyard doors made from oak, beech and pine. As visitors leave the town they will pass an exotic butterfly garden, **Jardin des Papillons** *(open daily Easter–Oct).*

🚗 *In Hunawihr, behind the Cave Vinicole de Hunawihr turn left into the Grande Rue and follow it to the top of the village until the tiny turning on the left, the Rue de Riquewihr. Follow into Riquewihr. There are paid car parks at the main entrances to the old town and around the ramparts. There is also a free car park on Avenue Mequillet.*

EAT AND DRINK

ANDLAU

Au Boeuf Rouge *inexpensive–moderate*
The restaurant is known for its Alsace dishes and traditional brasserie-grill.
6 rue du Docteur-Stoltz, 67140 ; 03 88 08 96 26; closed Wed night, Thu from Oct–Jul 11

Val d'Eléon *inexpensive–moderate*
This colourful cellar-restaurant serves Alsace specialities.
19 rue du Docteur Stoltz, 67140; 03 88 08 93 23; www.valdeleon.com; closed Sun evening, Mon

A La Couronne *inexpensive–moderate*
Alsace specialities and vegetarian dishes are the highlights here.
4 rue du Maréchal Foch, 67140; 03 88 08 93 24; closed Wed and Thu

Top left Pink sandstone Château de Haut-Koenigsbourg **Top right** Rolling hills lead up to the Château de Haut-Koenigsbourg **Below left** Steeple of the Église Saint-Grégoire in Ribeauvillé **Below right** Café in Ribeauvillé

Above Vineyards surrounding the pretty town of Riquewihr **Below** *Colombage* house in Riquewihr

WHERE TO STAY

RIQUEWIHR

Hôtel-Restaurant Au Dolder
inexpensive
Small and intimate, Au Dolder has a dozen cosy rustic rooms.
52 rue du Général de Gaulle, 68340; 03 89 47 92 56; www.dolder.fr

KIENTZHEIM

Hostellerie Schwendi
inexpensive–moderate
This hotel in a *colombage* house has modernized rooms with balconies.
2 place Schwendi, 68240; 03 89 47 30 50

EGUISHEIM

L'Hostellerie du Château *moderate*
The small, welcoming establishment has neat, bright rooms.
2 rue du Château, 68420; 03 89 23 72 00

⑫ Riquewihr
Haut-Rhin, Alsace; 68340
Every time Riquewihr was assailed by enemies, winemakers doggedly rebuilt it so it would be more attractive than before. Pass through the late 13th-century watchtower entrance, the **Dolder** (home to a local history museum), and take Rue du Général de Gaulle. The tightly packed *colombage* houses are among the most beautiful in Alsace: multicoloured with sculpted wood beams, ornate overhanging windows, courtyards, wells and fountains. The town, known as "the pearl of Alsace's vineyards", boasts many cellars in small side *ruelles* showcasing the prized *grand cru* Riesling Schoenenbourg. Children will love the **Maison de Hansi** *(open daily except Mon mornings Jul–Aug)* which displays the delightful work of Alsatian illustrator Jean-Jacques Waltz, affectionately known as Uncle Hansi.

🚗 *From the avenue Mequillet turn southwards into the chemin de Kientzheim and continue along the Route du Riquewihr to Kientzheim.*

⑬ Kientzheim
Haut-Rhin, Alsace; 68240
A buttonhole of a place in a sea of vines, Kientzheim has a fortified gateway, **Porte du Lalli**, whose grimacing stone figurine was designed to scare off the town's aggressors. Pass through it to reach the **Château Schwendi**, named after an Alsace

hero credited with returning from wartime Hungary with cuttings of the Tokay-Pinot Gris vine. Today the château houses a wine museum. The fountain on the Place Schwendi is surrounded by wine cellars and *colombage* houses. The square opens on to the countryside, and the benches along the city walls are a nice place to sit and take in the view. Exiting Kientzheim, visitors will see an army tank that is part of a World War II memorial park along the town's western ramparts.

🚗 *Take the D28 to Kaysersberg. There is a big free car park outside the city walls requiring a 10-minute walk to the furthest sites. The other option is paid car parks in the town centre.*

⑭ Kaysersberg
Haut-Rhin, Alsace; 68240
Kaysersberg – Mountain of the Emperor – was named when the son of the 13th-century German ruler bought the castle whose ruins now loom over the town. Take the fortified **Porte des Pucelles** – Door of the Maidens – to the main street, Rue du Général de Gaulle and pass the **Église Sainte-Croix** and **Place Gouraud**. Near here is a museum dedicated to 1954 Nobel Peace Prize winning doctor Albert Schweitzer, who established a hospital in Gabon. From here follow the marked trail along the Weiss river which flows through the village, bordered by parklands, remains of ramparts, towers and dungeons and charming houses.

An illustration inside the Maison de Hansi

🚗 *Take the D415 via Ammerschwihr. At the roundabout turn right to Ingersheim. In the village turn right onto the D11(2).*

⑮ Niedermorschwihr
Haut-Rhin, Alsace; 68230
Alsatian place names can be a mouthful. Niedermorschwihr's original name Morswilre – Farm of Maur – was changed to stop it being confused with nearby Obermorschwihr. The town, cupped in a small valley, is bisected by the Grande Rue which features several beautiful houses with overhanging oriel windows, carved

wood balconies and vividly painted *colombage* wine cellars and restaurants. Turn the corner onto the Place de l'Eglise to see the **Église Saint-Gall** and its incredibly tall and twisted Gothic steeple.

🚗 *Take the D10 (7) to Turckheim. Turn left onto the D11(Route de Colmar) by the station. At the next roundabout turn right onto the D83. Continue past turnings to Wintzenheim and Wettolsheim and take the D1bis into Eguisheim. There are three easily accessed free car parks in Eguisheim: in the town centre on the Grande Rue (at the town hall), on Rue des Fleurs and the "Parking Marronniers" on the Rue des Trois-Châteaux on the edge of the town.*

🔟 Eguisheim
Haut-Rhin, Alsace; 68420
The birthplace of Pope Saint Léon IX has several sites named after him: the **Château Saint-Léon** is located at the heart of the village on the Place du Château Saint-Léon, which merges with the old marketplace, Place du Marché aux Saules. Its pastel *colombage* houses enclose the

Fontaine Saint-Léon, a historic monument which holds up to 80,000 litres (21,000 gallons) of water. From here take the Grand'Rue, the main axis, past other petite public squares and fountains and be sure to stop at one of the excellent *boulangeries-pâtisseries*. Arriving at the village ramparts turn left and head around to the Place de l'Église and the church **Saint-Pierre et Saint-Paul**. Continue along Rue des Ramparts to do a full circle.

EAT AND DRINK

RIQUEWIHR
La Grappe D'or Restaurant-Winstub
inexpensive–moderate
This rustic decor restaurant has a traditional menu.
1 rue des Ecuries Seigneuriales, 68340; 03 89 47 89 52; www.restaurant-grappedor.com; closed Wed from mid-Nov–end Mar, Thu

KAYSERSBERG
Le Chambard *expensive*
This restaurant serves sophisticated versions of rural Alsace food.
9-13 rue du Général de Gaulle, 68240; 03 89 47 10 17; closed Mon–Wed lunch and Jan

EGUISHEIM
A La Ville de Nancy
inexpensive–moderate
This restaurant-bistro in the village serves regional food with local wines.
2 place Charles de Gaulle, 68420; 03 89 41 78 75; www.villedenancy-eguisheim.com

---

DAY TRIP OPTIONS
Visitors staying in the Bas-Rhin can head to Mont Sainte-Odile for the day; Château de Haut-Koenigsbourg is easy to access from any base along the itinerary; the wine route of the Haut-Rhin makes for a perfect day trip for those based in the south.

Monastery and megalithic wall
Visit the monastery and wander through the trails of Mont Sainte-Odile ❷ leading to the springs or the *mur païen*, the megalithic wall built by the Celtic tribes.

Coming from the north follow the directions in the itinerary arriving via Ottrott; from the wine route to the south access is via Barr: take the D35, then at the roundabout take the third exit and continue on the D109 and pass through St-Nabor.

Medieval château and walking trails
For a great day trip, head to the Château de Haut-Koenigsbourg ❽. Marvel at the medieval decor, then picnic amidst nature and explore a few of the walking trails.

Coming from the north, follow the itinerary; from Ribeauvillé on the wine route to the south, take the D1bis, pass through Bergheim, Saint-Hippolyte and Kintzheim.

Grand Cru villages
The wine route from Ribeauvillé ❿ to Riquewihr ⓬ via Hunawihr ⓫ is a treasure chest of delightful villages, museums and vineyard walks.

Follow the directions in the itinerary. The best roads to take are the signed Route du Vin/wine route.

Eat and Drink: inexpensive, under €20; moderate, €20–€40; expensive, over €40

The Land of Three Frontiers

Côtes de Toul to Dabo

Highlights

- **Historic fortified town**
  Explore the Vauban fortifications, moats and a Gothic cathedral in Toul

- **Scenic wine route**
  Traverse the vineyards of Côtes de Toul on the Route du Vin et de la Mirabelle

- **Architectural gems**
  Marvel at the Classical and Art Nouveau architecture of Nancy

- **Quiche Lorraine**
  Savour the famous French tart made with bacon and Gruyère cheese

Picturesque route through the vineyards in Côtes de Toul

The Land of Three Frontiers

Lorraine is a major European crossroads as it shares its borders with Germany, Belgium and Luxembourg. The region's landscapes change dramatically over a short distance – from the gentle slopes of the Côtes de Toul to the very scenic forested valley of the Moselle river. While Metz to the north is Lorraine's administrative capital, Nancy strongly contends to be the cultural and culinary one, basking in the splendour of its regal square, Place Stanislas. Head east and Lorraine transforms into a wild natural area of mountain passes, ravines and pine forests.

0 kilometres 10

0 miles 10

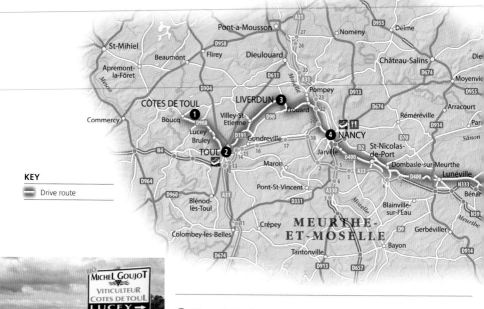

KEY

▬▬ Drive route

Above Signpost pointing towards a wine domaine in Lucey, Côtes de Toul

WHERE TO STAY

TOUL

La Villa Lorraine *inexpensive*
In the historic heart of Toul, the 21-room hotel has old-world charm, with lots of pastels, pinks and mauves in the decor. The rooms are simple, yet well furnished and have satellite TV. Meals are served to the room on request.
15 rue Gambetta, 54200; 03 83 43 08 95; www.hotel-villa-lorraine.com

❶ Côtes de Toul

Meurthe-et-Moselle, Lorraine; 54200
The grape-growing hills of the Côtes de Toul lie on the lip of the Lorraine plateau, at the southern edges of the forests of the **Parc Naturel Régional de Lorraine**. Wine culture prospered under the dukes of Lorraine and bishops of Toul and by the mid-1800s there were 110 sq km (43 sq miles) of grapes. A century later, in the aftermath of grape plagues, the ravages of World War I and rural exodus, only 0.3 sq km (0.12 sq miles) remained. The **Route du Vin et de la Mirabelle**, which traverses the vineyards and orchards of cherry plum trees between Boucq, Lucey and Bruley, symbolizes the comeback by local winemakers. **Bruley** is a typical Toulois village with its vaulted wine cellars and houses with white

stone and rounded roof tiles. There is a lovely view from its hillside chapel.

🚗 *The Route du Vin et de la Mirabelle follows the D908 from Boucq to Lucey and Bruley. From Bruley, continue on the D908. At the first major intersection on the approach to Toul, turn left and follow the signs first to the "Centre Ville" then towards the "Cathedral/ Tourism Office" to park.*

❷ Toul

Meurthe-et-Moselle, Lorraine; 54200
The best view of Toul is from the Boulevard Aristide Briand. The Gothic towers and Romanesque spires of **Cathédrale Saint-Etienne** loom above the city walls. The cathedral and town hall rub shoulders with the **Place Charles de Gaulle,** surrounded by gardens, canalside quays and stone ramparts. Wander around the

Where to Stay: inexpensive, under €70; moderate, €70–€150; expensive, over €150

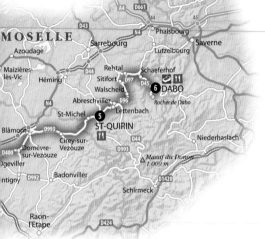

PLAN YOUR DRIVE

Start/finish: Côtes de Toul to Dabo.

Number of days: 2.

Distances: 155 km (96 miles).

Road conditions: Vary from excellent to ordinary between *départements*.

When to go: Summer is the best time to visit Lorraine.

Opening times: Vary greatly between individual sights and museums. Generally from 10am to 5pm. Most sights close on Mondays and major public holidays. Check ahead before visiting.

Main market days: Toul: Wed; **Nancy:** Tue–Sun; **Dabo:** Sat.

Shopping: In the countryside buy Côtes de Toul wines, Mirabelle eau-de-vie, Crème de Mirabelle, tarts, cakes and *confitures* (jams); in Nancy shop along the glamorous Rue des Dominicains and Rue Gambetta and in Place Stanislas for clothing, Art Nouveau objects and glassware and crystal such as Baccarat and Daum. Buy local honey from Dabo.

Major festivals: Toul: Fete du Vignoble, Sep; **Nancy:** Rendez-Vous place Stanislas, Aug–Sep; Aye Aye Film Festival, Sep; Le Livre sur Place, Sep; Jazz Pulsations, Oct.

Above Scenic countryside of the Moselle near St Quirin, *see p43* **Below left** Cathedralé Saint-Etienne standing behind the city walls in Toul **Below right** Porte Haute, the fortified gateway of Liverdun

church cloister and the Classical sandstone passages and façade of the **Hôtel de Ville** – once the Episcopal palace of Toul.

🚗 Take the D191 through Villey-St-Etienne, then the rue de la Porte Haute to the signposted Liverdun.

Liverdun

Meurthe-et-Moselle, Lorraine; 54460
Built on a rocky spur, Liverdun was a garrison for Toul's bishops. The views from alongside the Porte Haute, the fortified gateway of the upper town, take in the thick bends of the Moselle. The **tourist office** *(closed Sun; low-season)* is in L'Hôtel de Camilly, once the bishop's summer residence. Also see the pretty **Place de la Fontaine** with its arcades and statuettes. The stairway, **La Côte au Laye**, leads to the lower town where there is a marked

walking trail – the **Itineraire de la Boucle de la Moselle** – along the canals and riverbanks.

🚗 Descend to the lower town and cross the bridge over the Moselle. Turn left onto the D90, pass through Frouard. Continue on the A31 towards Nancy. Exit at junction 20 for Nancy.

Above Arc de Triomphe in Place Stanislas, Nancy

VISITING NANCY

Tourist Information
*Place Stanislas, 54011; 03 88 35 22 41;
www.ot-nancy.fr*

Parking
Meter parking near Place Stanislas/
Hôtel de Ville.

WHERE TO STAY

NANCY

Maison d'Hôtes de Myon *moderate*
This is an 18th-century townhouse
transformed into a bed-and-breakfast.
*7 rue Mably, 54000; 03 83 46 56 56;
www.maisondemyon.com*

Hôtel des Prélats
moderate–expensive
Housed in a 16th-century Episcopal
palace, this classy hotel has French
provincial furnishings and artworks.
*56 place Monseigneur Ruch, 54000; 03
83 30 20 20; www.hoteldesprelats.com*

DABO

Hotel-Restaurant Des Vosges
inexpensive
Family-run hotel with nine rooms,
some with views, and a restaurant.
*41 rue de la Forêt Brûlée, 57850, Dabo
la Hoube; 03 87 08 80 44; www.hotel-
restaurant-vosges.com*

❹ Nancy

Meurthe-et-Moselle, Lorraine; 54000

Beyond the Classical riches of Place Stanislas, Nancy's old town is a
hive of antiquity, while the "new town" is scattered with exquisite
works of Art Nouveau. Basking in its royal history, Place Stanlisas
truly became a public square when it was pedestrianized in 2004.

A one-hour walking tour

Nancy does not have a great climate,
and visitors may have to do the walk
under grey skies or drizzle. The tourist
office is on the corner of Rue des
Dominicains and **Place Stanislas** ①.
The royal square was inaugurated in
1755 by the Duke of Lorraine and former Polish king, Stanislas Leszczynski.
Its Classical stone façades are clad in
gold-embossed wrought iron railings
and Art Nouveau lamps. The sweep
of grand edifices around the square
include the Hôtel de Ville, Opera-
Theatre, Beaux-Arts Museum, the
Grand Hôtel and Grand Café Foy. The
ensemble is now a UNESCO World
Heritage Site. Pass through the **Arc
de Triomphe** ② – an imitation of
Rome's Arch Septimius Severus – to
the **Place de la Carrière** ③ – once a
jousting field, it is now the government and justice hub, with the Appeal
Court in the Hôtel de Craon and the
Administrative Tribunal in the former,
Bourse de Commerce. At the far end,
the **Palais du Gouvernement** ④ is
set within a semicircular colonnade.
Behind it off Rue des Ecuries is the

Parc de la Pépinière ⑤, a park first
established by Stanislas as a tree
nursery to line the roads of Lorraine –
now open to the public. Head back
past the Hemicycle and turn right into
Grande-Rue, a long narrow street
of medieval houses, which leads
to the Cordeliers quarter with its
convent and church, old marketplace
Place Saint-Epvre ⑥ and the **Palais
Ducal** ⑦. A bit further north are the
old city gates – the 14th-century
Porte de la Craffe ⑧ and **Porte de
la Citadelle** ⑨ with its Jardin del la
Citadelle. Head back down Rue du
Haut Bourgeois to the Cours Leopold;
its villas are the beginning of a promenade through Nancy's Art Nouveau
riches. The interiors and exteriors of
the **Brasserie Excelsior** ⑩ *(open daily)*
are the result of work by a group of
artists from the Ecole de Nancy – an
Art Nouveau movement born in 1901,
which set to decorating the town with
beautiful elements and forms, ceramic
architecture, iron and stained-glass
work. The **Chambre de Commerce** ⑪
opposite is another example of their
legacy. Take Rue des Dominicains and

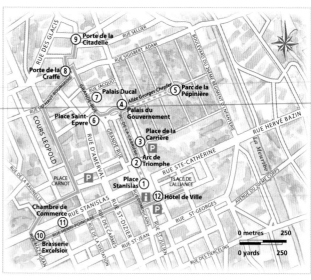

then the Rue Fourier past the **Hôtel de Ville** ⑫ to Place de l'Alliance to see a splendid fountain. Walk back to the Hôtel de Ville for the car park.

🚗 *Take the direction towards Jarville; continue on the D400 through Lunéville to Blâmont. Take the D993, pass Cirey-sur-Vezouze and St Michel. Turn left onto the D96 for St-Quirin.*

⑤ St-Quirin

Moselle, Lorraine; 57560

Crouched at the base of the Donon mountain, St-Quirin could just as easily be classified as one of France's most beautiful villages for its natural environment as for its architecture. This village of "seven roses" or churches is hemmed in by greenery. Climb to the **Haute Chapelle** for excellent views. The Valley of Abreschviller and the Donon in the Massif des Vosges offer excellent trekking. Do not miss a visit to a glass workshop – together with faïence and crystal, glasswork has been a craft in Lorraine for centuries. An archaeological site of a 1st–3rd

century AD Gallo-Roman settlement can be seen at Croix-Guillaume, 4 km (2 miles) east of the village.

🚗 *Continue along the D96 through Abreschviller and Walscheid, then the D97 to Rehtal; turn right into the D45 and continue straight via Schaeferhof. After Dabo turn off to the right on the D45A to reach Rocher de Dabo.*

⑥ Dabo

Moselle, Lorraine; 57850

The 30-m (100-ft) high, 80-m (260-ft) long and 26-m (85-ft) wide mass of Rocher de Dabo's crimson sandstone protrudes from the surrounding mountain peaks on a raised crown of forest. Roman temples, medieval burgs and castles once occupied the site, but were all destroyed by wars before the **Chapelle Saint-Léon** was built. Take the stairs to the platform for a view over the Lorraine plateau and try to see the chapel lit up at night. The area around the mountains is great for fishing, mountain biking, hiking and rock climbing.

ACTIVITIES

DABO

Tourist Information
10 place de l'Église, 57850; 03 87 07 47 51; www.ot-dabo.fr

EAT AND DRINK

NANCY

Les Petits Gobelins *moderate*
Traditional French food is served according to the season. The kitchen also produces home-made bread and delicious desserts.
18 rue de la Primatiale, 54000; 03 83 35 49 03; www.lespetitsgobelins.fr; closed Sun and Mon

Stanislas *expensive*
Prestigious chef Patrick Fréchin runs this fine dining restaurant on the terrace of the Grand Hotel de la Reine.
2 place Stanislas, 54000; 03 83 35 03 01; closed Sun and Mon

ST-QUIRIN
Hostellerie du Prieuré
inexpensive–moderate
Superb local produce forms the basis of the simple but generous *plats du jour* and more refined menus.
169 avenue du Général de Gaulle 57650; 03 87 08 66 52; www.saint-quirin.com; closed Tue evenings, Wed and Sat lunch

DABO

Auberge le Katz
inexpensive–moderate
On the village square, this traditional place serves pizzas and the local equivalent *flammekuche*. There is also a terrace and a bar.
2 place de l'Eglise, 57850; 03 87 07 40 04

Eat and Drink: inexpensive, under €20; moderate, €20–€40; expensive, over €40

The Champagne Route

Reims to the Montagne de Reims

Highlights

- **Coronation city**
  Marvel at Reims' cathedral where many French kings were crowned

- **Cellar tours**
  Step inside the Champagne Houses of famous brands, from Ruinart to Veuve Clicquot to Taittinger

- **Grape estates**
  Admire the sight of grapes growing from hilltop to valley, as far as the eye can see

- **Champagne gastronomy**
  Savour the local *cuisine champenoise* with some of the best champagne

Pretty hamlet of Verzenay with the vineyards merging into the horizon

The Champagne Route

More than 600 km (373 miles) of countryside roads – from Reims to the Côte de Blancs, south of Épernay, and through the Grande Vallée de la Marne – make up the famous Route Touristique du Champagne. The drive through the Montagne de Reims reveals one of France's most picturesque grape-growing regions: villages and forests roll into each other between vineyards owned by the most famous champagne names and those of small independent growers. Romans planted the first vines in the chalky limestone soil and grape culture flourished under the care of the clergy, especially the bishops of Reims and Châlons-en-Champagne.

Above Village of Ludes at the heart of the finest champagne-making territory, see p50 **Below right** Rows of grape vines in the Côte des Blancs, see p51

ACTIVITIES

Sit and sip champagne in one of Reims' Art Deco brasseries

Visit as many champagne cellars as possible

Enrol in a short course at Aÿ's Ecole des Vins de Champagne

Take a guided tour on the winemaker's trail, sentier du vigneron, in Côte de Blancs

Set off on a flowery walk, balade fleurie, from Oger

Hike or bike alongside the canals of the Marne

Balloon over the vines, especially at sunset

KEY

▬ Drive route

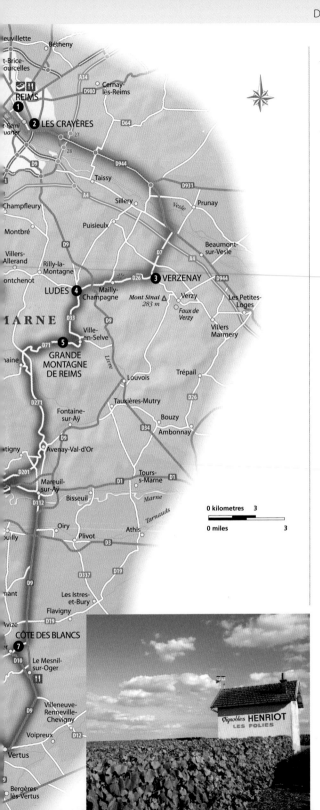

PLAN YOUR DRIVE

Start/finish: Reims to the Montagne de Reims.

Number of days: 4, allowing half a day to see the historic sights in Reims, two half days visiting the Champagne Houses in Reims and in Épernay, and 2 days to drive along the many detours of the Champagne Route.

Distances: 130 km (80 miles).

Road conditions: Roads are well signed. Expect heavy traffic near the cities especially in Épernay. Reims has very good urban planning, but making the transition from city to countryside can be wearing.

When to go: Given that the main attraction is champagne, any time of year will do. To see the vineyards, summer and autumn are the best time to visit. It also makes for a great winter escape.

Opening times: While visiting hours of individual Champagne Houses vary greatly, the famous brands are usually open daily from Feb/Mar–Nov with cellar visits conducted from 9 or 10am to noon and from 2 to 5 or 6pm. Ring ahead for precise times.

Main market days: Reims: daily.

Shopping: Buy champagne direct from the source, from the *maisons de Champagne* in Reims, Épernay and in the countryside of Champagne. The big brands also have great souvenirs for their fans.

Major festivals: Reims: Fêtes Johanniques, Jun; Flâneries Musicales d'été de Reims, Jun–Jul; Jonglissimo, Sep; Aÿ: Mai Musical, May; Fêtes Henri IV, Jul (biennial).

DAY TRIP OPTIONS

Day trips suitable for the whole **family** include the Musée de la Vigne on the Champagne Route near Reims and Épernay's avenue du Champagne; while Dom Perignon's village Hautvillers is for **history buffs**, **vineyard walkers** and **wine-lovers**. For details, *see p53*.

Above Dramatic Basilique de Saint-Remi **Below left** Magnificent Cathédrale de Notre-Dame in Reims **Below right** Statue of Louis XV at Place Royale, Reims

VISITING REIMS

Tourist Information
2 rue Guillaume de Machault, 51100; 08 92 70 13 51; www.reims-tourisme.com

Parking
There are 8,000 parking places including free open-air parking, and paid covered car parks and meters. It is easy to park within a few minutes' walk of the historic centre – the cathedral car park is on Rue des Capucins.

WHERE TO STAY

REIMS

Hotel Azur inexpensive
This personable non-smoking hotel with garden patio has 18 rooms including family rooms.
9 rue Ecrevées, 51100; 03 26 47 43 39; hotelazurreims.free.fr

Hôtel de la Paix expensive
This is an efficient and business-oriented hotel but still does not compromise on the luxuries.
9 rue Buirette, 51100; 03 26 40 04 08; www.bestwestern-lapaix-reims.com

AROUND REIMS

Château de la Muire
moderate–expensive
The main attraction of the family-run Château de la Muire is its 2-star Michelin restaurant. The dark leathered Le Bar is the icing on the cake.
40 avenue Paul Vaillant-Couturier, Tinqueux, 51430; 03 26 84 64 64; www.assiettechampenoise.com

❶ Reims

Marne, Champagne-Ardenne; 51100
Reims was founded by the Gauls and was a major city during the Roman Empire. Post-war restoration has created an elegant city of stately town squares and eclectic architecture: from salvaged Gothic marvels to Renaissance-style townhouses and Art Deco gems. On Place du Cardinal Luçon, the 13th-century **Cathédrale de Notre-Dame de Reims** (open daily), a UNESCO World Heritage Site, is adorned with over 2,300 statues including one known as the Smiling Angel. It was on this site that Clovis, the Frankish king, was baptized by Saint-Remi, Bishop of Reims, in AD 498. His conversion to Christianity led to Reims becoming the place where some 30 French kings were subsequently crowned. Next door is the **Palais du Tau**, once

the Archbishop's Palace. Do not miss the beautiful square, **Place Royale**, with the statue of Louis XV by 18th-century sculptor Jean-Baptiste Pigalle. After completing the tour of Reims Centre, drive down to the **Saint-Remi Quarter**, about 2 km (1 mile) away. From Place du Cardinal Luçon, take Rue Rockefeller and immediately turn left into Rue Chanzy and continue straight into Rue Gambetta. Then turn right into Rue du Ruisselet and left into Rue Simon to the Place Saint-Remi to find free parking next to the Basilique de Saint-Remi. Another of Reims' UNESCO World Heritage Sites, the Saint-Remi Quarter is centred on the dramatic Romanesque Benedictine abbey, the **Basilique de Saint-Remi**, with Gothic art additions built to house the bishop's tomb. Alongside the basilica is the grand Classical façade of the **Saint-Remi Abbey Museum**, which houses collections of history and archaeology, from prehistory to the Renaissance.

🚗 *From the car park by the basilica walk on Rue Saint-Julien; continue straight on Rue Jean Aubert and turn left to reach Les Crayères.*

Caves and Crayères

In the 17th century, Champagne Houses were built on top of massive subterranean chambers which were dug into the limestone during the Gallo-Roman era. The crayères – chalk pits – make perfect storage conditions for champagne to age slowly, in the humid, constant temperatures. They also served as a place to hide during World War I.

❷ Les Crayères

Marne, Champagne-Ardenne; 51100

Several of Reims' leading Champagne Houses are located in the city-edge neighbourhood known as Les Crayères. Some have regular public cellar tours in several languages; others are by appointment only. These are paid tours, and last an hour on average.

A 45-minute walking tour

Champagne House visits are perfect for any time of the year – as long as it fits in with the opening times of the *maisons de Champagne*. Start the tour at **Champagne Taittinger** ① *(9 place Saint Nicaise, 03 26 85 45 35)*, established in 1735 by champagne merchant Jacques Fourneaux. Visitors may want to see the house that produces Maxim's de Paris Champagne with its *belle-époque* labels. For this, descend Rue des Salines, and turn left into Rue Créneaux where there are cellar tours and tastings at **G H Martel & Co** ② *(17 rue des Créneaux, 03 26 82 70 67)*.

Turn back and follow Rue Goïot over Boulevard Victor Hugo to Boulevard Henry Vasnier, to pass by the small family-owned Champagne Drappier *(11 rue Goïot)*. **Charles Heidsieck** ③ *(4 boulevard Henry Vasnier, 03 26 84 43 50)* and **Piper-Heidsieck** ④ *(51 boulevard Henry Vasnier, 03 26 84 43 00)* spring from the same family; both are now part of the Rémy Cointreau group. Head up Boulevard Henry Vasnier to the intersection with Boulevard Pommery. **Champagne Pommery** ⑤ *(5 place du Général Gouraud, 03 26 61 62 63)*, a brand forged

by Louise Pommery, is on the corner. The grandiose castle is set in gardens behind a soaring black fence. The Pommery estate contains 18 km (11 miles) of cellars and Gallo-Roman chalk pits. There are 20 million bottles of Pommery lying 30 m (100 ft) underground. The gardens have several bright sculptures. Turn right into the Rue des Crayères and head to **Champagne Ruinart** ⑥ *(4 rue des Crayères, 03 26 77 51 51)*. The 18th-century mansion conceals a phenomenon: reached via a plummeting staircase and network of corridors, the *crayères* here are cathedral-like in proportion. Finally, head down the Boulevard Diancourt to **Veuve Clicquot-Ponsardin** ⑦ *(1 place des Droits de l'Homme, 03 26 89 53 90)*. The house is also involved in the arts and its innate design flair is reflected in the fabulously modernised interiors of the historic estate. From here head back to Rue Jean Aubert and turn left to reach the car park by the basilica.

🚗 *Leave on D951, then join the A4. Take exit 26 and continue on the D8E, towards Louvois. At the big roundabout turn left on the D9, then left on the D26 and pass through Mailly-Champagne to arrive at Verzenay.*

Above Grand Champagne Pommery, Les Crayères

VISITING LES CRAYÈRES

Parking
Boulevard Pommery, Boulevard Henry Vasnier and Rue des Crayères have many *maisons* which offer visitor parking. Visitors can also walk from the car park by the Basilique de Saint-Remi.

EAT AND DRINK

REIMS

La Brasserie du Boulingrin
inexpensive–moderate
Big choice of set menus, *a la carte* and *plat du jour* in a vibrant 1925 Art Deco brasserie of brass, wood and wall lamps. *48 rue de Mars, 51100; 03 26 40 96 22; closed Sun*

Bistro Henri IV *inexpensive–moderate*
This restaurant is known for its generous servings of traditional food. *29 rue Henri IV, 51100; 03 26 47 56 22; closed Sun–Mon.*

Café du Palais *inexpensive–moderate*
This theatrical café is loved by the art fraternity. It serves bistro food and has an extensive list of champagnes. *14 place Myron Herrick, 51100; 03 26 47 52 54; www.cafedupalais.fr; closed Tue night and Sun*

AROUND REIMS

L'Assiette Champenoise *expensive*
Enjoy an exquisite dining experience in the 2-star Michelin restaurant. *40 avenue Paul Vaillant-Couturier, Tinqueux, 51430; 03 26 84 64 64; www.assiettechampenoise.com*

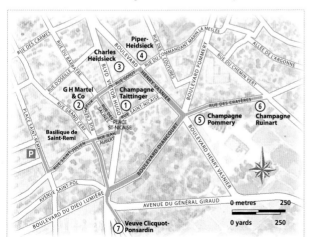

Eat and Drink: inexpensive, under €20; moderate, €20–€40; expensive, over €40

Above Village of Verzenay with stretches of vineyard in the background **Below left** *Jardiniere* in Ludes **Below right** Champagne House Forget-Chauvet in Ludes

🚗 *Back on the D26 drive about 2 km (1 mile) to see the Faux de Verzy – just opposite is the car park for Mont Sinai observation point – the highest point of the Montagne of Reims, at 283 m (928 ft). Return via the D26 to reach the next stop, Ludes.*

③ Verzenay

Marne, Champagne-Ardenne; 51360
Originally named Virdunacus from the Latin *viridium sanum*, meaning a luxuriantly verdant place, the village was partly destroyed when the World War I battlelines came too close to it. The landmark lighthouse, the Phare de Verzenay, was built in 1919 by champagne-maker Joseph Goulet as a publicity stunt. It has now been converted into a champagne museum. The **Museé de la Vigne** *(open Tue–Sun)* has historic frescoes, culinary exhibitions, audiovisual presentations and a vine garden displaying the different grape varieties grown in Champagne. Near the adjacent village, visit the **Faux de Verzy**, a conserved forest patch of twisted beech trees. Experts have not fully understood why the trees continue to grow in this fashion.

④ Ludes

Marne, Champagne-Ardenne; 51500
Ludes sits between the foot of the Montagne de Reims and the summit of the hillsides of Champagne vineyards. Its name is believed to have come from either Lucida or Lucus, both derived from a word meaning light. Ludes wines have been appreciated since the Middle Ages when it belonged to lords. Today it is among the class of elites – 17 villages of Champagne, many of them concentrated in the Montagne de Reims – which produce the some of the best *grands crus* champagnes.

🚗 *Exit Ludes at the top of the town via the D33 and continue to Ville-en-Selve, at the heart of Montagne de Reims. From here turn right onto the D71, towards Germaine, and pass through the Grande Montagne de Reims.*

Champagne Countryside

There are two explanations for the origin of the word champagne. One says that it comes from two Celtic words *kann* and *pann* meaning white countryside, referring to the chalky landscape. The second explanation is that it is from the Latin word for cultivated fields, *campagna*.

WHERE TO STAY

AŸ

Le Manoir des Charmes *moderate*
This upmarket bed-and-breakfast is furnished with refinement, taste and historic astuteness. The 1906-built stone manor is set in lovely gardens at the heart of the top champagne-making territory. The five rooms are romantically decorated with one-off antiques, vintage objects, and fresh, natural fabrics, linen and hand-embroidered bath towels.
83 boulevard Charles de Gaulle, 51160; 03 26 54 58 49; www.lemanoirdescharmes.fr

Hotel Castel Jeanson *moderate*
This is a small, charming and welcoming hotel in an elegant former Champagne House with swimming pool, stained-glass windows, drawing room and lounge, bar and private parking facilities. Run by a small friendly and efficient staff, there are 14 rooms, 3 suites, and a family room – some have rather florid decor and fabrics, but are nonetheless immaculate, cultivated and personal in style.
24 rue Jeanson, 51160; 03 26 54 21 75; www.casteljeanson.fr

Where to Stay: inexpensive, under €70; moderate, €70–€150; expensive, over €150

⑤ Grande Montagne de Reims

Marne, Champagne-Ardenne; 51160

The route from Ludes to Aÿ penetrates the forested highland between Reims and Epernay – the Grande Montagne de Reims. The hillsides and valleys are covered with Pinot Noir grapes, one of the three varieties used in the elaboration of champagne. Ten out of 17 *grand cru* territories are concentrated in this area. The region is also the greenest, wildest part of the drive – a mix of deep forest and voluptuous spreads of vines in the hills around the tiny *Hameau de Vauremont* where Moët & Chandon has some terrains. In the last forest fold is the pretty village of Avenay-Val-d'Or.

🚗 *Continue along the D271, pass Avenay-Val-d'Or onto the D201 and follow signs to Aÿ.*

⑥ Aÿ

Marne, Champagne-Ardenne; 51160

Between the Marne river and the southern slopes of the Montagne de Reims, Aÿ has 3.7 sq km (1.4 sq miles) of *grand cru*-classed vineyards and is the headquarters of the **Institut International des Vins de Champagne** *(15 rue Jeanson)* a perfect place to get an introduction to the wines of Champagne. With a map from the town hall in Place Henri Martin, follow the signed tourist trail around 19 interpretation panels, which has brief explanations in English. The rustic doorways of smaller family-owned Champagne Houses line the narrow cobble-stoned passages leading to the Gothic **Église Saint-Brice**, a classified historic monument. The streets just below the vine-covered hillsides are home to some of the biggest brands: Champagne Bollinger and Champagne Gosset Brabant on Boulevard de Lattre de Tassigny; Champagne Ayala on Boulevard du Nord and Deutz on Rue Jeanson. Visitors who are able to climb up to the hilltop will find fantastic views over the town and the countryside reaching as far as Epernay.

🚗 *Drive out of Aÿ on the D1 to Mareuil-sur-Aÿ and turn right onto the D112 to cross the Marne; continue onto the D9, twards Avize, to reach Oger.*

⑦ Côte des Blancs

Marne, Champagne-Ardenne; 51190

The Côte des Blancs extends for 15 km (9 miles) south of Epernay from the *grands cru* villages of Oger and **Le Mesnil-sur-Oger** through to Vertus. Dotted within a large amphitheatre, the hillside villages are the cradle of Chardonnay grapes, one of the vital champagne ingredients. Fine and elegant, these grapes are used in the preparation of some of the best champagnes.

In Oger, one of the prettiest villages in the region, people decorate their houses with barrels, troughs and grape-picking baskets which overflow with flowers. The town also has a 12th-century church.

🚗 *From Oger take the D10 to Vertus via Mensil-sur-Oger. Then take the D36 to Villers-aux-Bois and then the D38 to Chaltrait; there turn right onto the D40, towards Moslins, for Épernay.*

Above left Valley of Grande Montagne de Reims **Above** Charming town of Oger, Côte des Blancs **Below** Roofline of the town of Aÿ

EAT AND DRINK

AŸ

Le Vieux Puits *inexpensive–moderate* Various set menus are available, including the weekday lunch menu, which is excellent value for money. The *à la carte* dishes include *foie gras*, duck or goose liver and *escargot* (snails), and mirabelle plum tart for dessert.
Le Clos Saint Georges, 7 rue Jules Lobet, 51160; 03 26 56 96 53; closed Mon, Wed, Thu evening

AROUND CÔTE DES BLANCS

Le Mesnil *expensive* In the heart of the vines of the Côte des Blancs, the restaurant is lush, modern and elegant. The same *esprit* infuses the food.
2 rue Pasteur, Le-Mesnil-sur-Oger, 51190; 03 26 57 95 57; closed evenings Mon–Tue, Wed

Above Tower of Champagne de Castellanne in Épernay **Above right** Town hall at Hautvillers **Below** Vineyards in Champillon

WHERE TO STAY

ÉPERNAY

Le Clos Raymi *moderate*
Housed in a mansion, this breezy place has lots of art and white furnishings.
3 rue Joseph de Venoge, 51200; 03 26 51 00 58; www.closraymi-hotel.com

La Villa Eugène *moderate–expensive*
Housed in a villa formerly owned by the Mercier Champagne family, the hotel has 15 rooms, ranging from standard to luxury.
82 avenue du Champagne, 51200; 03 26 32 44 76; www.villa-eugene.com

AROUND ÉPERNAY

Les Grains d'Argent *moderate*
Situated 4 km (2 miles) from Épernay towards Hautvillers, this hotel's 21 rooms are furnished with fresh, unfussy elegance. The in-house restaurant serves delicious dishes.
1 allée du Petit Bois, Dizy, 51530 (); 03 26 55 76 28; www.lesgrainsdargent.fr

8 Épernay

Marne, Champagne-Ardenne; 51200
The town is at the heart of 300 sq km (115 sq miles) of vineyards, on the crossroads of the tourist routes through the Montagne de Reims, Marne and Côtes des Blancs. Winston Churchill called its **Avenue du Champagne**, which is lined with grand *maisons de Champagne*, "the most drinkable avenue in the world". From Place de la République and Hôtel de Ville, the avenue starts with Moët & Chandon which dates back to 1743 and is the largest of the Champagne Houses. It continues past some of the most prestigious Champagne names, including Perrier-Jouët, De Venoge, Pol Roger, Demoiselle, Boizel, Martel, de Castellane and Mercier. The 110-km (68-mile) network of champagne storage cellars nearly outstrips the total length of Épernay's footpaths. In all there are some 200 million bottles of champagne stored underground.

🚗 *From the Avenue du Champagne, take the Rue de Reims and pass through Magenta cross the railway and the river, veer left to take the N2051. At Dizy turn left onto the D386 uphill following signs to Hautvillers. This village is best discovered on foot. There are several parking areas including one at the top of the village, near the church.*

9 Hautvillers

Marne, Champagne-Ardenne; 51160
The highlight of Hautvillers is the Benedictine abbey, **St-Pierre d'Hautvillers**, founded in AD 650 by Saint Nivard, Bishop of Reims. The Champagne region at this time was subject to many invasions, and people from the nearby village of Villare had been forced to take shelter up in the hills. This new community came to be known as Alta Villare and subsequently Hautvillers. Perched above a patchwork of Marne valley countryside, the immaculately groomed village is crowned by forest. Starting from the tourist office on Place de la République, follow the signs on a walk along the Rue des Buttes and Rue de Bacchus, and other streets full of medieval houses and some 140 forged iron signs. The self-proclaimed "cradle of champagne" has over a dozen Champagne Houses to visit and there are walking trails in the forest and among the vines.

🚗 *Instead of leaving Hautvillers via the D386, turn left at the car park by the cemetery, in the lower part of the village, and then immediately right onto the Route de Champillon, which passes under the main road and arrives in Champillon.*

Father Dom

Benedictine monk Dom Pierre Pérignon is credited with putting the bubble and the cork into champagne in the 17th century while he was the cellar master of the Abbey of Hautvillers. He transformed dull "grey wine" into a sparkling wine by marrying high quality grapes, extracting the juice under the right pressure, choosing thick resistant glass bottles and using a Spanish cork. Legend has it that on tasting champagne for the first time, he cried out "Come quickly, I am drinking the stars!"

⑩ Champillon

Marne, Champagne-Ardenne; 51160

The Rue du Paradis is a perfect way to describe the drive through sweeping hillsides of vineyards. One of the highest points in the Montagne de Reims, Champillon has panoramic views that cover the entire Marne valley, the vineyards and the village of Dizy through to Épernay. As writer Victor Hugo observed in the 1840s, "It is the town of champagne wine – nothing more, nothing less". The church of Saint Barnabé has a wooden Louis XIV altar offered to the noble seigneurs by Dom Pérignon.

🚗 *Turn left out of the village and join the D951; continue to Montchenot. Just at the entrance to the village take the sharp turn left to Sermiers onto the D26. Take the D22 through Nogent and then turn left back onto the D26 to Coulommes-la-Montagne. The villages on this route form the Montagne de Reims wine producing region.*

⑪ Montagne de Reims

Marne, Champagne-Ardenne, 51480

The Champagne Route is split into five wine producing regions, of which one is the Montagne de Reims. This route passes through the small villages on the slopes of the **Parc Naturel Régional de la Montagne de Reims**: Montchenot, Chamery, Sacy, Villedommange and Coulommes-la-Montagne. There are several *vignerons indépendants,* small independent champagne-makers, flagged along the way. Their logo depicts a winemaker carrying grapes from the field – symbolic of the

ethos *propriétaire-récoltant* – owner-grower. The hilltop **Chapelle Saint-Lié** at Villedommange has a viewpoint over the forested hillsides and the Plain of Reims. The 12th-century church of **Saint-Remi Coulommes** in Coulommes-la-Montagne is set among the vines on a hillside from where several walking trails begin.

Above left Mural in Champillon depicting the production of champagne **Above right** Town signs in Hautvillers **Below** Pretty tourism office in the Montagne de Reims

---

EAT AND DRINK

ÉPERNAY

Restaurant Le Théâtre
inexpensive–moderate
The restaurant, housed in a renovated theatre, serves food such as veal with local mustard. Another delicacy is duck and game in season.
8 place Mendès, 51200; 03 26 58 88 19; www.epernay-rest-letheatre.com; closed Sun and Tue nights, Wed

La Table Kobus *moderate*
In this old brasserie-style eatery with its marble tables, small wooden bar and vintage photos, the chef recalls the traditional French flavours – *entrecôtes,* goat's cheese tart and *mousse au chocolat.*
3 rue Dr Rousseau, 51200; 03 26 51 53 53; www.latablekobus.com; closed Thu and Sun nights, Mon

---

DAY TRIP OPTIONS

Wherever visitors happen to be based on the Champagne Route, the following day trips to Verzenay, Hautvillers and Epernay are within easy reach.

Musée de la Vigne

The Musée de la Vigne at Verzenay ③ is good entertainment and educational for children and adults, with Champagne Houses and forest walks right alongside.

Verzenay lies along the Route Touristique du Champagne. From

Reims, follow the driving instructions in the itinerary. Those based in Ludes need to take the D26.

Dom Pérignon territory

The town of Hautvillers ⑨ offers a historic village and abbey, Champagne Houses and walking among the vines and forest; all make for a well-rounded day out.

From Épernay take the Rue de Reims, pass through Magenta and continue on the N2051. At Dizy, take the Avenue du General Leclerc, and continue on the D386.

Avenue du Champagne

While adults may find cellar tours in Reims amazing, children will love the visit to Champagne Mercier in Épernay ⑧ especially the train trip through its storage galleries *(68 avenue du Champagne, 03 26 51 22 22; www.champagnemercier.fr).*

Follow the signs to the Avenue du Champagne and enter the visitor parking at Mercier. From Reims take the D951 in the direction of Épernay. Approaching the city take the 4th exit at the roundabout and continue on the D301.

Eat and Drink: inexpensive, under €20; moderate, €20– €40; expensive, over €40

Discovering the North

Calais to Baie de la Somme

Highlights

- **Historic towns**
  Discover fine architecture and superb food in Boulogne and Montreuil

- **Stunning cities**
  Marvel at the Grand'Place of Arras and the cathedral of Amiens, the centrepieces of two distinctive French cities

- **Moving memories**
  Explore the past through the poignant World War I memorials of Vimy and the Somme

- **Misty Wilderness**
  Experience tranquility in the hidden villages of the Pas-de-Calais and the Baie de la Somme

Rooftops of a pretty little village
in the Pas-de-Calais

Discovering the North

The northern region of France has many charms to explore. All along the coast there are fine beaches. Inland the broad downland is punctuated by hidden valleys with quick-flowing rivers and flower-filled villages. This region has always played a major role in European history and trade. In the 20th century, this was one of the great crucibles of World War I. To the south, the Somme river enters into one of Europe's largest wetlands. Cuisine highlights here include fine seafood and cheese.

Above Picturesque village of Beussent in the Vallée de la Course, see p58

ACTIVITIES

Take a stroll along the beach at Wimereux before sampling some seafood in one of its brasseries

Hunt for the best cheeses, hand-made sausages and other tempting delicacies in the shops and markets of Boulogne

Spend some time in a sleepy local café in the Vallée de la Course to get the pace of village life

Learn about the realities of trench life during World War I at the top of Vimy Ridge

Pick out all the many figures of medieval life carved in the little medallions around the portals of cathedral of Amiens

Rent a bike in St-Valery-sur-Somme and ride around the huge, flat bay, looking out for birds and seals

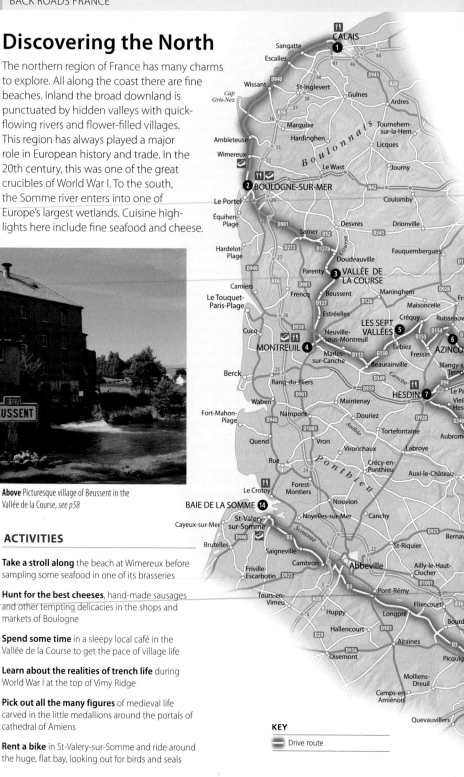

KEY

Drive route

Above French memorial of Notre-Dame de Lorette, *see p61* **Below** Terrace at Chez Jules, Boulogne-sur-Mer, *see p58*

0 kilometres 10

0 miles 10

PLAN YOUR DRIVE

Start/finish: Calais to Baie de la Somme.

Number of days: 3–4, with half a day each to explore Arras and Amiens.

Distances: 400 km (250 miles).

Road conditions: Roads are in good condition and well signposted.

When to go: May to June and September are ideal, when the weather is pleasant. Winter is another good time to visit for the Christmas markets.

Opening hours: Museums and sights generally open from 9 or 10am to 6 or 7pm with a 1- or 2-hour lunch break. World War I memorial sites generally do not close for lunch. Many attractions have shorter hours at weekends and in winter.

Main market days: Boulogne: Wed, Sat; **Montreuil:** Sat; **Hesdin:** Thu; **Arras:** Wed, Sat; **St-Valery-sur-Somme:** Wed, Sun.

Shopping: Northern France is known for its strong cheeses and chocolates.

Major festivals: Arras: Main Squares Festival, Jul; **Amiens and other places throughout Picardy:** Picardy Cathedrals Festival, Sep–Oct; **St-Valery-sur-Somme:** Fête de la Mer, Aug.

DAY TRIP OPTIONS

Visitors can explore the area on separate day trips. **Families** can enjoy a taste of French ambience between the Côte d'Opale and Montreuil; **history enthusiasts** can spend their time at the battlefields; **art and nature lovers** will have a lot to see at Amiens and the Baie de la Somme. For details, *see p63*.

Above left Château-Musée, Boulogne-sur-Mer **Above right** Beach-huts along the beach of Calais **Top right** Façade of one of Montreuil-sur-Mer's historic houses

WHERE TO STAY

AROUND CALAIS

Hotel Atlantic *moderate*
This Art Deco hotel, 30 km (20 miles) south of Calais, has been modernized, and has wonderful sea views from many rooms. It has a fine restaurant.
Digue de Mer, Wimereux, 62930; 03 21 32 41 01; www.atlantic-delpierre.com

BOULOGNE-SUR-MER

L'Enclos de l'Evêché *moderate*
A delightful *chambre d'hôtes* in a finely restored town house, it has five rooms decorated on historical themes.
6 rue de Pressy, 62200; 03 91 90 05 90; www.enclosdeleveche.com

MONTREUIL

Le Coq Hôtel *moderate*
This cosy traditional hotel in the heart of old Montreuil has been thoroughly renovated, but without losing its small-town charm.
2 place de la Poissonnerie, 62170; 03 21 81 05 61; www.coqhotel.fr

AROUND LES SEPT VALLÉES

La Cour de Rémi *moderate*
Very stylish design and rural tranquility are effectively combined at this hotel. There is a very romantic treehouse.
1 rue Baillet, Bermicourt, 62130; 03 21 03 33 33; www.lacourderemi.com

① Calais
Pas-de-Calais, Nord-Pas-de-Calais; 62100
Calais was rebuilt in functional style after World War II. The **Musée des Beaux Arts et de la Dentelle** *(open daily)* has some fine paintings and displays of local lace. By the **Hôtel de Ville** is the original casting of Rodin's 1888 sculpture, the *Burghers of Calais*. Calais also has a beach which leads to the coast road for Boulogne along the Côte d'Opale. **Wimereux** is a charming traditional seaside resort and **Ambleteuse** has a rugged 1680s fort.

🚗 *Leave Calais along Digue Gaston Berthe and follow signs for "Boulogne par le Côte" onto the D940. In Boulogne, head for "Centre Ville".*

② Boulogne-sur-Mer
Pas-de-Calais, Nord-Pas-de-Calais; 62200
The most historic of France's cross-Channel ports, Boulogne has at its heart the hilltop old town or Haute Ville, enclosed within massive walls begun in the 1230s. A walk around the ramparts is a delightful way to get a feel of the old town. In a corner of the ramparts is the **Château-Musée**, *(open Wed– Mon)*, an eclectic museum.

Down the hill from the Haute Ville, **Place Dalton** hosts the area's liveliest market. Round the corner is Philippe Oliver, the best cheese shop in France. Beside the harbour is **Nausicaà** *(open daily)*, a dynamic sealife centre.

🚗 *Follow the main road south out of Boulogne, then the D901 as far as Samer. Turn left onto the D215 to "centre town" and then continue on the D52 for Desvres, but after 2.5 km (1.5 miles) look for a sharp right turn onto the D127A, which joins the Vallée de la Course road at Doudeauville.*

Philip Frizzy-Hair

Boulogne's massive ramparts and many of its oldest buildings, such as the looming stone belfry, were begun for Philippe Hurepel, or "Frizzy Hair", Count of Boulogne. A younger son of King Philippe-Auguste, he married the Countess of Boulogne in 1223. He had ambitions of becoming king but failed in his attempts.

③ Vallée de la Course
Pas-de-Calais, Nord-Pas-de-Calais; 62650, 62170
A climb up and over a hill from the Desvres road leads into a hidden

Above Cosy little cottages line the Course river in Doudeauville, Vallée de la Course

valley. The Course river runs through the middle of the valley's villages, between red-roofed white cottages. **Doudeauville** is one of the prettiest, with a grey-walled church and the remains of a medieval fortress. **Beussent** is the home of the renowned producer of handmade chocolates, **Chocolaterie de Beussent**. 🚗 *Rejoin the D901 south of Estréelles. Turn right into Montreuil. Follow the road uphill into the old town, and park in one of the squares off Rue Ledent.*

Above Row of cottages along a cobblestoned road in Montreuil-sur-Mer

4 Montreuil
Pas-de-Calais, Nord-Pas-de-Calais; 62170
Montreuil has a dramatic approach to its old town around hairpin bends and through the imposing **Porte de Boulogne** gate in the town walls, built in the 1540s for King François I. There are fabulous views over the Canche valley from the ramparts. Inside the walls are cobbled alleys of tiny cottages, 18th-century town houses and Gothic churches. Today, Montreuil is a popular stopping-place and has a wide range of restaurants. 🚗 *Retrace the same road out of Montreuil; cross over the D901 into Neuville-sous-Montreuil. Turn right onto the D113 through Marles-sur-Canche. From Beaurainville, turn left onto the D130 up the Créquoise Valley as far as Créquy, then right onto the D155 for Fressin.*

5 Les Sept Vallées
Pas-de-Calais, Nord-Pas-de-Calais; 62140
The "Seven Valleys" of Artois are wooded clefts cut by a set of rivers – the **Créquoise**, **Planquette** and

Ternoise are the most attractive. Lush and tranquil, they offer lovely walking routes and fishing spots between the ancient villages. **Fressin**, home of the novelist Georges Bernanos (1888–1948), has an imposing ruined castle and, in the **Église St-Martin**, an exquisite Gothic funeral chapel. 🚗 *From Fressin take the D154 north-east to meet the D928 at Ruisseauville. Turn right, and immediately left onto the D71 for Azincourt.*

6 Azincourt
Pas-de-Calais, Nord-Pas-de-Calais; 62310
Known in English as Agincourt, this was the site of the battle where, in October 1415, Henry V of England defeated Charles VI of France. There is an informative museum, the **Centre Historique Médiéval** (*open daily Apr–Oct; closed Tues, Nov–Mar*). A walk around the battlefield, between Azincourt and the next village of **Maisoncelle**, gives a vivid impression of the events even after 500 years. 🚗 *From the battlefield at Maisoncelle continue along the D104 to Blangy-sur-Ternoise and the D94. Turn right for Hesdin and follow the road to the main square, Place d'Armes.*

7 Hesdin
Pas-de-Calais, Nord-Pas-de-Calais; 62140
The town was laid out in 1554 for Charles V after he made it a part of the Spanish Netherlands. This gave the town its distinctive Dutch appearance. The Canche river appears in many places around Hesdin, glittering under humpback bridges. 🚗 *Leave Place d'Armes by Rue André Fréville; follow signs for Frévent onto the D340. Continue along it to Arras via Frévent, where it becomes the D339. Then take the D68 and D59 for Arras. Follow signs to Grand' Place to park.*

Above Nineteenth-century memorial commemorating the battle at Azincourt in 1415

Above Hôtel de Ville on Place d'Armes, a great example of Flemish architecture in Hesdin

EAT AND DRINK

CALAIS

La Pléiade *moderate–expensive*
The cooking here is inventive and extremely refined, seen at its best in subtly-flavoured fish dishes.
32 rue Jean Quéhen, 62100; 03 21 34 03 70; www.lapleiade.com; closed Sun evening, Mon

BOULOGNE-SUR-MER

Chez Jules *inexpensive–moderate*
A big, classic town brasserie, with an unbeatable position for its bustling terrace on the market square. Everything from snacks to intricate dishes are served.
8 place Dalton, 62200; 03 21 31 54 12; www.chez-jules.fr; closed Sun evening

MONTREUIL

Auberge de la Grenouillère *moderate–expensive*
Set in a pretty old farmhouse, this is one of the finest restaurants in the north of France. It serves an array of distinctive creations.
La Madeleine-sous-Montreuil, 62170; 03 21 06 07 22; www.lagrenouillere.fr; closed Tue, Wed

HESDIN

L'Écurie *inexpensive–moderate*
A pleasant restaurant in a converted 16th-century stable, with attractively varied menus and a quality wine list.
17 rue Jacquemont, 62140; 03 21 86 86 86; closed Sun evening, Mon, Tue

Eat and Drink: inexpensive, under €20; moderate, €20–€40; expensive, over €40

Above People relaxing at the casual bars lining the Place des Héros, Arras

VISITING ARRAS

Parking
There are paid parking places in the Grand'Place except during the Wednesday and Saturday markets. There is also an underground car park beneath the square, open at all times except on Sundays.

Tourist Information
Hôtel de Ville, Place des Héros; 03 21 51 26 95; www.ot-arras.fr

WHERE TO STAY

ARRAS

Les Agaches inexpensive
A charming bed-and-breakfast in the centre of Arras, with just two pretty rooms and a garden.
17 Rue des Agaches, 62000; 03 21 23 15 03; www.lesagaches.fr

Ostel les Trois Luppars
inexpensive–moderate
The oldest house in Arras, with a Flemish Gothic gable façade from 1467, contains this very popular hotel. Rooms are small, but has plenty of character.
49 Grand'Place, 62000; 03 21 60 02 03; www.ostel-les-3luppars.com

La Maison d'Hôtes moderate
The most stylish and friendliest option in Arras, this 18th-century town house is furnished with a luxurious mix of antiques and chic modern touches to create a very special ambience.
1 place Guy Mollet, 62000; 03 21 58 85 94; www.lamaisondhotes.com

⑧ Arras
Pas-de-Calais, Nord-Pas-de-Calais; 62000

Visitors to Arras are often stunned by their first view of the town's Grand'Place, one of the largest market squares in Europe, lined by gable-topped Flemish houses. Two other squares nearby seem small only by comparison. Devastated in World War I, all three were restored brick-by-brick in the 1920s. Today, the arcades beneath the gables host beguiling shops and restaurants and a vibrant streetlife.

A 90-minute walking tour

The best time to do the walk is in the morning or during the afternoon. Begin by taking in the scale of the **Grand'Place** ①. A market has been held here since AD 828. The square grew to its present size in the 15th century. Look out for the intricate details on the many façades, such as the two sheep carved on No. 54. No. 49, dating from 1467, is the oldest house in Arras. Today it is the Trois Luppars hotel.

Lively Rue de la Taillerie connects the Grand'Place to the second square, **Place des Héros** ②, also known as the Petit-Place. It is more intimate, and has a more individual range of shops.

Walk across to the **Hôtel de Ville** ③, with its extraordinary Gothic façade. First completed in 1506, it too was rebuilt in the 1920s. The tourist office here offers two trips within the building, one up to the top of the giant belfry for a panoramic view, and another down to the mysterious Boves (chalk tunnels that run beneath Arras).

Belfry of Hôtel de Ville, Arras

Back on ground level, walk around the Hôtel de Ville into Place de la Vacquerie. Walk out of it on the right-hand side up Rue Désiré-Bras to reach the Neo-Classical Cathédrale Notre-Dame-et-St-Vaast d'Arras on Rue des Teinturiers, built between 1770 and the 1830s. Next to it is the similarly huge **Abbaye St-Vaast** ④, also built in Neo-Classical style in the mid-18th century. It now houses the Musée des Beaux Arts (open Wed–Mon), with notable 17th- and 19th-century paintings, fine porcelain and some medieval sculptures. Leaving the complex on Place de la Madeleine, walk down Rue Maximilien Robespierre to pass **Maison Robespierre** ⑤ where the revolutionary lived before 1789. On **Place du Théâtre** ⑥ is the elegant 1785 theatre. Across Rue Ernestale, streets lead towards **Place Victor Hugo** ⑦, an octagon of symmetrical houses around an obelisk. Retrace the route to Rue Ernestale; turn right and then left onto Rue Désiré de Lansomme

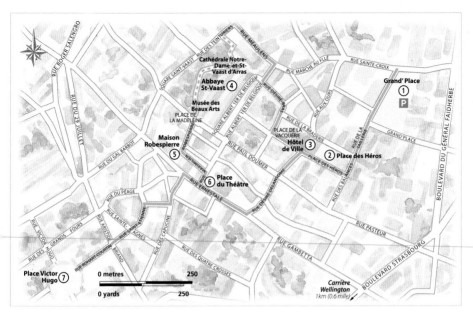

Map showing Arras town centre with numbered points of interest:
- **Grand' Place** ①
- **Cathédrale Notre-Dame-et-St-Vaast d'Arras**
- **Abbaye St-Vaast** ④
- **Musée des Beaux Arts**
- PLACE DE LA MADELEINE
- **Maison Robespierre** ⑤
- PLACE DE LA VACQUERIE
- **Hôtel de Ville** ③
- **Place des Héros** ②
- **Place du Théâtre** ⑥
- **Place Victor Hugo** ⑦
- **Carrière Wellington** 1km (0.6 mile)
- 0 metres 250
- 0 yards 250

for a drink in the Place des Héros before heading back to the car park in Grand' Place and driving to the Carrière Wellington *(open daily)*. Follow the D917 from Boulevard Strasbourg and look for signs on the left.

During World War I, British and New Zealand troops extended the chalk tunnels beneath Arras as part of the front line, and thousands lived for months here. The Carrière Wellington has been made into a very moving memorial to trench life, with remarkable mementoes such as drawings carved into the tunnel walls.

🚗 *Leave the Grand' Place towards Lens; turn right on road signposted A1 towards Lille. Then turn left on D917 and left again on N17 for Vimy.*

⑨ Vimy Ridge and Notre-Dame de Lorette
Pas-de-Calais, Nord-Pas-de-Calais; 62580
Bitter fighting went on around Arras throughout World War I. To the north is one of the most powerful war monuments, the **Canadian National Memorial** *(visitor centre open daily)* at the top of Vimy Ridge. From the base of the austere monument, inscribed with the names of the 11,285 Canadian dead, there is an immense view to the east. The visitor centre provides vivid tours. To the northwest, the French memorial of **Notre-**

Dame de Lorette contains over 40,000 graves, while by the D937 road near Neuville-St-Vaast there is a sombre German cemetery.

🚗 *Return to Arras on the D937, and follow the boulevards round to Place Foch. Take the D917 Bapaume road; immediately turn right onto the D919, signed for Bucquoy. After 28 km (17 miles) turn left for Beaumont-Hamel and Thiepval, further east along the D73.*

⑩ Beaumont-Hamel and Thiepval
Somme, Picardie; 80300
The Somme battlefield sites, memorials and cemeteries from World War I extend over the rolling green countryside east of Amiens. The **Newfoundland Memorial** *(visitor centre open daily, except mid-Dec–mid-Jan)* at Beaumont-Hamel brings home the horror of the 1916 battle. Visible from a great distance at Thiepval is the main British Somme memorial, an awe-inspiring arch bearing the names of 73,367 men whose bodies were never found.

🚗 *Continue on the D73 to Pozières and turn left on the D929, then right at Martinpuich onto the D107. Drive onto Longueval, then turn left in Guillemont, to Rancourt across the A1, then take the D1017 into Péronne.*

Above Canadian National Memorial, Vimy Ridge **Below left** Panoramic view of the town of Arras from the belfry of the Hôtel de Ville

SHOPPING IN ARRAS

Au Bleu d'Arras
A great place to buy hand-decorated blue-and-white porcelain.
32 place des Héros, 62001

S. Thibaut
The best place to find traditional spiced biscuits and chocolate rats.
50 place des Héros, 62001

EAT AND DRINK

ARRAS

La Faisanderie *expensive*
This gourmet restaurant offers modern variations on classic French cuisine.
45 Grand' Place, 62000; 03 21 48 20 76; www.restaurant-la-faisanderie.com; closed Thu pm, Sun eve and Mon

Eat and Drink: inexpensive, under €20; moderate, €20–€40; expensive, over €40

Above left Historial de la Grande Guerre museum, Péronne **Above right** Rifles displayed in the tunnels of Musée Somme 1916, Albert

VISITING AMIENS

Parking
Parking is controlled within the ring of boulevards around the city centre. The most convenient large car park is St-Leu, on rue Vanmarke near the river. There is free parking outside the boulevards, but spaces are often hard to find.

Tourist Information
40 Place Notre-Dame ; 03 22 71 60 50; www.amiens-tourisme.com

WHERE TO STAY

AROUND ALBERT

Le Macassar expensive
This luxury boutique hotel,18 km (11 miles) south of Albert, is housed in a lavishly restored 1930s house.
8 Place de la République, Corbie, 80800; 03 22 48 40 04; www.lemacassar.com

AMIENS

Hôtel Le Prieuré
inexpensive–moderate
This atmospheric old Logis hotel, an inn since the 18th century, is very close to the cathedral of Amiens.
17 rue Porion, Amiens, 80000; 03 22 71 16 71; www.hotel-prieure-amiens.com

Hotel Victor Hugo inexpensive
This is a good-value family hotel in the centre of the city, it is within walking distance of the Cathedral, other tourist areas and the station.
2 rue de l'Oratoire, 80000; 03 22 91 57 91; www.hotel-a-amiens.com

AROUND BAIE DE LA SOMME

Hôtel Picardia moderate
A rather chic little hotel in a renovated old inn near St-Valery's waterfront, with a fresh, youthful feel. Several rooms are very large and excellent for families.
41 Quai Romerel, St-Valery-sur-Somme, 80230; 03 22 60 32 30; www.picardia.fr

⑪ Péronne
Somme, Picardie; 80200
The historic town of Péronne suffered terribly during World War I. The walls of its ruined medieval castle now form the base for the innovative **Historial de la Grande Guerre** museum (open daily, mid-Jan–mid-Dec), covering every aspect of the war with original exhibits. Around Amiens and Péronne, the Somme forms several étangs (ponds) – natural sites that host a range of flora and fauna. At the back of the museum is a walk that takes visitors through some of these étangs.

🚗 Follow Avenue de la République out of Péronne onto the D938 for Albert, via a left turn in Fricourt onto the D64.

⑫ Albert
Somme, Picardie; 80300
Albert was the main British base during the Somme battles of 1916. Its **Musée Somme 1916** (open daily Feb–mid-Dec) has a large number of military relics and reconstructions of trench life. South of Corbie at Villers-Bretonneux, is the **Australian National Memorial** and the **Musée Franco-Australien** (open Mon–Sat) commemorating the role of the Australian troops in the Somme.

🚗 From Albert town centre follow signs for Corbie onto the D42 and then right onto the D1. Go through Corbie, then turn left on the D23 to Villers-Bretonneux; there turn right on the D1029 for Amiens.

⑬ Amiens
Somme, Picardie; 80000
"My little Venice" was what the 15th-century King Louis XI called Amiens.

The Somme river runs through the centre in canals and marsh-gardens, creating a relaxed ambience within the city. At its heart is the largest of France's cathedrals, **Cathédrale Notre-Dame d'Amiens**. The carvings on the west front of the cathedral are stunning, from intricate biblical scenes to the roundels around the portals that show a panorama of 13th-century life. Every evening during summer and around Christmas the west front is spectacularly illuminated with a re-creation of the rich colours with which it was painted when first built in the 13th century. There is more superb carving inside, especially in the scenes of the lives of St John the Baptist and St Firmin around the ambulatory. Below the cathedral, lively Place du Don leads to the **Quartier St-Leu**, a charming, car-free district of canals, tiny colombage houses and craft shops that is ideal for strolling. Its social centre is the **Quai Bélu**, with a line of waterside restaurants. Amiens' marsh gardens, the **Hortillonnages** (open daily, Apr–Oct), have existed since Roman times, and form a separate, placid world within the city east of Quartier St-Leu. A unique environment, full of birdlife, they are popular as leisure and market gardens, and famous for producing high-quality vegetables. The Hortillonage owners' cooperative provides tours in punt-like boats.

Bas relief in Amiens Cathedral

Above One of many waterside gardens in the Hortillonnages of Amiens

Where to Stay: inexpensive, under €70; moderate, €70–€150; expensive, over €150

The Ficelle Picarde

The *ficelle* is Picardy's most famous dish, and appears on most restaurant menus around the region. It is a rather thick crêpe covered with a slice of ham, filled with chopped or sliced mushrooms that are usually pre-sautéed, often with garlic. It is then rolled up, covered in crème fraîche and topped with grated cheese. Finally it is baked until golden and bubbling.

South of the cathedral, the **Musée de Picardie** (*open Tue–Sun*) has finds from excavations of the nearby Roman city of Samara, medieval sculpture and an impressive range of paintings. Another museum commemorates one of Amiens' most famous citizens, the author Jules Verne (1828–1905). The **Maison de Jules Verne** (*open daily Easter–mid-Oct, Wed–Mon mid-Oct–Easter*), where he lived for many years, has a reconstruction of his study and artifacts related to his life and ideas.

🚗 *Leave Amiens on the main riverside boulevard on the south bank of the Somme; follow signs for Picquigny onto the N235 and then D1235. In Picquigny, fork right onto the D3, through Abbeville to St-Valery-sur-Somme.*

⑭ Baie de la Somme
Somme, Picardie; 80230, 80550

The Somme river meets the sea in a huge arc of salt marsh, dunes and sand flats. Here at low tide, the sea can retreat 12 km (7 miles), leaving behind vast horizons and a wonderful tranquility. Ringed by footpaths, the Baie de la Somme is ideal for walking, cycling and bird-watching. On either side of the bay are two charming towns. **St-Valery-sur-Somme** is a tiny, ancient walled town, and has a tree-shaded bayside promenade, while **Le Crotoy**, opposite, has a great choice of fish restaurants. Its beach is popular for sand-yachting, and **Marquenterre** (*open daily*), a wildlife reserve to the north, is home to millions of birds.

Exploring the Bay

One of the greatest experiences in the Baie de la Somme is to walk into or even across it at low tide, in the Traversée de la Baie. Several organizations offer walks, including Rando-Nature en Somme (*www.randonature-baiedesomme.com*) and Promenade en Baie (*www.promenade-en-baie. com*). No one should ever try the walk without a guide, as the changing tides can be dangerous.

Above left Stone carving decorating Amiens Cathedral **Above right** Buildings in the walled town of St-Valery-sur-Somme

EAT AND DRINK

PÉRONNE

Bistro d'Antoine *inexpensive–moderate*
A traditional bistro located opposite the l'Historial de la Grande Guerre.
8 Place André Audinot, 80200; 03 22 85 84 46; www.bistrot-antoine.fr

AMIENS

Brasserie Jules *inexpensive–moderate*
Jules Verne provides the theme for this huge, bright modern brasserie.
18 boulevard Alsace-Lorraine, 80000; 03 22 71 18 40; www.brasserie-jules.fr

AROUND BAIE DE LA SOMME

Les Tourelles *moderate*
The brilliant light of the bay floods into the dining room at Les Tourelles. Its seafood specialities are delectable.
2–4 rue Pierre Guerlain, Le Crotoy, 80550; 03 22 27 16 33; www.lestourelles.com

DAY TRIP OPTIONS

This route conveniently breaks down into separate parts, for those with less time or a special interest to follow. For anyone approaching the area from Paris and central France, the most convenient route can be to take the A16 *autoroute* to Amiens, and begin from there.

Along the Côte d'Opale

For immediate relaxation spend some winding-down time on the beach at Wimereux, then explore Boulogne ❷ before driving down the Vallée de la Course ❸ to end the day with a gourmet meal at Montreuil ❹.

For a faster start from Calais, take the (partly toll-free) A16 autoroute from Calais rather than the coast road, and take the Wimereux exit. Follow the directions from Boulogne for the Vallée de la Course and Montreuil, but for a change return on the D940 up the coast.

The battlefields

History enthusiasts can easily spend a whole day or more exploring the World War I sites. Begin at Arras ❽ to take in Vimy ❾ and then continue down to the Somme ⑭.

To go directly to Arras, take the A26 autoroute from Calais, or the A1 from Paris. From Arras head south to

Beaumont-Hamel on the D919, then follow the Circuit du Souvenir to Péronne and Albert. From Paris, visitors can take the A16 to Amiens and begin a battlefield tour from there.

Amiens and the bay

Admire the cathedral at Amiens ⑬ and take in the city's atmosphere in the morning, and then head to the Baie de la Somme ⑭ for an invigorating walk and a stunning sunset.

Amiens can be reached very fast on the A16 autoroute from Calais or Paris and the south. From the city, follow the minor roads on the south of the Somme (D1235 and D3) for the best views.

Eat and Drink: inexpensive, under €20; moderate, €20–€40; expensive, over €40

Forests and Gardens

Giverny to Varengeville-sur-Mer

Highlights

- **Impressionist Giverny**
  Visit the house and garden that inspired Claude Monet

- **Deep countryside**
  Wander off the beaten track into a world of forests and sleepy villages

- **Magical gardens**
  Explore creative natural spaces, from a wacky art garden to exuberant banks of exotic orchids

- **Pleasures of the harbour**
  Soak in the light from atop the cliffs while savouring a delicious meal by the quayside in the old ports of Dieppe and Le Tréport

Japanese water garden and lily pond at the Fondation Claude Monet

Forests and Gardens

Between Paris and France's northern coast is a swathe of territory that contains a remarkable variety of landscapes and atmospheres. The beauties of the Seine valley are inseparably associated with the Impressionist painters, while the coastal light of maritime Dieppe has inspired many artists. In between them lies the Pays de Bray, called the *boutonnière* (buttonhole) because it is a depression of soft, rolling green valleys between the flat plains to east and west. Around the Bray towns are huge stretches of beech forest, leading up to the white chalk cliffs of the coast and towns rich in historical memories such as Eu and Dieppe itself. This region is also home to an extraordinary collection of very distinctive green havens from the Pays de Bray to the Varengeville cliffs.

Above Picturesque Vallée de l'Héron, *see p69* **Below right** People relaxing at a bar in the village square of St-Saëns, *see p70*

ACTIVITIES

Scale the ramparts of Richard the Lionheart's castle of Château Gaillard

Count the varieties of half-timbering around the square in Lyons-la-Forêt

Wander through miles of beech forest around Lyons or St-Saëns

Discover the gardens of L'Agapanthe and Bellevue

Get a taste for Neufchâtel cheese and farm-fresh terrines at the market in Neufchâtel-en-Bray

Shop for gourmet produce in the old town of Dieppe

Run into the sea at Pourville-sur-Mer, then head up to Varengeville for a panoramic sea view

KEY

▬▬▬ Drive route

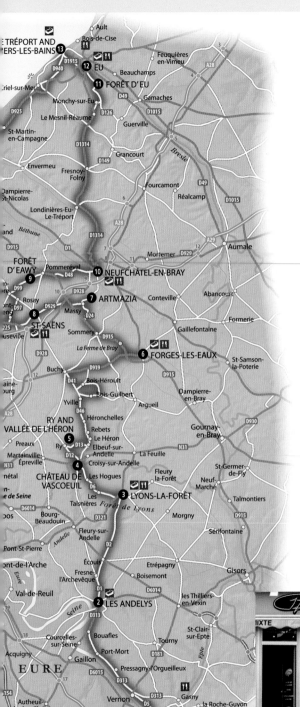

PLAN YOUR DRIVE

Start/finish: Giverny to Varengeville-sur-Mer.

Number of days: 3–4, with extra time to relax in Dieppe.

Distances: 230 km (145 miles).

Road conditions: Roads are in good condition and usually well-signposted.

When to go: April to September is generally bright and sunny.

Opening hours: The Fondation Monet is open from April to October and other attractions at Giverny are only open from May to October.

Main market days: Les Andelys: Sat; Lyons-la-Forêt: Thu, Sat, Sun; Forges-les-Eaux: Thu, Sun; St-Saëns: Thu; Neufchâtel-en-Bray: Sat; Eu: Fri; Le Tréport: Tue, Sat; Dieppe: Tue, Thu, Sat.

Shopping: Dieppe has excellent gourmet food stores around Grande Rue and Rue St-Jacques.

Major festivals: Giverny: Chamber Music Festival, Aug; Forges-les-Eaux: Juillet en Fête, Jul; Neufchâtel-en-Bray: Cheese Festival, Sep; Dieppe: International Kite Festival, Sep.

DAY TRIP OPTIONS

This area can be visited in three or more day trips. **Lovers of art** and spectacular scenery can stay between Giverny and Lyons-la-Forêt; **garden and food enthusiasts** can explore the Pays de Bray; and for **families** the stunning coast from Le Tréport to Dieppe has many attractions. For details, *see p75*.

Towering above are the ruins of **Château Gaillard** *(open Wed–Mon, Mar–Nov)*, with a breathtaking view across the valley. With walls 5 m (16 ft) thick, this massive castle was built in just one year in 1196–7 for Richard the Lionheart, King of England, to resist French attacks on Normandy. However, King Philippe Auguste of France finally captured Château Gaillard in 1204, ending the rule of the descendants of William the Conqueror in Normandy and incorporating it into France.

🚗 *From Les Andelys' main street, Avenue de la République, look for the D1 (Rue Hamelin), signed for Écouis and Lyons-la-Forêt. In Fresne-l'Archevêque, fork right to stay on the Écouis road, which then becomes the D2.*

Top Fondation Claude Monet standing amid its gardens **Above** Panoramic vista of Château Gaillard **Below** View of Les Andelys from Château Gaillard

WHERE TO STAY

GIVERNY

Moulin des Chennevières *moderate*
This 17th-century mill has four attractive bed-and-breakfast rooms.
34 chemin du Roy, 27620; 02 32 51 28 14; www.givernymoulin.com

La Réserve *moderate–expensive*
An enchanting *chambre d'hôtes* surrounded by ample grounds on the hill behind Giverny.
Chemin Blanche Hoschedé-Monet, 27620; 02 32 21 99 09; en.giverny-lareserve.com; closed Jan–Feb

LES ANDELYS

La Chaine d'Or *moderate*
This charming hotel has been converted from an 18th-century toll house near the Château Gaillard.
27 rue Grande, 27700; 02 32 54 00 31; www.hotel-lachainedor.com

LYONS-LA-FORÊT

Hostellerie de la Licorne *moderate–expensive*
The grand half-timbered La Licorne has been an inn since 1610; it has very elegant modern rooms, exceptional service and a gourmet restaurant.
Place Benserade, 27480; 02 32 48 24 24; www.hotel-licorne.com

① Giverny
Eure, Haute-Normandie; 27620
The charming house of painter Claude Monet has been beautifully restored as the **Fondation Claude Monet** *(open daily Apr–Oct)*, with its unusually fresh, bright colours – blue for the kitchen, yellow for the dining room – and Monet's superb collection of Japanese prints. Alongside it is the exquisite garden he created, including the Japanese water garden and lily pond that he painted countless times. Also on display are copies of some of his major paintings.

Following Monet, many other artists visited Giverny, and the passage from Impressionism to 20th-century art is commemorated in the **Musée des Impressionnismes** *(open daily Apr–Oct).*

🚗 *Follow the D5 north out of Giverny village to Vernon, then turn right on the D181 and immediately left onto the D313, a much calmer Seine-side route than the left-bank D6015. Take a right turn in Bouafles for Les Andelys.*

② Les Andelys
Eure, Haute-Normandie; 27700
Les Andelys is a classic Seine Valley town, with lovely views from the riverside quarter of **Le Petit-Andely** and its delightful restaurant gardens.

Monet's Little Paradise
The great Impressionist painter Claude Monet first saw Giverny from a train window, when he was looking for a place to live in the country. He had a large household to accommodate: his two sons by his first wife, who had recently died, and Alice Hoschedé, a friend of his first wife whose husband had left her and her six children. Monet and Alice later married, in 1892. They first moved into the house that is now the **Maison Claude Monet** in 1883 as tenants, but later bought it and acquired additional land in which to create Monet's astonishing garden. He was visited here by many famous artists, including Gauguin, Renoir and Pisarro.

④ Château de Vascoeuil

Vascoeuil, Eure, Haute-Normandie; 27910

Built from the 12th to the 17th centuries, this impressive turreted stone manor house became famous as the home of the historian and writer Jules Michelet (1798–1874), and part of it is now a museum dedicated to him. Since the 1970s, Vascoeuil has also hosted contemporary art exhibitions. Around the château there is a sculpture garden, with works by Dalí, Vasarely, Léger and other artists distributed around the lawns.

🚗 *On the right while leaving the castle, cross over the N31 onto the D12 for Ry.*

⑤ Ry and Vallée de l'Héron

Seine-Maritime, Haute-Normandie; 76116, 76750

The suicide of a doctor's wife at Ry in 1848 was the incident that inspired Gustave Flaubert's novel *Madame Bovary*, and many of the town's buildings can be closely identified with those in the book. Follow signs to Elbeuf-sur-Andelle (D13) and turn left to the east onto the Héron valley road, the D46, towards Buchy. The road runs by the Héron river up one of the region's prettiest valleys, with lovely views near **Le Héron**, **Héronchelles** and **Yville**. Detour right above Yville to Bois Guilbert and Bois-Héroult before rejoining the D41 to Buchy. **Bois-Guilbert** and **Bois-Héroult**, outside the main valley, each have 17th- and 18th-century châteaux amid fine gardens, and **Buchy**, has a 17th-century timber-frame market hall.

🚗 *At the crossroads in the centre of Buchy take the D919 to reach Forges-les-Eaux.*

③ Lyons-la-Forêt

Eure, Haute-Normandie; 27480

This astonishingly well-preserved village of Norman *colombage* houses has often been used as a film set, especially the stunning main square with its 18th-century timber **Halles** (market hall). The village has had a varied history: Henry I, King of England and ruler of Normandy, died here in 1135, and composer Maurice Ravel came here to write amid rural tranquillity in the 1920s. The **Forêt de Lyons** around it, once a hunting-ground of the Norman dukes, is one of the largest and densest beech forests in Europe, crossed by excellent walking and cycling routes.

🚗 *Take "Toutes directions"; take the first left and then right onto the D321. Take a left onto the D6, signed for Les Taisnières, Les Hogues et Château de Vascoeuil. Take the road right in Les Hogues, then left in Vascoeuil.*

Henry and the Lampreys

Henry I of England died in 1135 in Lyons-la-Forêt's now long-destroyed castle, supposedly from eating too many lampreys, the river eels that were considered a delicacy at medieval courts. Known as Henri Beauclerc because of his reputation for learning, he was also extremely cruel. He had more illegitimate children than any other English king.

EAT AND DRINK

GIVERNY

Ancien Hôtel Baudy *inexpensive–moderate*
Painters such as Cézanne and Sisley often stayed at this historic village hotel when they came to visit Monet at Giverny. The bar, dining room and gardens have a bohemian feel, with paintings around the walls. It offers good value dishes and *plats du jour*.
81 rue Claude Monet, 27620; 02 32 21 10 03; closed Sun evenings and Mon, and Nov–Mar

AROUND GIVERNY

Auberge du Prieuré Normand *moderate– expensive*
Philippe Robert prepares some of the best food in the area at this unassuming, comfortable restaurant, 7 km (4 miles) north of Giverny.
1 place de la République, Gasny, 27620; 02 32 52 10 01; closed Wed and Aug

LYONS-LA-FORÊT

Les Lions de Beauclerc *inexpensive–moderate*
Menus here are an attractive mix, from substantial grills or roasts to crêpes, salads and other light dishes. It is also an enjoyable hotel, with six charming rooms plushly decorated with antiques.
7 rue de l'Hôtel de Ville, 27480; 02 32 49 18 90; closed Tue

La Halle *inexpensive–moderate*
Friendly young staff give this bar-bistro a fresh style, so the menu might include light pasta dishes with seafood as well as Norman meats in cider sauces. The terrace in front is a great spot for admiring the village architecture.
6 place Benserade, 27480; 02 32 49 49 92; closed Sun evenings and Wed

Top Turreted Château de Vascoeuil **Above** Thatched cottage, Lyons-la-Forêt **Below left** Château de Bois-Guilbert **Below right** Fresh strawberries on sale

Above left Part of the art maze at Artmazia
Above right Gothic church at St-Saëns
Below Grand Casino at Forges-lès-Eaux

WHERE TO STAY

FORGES-LES-EAUX

Forges Hotel *moderate–expensive*
A sleek modern spa hotel. It has a
whole range sports facilities too.
*Avenue des Sources, 76440; 02 32 89
50 57; www.forgeshotel.com*

ST-SAËNS

Le Logis d'Eawy
inexpensive–moderate
A *colombage* former coaching inn has
been tastefully renovated into this
chambre d'hôtes. There is an antique-
furnished breakfast room, a bright
courtyard and a large garden. The four
bed-and-breakfast rooms have plenty
of charm.
*1 rue du 31 Août 1944, 76680; 06 19 15
52 04; www.logisdeawy.com*

NEUFCHÂTEL-EN-BRAY

Le Grand Cerf *inexpensive*
This traditional hotel is a very likeable
local institution. The rooms are
comfortable and the hotel now has
some modern extras (even Wi-Fi), and
the staff is very helpful. The restaurant
has enjoyable, good-value local cuisine.
*9 Grande Rue Fausse Porte, 76270; 02
35 93 00 02; www.logis-de-france.fr*

Le Cellier du Val Boury *inexpensive*
This huge farm is on the edge of the
town, but feels very rural, with ample
space for relaxing. The rooms are in an
impressive 17th-century wine store.
*3 rue du Val Boury, 76270; 02 35 93
26 95; www.cellier-val-boury.com*

6 Forges-les-Eaux

Seine-Maritime, Haute-Normandie;
76440
One of the main towns of the Pays
de Bray, Forges-les-Eaux became a
fashionable spa in the 17th century.
The town has a 19th-century casino
and there are some pretty walks in
the **Bois d'Epinay** woods. To the
north near Sommery is the **La Ferme
de Bray**, owned by the Perrier family
for generations and now a remarkable farm-museum *(open daily Jul–Aug,
and Sat, Sun, holidays Easter–Oct)*, with a
15th–18th century watermill, cider-
press and dairy. It houses fascinating
exhibits on rural life. Ferme de Bray
also has very pretty bed-and-
breakfast rooms. There are amazing
views over the Bray valleys from the
D915 heading north.

🚗 *Retrace the route out of Forges-les-
Eaux, but turn right onto the D915
Dieppe road for La Ferme de Bray.*

*Drive on along this road and look out
for a right turn, the D24, to Massy.
Follow signs through Massy village to
arrive at Artmazia.*

7 Artmazia

Seine-Maritime, Haute-Normandie;
76270
This huge spiral "art-maze" has been
created out of 5,000 beech trees by
British artist Geoff Troll *(open daily Jul–
Aug, Sat & Sun May–Jun and Sept–Oct)*.
As visitors make their way around it,
they discover all kinds of colourful
and offbeat artwork, animals and
beautiful vistas, and it is great fun for
children. There are also innovative
exhibitions and a relaxing little
café, which hosts concerts and
other entertainment.

🚗 *Take the C3 Bellozane and at the
roundabout, turn left onto the D928,
then right onto the D929 for St-Saëns.
Take the D225 to Grigneuseville and
Étaimpuis. After visiting the gardens
there, turn back along the D929 and
then left (north) onto the D97 for
Beaumont-le-Hareng.*

8 St-Saëns

Seine-Maritime, Haute-Normandie;
76880
St-Saëns is one of the prettiest Bray
towns, with a charming old town
square. In the countryside to the
west are three remarkable gardens.
L'Agapanthe at Grigneuseville *(open
Thu–Tue Apr–Nov)* is a labyrinth of
intimate spaces overflowing with
roses, agapanthus and other flowers.
Le Clos du Coudray at Étaimpuis
(open daily Apr–Oct) is a more conven-
tional, elegant garden. **Les Jardins de**

Bellevue at Beaumont-le-Hareng (*open daily*) is quite the opposite. It is an extraordinary hillside estate created by the Lemonnier family with rare and exotic trees and plants from around the world. Unusually, it has different plants in bloom all year round.

🚗 *Drive on from the Jardins de Bellevue up the D97 to Rosay, and turn left on the D154 to Bellencombre. Turn up the steep, winding D99 for Pommeréval to cross the Forêt d'Eawy.*

⑨ Forêt d'Eawy

Seine-Maritime, Haute-Normandie; 76680

Extending north from St-Saëns, the Forêt d'Eawy is another of this region's giant beech woods, once a royal hunting-ground. It stretched over an area of 65 sq km (25 sq miles). With its church nestling in a valley, **Bellencombre** is one of its loveliest villages. Visitors should look out for superb views as they climb out of the village on the D99, which crosses the **Allée des Limousins**, a splendid bridle path that cuts through the forest for 14 km (9 miles). In the shade of the trees by the roadside at **Val-Ygot** is an unusual World War II site with a reconstruction of a V1 bomb and the ramp from which it was launched. In 1944, the Germans used this as a base to bombard London.

🚗 *At Pommeréval, turn right onto the D915, and then left onto the D48 following signs for Neufchâtel.*

Cheese With a Heart

First recorded in 1035, Neufchâtel is by far the oldest of the great Norman cheeses, and the only one from north of the Seine. It is still only produced on small farms in the Pays de Bray. With a soft, powdery texture and a subtly dry taste, for aficionados it has more character than the creamier Norman cheeses. Excellent for cooking, most Neufchâtel is white and has a short life; aged or *vieux Neufchâtel* takes on a brown colour, and is extremely strong. Neufchâtel is made in several traditional shapes – cylinders, rectangles and, the best known, hearts (*coeurs*). According to legend, this shape was invented by Norman milkmaids during the Hundred Years' War in order to "soften the hearts" of English soldiers.

⑩ Neufchâtel-en-Bray

Seine-Maritime, Haute-Normandie; 76270

Neufchâtel-en-Bray was the former capital of the Pays de Bray region. It holds the region's largest market every Saturday, with a special section for local products. The town is the best place to find the area's specialities such as duck terrines and Neufchâtel cheese. It is enjoyable to explore the surrounding villages and to find farms that sell cheeses or meats directly to visitors. There are also fine cider and Calvados producers, like the **Clos du Bourg** at **St-Saire**. Enquire at the Neufchâtel tourist office for details.

🚗 *Leave Neufchâtel on the D1314, for Londinières-Eu-Le Tréport. At Le Mesnil-Réaume, take the D58 right to Monchy-sur-Eu, follow it through the village and into the small road on the left at the start of the forest, then turn left at the "Carrefour Isabelle" to join Route de la Poterie. Follow this forest road, and park in the clearing where it meets the road from Eu.*

Above La Ferme de Bray, a remarkable farm-museum **Below** Reconstruction of a World War II V1 bomb at Val-Ygot

VISITING NEUFCHÂTEL-EN-BRAY

Tourist Information
6 place Notre-Dame, 76270; 02 35 93 22 96; www.ot-pays-neufchatelois.fr

EAT AND DRINK

FORGES-LES-EAUX

Hôtel de la Paix *inexpensive–moderate*
This cosy hotel-restaurant has long been renowned for the fine cooking of chef Rémy Michel and his team – from Norman classics to intricate fish dishes.
17 rue de Neufchâtel, 76440; 02 35 90 51 22; www.hotellapaix.fr; closed Sun evenings

ST-SAËNS

Le Relais Normand *inexpensive–moderate*
With tables on St-Saëns town square in summer, this popular restaurant offers enjoyable menus of skilfully-prepared Norman dishes and a good range of one-course options.
21 place Maintenon, 76680; 02 35 34 38 93; closed Sun evenings and Wed

NEUFCHÂTEL-EN-BRAY

Les Airelles *inexpensive–moderate*
A great €17 menu is available from Tuesday evening to Friday midday, serving *cuisine moderne* dishes such as rump steak with forest herbs and lamb flavoured with thyme, all in a pleasant terrace setting.
2 Passage Michu, 76270; 02 35 93 14 60

Eat and Drink: inexpensive, under €20; moderate, €20–€40; expensive, over €40

Above Rows of trees in the dense Forêt d'Eu

⑪ Forêt d'Eu

Seine-Maritime, Haute-Normandie; 76260

The Forêt d'Eu is the largest of northeast Normandy's great beech forests, extending in several sections over 93 sq km (36 sq miles) on a long ridge between the valleys of the Yères and Bresle rivers. The dark, dense forest was once a home for the Gauls and Romans and later a hunting estate for the Dukes of Normandy and a source of charcoal for the early glassmakers of the Bresle valley. It is also one of the largest intact native forests left in Europe, and a walk through it is a marvellous way to discover its fascinating landscape.

A 90-minute walking tour

Leave the car in the parking area where the forest road from Monchy meets the Route de Beaumont from Eu, and take the path to the left, looking into the forest, the Route Clémentine. The main tracks in this part of the forest, Clémentine and Louise, are named after the daughters of King Louis-Philippe (1773–1850), a great lover of Eu, who often came to the forest for family outings and picnics. Follow the path along until it bends to the right around an escarpment known as La Houblonnière, which has superb views over the Vallée de la Bresle, with large ponds between the viewpoint and the village of Bouvaincourt-sur-Bresle.

The Vallée de la Bresle has been a centre of glassmaking since the early Middle Ages when it was a cottage industry, making use of the area's sandy soil. Today, there are huge glass

Road sign pointing to Bois-l'Abbé

factories towards Mers-les-Bains. Continue on the Route Clémentine as it turns back into the forest and winds around the sides of the escarpment. To the left, at every break in the trees, there are more superb views.

In late spring, there are often great banks of bluebells around the paths; in autumn, the colours of the golden beeches are stunning. Look out too for wildlife: deer and wild boar are quite common in the forest, and there is an enormous range of birds, including warblers, woodpeckers and orioles. At the end of a steep cleft where the path hairpins left there is one of the forest's most intriguing monuments, the **Pierre Bise** ①, a stone column believed to be a Druidic monument dating from Gaulish times. A little further on are the giant remains of one of the forest's largest and most famous trees, the **Quesne à Leu** ②, which fell

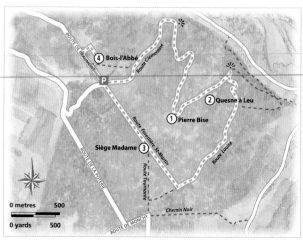

in 2008 after standing for over 300 years. Follow the path through more twists and turns and viewpoints over the village of Incheville to meet the Route Louise at one of the forest's main junctions, indicated by metal *poteaux* or signposts. Take this path to the right, and follow it through the woods above Incheville until it meets the Route Forestière St-Martin. Turn right to head straight back to the car through the heart of the forest, one of the best places in the forest for seeing wildlife. On the way, at **Siège Madame ③**, a *sentier botanique* or botanical path has been marked out off the main track, indentifying over 40 different plants.

For a longer walk stay on Route Louise and turn left onto Route Tournante, then right on Route de Monchy and right again onto Route de la Poterie to follow this track back to the parking area along the Yères valley side of the forest. Before getting back into the car, walk down the Route de Beaumont a little way to look across at the excavations of **Bois-l'Abbé ④**. Mainly excavated over the last 20 years, this is believed to have been a major Gallo-Roman city between the 1st and 3rd centuries AD. Excavations are ongoing, but have already revealed the city's forum, a theatre and a large Roman bath complex. Visitors can see a lot of the site from beside the fence around it. From June to September guided tours are provided every Tuesday and Sunday afternoon.

🚗 *Take the Route de Beaumont from the forest past Bois l'Abbé, which joins the D49 road into the centre of Eu. Except during the Friday market, there is ample parking around the château.*

⑫ Eu

Seine-Maritime, Haute-Normandie; 76260

Thanks to its special history, Eu looks surprisingly grand for a small town. The Irish saint, Laurence O'Toole, died here in 1180, and the magnificent Gothic **Collégiale** church was built over his tomb. The splendid 16th-century French-Renaissance-style **Château d'Eu** *(open Wed–Mon Mar–Nov)* was the favourite home of King Louis-Philippe. Among the items on display inside are mementoes of the 1843 visit of Queen Victoria. There are more distinguished buildings around Eu's streets, and the Friday market is very popular.

🚗 *From the Château d'Eu the Route du Tréport, D1915, leads directly to Le Tréport, where a curving bridge by the quais crosses over to Mers-les-Bains.*

⑬ Le Tréport and Mers-les-Bains

Seine-Maritime, Haute-Normandie; 76470. Somme, Picardie; 80350

On either side of the Bresle river, these two towns were among France's first seaside resorts. **Le Tréport** to the west is an important fishing port, and fresh fish and seafood are the mainstays of the bustling restaurants along the quayside. **Mers-les-Bains**, on the Somme side, has the best beach and a long seafront of extraordinary 1900s Art Nouveau houses, with ornate balconies and gorgeous tilework.

🚗 *Take the D940 for Dieppe from Le Tréport's main avenue; as it climbs look for a right turn onto Boulevard du Calvaire for a spectacular route along the cliffs. This rejoins the main D925 Dieppe road at Criel-sur-Mer.*

Above Collégiale church in Eu built over the tomb of St Laurence O'Toole **Below** Art Noveau houses on the seafront, Mers-les-Bains

EAT AND DRINK

EU

Domaine de Joinville
moderate-expensive
This excellent and surprisingly reasonably priced restaurant is located in Château d'Eu's 19th-century hunting lodge housed in the heart of the forest of Eu.
Route du Tréport, 76260; 02 35 50 52 52; www.domainejoinville.com

AROUND LE TRÉPORT

Le Cise *moderate*
A stunning restaurant at Bois de Cise, a curious little Art Nouveau holiday village concealed in a sheltered wooded inlet in the cliffs north of Mers-les-Bains. The clifftop restaurant has a superb panoramic seaview from the dining room and terrace. The adventurous modern cooking is full of enticing flavours, especially the catch-of-the-day fish and seafood.
Route de la Plage, Bois de Cise, Ault, 80460; 03 22 26 46 46; www.lecise. com; closed Mon

Above Pinnacle-roofed turrets of Château-Musée, Dieppe **Below left** Yachts line the harbour at Dieppe **Below right** Café des Tribunaux, Dieppe

VISITING DIEPPE

Tourist Information
Pont Jehan-Ango; 02 32 14 40 60;
www.dieppetourisme.com

Parking
There is plenty of parking, some for free, in Dieppe on the seafront, along Boulevard Verdun and Boulevard Maréchal Foch.

Shopping
L'Epicier Olivier has magnificent displays of fine wines, ciders, preserves and Normandy cheeses, including best-quality Neufchâtel.
16 rue St-Jacques

WHERE TO STAY

DIEPPE

Au Grand Duquesne *inexpensive*
The most characterful of Dieppe's hotels, located right on the main shopping street.
15 place St-Jacques, Dieppe, 76200; 02 32 14 61 10; augrandduquesne.free.fr

Villa des Capucins
inexpensive–moderate
A wall in the fishing quarter of Pollet conceals the garden of this splendid 19th-century house. The rooms, alongside the garden, are snug and pretty.
11 rue des Capucins, Dieppe, 76200; 02 35 82 16 52; www.villa-des-capucins.fr

⑭ Dieppe

Seine-Maritime, Haute-Normandie; 76200

Dieppe's giant harbour is the source of its distinctive maritime character. It has enabled Dieppe to play many roles, from Viking stronghold to home port for explorers and pirates and, later, a link between France and Britain. It also became France's first-ever beach resort, and has retained its mix of energy and easy-going streetlife.

Quai Henri IV, along the north side of the port, is lined with cafés and restaurants that are ideal places to relax and watch the movement in the harbour. Rising up above the east side of the port is the tower of the regal Gothic church of **St-Jacques**. Its size and opulence reflect the wealth of Dieppe's shipowners in the 15th and 16th centuries, when they sailed to Canada, Africa and Brazil and engaged in piracy as well as trade.

On three days each week the squares and streets around St-Jacques are filled with a wonderful market, with every kind of local product. There are also many eye-catching permanent shops along the **Grande Rue** and adjacent streets, especially for luxury foods such as fine wines, cheeses and high-quality chocolates.

Throughout the 19th century Dieppe was an important point of contact between the French and British artistic worlds. The **Café des Tribunaux** with its clock tower above Place du Puits Salé, where the Grande Rue meets Rue St-Jacques, is one of France's most imposing grand cafés. It was a celebrated artists' meeting-place and is most associated with writer Oscar Wilde, who fled to Dieppe after he was released from

prison in England in 1897. Rising up on a lofty crag beside the old town is the 15th-century **Château-Musée** *(open daily Jun–Sep, Wed–Mon Oct–Mar)*, with pinnacle-roofed turrets and a sweeping view. Highlights of the collection inside are paintings by artists associated with Dieppe such as Pisarro, Braque and Sickert, and relics of the town's maritime past, including an astonishing collection of intricately carved ivory pieces.

The Duchesse de Berry introduced the new fashion for sea-bathing to France in Dieppe in 1824. The beach is a long shingle bank, with a promenade separated from the town by a swimming pool, a playground, gardens and other attractions. A garden at one end of the beach below the château is now the **Square du Canada**, in memory of the losses suffered by Canadian troops in the Dieppe Raid of August 1942. There is also a nearby museum, the **Mémorial du 19 Août 1942** *(open Wed–Mon Jun–Sep, Sat & Sun Easter–May and Oct–Nov)*. 🚗 *Just below the Château-Musée at Place des Martyrs, take the D75, signed for Pourville, which runs steeply uphill and out of Dieppe towards Pourville-sur-Mer and the next stop at Varengeville.*

⑮ Varengeville-sur-Mer

Seine-Maritime, Haute-Normandie; 76119

The coast road west of Dieppe has magnificent views, especially above the beach of **Pourville-sur-Mer**. The beauty of Varengeville, spread through woods above the cliffs further on, has long attracted artists and the wealthy. The 12th-century clifftop church has windows by modern artist Georges Braque (1882–1963), who is buried in the churchyard. Inland from the village is the **Manoir d'Ango** (open daily May–Sep), a mix of Norman farm and Renaissance manor, built for Dieppe shipowner-buccaneer Jehan Ango in the 1540s. More unusual are the house and gardens of the **Bois des Moutiers** (open daily mid-May–mid-Nov; house by appointment), built in 1898 by English architect Edwin Lutyens and garden designer Gertrude Jekyll for banker Guillaume Mallet, to reflect his theosophist beliefs.

Above Clifftop church at Vargenville-sur-Mer
Below Gardens at Bois des Moutiers

Pirate Dieppe

In the 16th century, Dieppe's hardy seamen made voyages of exploration virtually on their own account and carried on their own private wars. They sailed to the Americas, Africa and East Asia, bringing back spices, ivory and tropical woods. Many voyages were sponsored by the legendary shipowner Jehan Ango (1480–1551), the richest man in Dieppe. He was given permission by King François I (1494–1547) to attack ships, other than the French ones, and his voyages were a combination of commercial venture and pirate raid. In the 1520s, he fought his own war with Portugal off the coast of Brazil. Ango spread the loot he gained widely around his hometown, and ever since has been remembered as a local hero.

EAT AND DRINK

DIEPPE

Restaurant du Port
inexpensive–moderate
Chef Michel Mouny's Du Port has fish dishes as a highlight.
99 quai Henri IV, 76200; 02 35 84 36 64; closed Wed evening and Thu

Café des Tribunaux
inexpensive–moderate
Having a coffee at the Tribunaux is obligatory just to take in its historical associations, but it also has brasserie-style menu of grills and snacks.
1 place du Puits-Salé Dieppe, 76200; 02 32 14 44 65

VARENGEVILLE-SUR-MER

Auberge du Relais
inexpensive–moderate
Excellent seafood dishes are served on a pleasant terrace close to the sea. There's a reasonable wine list, too.
Route Dieppe, 76119; 02 35 83 64 04; closed Jan, Sun evening and Mon out of season

---

DAY TRIP OPTIONS

To go directly to the Pays de Bray from the Paris area, take the A16 *autoroute* to Beauvais (exit 14) and then the Gournay-en-Bray road to Forges-les-Eaux; from the north, take the A28 and leave at exit 10. For the coast, follow the A28 from either direction, and take exit 5 for Eu and Le Tréport.

Monet and the forest

Get to Giverny ❶ early to avoid the crowds, and then wander up the Seine to Les Andelys ❷ for lunch by the river. Then visit Château-Gaillard, before ending the day with a walk in the dense woods around Lyons-la-Forêt ❸.

From Lyons, take the D31 road through Fleury-sur-Andelle to return to the Seine valley and the main north–south autoroute.

The Bray countryside

Those looking for a real sense of the countryside have the option of spending a day in the Bray valleys between Forges-les-Eaux ❻, St-Saëns ❽ and Neufchâtel-en-Bray ❿. Visitors will have the opportunity to see the remarkable gardens here and buy fine cheeses and other country foods from the small-town markets.

From Neufchâtel, make a quick return to the A28 autoroute at junction 9.

The Alabaster Coast

Beaches, sea views, fine food and history can all fill a day beginning with an exploration of the little-known charms of Eu ⓬ before going on to Le Tréport ⓭ and Dieppe ⓮.

From Dieppe, take the D927 Rouen road for Paris and the south, or the D915 Forges road, back to the A28 for the route to the north and east.

Eat and Drink: inexpensive, under €20; moderate, €20–€40; expensive, over €40

The Essence of Normandy

Honfleur to Falaise

Highlights

- **Maritime Honfleur**
  Stroll around this unique old harbour town and marvel at its architecture

- **Chic resorts**
  Be a part of Deauville's glamour, and enjoy superb seafood in Trouville

- **Green paradise**
  Forget the everyday and find perfect peace among the dense green lanes and tiny villages of the Pays d'Auge

- **Norman delights**
  Discover the bounty of the Auge countryside: wonderful cheeses, ciders and farm-fresh produce

- **Entrancing gardens**
  Wander around the elegant gardens at Château de Canon

Idyllic gardens of the 18th-century Château de Canon

The Essence of Normandy

Located between the sea, Caen and the Seine river, this area distils into one space the prime attractions of one of France's most distinctive regions. On the coast is the old granite port of Honfleur, evocative of explorers, artists and eccentrics. To the west are the resorts of Deauville and Trouville, still with plenty of verve after over a century in fashion. Inland is the Pays d'Auge, so idyllically pretty it almost seems unreal, with deep green orchards, half-timbered farms and winding tree-lined lanes, at the end of which is the promise of France's finest cheeses and ciders and an original cuisine, for this is also a land of great natural abundance.

Top Relaxing terrace at one of Honfleur's many small restaurants, *see p80*
Above Equestrian statue of William the Conqueror in Falaise, *see p85*

ACTIVITIES

Enter the unique world of Erik Satie, and listen to his music, at Honfleur's Maison Satie museum

Play on the beach with a Monet view as a backdrop on Trouville's famous *planches*

Sample ciders from the barrel in the giant-timbered barns of a Pays d'Auge farm

Walk through the woods and lanes around Beuvron-en-Auge

Absorb the atmosphere of rural Normandy at St-Pierre-sur-Dives' wonderful market

See two sides of the Ancien Régime at the contrasting châteaux of Canon and Vendeuvre

Get a feel of the Middle Ages on the mighty towers of Falaise castle

KEY

Drive route

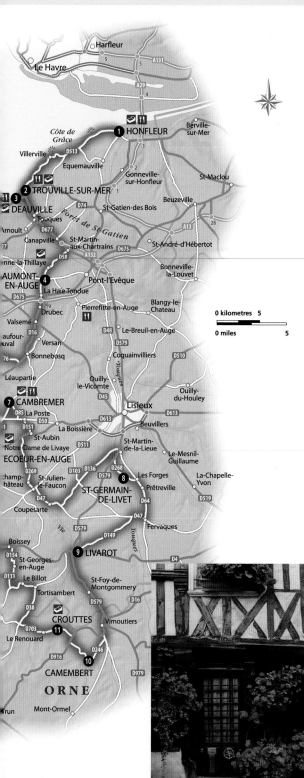

PLAN YOUR DRIVE

Start/finish: Honfleur to Falaise.

Number of days: 3–4, allowing for at least a half-day in Honfleur.

Distances: 195 km (120 miles).

Road conditions: In good condition, but signposting in the tiny lanes of the Pays d'Auge can be inconsistent. D roads change numbers when they cross into a different *département*.

When to go: The weather is generally good from May to September, and everywhere is open. From late July through August all major tourist spots are crowded. September to November is the cider apple harvest season.

Opening hours: Museums and sights in the region usually open from about 9 or 10am to 6 or 7pm, with a 1- or 2-hour lunch break. Some stay open without a lunch break in July–August. Many sites have shorter hours at weekends, and many close completely over December–January.

Main market days: Honfleur: Sat; Trouville-sur-Mer: Wed, Sun; Beuvron-en-Auge: Sat; Cambremer: Fri; Livarot: Thu; St-Pierre-sur-Dives: Mon; Falaise: Sat.

Shopping: Shop for idiosyncratic jewellery, art and accessories in Honfleur; traditionally chic fashion and gourmet foods in Deauville; and cheeses and ciders in the Pays d'Auge.

Major festivals: Deauville: horse-racing, Jul–Aug, Festival du Cinéma Américain, Sep; Beuvron-en-Auge: Cider Festival, Oct; Falaise: Fêtes Guillaume-le-Conquérant, Aug.

DAY TRIP OPTIONS

This area can be divided into different day trips. **Families** can spend a whole day in Honfleur and on the beaches further west; **food and countryside lovers** are in heaven around Beuvron and Cambremer; and those who just want to **get away from it all** can find plenty to explore around St-Germain-de-Livet. For details, see *p85*.

Left Typical Norman *colombage* house near Beaumont-en-Auge, *see p82*

Map labels

Harfleur
Le Havre
A131
A29
Côte de Grâce
1 HONFLEUR
Berville-sur-Mer
Villerville
D513
Equemauville
Gonneville-sur-Honfleur
St-Maclou
2 TROUVILLE-SUR-MER
Beuzeville
3 DEAUVILLE
Touques
D74
St-Gatien-des-Bois
Arnoult
D677
Forêt de St-Gatien
A13
Canapville
St-Martin-aux-Chartrains
D675
St-André-d'Hébertot
nne-la-Thillaye
D58
A132
AUMONT-EN-AUGE 4
Bonneville-la-Louvet
D675
La Haie Tondue
Pont-l'Évêque
Drubec
Pierrefitte-en-Auge
Blangy-le-Château
Valsemé
D16
Versan
D48
Le-Breuil-en-Auge
aufour-uval
Bonnebosq
D579
Coquainvilliers
D510
Léaupartie
Quilly-le-Vicomte
D45
Ouilly-du-Houley
7 CAMBREMER
La Poste
Lisieux
D85
D50
D613
D613
D151
La Boissière
Beuvillers
St-Aubin
D511
St-Martin-de-la-Lieue
Notre-Dame de Livaye
Le-Mesnil-Guillaume
ECOEUR-EN-AUGE
D269
D103
D136
D579
D268
Les Forges
La-Chapelle-Yvon
champ-hâteau
St-Julien-le-Faucon
8
Prêtreville
ST-GERMAIN-DE-LIVET
D47
D64
D519
Coupesarte
D47
Fervaques
Vie
D579
D149
Boissey
D154
9 LIVAROT
St-Georges-en-Auge
D4
D111
Le Billot
St-Foy-de-Montgommery
Tortisambert
D579
D16
D38
CROUTTES 11
Vimoutiers
D703
Le Renouard
D246
D916
10
CAMEMBERT
D979
ORNE
Mont-Ormel
run

0 kilometres 5
0 miles 5

Above Steps leading up to the impressive 16th-century Lieutenance **Below** Boats anchored in the Vieux Bassin in Honfleur

VISITING HONFLEUR

Tourist information
Quai Lepaulmier, 14600; 02 31 89 23 30; www.ot-honfleur.fr

Parking
There are large paid car parks around the old town, the most convenient next to Quai de la Tour. There are some free car parking spaces on Rue Haute and off Boulevard Charles V, but they are in great demand, especially in summer.

WHERE TO STAY

HONFLEUR

Hôtel des Loges moderate
Very chic modern design and subtle colour schemes combined with a splendid old Honfleur house.
18 rue Brûlée, 14600; 02 31 89 38 26; www.hoteldesloges.com

L'Absinthe moderate–expensive
A special hotel in a restored 16th-century presbytery, it luxuriously blends modern features with the style of the original building. The nearby Absinthe restaurant is one of Honfleur's most refined.
1 rue de la Ville, 14600; 02 31 89 23 23; www.absinthe.fr

TROUVILLE-SUR-MER

Hôtel Le Central moderate
The location is excellent for getting in touch with Trouville's buzzy joie de vivre, with rooms right above one of the classic brasseries.
5–7 rue des Bains, 14360; 02 31 88 80 84; www.le-central-trouville.com

① Honfleur
Calvados, Basse-Normandie; 14600

Honfleur is unique. Its inner harbour or Vieux Bassin is flanked by slate-fronted six- or seven-storey houses, bizarrely tall for the time when they were built in the 17th century. Later, the town became a hub for Impressionist painters, first led here by artist Eugène Boudin, born in Honfleur in 1824. Today, the town offers a huge choice of restaurants and some of Normandy's most stylish hotels.

A two-hour walking tour

Try to park by Quai de la Tour, on the east side of the old town. Walk along Cour des Fossés past the tourist office and turn right onto Rue de la Ville, the oldest part of Honfleur. On the right is the massive **Greniers à Sel** ① or salt warehouse, built in 1670 when salt was a royal monopoly. It is now used for exhibitions. Turn down the alley opposite the Greniers and turn left down Rue de la Prison towards the two parts of the **Musées du Vieux Honfleur** ②. The first includes part of the old town prison and engaging reconstructions of rooms in traditional Augeron houses. Beyond it is the Quai St-Etienne, where visitors get the first spectacular view of the **Vieux Bassin** ③. To the left is the other half of the museum on maritime history, in the former church of St-Etienne.

Walk around the quays, checking out which of their terrace restaurants to come back to for lunch. The most unusual multistorey houses line Quai Ste-Catherine on the west side, built

Typical façade of a building, Honfleur

against the steep sides of the harbour to maximize space, and with roofs that are a crazy mixture of heights. At the end of the quay, guarding the entrance to the Vieux Bassin, is the imposing stone **Lieutenance** ④, the 16th-century former governor's residence. In 1608, Samuel Champlain sailed from here to found the French colony of Québec.

Turn left at the end of Quai Ste-Catherine and cross Place Hamelin to walk up Rue de l'Homme-de-Bois, which has intimate restaurants and fine craft jewellers. A short way along is the **Musée Eugène Boudin** ⑤, with works by Boudin and other artists associated with Honfleur, including Monet, Jongkind, Courbet and Dufy.

Walk down the alley opposite the Musée Eugène Boudin and turn left on Rue Haute to pass the **Maisons Satie** ⑥, birthplace of the eccentric composer Erik Satie (1866–1925). It is now a museum that gives a wonderful insight into his special world. Continue along Rue Haute and take the next

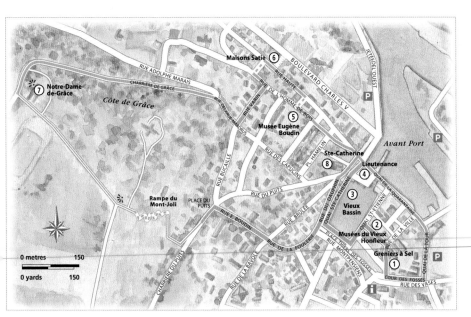

stairway on the left back to Rue de l'Homme-de-Bois. Turn left, and then right again up Rue Varin, past the gardens of old Honfleur houses. Next, turn right on Rue Delarue-Mardrus, and look on the left for the long ramp of the Charrière de Grâce, which will take visitors to the very top of the escarpment above Honfleur, the Côte de Grâce. Take in the fabulous view of the Seine, the Pont de la Normandie bridge and modern Le Havre across the river. At the top is the tranquil Baroque sailors' chapel of **Notre-Dame-de-Grâce** ⑦.

Walk on past the chapel and look out on the left for another viewpoint, which leads to a precipitous zigzag path, the Rampe du Mont-Joli, back down to the town and the pretty Place du Puits. Turn right down Rue Eugène Boudin and follow the street past more fine old houses, a stone Lavoir or traditional washhouse and the tempting shops of Rue du Dauphin. This street ends at the delightful sloping squares around the glorious church of **Ste-Catherine** ⑧, built entirely out of wood by local shipwrights in the 1470s. Leave the square on the right to rejoin the harbour by the Lieutenance, and walk on across the mouth of the

Restaurant sign, Honfleur

Vieux Bassin to return to Quai de la Tour.

🚗 *Follow Honfleur harbour seawards and turn left onto Boulevard Charles V to join the D513, which runs into Trouville. Parking can be found on the streets uphill from the beach.*

Honfleur Characters

Honfleur has been the hometown of two great eccentrics. Composer Erik Satie for a time wore only black clothes and ate only white food. His contemporary, humourist Alphonse Allais (1854–1905), staged the world's first abstract art show with paintings such as an entirely red canvas titled *Apoplectic Cardinals Harvesting Tomatoes by the Red Sea*.

② Trouville-sur-Mer
Calvados, Basse-Normandie; 14360
Trouville was the first resort at the mouth of the Seine to become popular in the 1850s, and its beach was painted by famous artists such as Boudin, Monet and Renoir. It has still retained a laid-back, bohemian appeal and is home to some of France's liveliest and most enjoyable brasseries.

🚗 *Cross the Pont des Belges across the Touques river to enter Deauville.*

EAT AND DRINK

HONFLEUR
Le Bréard *moderate*
Among the region's best for inventive, original cooking. Fabulous value.
7 rue du Puits, 14600; 02 31 89 53 40; www.restaurant-lebreard.com; closed Tue lunch, Wed–Thu lunch except Jul–Aug

TROUVILLE-SUR-MER
Bistrot les Quatre Chats
inexpensive–moderate
This popular bistro has an excellent wine selection and a chalked-up menu of tapas, salads and larger dishes.
8 rue d'Orléans, 14360; 02 31 88 94 94; closed Wed, Jan

Les Vapeurs *moderate*
Savouring a bowl of *moules et frites* and chilled white wine on the terrace of Les Vapeurs is one of the essential experiences of the Normandy coast.
160–162 quai Fernand Moureaux, 14360; 02 31 88 15 24; www.lesvapeurs.fr

Eat and Drink: inexpensive, under €20; moderate, €20–€40; expensive, over €40

Top Pigeon-loft and former barn at Crèvecoeur's château **Above left** Cambremer's village square **Above right** Beuvron-en-Auge, a classic Norman village

Apple Magic

The Pays d'Auge is credited with producing the best of all Normandy ciders and Calvados (apple brandy), and is the only area with an official *appellation contrôlée* for both. The local tourist office has marked out a Route du Cidre of farms that welcome visitors for tastings and sales.

4 Beaumont-en-Auge

Calvados, Basse-Normandie; 14950

South of Deauville visitors rapidly enter the rolling Pays d'Auge countryside, and traffic thins out as they turn off the main road and climb up winding lanes into a world of soft green fields, orchards and unshakeably peaceful villages. Beaumont makes an attractive entry point, dubbed the "balcony of the Pays d'Auge" due to its remarkable location on a lofty ridge, with an immense view east across the Touques valley and to Deauville and the sea.

Continue on the D58 to La Haie Tondue and cross over the D675 to take the D16 as far as Bonnebosq. After Bonnebosq, turn right onto the D276 for Beaufour-Druval, and then left onto the D146, to Beuvron.

5 Route du Cidre and Beuvron-en-Auge

Calvados, Basse-Normandie; 14430

The signposted "cider route" runs around the lushest, greenest part of the Pays d'Auge with some of its finest old *colombage* farms and giant manor houses. Off the road west of **Beaufour-Druval** is the rambling farm of one of the best small cidermakers, **Gerard Desvoyé**.

3 Deauville

Calvados, Basse-Normandie; 14800

Created as a new town in the 1860s, Deauville became the most fashionable holiday resort for rich Parisians, and has never lost its upmarket cachet. Horse-racing at the town's two tracks is a major social focus, and there is an opulent golf course. The seafront is dominated by the **Casino** and two giant luxury hotels, the **Normandy** and the **Royal**, and there are glamorous cafés along the famous promenade **Les Planches**.

Leave Deauville on the D677 south beside the Touques, for Pont-l'Evêque and Paris. In St-Martin-aux-Chartrains, turn right onto the D58 for St-Etienne-la-Thillaye and Beaumont-en-Auge.

WHERE TO STAY

DEAUVILLE

Le Mascaret de Deauville *moderate*
This *chambre d'hôtes* is housed in a 1930s villa with a large garden.
115 avenue de la République, 14800; 02 50 66 80 39; www.location-vacances-deauville.com

BEUVRON-EN-AUGE

Aux Trois Damoiselles *moderate*
The rooms of this engaging little hotel are charming with traditional furniture.
Place Michel Vermughen, 14430; 02 31 39 61 38; www.manoirdesens.com

Le Pave d'Hôtes *expensive*
This elegantly modernised 18th-century Norman house has luxurious features and views of the countryside.
Le Bourg, 14430; 02 31 39 39 10; www.pavedauge.com

AROUND CRÈVECOEUR-EN-AUGE

Aux Charme des Pommiers *moderate*
This bed-and-breakfast, 2 km (1 mile) east of Crèvecoeur, has pretty rooms.
Notre-Dame de Livaye, 14340; 02 31 63 01 28; http://bandb.normandy.free.fr

CAMBREMER

Château Les Bruyères *expensive*
The country house hotel comes with a swimming pool in its large gardens.
Route du Cadran, 14340; 02 31 32 22 45; www.chateaulesbruyeres.com

Above Tractor at the cider shed of a Pays d'Auge farm

Where to Stay: inexpensive, under €70; moderate, €70–€150; expensive, over €150

At Clermont-en-Auge a path leads to the **Chapelle de Clermont**, a 12th-century chapel on a crag with a wonderful panoramic view. The road leads down to the pretty Beuvron-en-Auge, with a famous flower-decked square of half-timbering in varying colours and patterns.

🚗 *Fork left in Beuvron onto the D49; follow the road through Victot-Pontfol to meet the D16 and then the main D613 from Caen at Carrefour St-Jean. Turn left for Crèvecoeur.*

⑥ Crèvecoeur-en-Auge
Calvados, Basse-Normandie; 14340
Crèvecoeur's château is an amazingly intact example of a classic Norman medieval castle, with an inner keep, or *motte*, and a farm, pigeon-loft and other rustic buildings around a grassy outer enclosure or bailey. Inside are exhibits on the castle's history and traditional building techniques, as well as a display on the engineering work of the Schlumberger Foundation, which restored the castle in the 1970s.

🚗 *From the château, turn left into Crèvecoeur village, and left again towards Cambremer on the D101.*

⑦ Cambremer
Calvados, Basse-Normandie; 14340
Cambremer is the chief market town of the northern Pays d'Auge and hub of the Route du Cidre, with a charming main square. Just south of town, the **Jardins du Pays d'Auge** form a maze of luxuriant themed gardens, with a lovely *salon de thé*. Nearby is **Calvados Pierre Huet**, one of the most

prestigious makers of fine ciders and Calvados, run from a magnificent *colombage* manor. Illuminating tours generally end with a tasting.

Along the road south are more fine houses (not open to visitors) such as the refined 17th-century **Château de Grandchamp** and the massive 15th-century rustic manor at Coupesarte.

🚗 *Leave Cambremer on the D85. Turn left on D50 toward Lisieux; at La Poste turn right on D151 to St-Aubin then take D613 to Crèvecoeur and left on D269 to Grandchamps-le Château. When road meets D269A turn left; at St Julien Le Faucon take D47 for Coupesarte. Turn left onto D136; crossing over D103, turn right on the D579 and then left onto D268 to St-Germain.*

⑧ St-Germain-de-Livet
Calvados, Basse-Normandie; 14100
Nestling in a sheltered valley, this romantic 16th-century château is a beguiling blend of a traditional Pays d'Auge *colombage* manor and French Renaissance architecture, with pepperpot turrets and fascinating check-pattern stonework. Surrounding it are lovely gardens and a moat, and inside there are original 16th-century frescoes and many mementos of the painter Eugène Delacroix (1798–1863), who often visited here. There are especially pretty views over the upper Touques Valley along the road south of St-Germain, particularly between Prêtreville and Fervaques.

🚗 *Continue on the same road to meet the D64 at Les Forges, turn right and drive down to Fervaques. In the village turn right onto the D47, and then left onto the D149 for Livarot.*

Above Château of St-Germain-de-Livet
Left Willows and waterlilies around the Château de Grandchamp, near Cambremer **Below** Cambremer's church tower

EAT AND DRINK

AROUND BEAUMONT-EN-AUGE
Auberge des Deux Tonneaux
inexpensive–moderate
This house, 10 km (6 miles) east of Beuvron, has been an auberge since the 17th century. Enjoy classic Norman dishes rich in cream, cheese and cider.
Pierrefitte-en-Auge, 14130; 02 31 64 09 31; www.aubergedesdeuxtonneaux. com; closed Mon Sep–May

BEUVRON-EN-AUGE
Le Pavé d'Auge *moderate–expensive*
The number-one gourmet choice in the area is this postcard-pretty restaurant in Beuvron's historic market hall.
Le Bourg, 14430; 02 31 79 26 71; www.pavedauge.com; closed Mon, Tue

CAMBREMER
Au P'tit Normand
inexpensive–moderate
Bright and friendly, this little restaurant is a great-value choice for varied menus including local classics.
Place de l'Église, 14340; 02 31 32 03 20; closed Sun evening, Mon

Above left Delightful green fields around Crouttes **Above right** Arlette Fountain in Falaise **Below** Colourful stalls in the market at St-Pierre-sur-Dives

WHERE TO STAY

CROUTTES

Le Prieuré St-Michel *moderate*
A marvellously peaceful place, this offers five very special bed-and-breakfast rooms and two self-contained *gîtes* in the 18th-century abbot's residence attached to the medieval priory of St-Michel. Breakfast is served in the 15th-century cider press.
Crouttes, 61120; 02 33 39 15 15; www.prieure-saint-michel.com

AROUND ST-PIERRE-SUR-DIVES

Le Pressoir de Glatigny *inexpensive*
Rooms are traditionally furnished at this tranquil *chambre d'hôtes* on a sprawling 18th-century stone farm, 3km (2 miles) north of St-Pierre.
Bretteville-sur-Dives, 14170; 02 31 20 68 93; www.gites-de-france.com

Ferme de l'Oudon
moderate–expensive
Designer furniture and subtle colour schemes combine with the massive timbers and stone walls of a grand old farm in the rooms and suite-like *gîtes* here, 3 km (2 miles) south of St-Pierre. Some have their own entrances onto the gardens and large tracts of fields.
12 route d'Ecots, Berville l'Oudon, 14170; 02 31 20 77 96; www.fermedeloudon.com

AROUND FALAISE

Domaine de la Tour *moderate*
This hotel is located in beautifully restored 18th-century buildings that form part of the former hunting lodge and stables of the Château de la Tour, just outside Falaise. Good for families, as extra beds can be provided in rooms for a small charge.
Sainy-Pierre-Canivet, 14700; 02 31 20 53 07; www.domainedelatour.fr

⑨ Livarot
Calvados, Basse-Normandie;14140
The southern Pays d'Auge is most famous for its cheeses. At Livarot, which gave its name to one of the great Norman cheeses, **Le Village Fromager** offers free tours and tastings, and has a shop. A short distance from Livarot along the D579 is **Vimoutiers**, where there is a statue of Camembert's inventor, Marie Harel, in the main square. Nearby, the **Musée du Camembert** has exhibits on the region's folk traditions and on cheese.
🚗 *Take the D916 out of Vimoutiers; turn left on the D246 for Camembert.*

⑩ Camembert
Orne, Basse-Normandie; 61120
The village where little Marie Harel is said to have invented Camembert in 1791 is tiny, climbing up a steep hill with lofty views. The official **Maison du Camembert** presents a modern exhibition on the cheese and its history, and the **Ferme Président**, run by a major cheese producer, has a more extensive cheese and folk museum in a restored 17th-century farm. South of the village, **Fromagerie Durand** is a traditional Camembert farm that admits visitors for tours, tastings and sales.
🚗 *Continue along the road uphill from Camembert, turn left to rejoin the D916. Turn right, and then left onto the D703 for Crouttes.*

⑪ Crouttes
Orne, Basse-Normandie; 61120
The road twists and climbs still more steeply up to this delightful village, on a ridge with a breathtaking view over the narrow Monne Valley. Just across the valley is the **Prieuré St-Michel**, a restored 13th-century

priory with a splendid chapel, barns and cider-press, and exquisite modern gardens and lily ponds. Northwest of Crouttes is some of the leafiest Auge countryside, with woods and villages that are delightful to explore. By the road outside **Boissey** is Fromagerie **de la Houssaye**, makers of fine Livarot and Pont-l'Evêque cheeses.
🚗 *Follow the D703 past the Prieuré St-Michel and through Le Renouard until the D38. Turn right for Tortisambert, then left through Le Billot and follow signs for St-Georges-en-Auge to the right onto the D111. From St-Georges take the D154, which meets the D4 at Boissey. Turn left for St-Pierre-sur-Dives.*

Land of Cheese

Three of the four great Norman cheeses originated in the Pays d'Auge – Camembert, softer, slightly browny-white Pont l'Evêque, and Livarot, with its distinctive orangey rind wrapped in paper strips. Real Norman Camembert is labelled *Camembert de Normandie* or, even better, *Camembert de Normandie Fermier*. Tourist offices (*21 place du Mackau, Vimoutiers, 02 33 67 49 42*) have leaflets listing those farms that are open for visits and direct sales.

⑫ St-Pierre-sur-Dives
Calvados, Basse-Normandie; 14170
The centre of St-Pierre is the **Halles**, the giant timber-frame market hall, first built in the 11th century, which hosts the Pays d'Auge's largest

traditional country market every Monday. Nearby is the **Abbatiale** church, founded in 1012 and a classic example of Norman architecture. The Gothic chapter house and part of the cloister now house exhibitions, the tourist office and a cheese museum.

🚗 *Take the main road north out of St-Pierre, the D16, signed for Crèvecoeur. At Les Quatres Routes crossroads turn left on the D47 for Mézidon-Canon, and follow the road all the way through the town to the château.*

⑬ Château de Canon

Calvados, Basse-Normandie; 14270

This elegant 18th-century mansion was the home of the liberal thinker J-B Élie de Beaumont (1732–86) and his wife, who laid out its entrancing gardens influenced by the philosophical ideas of the Enlightenment. The house is closed to visitors, but they can wander around the gardens *(open Wed–Mon Jun–Sep, Sat–Sun Apr–May)* passing sculptures, secluded groves, and a Chinese-style summerhouse. The estate has a very special treehouse guestroom.

🚗 *Turn left from the château, cross over the D47 and turn right onto the D152 signed to Vieux-Fumé. Follow signs for Condé-sur-Ifs and then Ernes, and turn left onto the D253 for Vendeuvre, arriving almost opposite the château.*

Old bell from a Pays d'Auge inn

⑭ Château de Vendeuvre

Calvados, Basse-Normandie; 14170

The Vendeuvre family reclaimed this refined 1750s château after the French Revolution. Badly damaged in World War II, it has been sumptuously restored with originals or replicas of its delicate, colourful decor. On display in the **Orangerie** *(open daily May–Sep, Sun Oct)* is the world's largest collection of miniature furniture. The gardens have mazes, a grotto and ponds.

🚗 *Leaving the château, turn left to join the main D511 at Jort, and follow it into Falaise.*

⑮ Falaise

Calvados, Basse-Normandie; 14700

Falaise's **Château Guillaume-le-Conquérant**, on a crag with a view of the surrounding plain, is one of the most formidable of Norman castles. William the Conqueror was born here in 1028, and his mother Arlette, then only 17, was the daughter of a local tanner. The town and castle were terribly damaged in World War II, but the château's keep and giant tower were restored in the 1980s. Falaise was the key point in the last stage of the 1944 Battle of Normandy, commemorated in the **Musée Août 1944** *(open daily Jun–Aug, Wed–Mon Apr–May and Sep–early Nov)* near the castle.

Above Grand Château de Vendeuvre

EAT AND DRINK

ST-PIERRE-SUR-DIVES

Aux Plaisirs des Mets *inexpensive–moderate* Chef Franck Dick has brought a new culinary sophistication to St-Pierre with this brightly stylish restaurant. *2 rue de Lisieux, 14170; 02 31 90 33 05; closed Tue, Wed*

FALAISE

La Fine Fourchette *moderate* Plush traditional comfort and fine Norman cuisines are the keynote here. *52 rue Georges Clémenceau, 14700; 02 31 90 08 59; closed Tue evenings, Feb*

DAY TRIP OPTIONS

Those approaching from Paris on the A13 should turn onto the A29 for Honfleur, or, if they wish to miss out the coast, stay on until exit 29, to Pont l'Evêque, and turn onto the D675 Caen road as far as Drubec.

A Tang of the sea

The Côte Fleurie from Honfleur ❶ west to Trouville-sur-Mer ❷ and Deauville ❸ makes a natural trip on its own, with lovely views along the cliffs, and many pretty small resorts as well as the bigger names.

From Deauville continue along the D513 coast road to Villers-sur-Mer, Houlgate and Cabourg rather than

heading inland, and from there go on to Caen or return to Honfleur by the same route.

Cider country

Food and countryside lovers may wish to visit the heart of the Pays d'Auge around Beuvron ❺ and Cambremer ❼, and search for cider and cheese.

Drivers coming from the north on the A29 who wish to head straight for the countryside should stay on the autoroute after crossing the Pont de la Normandie bridge over the Seine and turn right onto the A13, exiting at Pont l'Evêque. Then take the D675 Caen road as far as Drubec, and turn left on

the D16 to join the main itinerary near Bonnebosq. From Cambremer, follow signs to Bonnebosq to retrace the same route.

Châteaux and lost villages

The southern half of the Pays d'Auge including St-Germain-de-Livet ❽ makes an intriguing area to explore, with an enjoyably remote feel, exquisite landscapes and unusual castles.

Whether entering from the north or from Paris and the south, leave the autoroute at Pont l'Evêque and take the D579 road through Lisieux towards Livarot; turn left onto the D268 for St-Germain-de-Livet to join the main route.

Eat and Drink: inexpensive, under €20; moderate, €20–€40; expensive, over €40

Normandy's Wild West

Bayeux to Mont-St-Michel

Highlights

- **The Middle Ages in full colour**
  Learn about medieval history from Bayeux's spectacular tapestry

- **Rugged coastline**
  Wander along the dunes and empty beaches of the Cotentin's west coast, stopping at harbours and resorts

- **Magic mountain**
  Circle the fascinating landscape of the bay of Mont-St-Michel to reach the extraordinary mountain-abbey

- **Normandy's wildernesses**
  Find your way through the lanes and hedgerows of the *bocage* country-side, to discover ruined abbeys, lost castles and irresistible country foods

View of the fascinating mountain-abbey of Mont-St-Michel

Normandy's Wild West

Western Normandy has far less of the luxuriant softness so prominent in the countryside east of Caen. The Cotentin Peninsula is a giant slab of granite, jutting out into the Atlantic, and this grey stone is a prime characteristic of its villages and sturdy manor houses. Its west coast has an invigorating wildness, with long stretches of underused beaches and windswept dunes punctuated by small-scale resorts and fishing harbours, leading down to vast sand flats and salt marshes of the bay of Mont-St-Michel. Behind the coast there are silent marshes and the dense land-scape of the *bocage*. At either end of this drive are two of the most astonishing sights – the Bayeux Tapestry and the island-abbey of Mont-St-Michel.

Above Calm waters of the bay of Mont-St-Michel, *see p95*

ACTIVITIES

Soak up the small-town atmosphere on a stroll around the charming streets of old Bayeux

Spot grebes, cormorants and marsh harriers on a boat trip through the Cotentin Marais

Surf or just splash in the waves on the beaches around Barneville-Carteret

Scan the horizon from the walls of the Château de Pirou

Dine on lobster fresh from the sea at Granville harbour, and gutsy sausages and cheeses at a village *auberge*

Get to the roots of French fashion at Granville's Musée Christian Dior

Listen to the silence and breathe the fantastically fresh air on a walk beside the bay of Mont-St-Michel

PLAN YOUR DRIVE

Start/finish: Bayeux to Mont-St-Michel.

Number of days: 3–4, with half a day each in Bayeux and on Mont-St-Michel.

Distance: 285 km (175 miles).

Road conditions: Roads are in good condition. In the *bocage* country, the maze of tiny lanes is sometimes erratically signposted.

When to go: From May to September it is usually bright and sunny, without being very hot. From late July through August the coast is very busy. In winter it is almost empty, but ocean winds make it very atmospheric.

Opening hours: Mont-St-Michel, the Bayeux Tapestry centre and other major museums in Bayeux are generally open daily all year, without closing for lunch. Many smaller châteaux, abbeys and other attractions are closed during the winter season.

Main market days: Bayeux: Sat; Barneville-Carteret: Thu, Sat; Coutances: Thu, Sat; Granville: Wed, Sat; Avranches: Sat.

Shopping: There are many farms around the Cotentin peninsula that sell their own produce direct to callers – especially ciders, Calvados, fruit preserves and meats such as duck pâtés and rillettes or Andouille sausages.

Major festivals: Bayeux: D-Day festival, Jun; Fêtes Médiévales, Jul; **Cerisy-la-Forêt, Lessay, Hambye, La Lucerne:** Abbayes Normandes festival, Jun–Sep; **Granville:** Carnival, Feb; Shellfish festival, Oct; **Mont-St-Michel:** Nocturnes, Jul–Aug.

DAY TRIP OPTIONS

This route easily divides into three separate day trips. **History enthusiasts** can spend a day in and around Bayeux; **families** can enjoy the Cotentin coast; and Mont-St-Michel and its bay are ideal for **nature lovers**. For details, see *p95*.

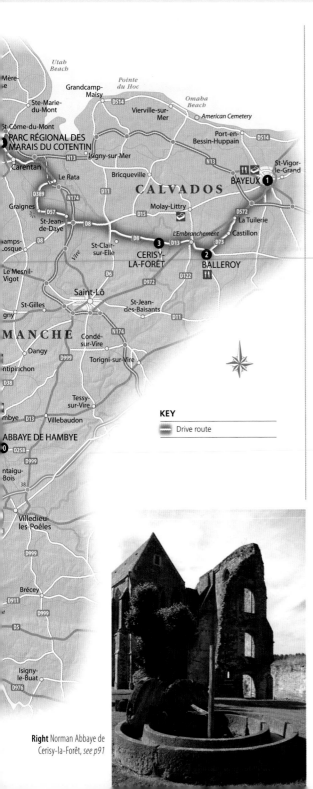

Right Norman Abbaye de Cerisy-la-Forêt, *see p91*

Above The majestic Cathédrale Notre-Dame de Bayeux **Below** Rue St-Martin, one of Bayeux's main streets

VISITING BAYEUX

Tourist Information
Pont St-Jean; 02 31 51 28 28;
www.bessin-normandie.fr

Parking
There is plenty of free parking on Rue Larcher, the main entrance to the Centre Guillaume-le-Conquérant and the cathedral, and in other streets around the centre.

WHERE TO STAY

BAYEUX

Le Petit Matin *inexpensive–moderate*
A very friendly *chambre d'hôtes*, a short walk from Bayeux's main street.
2 bis rue Quincangrogne, 14400; 02 31 10 09 27; www.antpas.com

Hôtel d'Argouges
moderate–expensive
There is a real touch of *ancien régime* elegance in this 18th-century mansion. Rooms have plenty of modern extras.
21 rue St-Patrice, 14400; 02 31 92 88 86; www.ohotellerie.com/dargouges

AROUND BALLEROY

Le Prieuré *inexpensive*
Very comfortable bed-and-breakfast rooms in a venerable old stone house, 8 km (5 miles) north of Balleroy.
Rue Retot, Le Molay-Littry, 14430; 02 31 51 91 97

① Bayeux
Calvados, Basse-Normandie; 14400

Compact and easy to explore, Bayeux has retained more of its historic character than perhaps any other city in western Normandy. This is partly because it escaped remarkably unscathed from the cauldron of the Battle of Normandy in World War II. It also possesses two special treasures – one of the finest of all Norman cathedrals and an extraordinary medieval picture-book, the Bayeux Tapestry.

Bayeux suffered so little destruction in the war because it was liberated by the Allies on the second day after the Normandy landings, on 7 June 1944. Consequently it has retained many of its picturesque old buildings, many of them along the long main street that runs roughly east-west through the town, a natural route for strolling. The oldest house in Bayeux is at the corner of **Rue St-Martin** and **Rue des Cuisiniers**, a huge stone and *colombage* 14th-century townhouse, and on **Rue St-Patrice** is the **Hôtel d'Argouges**, a stately 16th-century mansion in stone. Other historic houses can be found in the surrounding streets and alleys, and at many places, 14th-century watchtowers, built during the Hundred Years' War, can be seen.

The Bayeux Tapestry is housed in the **Centre Guillaume-le-Conquérant**, a little south of the main street. It is thought to have been made in England around 1070, commissioned by Odo, half-brother of William the Conqueror and Bishop of Bayeux, to hang in Bayeux Cathedral. It recounts in graphic detail all the events leading up to and during the Norman invasion of England in 1066, very much from the Norman point of view. In the process, it gives a vivid picture of 11th-century life. An exhibition and a film shown on other floors add to the historical context.

The **Cathédrale Notre-Dame de Bayeux** is just a short walk away uphill. The two giant towers of the main façade, the crypt and much of the nave are survivors from the cathedral built for Bishop Odo and completed in 1077 in a majestically simple Norman-Romanesque style. Other Gothic sections were added from the 13th to the 15th centuries, like the main portals and the apse at the back. The dome on the central tower was only added in the 19th century. Leaving the cathedral, look out for the 16th-century **Maison d'Adam et Eve** across the street, named because it has the figures of Adam and Eve carved on its façade. The building houses the Conservatoire de la Dentelle de Bayeux, a showcase for the town's traditional lacemaking skills. On the Boulevard Fabian Ware on the southwest side of the town is the large **Musée-Memorial de la Bataille de Normandie**, which covers the entire campaign in great detail.

🚗 *Take the St-Lô exit off Bayeux's ring of boulevards, the D572. Turn left in La Tuilerie onto the D73 (Route Touristique) for Castillon and the next stop, Balleroy.*

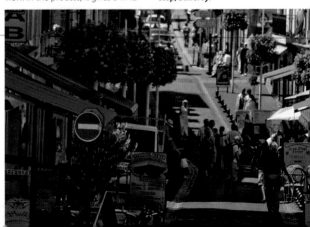

Bayeux is a natural base for visiting the beaches that were the scene of the Normandy landings of D-Day on 6 June 1944. **Arromanches**, centre of the British landings on Gold Beach, is to the north; **Omaha Beach** and the sombre American Cemetery are to the northwest. The D514 coast road runs all along the beaches from above Caen to Pointe du Hoc.

② Balleroy

Calvados, Basse-Normandie; 14490
The village of Balleroy was laid out around its château to create a spectacular approach on the road from Bayeux. Designed in 1631 by architect François Mansart, it is a classic of the Louis XIII style. In the 1970s the château was opulently restored by American press magnate and ballooning enthusiast, Malcolm Forbes, who installed the **Musée des Ballons** *(open mid-Mar–Oct)* in the stables.

🚗 *Facing the château in Balleroy, turn right down the D13 to reach a five-way junction in the Forêt de Cerisy, known as L'Embranchement. Take the Cerisy-la-Forêt exit, still the D13, and in the village follow the "Abbaye" signs.*

③ Cerisy-la-Forêt

Manche, Basse-Normandie; 50680
The sublime **Abbaye de Cerisy-la-Forêt** is one of the finest Norman abbeys. Founded in 1032 by Robert the Magnificent, it has been damaged over the centuries, but most of its great church, a court room and a Gothic chapel from 1260 are intact. The best views of the abbey are from around the pond below it.

🚗 *From Cerisy village follow signs for St-Clair-sur-Elle on D8, beyond which the road meets the D6. Turn right onto D6, then left onto the D8, then right onto the D974. Turn right again, but make a detour left to Graignes on D57, following the road back to the N174 at Le Rata. Then turn left to drive past Carentan, and look out for a turning left for Les Ponts d'Ouve.*

④ Parc Régional des Marais du Cotentin

Manche, Basse-Normandie; 50500
A protected nature park, the Cotentin Marais is a peaceful expanse of wetland, full of birds, extending across the base of the Cotentin Peninsula. In and around **Graignes** there are fine views over the marshes. The main park information centre is at **Les Ponts d'Ouve** near St-Côme-du-Mont. The town of **St-Sauveur-le-Vicomte** is centred around a 12th-century castle.

🚗 *From Les Ponts d'Ouve, drive to St-Côme-du-Mont; turn left onto D270 through Carquebut, towards Houesville. Turn left again onto D70 before Chef-du-Pont, and follow this road through Pont-l'Abbé, past Crosville to St-Sauveur-le-Vicomte. Follow signs to Barneville-Carteret on D15, continue on D903, then D650.*

Top Cattle grazing in the Marais wetlands **Above left** Old watermill in Bayeux **Above right** Typical Cotentin stone house **Below** Seventeenth-century Château de Balleroy

---

EAT AND DRINK

BAYEUX

La Table du Terroir
inexpensive–moderate
Meat dishes are the mainstay of this convivial restaurant.
42 rue St-Jean, 14400; 02 31 92 05 53; closed Sun evening

La Coline d'Enzo
moderate–expensive
Haute cuisine, Norman traditions and international influences are inventively combined here.
2–4 rue des Bouchers, 14400; 02 31 92 03 01; closed Sun, Mon

BALLEROY
Manoir de la Drôme *expensive*
One of Normandy's finest gourmet restaurants. Follow suggestions for the day's market specials.
129 rue des Forges, 14490; 02 31 21 60 94; www.manoir-de-la-drome.com; closed Sun evening, Tue lunch, Mon, Wed and Feb

Eat and Drink: inexpensive, under €20; moderate, €20–€40; expensive, over €40

WHERE TO STAY

BARNEVILLE-CARTERET

Hôtel des Isles *moderate*
A stylishly renovated hotel right on the Barneville beach, with comfortable, nautical-themed rooms.
9 blvd Maritime, 50270; 02 33 04 90 76; www.hoteldesisles.com; closed Feb

AROUND COUTANCES

Manoir de la Foulerie *inexpensive*
A formidable stone tower is one of the first things noticeable at this rugged 16th-century farm 8 km (5 miles) north of Coutances. There are self-contained *gîtes* and bed-and-breakfast rooms.
Ancteville, 50200; 02 33 45 27 64; www.manoirdelafoulerie.com

Le Castel *moderate–expensive*
This château, 15 km (9 miles) south of Coutances, has been transformed into a luxurious retreat with six opulent rooms.
Montpinchon, 50210; 02 33 17 00 45; www.le-castel-normandy.com

HAMBYE

Auberge de l'Abbaye *inexpensive*
This long-running little hotel is a favourite of many regular visitors. The traditionally-styled rooms are pretty.
5 route de l'Abbaye, 50450; 02 33 61 42 19; www.logis-de-france.fr

AROUND LA LUCERNE D'OUTREMER

Ferme de la Butte *inexpensive*
Rural tranquility is guaranteed in this bed-and-breakfast at a farm 12 km (7 miles) north of La Lucerne.
La Meurdraquière, 50510; 02 33 61 31 52; www.gites-de-france.com

Logis d'Equilly *inexpensive*
This splendid 17th-century manor, 13 km (8 miles) north of La Lucerne, has a huge double bed-and-breakfast suite, with a grand living room.
Equilly, 50320; 02 33 61 04 71

Above Partly ruined medieval Château de Gratot **Below** Jardin des Plantes in Coutances

⑤ Barneville-Carteret
Manche, Basse-Normandie; 50270
This charming seaside resort has three parts, the hilltop village of Barneville, the beach area of Barneville-Plage and the pretty harbour of Carteret, nestled against the rocky headland of **Cap Carteret**. There are excellent fish restaurants, and to the north, past the cape, there is an endless, windswept beach. To the south, **Portbail** is a tiny port with a fascinating fortified church from the 11th-century and a long shingle beach reached by a causeway.

🚗 *From Barneville take the D124 for St-Georges-de-la-Rivière down to Portbail. Turn inland, and outside the village turn right onto the D650. After St-Germain-sur-Ay, turn left on the D652 for Lessay, and follow signs for "Centre Ville".*

⑥ Lessay
Manche, Basse-Normandie; 50430
The centre of this placid market town is dominated by the majestic abbey church, the **Abbatiale de la**

Stained-glass window of the abbey in Lucerne

Ste-Trinité. First built in the 11th century, it was terribly damaged in World War II, but has been beautifully restored. It was the first Norman church with a roof of ribbed vaults, and it has one of the longest naves of any Norman church.

🚗 *Retrace the same route out of Lessay to the D650. Turn left, drive on past Pirou village and look for a turning inland, about 2 km (1 mile) up this road, signed to Château de Pirou.*

⑦ Château de Pirou
Manche, Basse-Normandie; 50770
One of the oldest Norman castles in the region, rugged **Pirou** looks like a model of a warrior stronghold. Its oldest parts are from the 9th century, but most of the granite walls date from three centuries later. To enter the castle, visitors must walk through several gates and all the way around the green-water moat. Inside, the rooms include a medieval guardhouse with a giant fireplace. Narrow stairways lead to the ramparts, which offer panoramic views.

🚗 *Get back onto the D650 and turn left. In Gouville-sur-Mer, turn left onto the D268, towards Gouville-Bourg and Coutances. In Gratot, park next to the church and follow signs to the château.*

Ciders of the Bocage
The Cotentin peninsula produces fine ciders and Calvados. They are generally drier and more astringent than the better-known ciders of the Pays d'Auge, which many aficionados think makes them more interesting. The farms here tend to be very small and seeking them out is a great way to discover the countryside.

⑧ Château de Gratot

Manche, Basse-Normandie; 50200

Although partly in ruins, this 14th-century château can still give a powerful impression of life in a medieval castle, with its towers, pepperpot turrets and broad moat. Several buildings have been restored and now house a display on the history of the castle and the Argouges clan, lords of Gratot. Soaring up above Gratot is the strange one-room *Tour à la Fée* (Fairy Tower), so-called because a local legend has it that a fairy who married an Argouges is said to have disappeared out of its window when he mentioned death in her presence.

🚗 *Follow the same road into Coutances, and then signs for "Centre Ville" to the cathedral. Except during the Thursday market, there is free parking in the squares beside it.*

From the Cotentin to Sicily

In 1036, Tancrède de Hauteville, a minor Cotentin lord, left with his sons for Italy, where they got work as mercenaries. After fighting for local kings for a while, and gaining a fearsome reputation, they began to go into business for themselves. One son became King of Apulia, and two others set up a Norman kingdom in Sicily that lasted over 150 years. Pirou is believed to have been one of the Hautevilles' possessions, and the story of their adventures is told on a modern embroidery at the château.

---

⑨ Coutances

Manche, Basse-Normandie; 50200

The old town of Coutances sits atop a massive hill. Its height seems to be raised even higher by its unique **cathedral**, with a soaring Gothic-Romanesque façade of extraordinarily tall, thin towers and columns. Informative guided tours allow visitors to see every part of the cathedral.

🚗 *Follow signs for Granville and Avranches out of Coutances, but fork left onto the D7, signed for Villedieu-les-Poêles. At Les Hauts Vents (the sign is very small) turn off left on the D49 to St-Denis-le-Gast. Next, turn left and right onto the D38, before turning left on the D238 for La Baleine. Follow this lane and then the D398 to join the D13 to Hambye village. Turn right onto the D51, then left onto the D258 to the Abbaye de Hambye.*

⑩ Abbaye de Hambye

Manche, Basse-Normandie; 50450

The 12th–13th-century **Abbaye de Hambye** *(open daily Jul–Aug, Wed–Mon Apr–Jun and Sep–Oct)* was one of the largest Benedictine abbeys in Normandy. It was closed after the 1789 Revolution, and the abbey church is now an atmospheric ruin, rising up among the woods. Around Hambye and to the south is one of the densest and most picturesque stretches of *bocage* countryside.

🚗 *From the abbey return to the D51 and turn left and then right onto the D198 for Gavray. At the next fork join the D238; when this meets the D9 turn right into Gavray. Turn left in the town on the D7, and drive on down this road to La Haye-Pesnel, where the D35 to La Lucerne is signed on the right.*

⑪ La Lucerne d'Outremer

Manche, Basse-Normandie; 50320

In an idyllic setting in a wooded valley stands the 12th-century **Abbaye de la Lucerne d'Outremer**. It gained its title 'd'Outremer' ("overseas") because it stayed loyal to the Kings of England even after King Philippe-Auguste of France took over Normandy in 1204. La Lucerne was reduced to ruins after the Revolution, but is now being restored. There are lovely walks in the woods around La Lucerne.

🚗 *Turn right out of the abbey, take the road uphill and follow signs to St-Jean-des-Champs on the D105 to meet the D924. Turn left into Granville.*

Above Gardens at the Abbey de la Lucerne d'Outremer **Below** Abbatiale de la Ste-Trinité, Lessay

---

EAT AND DRINK

BARNEVILLE-CARTERET

La Marine *moderate–expensive*
This place is the town's number-one choice for gourmet cuisine.
11 rue de Paris, 50270; 02 33 53 83 31; check opening hours before visit

AROUND BARNEVILLE-CARTERET

Le Hamelinet *inexpensive–moderate*
A laid-back atmosphere is the keynote at this pub-like village restaurant, 16 km (10 miles) south of Barneville.
La Rue de Surville, 50250; 02 33 07 10 84

AROUND HAMBYE

Auberge de l'Abbaye de Hambye *moderate*
This local restaurant serving traditional cuisine is located in a classic old stone Norman establishment next to the Abbaye d'Hambye.
5 route de l'Abbaye, 50450; 02 23 61 42 19; closed Sun evening, Jan

LA LUCERNE D'OUTREMER

Le Courtil de la Lucerne *inexpensive–moderate*
A lovely garden leads guests to this charming inn. Norman hams, cheeses and Calvados feature on the menu.
La Lucerne d'Outremer, 50320; 02 33 61 22 02; closed Tue, Wed (low season)

AROUND LA LUCERNE D'OUTREMER
Auberge du Mesnil-Rogues *moderate*
Known for fine quality, this *auberge*, 10 km (6 miles) west of La Lucerne, has comfortable dining rooms.
1 route de l'Auberge, Le Mesnil-Rogues, 50450; 02 33 61 37 12; www.aubergedumesnilrogues.com; closed Tue & Wed evening, Mon

---

Eat and Drink: inexpensive, under €20; moderate, €20–€40; expensive, over €40

⑫ Granville

Manche, Basse-Normandie; 50406

Founded as a fortress in the Hundred Years' War (1337–1453), Granville's old town or *haute ville* is an atmospheric knot of cobbled streets on a headland with superb sea views. The town has unusual museums, notably the **Musée d'Art Moderne Richard Anacréon** *(closed Jan)* for contemporary art, and the **Musée Christian Dior** *(open May–Sep)*, the fashion designer's childhood summer home.

🚗 *Take the road nearest the waterfront out of Granville onto the D911 coast road through St-Pair-sur-Mer. Climb up to the cliffs at Champeaux.*

⑬ Champeaux

Manche, Basse-Normandie; 50530

The coast road south enters the bay of Mont-St-Michel on top of massive cliffs at **Champeaux**, from where, like medieval pilgrims, visitors can get their first glimpse of the mount. There are more fine views as the road heads to St-Jean-le-Thomas. From there, follow signs for the *plage*, then turn left for **Genêts**. This village was once the main departure point for pilgrims walking across to Mont-St-Michel.

🚗 *From Genêts village follow signs to St-Léonard, but at the D41 turn right for Le Grand-Port, and follow this road to the Maison de la Baie de Vains.*

⑭ Grouin du Sud

Manche, Basse-Normandie; 50300

The silhouette of Mont-St-Michel, seen across the flat sands and channels, is one of its most extraordinary features. A walk along the bay allows visitors to absorb the rare calm of this place.

A 90-minute walking tour

Park by the **Maison de la Baie de Vains ①**. Take a look around the exhibition housed in this restored farm that also serves as an information centre and offers an introduction to the complex ecology of the place. Walk down the path to the right of the Maison de la Baie to meet the coastal footpath and continue along this path beyond the last houses, with the flat marshes and sandbanks to the right and lush cattle pastures to the left. A short distance ahead, the path meets a gate and climbs a little. After a second gate,

Top Road signs along the walk around the Grouin du Sud **Above** Path along the beach in Grouin du Sud

WHERE TO STAY

GRANVILLE

Hôtel L'Arivée *moderate*
A reasonably-priced hotel just two minutes' walk from the beach.
110 Avenue Libération, 50400; 02 33 50 03 00; www.hotelarivee.com

AROUND MONT-ST-MICHEL

Le Moulin *inexpensive*
The old granite water mill, 25 km (15 miles) north of Mont-St-Michel, hosts four traditionally-styled rooms.
93 Grand Rue, Genêts, 50530; 02 33 70 83 78; www.gites-de-france.com

Le Jardin Secret *inexpensive*
This bed-and-breakfast is housed in a lovely 19th-century house, 20 km (12 miles) northeast of Mont-St-Michel.
42 route de Granville, Marcey-les-Grèves, 50300; 02 33 51 92 47

Manoir de la Roche Torin *moderate*
One of the classic hotels for Mont-St-Michel visitors, this very comfortable, traditionally-styled manor, 10 km (6 miles) east of the shrine, has a marvellous setting by the bay's edge.
La Roche Torin, Courtils, 50220; 02 33 70 96 55; www.manoir-rochetorin.com

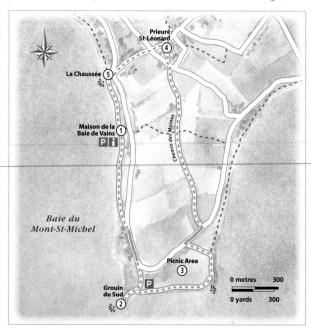

Prieuré St-Léonard ④
La Chaussée ⑤
Maison de la Baie de Vains ① 🅿️ ℹ️
Chemin des Moines
Baie du Mont-St-Michel
Picnic Area ③
Grouin du Sud ② 🅿️
0 metres 300
0 yards 300

Where to Stay: inexpensive, under €70; moderate, €70–€150; expensive, over €150

Above left Bay near Mont-St-Michel **Above right** La Merveille cloister at Mont-St-Michel

follow the path uphill past another car park to the **Grouin du Sud** ②. Follow the path to reach the little beaches either side of the jagged rocks. Climb down to the beach on the left and walk along it to rejoin the footpath, and then follow it along the shore's edge. Turn left away from the shore up a track between hedges to rejoin the road. Looking back, there is another view of the inner bay across to Avranches. The **picnic area** ③ near the parking offers the chance to take a short break. Turn right along the road, and then left up a wooded path marked Chemin des Moines. This path runs downhill to St-Léonard, a tiny cluster of farms and houses typical of the old stone villages around the bay. Turn right up Rue des Chevaliers to the **Prieuré St-Léonard** ④, a 11th-century chapel. From there, follow the road downhill to rejoin the shore at **La Chaussée** ⑤; turn left for a view of Mont-St-Michel on the way back to the parking.

🚗 **Turn back up the same road from the Maison de la Baie, then right through St-Léonard. Follow signs to Vains, and then D911 to Marcey-les-Grèves and uphill into Avranches on D973. Park in Place Valhubert, by the tourist office.**

⑮ Avranches
Manche, Basse-Normandie; 50300

This appealing old town is located on a rocky mound that towers above the bay. St Aubert, Bishop of Avranches, founded Mont-St-Michel in AD 708, and his skull is preserved in the church of **St-Gervais**.

🚗 **Follow signs for "Toutes Directions" – Mont-St-Michel to leave Avranches on rue General Patton. At the junction with the N175, take the D43E for Pontaubault; turn off right onto the D113 for Céaux. Follow the road around the bay (later the D313 and D275) through Courtils to join the causeway to Mont-St-Michel.**

⑯ Mont-St-Michel
Manche, Basse-Normandie; 50170

Soaring up to its pinnacle spire from out of the sea and sands, Mont-St-Michel is an astonishing sight. It began as a small hermitage, but developed into a major pilgrimage centre in the 11th century. It is an extraordinary feat of medieval engineering, as the abbey was built above rather than on top of the mount, resting on four giant pillars, and other later buildings were added around it to form an intricate labyrinth.

EAT AND DRINK

GRANVILLE
Le Phare *inexpensive–moderate*
One of the most enjoyable of the big seafood brasseries that line the harbour. *11 rue du Port, 50400; 02 33 50 12 94; closed Tue, Wed low season*

MONT ST-MICHEL
Auberge St-Pierre *moderate–expensive*
This place maintains high standards and serves quality food. *16 Grande Rue, 50170; 02 33 60 14 03*

AROUND MONT ST-MICHEL
Chez François *inexpensive–moderate*
Space at the long tables in this village café-bistro, 25 km (15 miles) north of the shrine, is often in great demand, so make sure to book. Meats grilled in the giant fireplace are the attraction here. *2 rue Jérémie, Genêts, 50530; 02 33 70 83 98; www.chezfrancois.fr; closed Wed, Thu*

L'Auberge du Terroir *moderate–expensive*
Chef Thierry Lefort presents some of the area's most skilful cooking here, 15 km (9 miles) east of Mont-St-Michel. *3 place St-Martin, Servon, 50170; 02 33 60 17 92; closed Wed, Thu and Sat lunch*

DAY TRIP OPTIONS
To get to the west Cotentin coast from Caen, Bayeux and central Normandy, take the D572 road from Bayeux through St-Lô and then the D900 to Lessay, and from there turn north to Barneville-Carteret. To go straight to the bay of Mont-St-Michel, take the A84 from Caen, but turn right at Avranches onto the D973 Granville road for the north side of the bay.

Bayeux's treasures
In a day, visitors to Bayeux ① can see the tapestry, the cathedral, Balleroy ② and the abbey of Cerisy ③.

From Cerisy, return to Bayeux through Le Molay-Littry on the D15.

Beaches and *bocage*
The beaches of Barneville-Carteret ⑤ are children's favourite. From Coutances ⑨, drive to Hambye ⑩ and La Lucerne d'Outremer ⑪ to

enjoy the countryside; take the D971 to Granville ⑫ for a seafood dinner.

Return on the D924 road to Villedieu-les-Poêles to join the A84 for Caen.

The bay of Mont-St-Michel
Drive around the bay and stop at the information centres to learn about the Abbey before reaching there.

Take the D275 following signs for Avranches, and then look for signs onto the A84 for Caen.

Eat and Drink: inexpensive, under €20; moderate, €20–€40; expensive, over €40

Côtes d'Armor: Land of the Sea

Saint-Malo to Trébeurden

Highlights

- **Historic fortifications**
  Explore the walled city of Saint-Malo, the ramparts of medieval Dinan and the ocean forts

- **Green corridor**
  Discover the Vallée de la Rance along the estuary of the Rance river

- **Pink granite**
  See the remarkable rock formations of the Côte de Granit Rose

- **Seafood platter**
  Savour the fresh local oysters, lobster, mackerel and shellfish accompanied by Breton beer and cider

View of Dinan and the medieval bridge that crosses the Rance river

Côtes d'Armor: Land of the Sea

From the Côte d'Emeraude, named after the colour of the sea off Saint-Malo, to the Côte de Granit Rose, northern Brittany has one evocatively named coastline after another. At midway point, the Côte des Ajoncs is characterized by the golden gorse flowers which thrive in the mild maritime climate. All these shorelines merge into the Côtes d'Armor, extending 350 km (210 miles) through a dramatic mix of capes, coves, cliffs and tidal phenomena. Named after the ancient Breton word *armorique*, land of the sea, this is a spirited region of countryside and sea, agriculture and aquaculture and a cuisine infused by both.

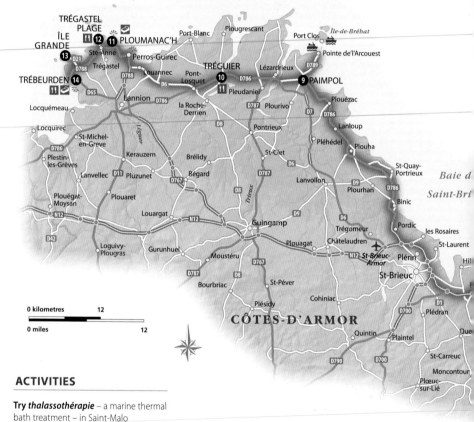

ACTIVITIES

Try thalassothérapie – a marine thermal bath treatment – in Saint-Malo

Cycle or walk in the Vallée de la Rance

Ramble, sail or kayak around the shores of Jugon-les-Lacs

Play golf between land and sea on Cap Fréhel

Catch a ferry to the Île de Bréhat

Navigate the northern Brittany coast on a crewed yacht or alone

Buy oysters at the marketplace or roadside stalls and wash them down with a dry white wine

Above Commanding fortress city of Saint-Malo, *see p100*

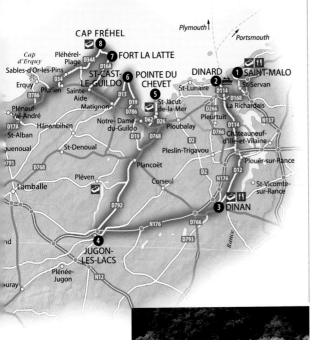

PLAN YOUR DRIVE

Start/finish: Saint-Malo to Trébeurden.

Number of days: 3–4, allowing half a day in Dinan, a full day between Dinan and Perros Guirec and a day at the Rose Granite coastline.

Distances: 260 km (160 miles).

Road conditions: Mostly very good roads; signage is not so good in some rural areas, especially on the coastal capes and headlands.

When to go: The maritime climate means fairly steady temperatures year round on the coast, with more rainfall and colder temperatures inland. The flora is wonderful in spring and summer months.

Opening hours: Generally from 10am to 6pm. Most sights close on major public holidays. Always check before visiting.

Main market days: Saint-Malo: Tue, Fri; Dinan: Thu; Jugon-les-Lacs: Fri; Saint-Cast-le-Guildo: Fri; Cap Fréhel: Tue; Paimpol: Tue; Tréguier: Wed; Tregastel Plage: Mon; Trébeurden: Tue.

Shopping: Follow the country road signs to the farm produce: *fromages fermiers* for farm cheeses, and *cidres fermiers* for artisan apple and pear juices and ciders. Buy Brittany coast-inspired artwork.

Major festivals: Saint-Malo: Route du Rhum (four-yearly trans-Atlantic race, next race Oct 2010); Etonnants Voyageurs, May; Quai des Bulles, Oct; Dinan: Fête des Remparts, Jul; Paimpol: Festival du Chant de Marin, Aug; Perros-Guirec: Festival de Musique de Chambre, Jul–Aug.

DAY TRIP OPTIONS

The Côtes d'Armor can also be explored on separate day trips: a trip to Saint-Malo's surrounds is ideal for **seafaring souls** and the Vallée de la Rance near Dinan is great for **maritime and rural peace**. The beaches of Tregastel on the Côte de Granit Rose is a great **family** destination. For more information, *see p105*.

KEY

 Drive route

Above Busy harbour of Trébeurden, *see p105* **Right** Granite cottages in the town of Jugon-les-Lacs, *see p102*

Top left View of the ramparts of the fortress town of Saint-Malo **Above left** Anglo-Breton houses in Dinard **Above right** Restaurant at Dinan port

VISITING DINAN

Tourist Information
9 rue du Château; 02 96 87 69 76; www.dinan-tourisme.com

Parking
There are car parks near the castle: Place du Guesclin and Place du Champ-Clos.

WHERE TO STAY

SAINT-MALO

Hotel Beaufort *moderate*
This is a fine newly redecorated hotel more like a private home in ambience.
25 chaussée du Sillon, 34500; 02 99 40 99 99; www.hotel-beaufort.com

Le Villefromoy *moderate–expensive*
Very welcoming small hotel in a mid-19th-century villa, located in the residential area of Rochebonne beach.
7 boulevard Hébert, 34500; 02 99 40 92 20; www.villefromoy.fr

DINAN

Hotel de la Porte Saint Malo
inexpensive
Small and personal hotel in a stone building in an old residential quarter.
35 rue de Saint-Malo, 22100; 02 96 39 19 76; www.hotelportemalo.com

Hotel le d'Avaugour
moderate–expensive
Relaxed hotel in a *maison bourgeoise*. Lovely communal spaces include a reading room and salon.
1 place du Champ-Clos, 22100; 02 96 39 07 49; www.avaugourhotel.com

① Saint-Malo
Ille-et-Vilaine, Bretagne; 35400
Saint-Malo is named after a Welsh monk, Mac Low, who arrived here in the 6th century. Built on a granite knoll over the ocean, Saint-Malo's allure comes from its eternal link with the sea. The fortress-town suffered enormous damage during World War II and the ancient ramparts were

---

A two-hour walking tour
From Place de Geusclin take Rue du Château to the Office de Tourisme. Next to it is Dinan's **castle dungeon** ① amid a cluster of rampart remnants, old city gates and towers. The Tour de Coetquen is home to the **Musée d'Art et d'Histoire** ②. Retrace the route up Rue du Château to Place du Champ-Clos where there is a statue of Bertrand du Guesclin, who was the French military commander during the Hundred Years' War and the Constable of France. From here enter the heart of Vieux Dinan – the old town – down Rue Sainte-Claire and left into Rue de Léhon which leads to Rue de l'Horloge. The street

---

nearly all that remained before reconstruction. A tour of the walls takes in the bastion, château and Bidouane tower and viewpoint.
🚗 *Head out of town on the Rue de la Rance which leads into the D168 to cross the Barrage de la Rance. At La Richardais take the D114 to Dinard.*

② Dinard
Ille-et-Vilaine, Bretagne; 35800
A nostalgic beach holiday ambience lingers among the seaside pavilions, casinos, café parasols and oyster bars along the main beach of this seaside resort. The Chemin de Ronde traces the old city walls and climbs up around the cliffs past handsome villas. Dinard is characterized by some 400 classified mansions, described as Anglo-Breton with their towers, turrets and Tudor wood features. Garden-lovers should not miss the **Parc du Port Breton** *(open daily)* and the **Jardin des Senteurs** *(open daily)*.
🚗 *From the seafront, turn left onto the D114 to Saint-Malo and continue straight ahead to La Richardais/Le Minihic-sur-Rance. After driving through Plouër-sur-Rance, follow the D12 to Dinan.*

---

③ Dinan
Côtes d'Armor, Bretagne; 22100
Dominating the Vallée de la Rance from its ancient fortifications, this medieval city is known for its art and history, with its architectural heritage remarkably preserved. The first Breton king Nominoë encouraged monks to establish a monastery here in the 9th century. Work on the ramparts began in 1283 and spanned four centuries.

is named after its 15th-century clocktower, the **Tour de l'Horloge** ③. It continues to the intersection with Rue de l'Apport. **L'Apport** ④ is an ancient trading square circled by porches, and three different types of wood-slat houses characteristic of Dinan. These include 15th-century houses with oriel windows, 16th-century houses with porches and 17th-century houses with decorative shop windows. On the opposite side of the street are two contagious squares testifying to Dinan's lively spiritual and trading history – the Place des Cordeliers and the Place des Merciers. From here, turn left into the Grande Rue which leads to the

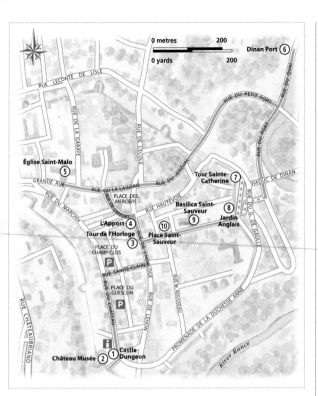

ACTIVITIES

MARINE SPAS

Thermes Marins de Saint-Malo
www.thalassotherapie.com

CRUISING

www.etoile-marine.com

EAT AND DRINK

SAINT-MALO

Crêperie Margaux *inexpensive*
Chirpy crêperie with home-made crêpes, *galettes*, and boutique cider, fruit juices and teas on the menu.
3 place du Marché aux Légumes, 34500; 02 99 20 26 02; www.creperie-margaux.com; closed Tue–Wed during low-season

Le Bistrot de Jean
inexpensive–moderate
Old-style bar-bistro serving grilled fish, fish tapenades and French classics.
6, rue de la Corne-de-Cerf, Saint-Malo, 34500; 02 99 40 98 68; closed Sun, Wed and Sat lunch

L'Entre Deux Verres *moderate*
Fresh *cuisine du marché*, meat and fish dishes are served in this bistro.
7 rue Grands Degrés, 34500; 02 99 40 18 91; www.restaurant-lentredeuxverres.com; closed Mon

DINAN

Crêperie Ahna *inexpensive*
Cheerful crêperie with big choice of crêpes and farm-fresh cider.
7 rue de la Poissonnerie, 22100; 02 96 39 09 13; closed Sun

Le Saint-Louis *inexpensive–moderate*
Organic and vegetarian dishes are served in a vibrant atmosphere.
9 rue de Léhon, 22100; 02 96 39 89 50; closed Tue nights, Wed

Below Boat approaches Dinan port, a lively dockside area

Gothic-Rennaissance church **Église Saint-Malo** ⑤. Retrace the route along Grande Rue, and continue straight ahead on Rue de la Lainerie, to reach the top of Rue du Jerzual. From here move downhill to the **Dinan Port** ⑥. The streets are packed with art and craft shops. Exiting the old city walls, the route continues along the Rue du Petit Fort past the Governor's Tower. This artillery tower is placed strategically between the two northern entries to the town – the Porte du Jerzual and the Porte Saint-Malo. They open onto the port on Rue du Quai, a lively area of restaurants and shops. Head down to the Rue du Port. To the left is La Maison de la Rance, a museum on the natural world in the Vallée de la Rance. Walk up to the end of Rue du Port along the river Rance, past the viaduct. On the right, a signed pathway leads to the **Tour Sainte-Catherine** ⑦ for an amazing view of the port and valley. Pass through the **Jardin Anglais** ⑧ – English gardens on the former parish cemetery – to the **Basilica Saint-Sauveur** ⑨, a melange of Roman, Gothic, Classical and Baroque layers from its 12th-century foundations. The walk ends at **Place Saint-Sauveur** ⑩, once home to the covered meat market and now a church square. From here take the Rue de l'Horloge and then the Rue Sainte-Claire and Rue du Château back to the parking.

🚗 *Take the Rue Sainte-Anne, at roundabout take second exit and continue on the Route de Dinan, turn right into the N176 then left into the D792.*

Above Fourteenth-century Fort la Latte on the Côte d'Émeraude **Below** Walking trail through the ecological zone in Pointe du Chevet near St-Jacut-de-la-Mer

WHERE TO STAY

AROUND JUGON-LES-LACS

Manoir du Vaumadeuc *moderate–expensive*
Twelve kilometres (7 miles) north of Jugon-les-Lacs, the 15th-century noble family château has chunky wooden beam ceilings, large fireplaces and French Renaissance gardens. The 11 rooms and two apartments are classily furnished with fine fabrics and wallpapers. Some of them have vintage bathtubs, stone fireplaces and antique writing desks.
Pléven, 22130; 02 96 84 46 17; www.vaumadeuc.com; closed Nov–Easter

AROUND POINTE DU CHEVET

Le Vieux Moulin *inexpensive*
The old stone walls of the *moulin du blé* – a wheat mill which operated from 1415 to 1918 – create enormous character in the small *hôtel de charme*. The 26 rooms are spic-and-span, and pleasantly furnished with antique beds and tables. The hotel interiors, from the bar to the restaurant, have an old-world style – dark wood, dark stones, bay windows and Art Deco floor tiles. The garden setting adds to the charm.
22 rue du Moulin, Saint-Jacut-de-la-Mer, 22750; 02 96 27 71 02; www.hotel-le-vieux-moulin.com

CAP FRÉHEL

Relais du Cap Fréhel *moderate*
Peace and greenery reign in this 19th-century farmhouse run by the Billets. Set in a wooded park, 2 km (1 mile) from the beach, the property includes bed-and-breakfast loft rooms cosily furnished, as well as two self-contained cottages. Evening meals area available on request.
Route du Cap, Plévenon, 22240; 02 96 41 43 02; www.relaiscapfrehel.fr

Where to Stay: inexpensive, under €70; moderate, €70–€150; expensive, over €150

4 Jugon-les-Lacs
Côtes-d'Armor, Bretagne; 22270
The granite cottages and castle of this once fortified little town nestle deep in a forested valley on the shores of a 4-km (2-mile) long lake. Its sheltered waters once acted as a natural moat to ward off invaders. They are now a haven for ramblers, anglers, canoeists and sailors. The village castle lies on a hillock between two rivers – Rosette and Arguenon. The old-world charm of the town, with its castle, town square and small cobblestoned *ruelles* full of artists' *ateliers* and *lavoirs* (communal washing places), has earned it the title "Petite City of Character".

🚗 *Take the D792 heading north and pass by Plancoët. Continue on the D768, then at the roundabout take the third exit; continue on the D26 to St-Jacut-de-la-Mer and follow signs through to the Pointe du Chevet, making a small detour to view the 5th-century Benedictine Abbaye de Saint-Jacut (not open to visitors).*

5 Pointe du Chevet
St-Jacut-de-la-Mer, Côtes-d'Armor, Bretagne; 22750
The narrow rocky isthmus of St-Jacut-de-la-Mer is wedged between two large inlets, the bays of Lancieux and Arguenon. Skirted by rocky beaches, dunes and vast tracts of oyster farms, the peninsula – which culminates in the Pointe du Chevet – is a protected ecological and flora zone, and a refuge for many migratory birds. The promontory looks over the **Île des Hébihens** and its 17th-century granite tower, built to ward off attacks by the English navy.

🚗 *Return to St-Jacut via the Boulevard du Chevet. Take Boulevard*

du Rougeret on the right and follow for about 1.7 km (1 mile); then turn left into Boulevard des Dunes, also called the D62. Continue until it meets the D786 and turn right; continue until Notre-Dame-du-Guildo and turn right onto the D19 which leads to Saint-Cast-le-Guildo.

6 Saint-Cast-le-Guildo
Côtes-d'Armor, Bretagne; 22380
Once a humble fishing village, Saint-Cast-le-Guildo was named after a Welsh monk, one of several who evangelized the area in the 6th century. It became a seaside resort in the late 1800s. The town is perched on a headland which separates the Baie de la Fresnaye from the Baie de l'Arguenon, with more than half a dozen beaches strung around its jagged coast. From the main beach, **Grande Plage**, it is just a short walk between the sand dunes and cliffs to the fishing and leisure port, and another short walk to reach the Point de Saint-Cast. The stunning panorama from here reaches the Channel Islands on a clear day.

🚗 *Exit on the D13, pass Chateau La Chesnaye, and turn right onto the D786. At Sainte-Aide turn right onto the D16/D16A and follow the road until the sign on the right for Fort la Latte is seen.*

Breton Identity

Language is at the heart of a very strong *identité bretonne*. Education, media, town names and street signs are bilingual – in French and Breton, or in Gallo, a Latin derived language spoken in eastern Brittany. Polls show that nearly 90 per cent of the population want the Breton language and culture to survive.

⑦ Fort la Latte

Côtes-d'Armor, Bretagne; 22240
Breathtakingly positioned 60 m
(197 ft) above the ocean on a rocky
outcrop, this 14th-century feudal
castle is separated from solid ground
by two huge crevasses, traversed by
drawbridges. Built for a French count,
the castle was modified in the 17th
century and fully restored in the early
20th century. From Le Chemin de
Ronde, the circular fort-top passageway, there are 360 degree views over
the Côte d'Émeraude.

🚗 *Return to the main road (D16A),
turn right and continue to Cap Fréhel
where visitors can either pay to pass a
toll gate and access the parking at the
end of the cape, or walk in.*

⑧ Cap Fréhel

Côtes-d'Armor, Bretagne; 22240
One of the largest moorlands in
Europe, Cap Fréhel is covered with
4 sq km (1.5 sq miles) of wild grass-
lands. The headland culminates in
pink sandstone cliffs which plunge
70 m (230 ft) to the sea. The cape
and its four islets, classified as an
ornithological reserve, is a great
place to spot some of the sea birds
which nest in the area. The 17th-
century granite lighthouse, **Tour
Vauban**, stands alongside its replace-
ment. Climb the 145 steps of the
lighthouse for a stunning view.

🚗 *Take the D34A direction Erquy/
Lamballe/Saint-Brieuc. At Pléhérel-
Plage continue on the D34 to Saint-
Brieuc. After Plurien turn right on the
D786 to Erquy/Saint-Brieuc. Continue
for 14 km (9 miles), then get on the*

dual carriage (N12/E50) to and around
Saint-Brieuc for another 14 km (9 miles).
Exit onto the coastal road, D786, and
drive 40 km (25 miles) to Paimpol. From
Paimpol follow signs to take the ferry
to Île-de-Bréhat on D789.

⑨ Paimpol

Côtes-d'Armor, Bretagne; 22500
At the height of its booming fishing
industry in the 19th century, Paimpol
was regularly flooded by high tides
until sea walls were built. From the
old port, stroll through the streets
of the Latin Quarter, admiring the
medieval houses on the Place du
Martray and particularly the **Maison
Jézéquel**. Three kilometres (2 miles)
from the port is another protected
building, the 13th-century monastery **Abbaye de Beauport**.
   Paimpol is the embarkation point for
those wanting to visit the **Île-de-
Bréhat**, two islands that are joined by
a bridge. The islands' landscapes vary
drastically. While the northern island
is wild and covered in heath, the
southern is more mild, flourishing with
mimosa, aloe, and palms. Several well-
signed walks take in villages, coastal
scenery and monuments such as the
citadel, lighthouse of Paon and **Moulin
à Marée** at Birlot.

🚗 *Take the Route de Kergrist, and turn
right onto the D786 to Tréguier.*

⑩ Tréguier

Côtes-d'Armor, Bretagne; 22220
With its immaculately landscaped port
and parklands facing the Jaudy river,
the medieval centre of Tréguier is a
treasure-chest of bell-towers and
Gothic arcades and courtyards. Key
sights include the three-steepled
Cathédrale Saint-Tugdual with its
Roman, Gothic and Classical towers;
the **Hôtel-Dieu**, the town hall housed
in a former Augustine convent; the
timber houses or *maisons en bois* on
Place Notre-Dame-de-Coatcolvezou
and the **Maison de Madame Taupin**
on the Place du Martray. Fifty-eight
elliptical prehistoric stones, the
Megaliths du Tossen Keller, are found
along the riverside on Rue du Port.

🚗 *Continue on the D786. Take the
first exit at the roundabout and
continue on the D6. Then turn right
to Perros Guirec, pass the town and
continue to Ploumanac'h.*

Top Cathédrale Saint-Tugdual in Tréguier
Above Panoramic view from Saint-Cast-le-
Guildo **Left** Handsome house in Paimpol

ACTIVITIES

GOLF

Fréhel Golf-Club des Sables d'Or
www.frehel-golfsablesdor.fr

EAT AND DRINK

TRÉGUIER

Crêperie du Cloître *inexpensive*
In the square facing the cathedral,
this crêperie is housed in an old stone
building with authentic Breton decor.
*1 place du Martray; 02 96 92 17 88;
closed Thu low season*

La Maison de Jeanne
inexpensive–moderate
This café-crêperie-gallery also serves
meat and vegetable dishes in a rustic
dining room with paintings based on
marine themes on the walls.
*24 rue Ernest Renan; 02 96 92 29 28;
closed Mon, Tue*

Eat and Drink: inexpensive, under €20; moderate, €20–€40; expensive, over €40

Above Left Megalithic site Allée Couverte de Ty-ar-kornandounezed **Above Right** Brick house in Trégastel **Below** Pink granite boulders on the beach in Ploumanac'h

⑪ Ploumanac'h
Perros-Guirec, Côtes-d'Armor, Bretagne; 22700

At the heart of the Côte de Granit Rose, the Grand Site National de Ploumanac'h is an extraordinary place with pink granite boulders randomly, and at times precariously, stacked along 30 ha (75 acres) of protected coast and beachfront. The natural sculpture of massive granite blocks and rock splinters has been shaped by 300 million years of erosion. The pink granite is a mix of quartz, mica and feldspar. The spectacle is best viewed in the evening when the setting sun bathes the granite formations in crimson hues with the lighthouse standing sentinel in the background.

🚗 *Take the D788 to Sainte-Anne, then continue to Trégastel Plage following the signs to Côte de Granit Rose. Note that the pretty town of Trégastel with its stone cottages is 2.5 km (1.5 miles) inland on the Route du Lannion.*

⑫ Trégastel Plage
Côtes-d'Armor, Bretagne; 22730

Trégastel's coastal splendour radiates from its stretches of dusky pink sand and granite rocks, a series of deep coves and inlets and a microclimate vegetation of exotic native plants, including mimosa, fig, hydrangea, aloe, wild rosemary, lavender, agave and yucca (bear grass). Visitors have the option of choosing from a dozen adjacent beaches by cove-hopping and coastal trekking. The main coastal promenade, the **Sentier Douanier** (customs trail), heads off in both directions, while the marked pathway around the Île Renote circumnavigates the conservation zone of this coastal outcrop. The **Aquarium Marin de Trégastel** *(closed Mon except Jul–Aug)* near the beach Coz-Pors has 28 exhibition ponds of marine fauna set within the rocks.

🚗 *Exit Trégastel Plage and Saint-Anne and take the D788. After the corniche roads, turn right and cross the bridge into the Rue de L'ile Grande which becomes the D21. To reach the megalithic site of Allée Couverte de Ty-ar-kornandounezed turn right at the tiny hamlet of Île-Grande and take the direction to Pors-Gelen; then some 300 m (328 yd) on the left is the road which leads to the site.*

⑬ Île Grande
Côtes-d'Armor, Bretagne; 22560

Despite its name, Île Grande is just 7 km (4 miles) in circumference, and connected by bridge to the mainland. The small port and village are

---

WHERE TO STAY

PLOUMANAC'H

Hotel Castel Beau Site *moderate*
Perched on the Côte de Granit Rose promenades, this handsome mansion has 40 (mostly sea-facing) rooms. The hotel has undergone a minimalist renovation including Ligne Roset furnishings. It also has an edge-of-water terrace restaurant.
Plage de Saint-Guirec Ploumanac'h, 22700; 02 96 91 40 87; www.castelbeausite.com

TRÉBEURDEN

Hôtel Le Toëno
inexpensive–moderate
Spirited seaside hotel with the basic facilities and bright rooms with sea-facing balconies.
Route de Trégastel Trébeurden, 22560; 02 96 23 68 78; www.hoteltoeno.com

Ti Al Lannec Hôtel Restaurant & Spa *expensive*
Serenity reigns in this 4-star "Relais du Silence", a hotel-restaurant located between huge cypress trees and with 180 degree sea views. The family mansion atmosphere and cliffside location mingle magically with flawless service and breezy, relaxed cordiality.
14 allée de Mézo-Guen, 22560; 02 96 15 01 01; www.tiallannec.com

Where to Stay: inexpensive, under €70; moderate, €70–€150; expensive, over €150

surrounded by a string of islets and the barren landscape is dramatically shaped by the tides. Up until 1910, millions of tonnes of blue and white granite were extracted from Île Grande's quarry helping to pave the streets of Paris and quays of Dunkerque. Now the **Kastel Erek** quarry is the heart of an ornithological reserve and bird hospital run by the League for the Protection of Birds. A megalithic site of standing stones – **Allée Couverte de Ty-ar-kornandounezed** – lies in the centre of the island. The site dates back to around 2,300 BC. Either drive there or pass it on a circular trek of the isle, which takes about 2 hours.

🚗 *Return via the D21, also known as the Rue de l'île Grande, and then turn right onto the D788 (Corniche de Goas Treiz). Next turn left onto the D65 to reach Trébeurden.*

⑭ Trébeurden
Côtes-d'Armor, Bretagne; 22560

From the densely forested cliffs above Trébeurden the seascape takes in multiple coves, beaches and islands, including the Île Milliau. The town is also home to the Holy Trinity Church, built in the shape of a Latin cross. Walk out to the granite outcrop, the **Presqu'île Le Castel**, where fabulous rock forms sculpted by the ocean have names such as Père Trébeurden. On the **Pointe de Bihit**, where visitors may catch otters sunbathing among the ferns and heather,there is an orientation table with views reaching as far as the Finistère coastline. From the main beach, **Goas Treiz**, head into the wetlands of the **Marais de Quellen**, a haven for birders and trekkers. Its hedged farmlands are home to a population of Camargue horses from the south of France, offering another way of visiting the area.

Above Seascape of Trébeurden as viewed from the cliffs Below Cosy little bar in Trégastel Plage

EAT AND DRINK

TRÉGASTEL PLAGE

Restaurant Les Triagoz
moderate-expensive
Waves will lap at diners' feet as they sip or eat on the terrace of this modern bistro, with a seafood-dominated menu and modern takes on traditional Breton dishes.
Place du Coz-Pors, 22730; 02 96 15 34 10; closed Tue, Wed lunch

TRÉBEURDEN

Manoir de Lan Kerellec *expensive*
Grand cuisine, seafood and rural produce, at 1-star Michelin hotel-restaurant with views towering over the coast.
Allee Centrale de Lan Kerellec, 22560 ; 02 96 15 00 00; www.lankerellec.com; closed Mon–Thu for lunch and Dec–Feb

---

DAY TRIP OPTIONS
The first two day trips work well for those who wish to stay near the Côte d'Emeraude. The ideas for the last two trips are for those who base themselves on the Côte de Granit Rose.

Trip to the beach
After exploring all of Saint-Malo's ➊ ramparts, drive to Cap Fréhel ➑ in the afternoon and take a cruise (www.compagniecorsair.com) to see the beautiful headlands from the sea.

From Saint-Malo take the D168 then the D768 towards St-Jacut, then the D786. At Sainte-Aide continue on the the D16/D16A to Cap Fréhel.

Vallée de la Rance
At the northern end of the Dinan ➌ port area, nature and maritime lovers can start exploring the Vallée de la Rance, its canals, cycle paths and riverbank walking trails. From there visitors can drive off to see the adjacent villages and countryside manors.

From Dinan port, the D12 heads off to Lehon, while the D676 leads to Lanvallay, and then to La-Vicomte-sur-Rance. The port is accessed from the old town via Rue du Général de Gaulle.

Île-de-Bréhat
The day trip to the île-de Brehat allows visitors to encounter the varied landscape between its wilder,

heath-covered north and the island of flowers in the south.

Head out of Perros-Guirec on the D6, turn left into the D786 and continue via Tréguier to Paimpol. Take the D789 to the Pointe de l'Arcouest where boats ply to Port-Clos.

Trégastel Plage
Children will love a lazy day on the beach and learning about the sea creatures, tidal phenomena and pink granite at the eco-friendly Marine Aquarium.

Take the Boulevard du Coz-Pors to Tregastel Plages and continue on the same road for the aquarium.

Eat and Drink: inexpensive, under €20; moderate, €20–€40; expensive, over €40

Rugged Coastline and Deep Valleys

Sizun to Aiguilles de Port Coton

Highlights

- **Spectacular landscapes**
  Explore the wild lunar landscape, woods and valleys of the Parc Naturel Régional d'Armorique

- **Finistère villages**
  Visit Le Faou and Locronan – two of France's most charming villages

- **Glorious vistas**
  Take in the dramatic views from Cap Sizun across the Atlantic

- **Britanny microcosm**
  Explore the island of Belle-Île-en-Mer that encapsulates the best of Brittany

Boats anchored in the port of Le Palais in Belle-Île-en-Mer

Rugged Coastline and Deep Valleys

Finistère – literally "the end of the earth" – is an isolated, ocean-swept region with 1,600 km (1,000 miles) of coastline. Here Breton culture is at its strongest. The Celts (called Gauls by the Romans) were the principal culture here by the 5th century BC, and their legends and megaliths endure. The Parc Naturel Régional d'Armorique is a forested spine running north to south, dotted with historic villages. Heading east, the Morbihan is tamer, with riverside towns and a coastal stretch of harbours, fortifications and leisure ports. Off the Gulf du Morbihan, Belle-Île-en-Mer, the biggest of Brittany's islands, is a haven of colourful fishing ports and craggy coastline.

Above View over Belle-Île-en-Mer from the Grand Phare de Kervilahouen, *see p115*

ACTIVITIES

Learn about the flora and fauna of the Pointe du Raz on a guided visit

Sit by the wild coast of Cap Sizun and listen to the seagulls and the sea

Go sea kayaking in the Baie de Concarneau

Follow in Gauguin's footsteps and grab a canvas or a sketch pad and capture Pont-Aven between art gallery visits

Explore the Carnac megaliths near the Gulf of Morbihan

Put on hiking boots and hit the trails around the Gulf of Morbihan

Bike around Belle-Île-en-Mer on the marked cycling circuit

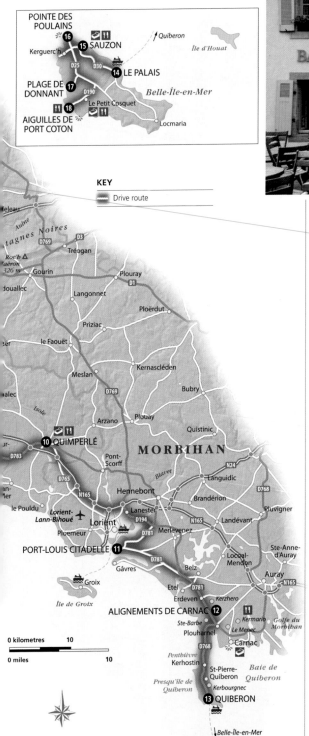

KEY

— Drive route

Above Delightful little bar in Locronan, see p111

PLAN YOUR DRIVE

Start/finish: Sizun to Aiguilles de Port Coton.

Number of days: 4–5, allowing one day to explore Cap Sizun and at least one day and night on Belle-Île-en-Mer.

Distance: 340 km (210 miles).

Road conditions: Generally good; traffic is particularly heavy during the summer, especially near towns.

When to go: The ideal time to undertake the drive is early summer, in May–June, just before the crowds start pouring in.

Opening hours: Monuments and shops are generally open from 10am to 6pm. During high season private museums stay open everyday and shops have longer hours.

Main market days: Le Faou: Fri; Douarnenez: Mon, Thu–Sat; Concarneau: Mon–Sat; Pont-Aven: Tue; Quimperlé: Fri; Le Palais: daily.

Major festivals: Sizun: Fête de la Nature, May; Douarnenez: Maritime festival, Jul (biennial, next in 2010); Concarneau: Breton Fête des Filets Bleus, Aug.

DAY TRIP OPTIONS

The Parc Naturel Régional d'Armonrique is ideal for **family** outdoor activities; Plage de Penthièvre makes for great picnics and swimming and the beaches of Belle-Île are a favourite with **surfers**. For more details, see p115.

Above Sign showing the direction to Roc'h Trevezel **Above right** Crêperie in a stone house in Locronan **Below** Communal well of Locronan

WHERE TO STAY

DOUARNENEZ

Le Clos de Vallombreuse *moderate*
This elegant early 1900s house has, spacious rooms with classical furnishings. There are also large gardens, a salon and a swimming pool.
7 rue d'Estienne d'Orves, 29100; 02 98 92 63 64; www.closvallombreuse.com

Hotel Ty Mad *moderate–expensive*
In a revamped 16th-century vicarage the old stone building of Ty Mad has been revamped with lots of white decor, 15 eclectically styled rooms, exotic furnishings, a gorgeous garden and a contemporary art gallery.
Plage St Jean, Treboul, 29100; 02 98 74 00 53; www.hoteltymad.com

① Sizun
Finistère, Bretagne; 29450
Sizun is a stunning ensemble of high walls, church towers and city gates. The parish enclosure, **l'Enclos Paroissial Saint-Suliau**, is classified as a historic monument. Named after a Welsh monk, it comprises the church, which was built between the 16th and 18th centuries, a sacristy and a 56-m (184-ft) tower. The centrepiece of the parish is the arched gateway, **l'Arc de Triomphe**, considered to be a jewel of Breton Renaissance art. A replica of it graced Paris' Jardins des Tuileries for the 1989 bicentenary celebrations of the French Revolution. Outside the town, along the D764, is **Ecomusée des Monts d'Arrée** *(open daily Jul–Aug, closed Sat Mar–Jun and Sep–Oct)*, with displays on ethnology and history.

🚗 *Exit Sizun and take the D764 passing through Commana, then turn right onto the D785.*

② Le Roc'h Trévézel
Finistère, Bretagne; 29410
The rocky outcrops and stunted heather of the massif of the Monts d'Arrée form the wildest part of the **Parc Naturel Régional d'Armorique** – France's second oldest national park created in 1969. The Roc'h Trévézel (383 m/1,257 ft) is its second highest point, and is known for its vistas of barren ridges, denuded hills and hedged farmland. Descending towards the Montagne St-Michel, the rocky escarpments are softened by forested valleys and streams. Also worth a vist is the **Domaine de Ménez-Meur** *(open daily May–Sep)*, which has flora and fauna trails, a short drive from Le Roc'h Trévézel.

🚗 *From Le Roc'h Trévézel, continue on the D785, then turn right onto the D42. Domaine de Ménez-Meur is off the D42 between the village of St-Rivoal and the commune of Rumengol. To reach Le Faou, continue along the D42.*

> ### Ronan's Hermitage
> Locronan's name comes from *Locus Ronani* – sacred place of Ronan – after a 7th century Irish bishop. Ronan came to Finistère to spread Christianity among the locals who practiced Druidism. He built a forest hermitage in Bois de Nevet where traces of the Druid's sacred site, Le Nemeton, still exist.

③ Le Faou
Finistère, Bretagne; 29590
At the head of the Aulne river, the main street of Le Faou, Rue du Général de Gaulle, is lined with gable-roofed granite and schist houses. The buildings have exquisite decorative details – corbelled features of carved wood and stone projecting from the façades – and small, pretty windows. Opposite the town's port, the Gothic steeple of **Saint-Sauveur** is reflected in the river. Just east of town near the Cranou forest, the **Église de Rumengol** is a historic monument – an eclectic mix of Gothic, Renaissance and Baroque styles – built on a Druidic site.

🚗 *Take the N165; then exit to the right onto the D770 and pass through Châteaulin, take the D7 on the left and continue via Kergoat to Locronan.*

④ Locronan
Finistère, Bretagne; 29180

The imposing 15th-century church of **Saint-Ronan**, communal well and fine granite townhouses on the **Grande Place de l'Église** were a backdrop in Roman Polanski's 1979 film *Tess*. The delightful square is crowded with cafés, bars and biscuit shops. Among them stands the former headquarters of the French East India Company and the **Bureau Royal des Toiles** which oversaw the town's thriving linen and hemp industry from the 14th century. Wander through the adjacent streets, from Rue des Charrettes with its attractive houses decorated with flowerpots, to Rue Moal, the old weavers' quarter. Rue Saint Maurice, the former craftsmen's street, leads to a viewpoint.

🚗 *Take Rue du Prieuré and continue straight ahead. At the roundabout take the second exit and continue on the D7 to Douarnenez.*

⑤ Douarnenez
Finistère, Bretagne; 29100

Set out on the Chemin de la Sardine – the Sardine Trail marked by 17 bronze fish – to get a taste of the city's fish-canning history. Do not miss the streets and houses around the old fishing port, **Porte de Peche du Rosmeur**; the gardens, Gallo-Roman archaeology and views from the **Belvedere des Plomarc'h**; and the **Port-Musée** *(open daily Jul–Aug, Tue–Sun Apr–Jun and Sep)*, a floating maritime museum.

🚗 *Continue along the D7 to the Pointe du Van. From there trace the waterfront and turn left onto the D607. Turn right into the Rue des Langoustiers and pass through Lescoff to reach Pointe du Raz.*

⑥ Pointe du Raz
Finistère, Bretagne; 29770

The mammoth granite spur at the end of Cap Sizun culminates in 70-m (230-ft) high cliffs which drop steeply to the Mer d'Iroise. The headland's flora and fauna – cormorants, gorse and heath – are part of a coastal conservation programme. The best way to view **Pointe du Raz**, the adjacent **Pointe du Van** and the eerily named **Baie des Trépassées** separating them is from one of the walking trails which crisscross the windswept headlands.

🚗 *Return to Lescoff (Rue des Langoustiers) and continue on the D784. After Audierne, take the second exit onto the D765 to Pont-Croix.*

⑦ Pont-Croix
Finistère, Bretagne; 29790

Take a tour of the village through the paved medieval *ruelles* (alleyways), such as the **Grand Rue Chère** which leads towards the river. The flower-covered stone walls and alcoves in Rue des Courtils are part of an old château. The 13th-century church, **Notre-Dame de Roscudon**, has intricate stonework. For a better understanding of Bigoudène folklore, stop by the **Musée du Patrimoine** *(open daily Jul–Aug, evenings Jun and Sep, Sun Oct–May)* in the Marquisat, once home of the noble seigneurs of Rosmadec. Finally head to the Goyen river, a habitat for herons, egrets and other sea birds.

🚗 *Continue on the D765, then turn right onto the D43 to Quimper. At the T-junction, turn right onto the D765 to Quimper. At the roundabout turn left onto the D100. At the next roundabout, take the N165 to Concarneau. Exit onto the D70, then onto the D783 to Concarneau.*

Above Scenic Pointe du Van by the Baie des Trépassées **Left** Boat in Porte de Peche du Rosmeur, Douarnenez **Below** l'Arc de Triomphe in l'Enclos Paroissial Saint-Suliau, Sizun

EAT AND DRINK

LOCRONAN

Crêperie Le Temps Passé *inexpensive*
This place stands among gorgeous little stone cottages and serves savoury *galettes* and sweet crêpes.
4 rue du Four, 29180; 02 98 91 87 29; www.creperie-letempspasse.fr

Crêperie Ty Coz *inexpensive*
Excellent crêperie. Imaginative fillings are on offer in this handsome 17th-century village house with two dining salons and a garden terrace.
Place de l'église, 29180; 02 98 91 70 79; http://creperietycoz.com

DOUARNENEZ

Crêperie Tudal *inexpensive*
This quaint 1950's crêperie and food store is a Breton jewel with daily specialities. The crêpes are filled with cheese, fruits and other sweet things.
36 rue Jean Jaurès, 29100; 02 98 92 02 74; www.augouterbreton.com; closed Sun

Le Bigorneau Amoureux *moderate*
The restaurant's name means "shellfish in love" and the specialities are potatoes with meat and seafood.
2 boulevard Richepin, Plage des Dames, 29100; 02 98 92 35 55; www.bigorneau-amoureux.com; closed Mon

Eat and Drink: inexpensive, under €20; moderate, €20–€40; expensive, over €40

Above left Maison des Archers on Rue Dom Morice, Quimperlé **Above right** Belfry of the walled city of Concarneau **Below** Creeper-covered millhouse on the Aven river at Pont-Aven

WHERE TO STAY

CONCARNEAU

Hôtel Kermor *moderate*
A wooden boat decor characterises this hotel overlooking the beach. The hotel doubles as an art gallery.
37 rue des Sables Blancs, 29900; 02 98 97 02 96; www.hotel-kermor.com

Les Sables Blancs *expensive*
This hotel has contemporary decor in the style of an ocean liner. There is a seaside bar and restaurant-lounge.
45 rue Sables Blancs, 29900; 02 98 50 10 12; www.hotel-les-sables-blancs.com

PONT AVEN

La Chaumière Roz-Aven
inexpensive–moderate
This hotel offers cosy rooms in a cottage on the banks of the Aven river.
11 quai Théodore Botrel, 29900; 02 98 06 13 06; www.hotelpontaven.online.fr

QUIMPERLÉ

Hotel Vintage *moderate*
The ten spacious rooms feature frescoes by contemporary artists.
20 rue Brémond d'ars, 29300; 02 98 35 09 10; www.hotelvintage.com

AROUND ALIGNEMENTS DE CARNAC

Hotel Tumulus *moderate–expensive*
Housed in a turreted white mansion facing Quiberon bay, this hotel has 23 large rooms and suites.
Chemin du Tumulus, 56340; 02 97 52 08 21; www.hotel-tumulus.com

8 Concarneau
Finistère, Bretagne; 29900

Between fishing and leisure ports stand the sea walls, bastions and towers of Concarneau's impressive *ville close*. This walled city was built in the 14th century on an islet in the bay of Concarneau, inhabited by fishermen since prehistoric times. The walled city is linked to the mainland by old drawbridges. Inside, visitors can discover its cobblestoned passageways and courtyards, parts of the old moat, a belfry and sundial. Within its walls there is a *colombage* château which was once the residence of the military governor. Before leaving visitors might want to see the **Musée de la Pêche** *(open daily Feb–Oct)*, a fishing museum.

🚗 *Take the D783 in direction of Pont-Aven. Parking in the centre during high season can be difficult; park wherever there is space and walk to the centre.*

9 Pont-Aven
Finistère, Bretagne; 29930

Over a century after Paul Gauguin sojourned here in the late 1800s and captured its pastoral beauty, Pont-Aven is still a living canvas. Wander along the banks of the Aven from the Rue des Meunieres to the **Place Royale** to see the rows of riverside dwellings which were once the homes of royal officers and millers. The Promenade Xavier Grall leads via quays and canals to the **Moulin de Poulhouars** mill, while **Jardin Excelmans** is located at the end of the port area. Other highlights are the **Église de Pont-Aven** painted by Gauguin, the **Musée des Beaux-Arts** *(open daily)* and the local butter biscuits, *galettes de Pont-Aven.*

🚗 *Continue on the D783, passing through Riec-sur-Belon to Quimperlé.*

10 Quimperlé
Finistère, Bretagne; 29300

Ravaged in the 14th century during the War of Succession battles over control of the Duchy of Brittany, this fortified town on the banks of the Odet river was rebuilt in the 17th century. From the hump backed medieval bridge, **Pont Fleuri**, head to the Art Nouveau covered market Les Halles and the abbatial **Église Sainte-Croix**, both on Place Hervo, on the way to the former aristocratic neighbourhood of Rue Bremond d'Ars, which is dubbed the Petit Marais. In Rue Dom Morice is the town's oldest building. To its left is the 1550 **Maison des Archers** which now holds temporary exhibitions. Visitors should not

miss the Gothic **Église Notre-Dame-de-l'Assomption** on Place St-Michel, and the Baroque-style **Chapelle des Ursulines** on Avenue Aristide Briand.

🚗 *Leave town on the D765; turn right onto the N165 and pass through Lanester. Continue on the D194E, into the D326 and D194. Turn right onto the D781 and continue to Port-Louis. Take the Avenue de Kerbel from here in the direction of "Citadelle musée" where there is space to park.*

⑪ Port-Louis Citadelle
Morbihan, Bretagne; 56290

Constructed at the end of a flat spit of land on the Atlantic coast, the stone citadel of Port-Louis is a monument of military architecture. Flanked by two natural harbours, the 17th-century bastion has views over the bay of Lorient, which it was intended to defend. The fort was named after French King Louis XIII, who ordered its construction. Work on it began in 1591 under the direction of Spanish architect Cristobal de Rojas, lending the building some features of Andalusian forts. Head to the dungeons where the **Musée National de la Marine** (open daily, closed Tue Sep–Apr, closed mid-Dec–Jan) chronicles the history of Port-Louis; there is also an Arsenal Room, Powder Magazine Room and exhibitions on ocean rescue.

🚗 *Continue on the D781 towards Quiberon and then Carnac. Watch for the signs to several sites with alignments between Erdeven and Ste-Barbe.*

⑫ Alignements de Carnac
Morbihan, Bretagne; 56340

The famous Carnac alignments – rows of megalithic standing stones – are seen in several fields over some 4 km (2 miles) around Carnac. In all there are about 3,000 menhirs (Breton for "long rock") up to 6 m (20 ft) high. While the big fields of alignments – **Kerlescan**, **Le Menec**, **Le Pett Menec** and **Kermario** – can only be visited in peak months on a guided tour, the smaller fields in **Sainte-Barbe** and **Kerzhero** can be easily explored independently. The 6,000-year-old alignments served a religious function – indicating the way to a sacred enclosure – while the dolmens were linked to burials.

🚗 *Take the D781 to Plouharnel and then the D768 to Quiberon taking in the views of the Penthièvre isthmus, Penthièvre fort, villages of Kerhostin and St-Pierre-Quiberon, and the megaliths of Kerbourgnec.*

⑬ Quiberon
Morbihan, Bretagne; 56170

At the tip of the **Presqu'île de Quiberon** isthmus, Quiberon is a mish-mash of modern beach resort and old-time fishing village in a splendid sea setting. Walk through the pedestrian zones of the city, then along the waterfront boulevard, taking in the **Mairie**, the **Église Notre-Dame de Locmaria** and the colourful houses of Port Maria, and views from Port Haliguen marina onto Quiberon Bay. The **Beg Er Lan** hill is home to the Anglo-Medieval **Château Turpault** and offers stunning panoramic views.

🚗 *Head to the Gare Maritime at Port Maria, from where car-ferries depart for Belle-Île-en-Mer.*

Above View of the port in Quiberon with the Château Turpault in the background **Below** Rows of menhirs in the famous alignments of Carnac

EAT AND DRINK

CONCARNEAU

Le Buccin *moderate–expensive*
In an alley, this restaurant serves succulent seafood and meat dishes.
1 rue Duguay-Trouin, 29900; 02 98 50 54 22

QUIMPERLÉ

Le Bistro de la Tour *moderate*
The menu here specializes in Breton seafood, cheese and meat.
2 rue Dom Morice, 29300; 02 98 39 29 58; www.hotelvintage.com; closed Sat lunch, Sun, Mon

AROUND ALIGNEMENTS DE CARNAC

La Côte *moderate–expensive*
This place offers refined Breton food such as camembert with cumin.
Kermario, 56340; 02 97 52 02 80; www.restaurant-la-cote.com; closed Sat lunch, Sun evening, Mon

Above Bright flowers, Pointe des Poulains

VISITING BELLE-ÎLE-EN-MER

Ferry Information
In summer and autumn regular car and passenger ferries link Gare Maritime at Port Maria in Quiberon with Le Palais. There are far fewer boats between Quiberon and Sauzon. Winter crossings are also less frequent. Reservation is mandatory for car crossings. www.compagnie-oceane.fr

WHERE TO STAY

SAUZON

Hôtel Le Cardinal
inexpensive–moderate
This contemporary residence has an ocean-liner design with sea views.
Port Bellec, 56360; 02 97 31 61 60; www.hotel-cardinal.fr

AROUND AIGUILLES DE PORT COTON

Hôtel La Désirade
moderate–expensive
The 32 rooms of the hotel are in cottages and have cool, marine decor.
Le Petit Cosquet, Bangor, 56360; 02 97 31 70 70; www.hotel-la-desirade.com; closed mid-Nov–Mar

⑭ Le Palais

Morbihan, Bretagne; 56360;
The old city gateways and ramparts of La Palais are threaded with gardens – a virtual forest of elms, acacia, willows, chestnuts and ash trees – and the bike paths which pass through them continue inland, or along the coast. Down at the port visitors can stroll the quays between the pubs and fishermen's cottages. Grafted onto a headland above the port of Le Palais, the **Citadelle Vauban** *(open daily Jul–Mar)*, a castle fortified in 1683 by France's leading military engineer, presides over Belle-Île's capital. Now privately owned, it houses a history museum and its ramparts are used as a fantastic outdoor stage for summer concerts, exhibitions and theatre performances.
🚗 *Take the D30 for Sauzon.*

⑮ Sauzon

Morbihan, Bretagne; 56360
Sauzon's colourful cottages are stacked up the hillside from the fishing port, where café chairs mingle with piles of fishing nets and crayfish pots. Between the green- and red-tipped dazzling white lighthouses at the entry to the harbour, the marina is full of bobbing leisure boats and fishing vessels. Stroll inland past the **Bassin de Pen-Prad** and catch the dusk views back over the town and port. Head up the steep Rue du Port Vihan and veer off to the right along the coastal track towards the **Pointe du Cardinal** for incredible views over the wooded hills and the ocean with its chain of deep water bays.
🚗 *From the D30 turn right into the Route de l'Apothicairerie and turn right onto the D25 for Pointe des Poulains.*

⑯ Pointe des Poulains

Morbihan, Bretagne; 56360
The Pointe des Poulains is likened to a ship's bow projecting into the ocean. The sheer cliffs and serrated rocks have been shaped by erosion into needles called "Polenn" in Breton. This was fancifully translated to French as the Pointe des Poulains, meaning point of the foals.

A 30-minute walking tour

From the large parking area at the entry to the point, join the trail which heads to the **Île des Poulains** ①. The islet with the lighthouse **Phare des Poulains** ② at its tip is isolated from the mainland during extremely high tides. For the rest of the time, it forms a concave sandy beach, with designated paths for people to stroll around. The cliff-edged, sea-sculpted promontory is an important natural site. The medley of flora, fauna and landscapes in this protected site includes schist rocks, coastal meadows and heather and a large variety of marine birds. The fragile and eroded habitat is in the midst of a coastal rehabilitation project and it is important to stick to the marked trails. The paths to the lighthouse intersect with those heading down the coast.

Once occupied by a camp of Neolithic Celts, the area is dominated by cushion-shaped lumps of vegetation dotted with many wild and aromatic flowers, including pink heather and gorse. On the cliffside, the sea spray is a catalyst for special vegetation: oval-leafed sea lavender and salt-loving plants such as saltwort. One plant, the deerhorn, has even adapted to being trampled upon and thrives in the most frequented zones.

Among the birds that can be seen here are seagulls, black-headed

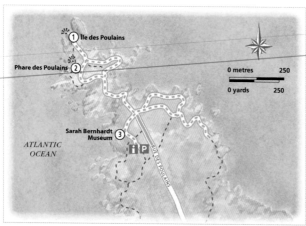

Île des Poulains ①

Phare des Poulains ②

Sarah Bernhardt Museum ③

ATLANTIC OCEAN

0 metres 250
0 yards 250

Where to Stay: inexpensive, under €70; moderate, €70–€150; expensive, over €150

warblers and purple herons. Chimney swallows nest in the sheltered cliffs; there are plenty of sparrows – pipit maritime and wheatears visit from Africa during spring and summer. Larger birds can be sighted if visitors leave the most commonly trodden paths around the lighthouse and extend their walk along the coast.

Either way visitors may choose to finish the walk with a visit to the **Sarah Bernhardt Museum** ③ *(open daily, Apr–Sep)*, the "Villa des Cinq Parties du Monde" dedicated to the flamboyant French actress who fell in love with the wildness of Belle-Île on her first visit in 1894 and built a home on the Pointe des Poulains. The visit is guided with a narration by contemporary French actress Fanny Ardant. From the museum walk back to the car park.

🚗 *Return and continue along the D25. On the way is another amazing coastal formation, l'Apothicairerie – turn right into the D30 and there is parking just after the village of Kerguerc'h. Further along the D25, on the right (between two megalithic standing stones) there is a road signposted towards Plage de Donnant. Further along turn left into a minor road which heads downhill to a large car park.*

⑰ Plage de Donnant
Morbihan, Bretagne; 56360

Donnant beach is set in a deep recession between headlands and hemmed in by high sand dunes. The dunes were formed 2,000 years ago, when there was a small drop in sea levels, leaving exposed sandy stretches which resemble sea-bed topography. Ongoing coastal

conservation work here aims to promote the growth of beach grass, blue thistle, dunal cloves and other vegetation which help anchor the dunes in place. The floral diversity is boosted by mineral rich sands. Within the dunes there are hawthorns, rare orchid species, burnet roses and blood-red sanguine geraniums.

🚗 *Return to the D25, turn right and continue until the intersection with the D190; turn right following the signs to Port Coton.*

⑱ Aiguilles de Port Coton
Morbihan, Bretagne; 56360

The beauty of Aiguilles de Port Coton, a chain of rocky teeth jutting out of the ocean, was captured by Claude Monet in several of his paintings. When the sea is whipped up by storms, the rocks sit in a mass of foam which looks like cotton wool – hence the name of the port. Time the visit with the opening hours of the 87-m (285-ft) high lighthouse, the **Grand Phare de Kervilahouen** *(open 2–4pm daily Jul–Aug)*. Climb its 213 granite steps to get an amazing view over the whole of Belle-Île.

Above left Citadelle Vauban as seen from the port of Le Palais **Above right** Rocks jutting out of the Atlantic Ocean, Port Coton

EAT AND DRINK

SAUZON
Café de la Calé *inexpensive–moderate*
This port side bistro, specializes in oysters and other fish dishes.
Quai Guerveur, 56360; 02 97 31 65 74; www.cafedelacale.pagecom.fr; closed Oct–Mar

AROUND AIGUILLES DE PORT COTON
La Désirade Restaurant *moderate–expensive*
The menu revolves around fresh produce from the market and the sea.
Le Petit Cosquet, Bangor, 56360; 02 97 31 70 70; www.hotel-la-desirade.com; closed mid-Nov–Feb

Castel Clara Hotel Spa *expensive*
From its cliff-top setting, the modern, castle-shaped hotel-restaurant has views over the port of Goulphar. Evening menus include spicy seafood and lobster dishes. Book for a thalasso treatment and lounge around the pool until dinner.
Port-Goulphar, Bangor, 56360; 02 97 31 84 21; www.castel-clara.com; closed mid-Nov–mid-Feb

---

DAY TRIP OPTIONS
For a day trip from Douarnenez, the Parc Naturel Régional d'Armorique is an ideal option. From Carnac, the wild coast of the Presqu'île Quiberon is a good choice and from Belle-Île head to the beach for the day to sun, surf and experience nature.

Hills and villages
Walk, mountain-bike or horse-ride on the hills and jagged cliffs in the morning and visit the beautiful Le Faou ③ while returning.

Take the D7 to Châteaulin, continue on the D770 to Le Faou, then the D42 towards Montagne and Roc Trevezel. A possibility for the return is to continue in a loop through the park, to Commana and Sizun, then return to Le Faou on the D18.

Quiberon waterfront
Plage de Penthièvre near Quiberon ⑬ is a favourite for picnics and swimming. Later in the day stroll around the waterfront of Quiberon, stopping at some of the boutiques on the way.

Take the D781 to Plouharnel. Then take the D768 to pass by the Penthièvre isthmus, and Kerhostin.

Surf and sand
Donnant beach ⑰ offers great surfing. Follow up with a visit to the Aiguilles de Port Coton ⑱.

Access is via the D25. There is a signed turn-off to Donnant Plage on a small road situated between two megaliths. Continue along the D25 and turn right at the intersection with the D190, towards Port Coton.

Eat and Drink: inexpensive, under €20; moderate, €20–€40; expensive, over €40

Valley of the Kings

Chartres to Blois

Highlights

- **Majestic Chartres**
  Gaze in wonder at the dazzling glass and intricate carvings of the most complete of all medieval cathedrals

- **Rural idyll**
  Discover gem-like villages, cave-houses and placid towns full of charm and treasures on the by-ways around the Loire

- **Gourmet pleasures**
  Sample rich delicacies and some of France's finest wines on a tour of the restaurants and vineyards of the Loire

- **Magnificent châteaux**
  Explore Chenonceau, Chambord, Blois, Montrésor – a collection of Renaissance palaces unique in Europe

Stately château of Montrésor overlooks the town

Valley of the Kings

The valleys of the Loire and its tributaries can seem like a special reserve of French delights. France's kings and nobles came to hunt here, and then made the valley their foremost pleasure-garden, lining it with palace-châteaux of stunning opulence. Royal extravagance is not the Loire's only attraction, though, for as well as the grand châteaux there are also ravishingly pretty villages, old stone manors and characterful medieval towns. In the north of the main Loire valley is the Loir, a much more intimate, snug green valley of 1,000-year-old churches, cave-villages and irresistible panoramas. Wines and fine foods also have an equal place among the Loire's great pleasures.

Top Stately château of Montpoupon, *see p124* **Above** Gardens in the pretty Place du Château in bloom, with the château of Blois in the background, *see p126*

ACTIVITIES

Learn the intricacies of the medieval mind from the exquisite stained-glass windows of Chartres cathedral

Tap into Proust's childhood memories in his bedroom at Illiers-Combray

Spend a night as a cave-dweller in the Loir valley

Compare *appellations contrôlées* on a tour of the vineyards around Bourgueil and Chinon

Walk through lush green woods beside the sparkling Indrois river from Montrésor

Get a taste of regal living at one of the Loire's sumptuous château hotels

Explore the great estates on a cycle ride around Chambord and Cheverny

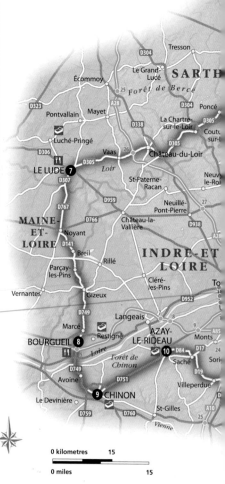

0 kilometres 15

0 miles 15

PLAN YOUR DRIVE

Start/finish: Chartres to Blois.

Number of days: 4–5, allowing half a day each for Chartres and Blois.

Distances: 470 km (290 miles).

Road conditions: The roads are excellent and well signposted.

When to go: The weather is generally fine from April to October. Avoid the peak season of late July and August.

Opening hours: Generally from 10am to 5pm. Most sights are closed on Mondays and major public holidays.

Main market days: Chartres: Tue, Thu, Sat; Châteaudun: Thu, Sat; Vendôme: Fri; Montoire-sur-le-Loir: Wed, Sat; Le Lude: Thu; Bourgueil: Tue, Sat; Chinon: Thu, Sat, Sun; Loches: Wed, Sat; Blois: Tue, Thu, Sat.

Major festivals: Chartres: Chartres en Lumières, Apr–Sep; Vendôme: Summer Music Festival, Jul–Aug; Blois: Son-et-Lumière at the château, Apr–Sep.

DAY TRIP OPTIONS

This area can be divided into separate day trips. **History enthusiasts** can devote a day to the magnificent cathedral in Chartres and to Châteaudun. Those **looking for tranquility** will enjoy the countryside of the Loir valley. **Wine and food aficionados** will love the vineyards of Bourgueil and Chinon; **lovers of architecture** will admire the châteaux along the Loire. For details, see p127.

Below left Crop fields along the Loire valley, see p121 **Below right** Remarkable windows and ceiling in the château at Chambord, see p126

KEY

▬▬ Drive route

❶ Chartres

Eure-et-Loir, Centre; 28000

It is hard to decide which is the finest, but there is no doubt at all that Chartres Cathedral is the most complete and majestic of all of France's great Gothic cathedrals, rising from the flat wheatfields of the Beauce plain. Around it, the streets and squares of old Chartres give a charming introduction to the life of a small French city.

Cathédrale Notre-Dame de Chartres is an extraordinarily fortunate survivor. Remarkably, it escaped the destruction wreaked elsewhere by religious wars, the French Revolution and the two World Wars. The Gothic cathedral was built surprisingly quickly after a fire destroyed most of an earlier Romanesque building in 1194, and was almost completed by 1250. The main entrance, known as the Royal Portal, and the bases of the two great towers are the few surviving parts of the 12th-century cathedral, but each tower looks different because they were rebuilt at different times, and the famous Gothic spire was added to the north tower later, in the 16th century. The intricacy of the carving all around the building is astonishing. Above all, Chartres has retained all its original medieval stained-glass windows. During both World Wars, the windows were dismantled and stored in a safe location. They present a staggering array of rich colours and complex imagery, from the giant rose windows to the side windows illustrating the lives of the saints. At Chartres it is easy to appreciate the way a medieval

Statues on the Royal Portal

cathedral worked as a giant illustrated book, embodying the Christian religion in stone and glass.

Just beside the cathedral on the north side, a restored medieval grain store houses the **Centre International du Vitrail** *(open daily)*, with a stained-glass workshop, an exhibition on the cathedral glass and displays of modern stained-glass. Behind the cathedral, the 17th-century former Bishops' Palace contains the **Musée des Beaux-Arts** *(open Wed, Sat & Sun)*, with beautiful Renaissance tapestries, 18th-century furniture and some modern paintings.

The streets of old Chartres are interesting to explore, with venerable timber and stone houses that have sharply sloping roofs, and steep narrow passageways called *tertres* leading down to the Eure river and the old artisan district or Basse Ville, where there is a lovely riverside walk along **Rue de la Tannerie**. At the southern end of the old town, the Gothic abbey church of **St-Pierre** also has fine stained glass from the 14th century.

Chartres puts on a spectacular display every evening from early

Above Magnificent stained-glass windows, Chartres Cathedral **Below** One of the stone bridges over the Eure river in the old town of Chartres

VISITING CHARTRES

Tourist information
Place de la Cathédrale, 28000; 02 37 18 26 26; www.chartres-tourisme.com

Parking
The most easily accessible car parks for the cathedral and old town are in Place Châtelet and Place des Épars.

WHERE TO STAY

CHARTRES

Les Conviv'hôtes *inexpensive*
The two bed-and-breakfast rooms in this pretty house are excellent value.
10 rue de Pot Vert, 28000; 02 37 90 88 62; http://lesconvivhotes.monsite.orange.fr

Hôtel Le Grand Monarque
moderate–expensive
This grand hotel has luxurious rooms and a renowned restaurant.
22 place des Épars, 28000; 02 37 18 15 15; www.bw-grand-monarque.com

AROUND CHÂTEAUDUN

La Chesnaye *inexpensive*
A peaceful former farm with three comfortable bed-and-breakfast rooms, 18 km (12 miles) north of Châteaudun.
2 La Chesnaye, Dangeau, 28160; 02 37 96 72 09

VENDÔME

Le Saint-Georges *moderate*
This hotel has comfortable rooms in lively colours and exceptional facilities.
14 rue Poterie, 41100; 02 54 67 42 10; www.hotel-saint-georges.com

April to late September in **Chartres en Lumières** when, from nightfall until after midnight, the cathedral, the abbey church of St-Pierre, the museum and other historic buildings are brilliantly illuminated in subtly changing colours and images evoking their past. The view of Chartres Cathedral from across the flat plains is a beautiful sight and a must-see for visitors. It is best viewed from the Orléans road to the south.

In Place des Épars, in Chartres' ring of boulevards, take the exit signed for Le Mans, but be ready to turn left shortly onto the D921, signed only to Illiers, for Illiers-Combray.

Above left Carved angel on Chartres Cathedral **Above right** Imposing château of Châteaudun

2 Illiers-Combray
Eure-et-Loir, Centre; 28120
The little town of Illiers was the home of the aunt of the writer Marcel Proust, who spent many childhood holidays here and evoked it as "Combray" in his novel *In Search of Lost Time*. So identified has it become with its fictional double, that it is now known as Illiers-Combray. His aunt's modest house, the **Maison de Tante Léonie** *(open mid-Jan–mid-Dec Tue–Sun)* is now a charming museum, and nearby are the **Pré-Catelan** gardens, designed by Proust's uncle.

From the centre of Illiers follow signs for Dangeau and Châteaudun onto the D941, and at Logron turn left on the D955. In Châteaudun, follow signs for "Centre Ville" and park in Place du 18 Octobre, by the tourist office.

3 Châteaudun
Eure-et-Loir, Centre; 28200
On the edges of the Beauce plain and the Loir valley, Châteaudun is presided over by its massive château *(open daily)*. Much of it, including a beautiful Gothic chapel with rare mural paintings, was built by Jean Dunois (1403–68), illegitimate brother of the Duke of Orléans and comrade-in-arms of Joan of Arc. His descendants added one of the earliest Renaissance staircases to a French castle, in 1508. Around the castle is an old town with many fine 16th-century houses.

From Place du 18 Octobre, take "autres directions", then the N10 for for Tours. Turn right onto the D35 to

Cloyes-sur-le-Loir. Once there, look for a right turn onto the D8 (1) when leaving Cloyes for La Ville-aux-Clercs. This road then becomes the D24. Drive through the Forêt de Fréteval, still on the D24, to Danzé. When leaving Danzé, turn left onto the D36 for Vendôme.

4 Vendôme
Loir-et-Cher, Centre; 41100
The road becomes much more wooded as visitors approach this appealing town. Vendôme was an important pilgrimage stop on the way to Compostela in Spain. Counts of Vendôme were important figures from the early Middle Ages. The town's 13th-century castle is an imposing ruin on a lofty crag, and the Loir river runs through the middle of Vendôme in a series of canals and placid streams, forming a lovely mirror to its stone and half-timbered buildings. Travellers can also discover many medieval relics, such as the 14th-century **Porte d'Eau** or water gate across one of the river's channels. The town's greatest treasure is the beautiful church of **La Trinité**, which was founded in 1034. Only the belltower survives from the original structure. During the 16th century an elaborate flamboyant Gothic façade was added to it.

From below Vendôme château follow signs for Montoire onto the D917. Stay on this road south of the river for the best views approaching Les Roches-l'Evèque, where the road turns left towards Montoire.

EAT AND DRINK

CHARTRES

Le Serpente *inexpensive–moderate*
A traditional brasserie-style restaurant with all kinds of choices on the menu including an imaginative list of enjoyable mixed salads.
2 cloître Notre-Dame, 28000; 02 37 21 68 81; http://leserpente.com

Le Bistrot de la Cathédrale *moderate*
This stylish modern restaurant has an ideal view of Chartres Cathedral. It serves various light dishes and there is a *menu terroir* featuring many rich local specialities.
1 cloître Notre-Dame, 28000; 02 37 36 59 60; closed Wed

VENDÔME

Le Moulin du Loir
inexpensive–moderate
An airy restaurant in a riverside mill, with a brasserie-style menu.
21–23 rue du Change, 41100; 02 54 67 13 51; www.le-moulin-du-loir.com; closed Mon

Eat and Drink: inexpensive, under €20; moderate, €20–€40; expensive, over €40

Above Clifftop château of Chinon **Below** Vineyards near Bourgueil

WHERE TO STAY

AROUND MONTOIRE-SUR-LE-LOIR

St-Eloy *inexpensive*
Three comfortable bed-and-breakfast rooms – one in a cave – situated 3 km (2 miles) to the east of Montoire.
Route des Reclusages, 41800; 02 54 72 65 38

TRÔO

B&B Cave *inexpensive*
This place has some of the most charming cave dwellings imaginable in one of Trôo's fascinating cave-houses.
Escalier St-Gabriel, 41800; 02 54 72 50 34; www.bandbcave.com

AROUND LE LUDE

Auberge du Port des Roches *inexpensive*
With just 12 cosy rooms, this modest little hotel, 10 km (6 miles) north of Le Lude, exudes a lot of charm.
Luché-Pringé, 72800; 02 43 45 44 48; www.logis-de-france.fr

AROUND BOURGUEIL

Manoir de Restigné *expensive*
Indulgent luxury awaits at this elegant 18th-century château, 5 km (3 miles) to the east of Bourgueil.
La Platerye, Rue de Tours, Restigné, 37140; 02 47 97 00 06; www.manoir derestigne.com

CHINON

Hôtel Diderot *inexpensive–moderate*
Rooms at this friendly small hotel are furnished in an old-world style.
4 rue de Buffon, 37500; 02 47 93 18 87; www.hoteldiderot.com

AZAY-LE-RIDEAU

Troglododo *inexpensive–moderate*
The hotel has three chic cave-rooms in a 16th-century vineyard farm.
9 chemin des Caves, 37190; 02 47 45 31 25; www.troglododo.fr

5 Montoire-sur-le-Loir
Loir-et-Cher, Centre; 41800
The villages along the north side of the Loir valley are among the region's oldest and there is a dramatic approach to the fortified **Les Roches-l'Evêque**. Montoire-sur-le-Loir contains the tiny, half-hidden **Chapelle St-Gilles**, with 11th- and 14th-century murals. Drive south on the well-signposted D108 to **Lavardin**, a gorgeous village of stone and caves nestling beneath a ruined castle, which crowns a steep hill. Lavardin is home to the wonderfully serene 11th-century chapel of **St-Genest**, entirely decorated with exquisite early medieval frescoes.
🚗 *Return to Montoire to rejoin the D917 for Trôo.*

6 Trôo
Loir-et-Cher, Centre; 41800
Trôo is the most complete and most fascinating of the Loir valley's cave villages. Far from being historical relics, its cave-dwellings are in big demand as homes, holiday *gîtes* and artists'

workshops. The **Cave-Exposition des Amis de Trôo** *(open daily Apr–Nov)* is a little museum of cave-village life.

Leaving Trôo, cross over to the valley's south side for a splendid view of the villages along the north flank. Near Couture-sur-Loir is **La Possonnière**, a gracious manor house with a gorgeous garden that was once the home of Pierre Ronsard, the Renaissance poet.
🚗 *Cross the Loir below Trôo on the D8 Ternay road, but turn right onto the D10 for Couture-sur-Loir and La Possonnière. From Couture take the D57 to rejoin the main valley road (now the D305) at Poncé, and turn left. At La Chartre sur le Loir, turn right in the direction of Château-du-Loir on the D256, which then becomes the D305. Before Château-du-Loir (24 km/15 miles), turn right at the roundabout onto the D338. In Château-du-Loir, turn left in the direction of Le Lude/La Flèche.*

7 Le Lude
Sarthe, Pays-de-la-Loire; 72800
Le Lude's château *(open daily mid-Jun–Aug, Thu–Tue Apr–mid-Jun and Sep, gardens all day, château evenings)* is a historic fortress that was rebuilt around 1500 for Jacques de Daillon, a courtier of King François I, and altered again for new owners in the 18th century. It can appear like two different châteaux in one, with the massive towers of the French Renaissance façade facing the town, and a contrasting 18th-century Neo-Classical façade overlooking the fine gardens.
🚗 *Leave Le Lude on the D307, which becomes the D767 in Maine-et-Loire before Noyant. Next follow signs for Breil onto the D141. Drive on through*

Parçay-les-Pins and Gizeux towards Bourgueil. The road then becomes the D749. At Marcé, cross the D35 down Rue Raymond Garrit to Bourgueil.

⑧ Bourgueil
Indre-et-Loire, Centre; 37140

The road southwards runs through the beech forest around Gizeux to the vineyards of one of the Loire's prime areas for red wines, with the adjacent *appellations contrôlées* of Bourgueil and St-Nicholas-de-Bourgueil. The wine cellars or *caves* of the Loire are real caves, and one contains the **Cave du Pays du Bourgueil** *(open daily Apr–mid-Nov, Sat–Sun mid-Nov–Mar)*, a lively wine museum. Follow signs to nearby **Restigné**, a classic wine country village, with fine vineyards such as Domaine de la Chevalerie *(open daily)*.

🚗 *Take the D749 out of Bourgueil to cross the Loire, and follow signs to Chinon. Turn uphill from the river following signs to the château, and park by the main entrance.*

⑨ Chinon
Indre-et-Loire, Centre; 37500

Chinon is one of the most historically enthralling of Loire valley towns. Most of its fierce-looking clifftop **château** *(open daily)* was built in the 1150s for Henry II, King of England, who made it his stronghold as he simultaneously ruled over England, Normandy, Anjou and Aquitaine. During the Hundred Years' War, Dauphin Charles of France took refuge in Chinon, and first met Joan of Arc here in 1429. She convinced him to provide her with an army to help drive the English out of France, and she defeated them at

Orléans. Ongoing archaeological work at the castle has lead to many new discoveries. Below the château, old Chinon is a huddle of medieval streets and is also the centre of an *appellation contrôlée*. Wine caves can be found all around old Chinon, such as the Couly-Dutheuil vineyard, which is right opposite the château. The great satirist and bon viveur François Rabelais (1483–1553) was born at **La Devinière**, south of Chinon. He has become a symbol of the town and the region, which is sometimes called La Rabelaisie.

🚗 *Stay on the same road past the château to meet the D751 Tours road to the château of Azay-le-Rideau.*

⑩ Azay-le-Rideau
Indre-et-Loire, Centre; 37190

A classic of French Renaissance style, the château of Azay-le-Rideau *(open daily)* sits like a jewel within its placid moat. It was begun in 1515 for Gilles Berthelot, treasurer to King François I, by his wife Philippa Lesbahy. However, it was confiscated by the king in 1527 when he accused Berthelot of corruption. The interior is delightful and there is a famous portrait of Gabrielle d'Estrées, mistress of King Henri IV. A short way from Azay is the **Château de Saché**, a stout 16th-century manor that was the country retreat of the writer Balzac, and is now the **Musée Balzac** *(open daily Apr–Sep, Wed–Mon Oct–Mar)*. The marshy **Sologne** region to the east is full of tranquil old villages, such as **Louans** and **Le Louroux**.

🚗 *Take the D84 to La Sablonnière and turn right to Saché. Turn left on the D17, then right onto the D19. After Louans, turn right on the D50, direction Le Louroux. Drive through Manthelan, and turn left at the roundabout onto the D760 towards Loches.*

Above left Frescoes in the chapel of St-Genest in Lavardin **Above right** Façade of the impressive Château du Lude **Below left** Charming château of Azay-le-Rideau

EAT AND DRINK

AROUND MONTOIRE-SUR-LE-LOIR

Le Relais d'Antan
inexpensive–moderate
Very popular with locals and visitors, this pretty restaurant, 3 km (2 miles) east of Montoire, has a terrace that offers great views. Other attractions are fine wines and refined Loire valley cuisine.
6 place Capitaine Vigneau, 41800; 02 54 86 61 33; closed Mon, Tue

TRÔO

Hôtel du Cheval Blanc
inexpensive–moderate
Hearty and meaty fresh local cooking is the mainstay at this friendly hotel.
47 rue Auguste Arnault, 41800; 02 54 72 58 22

LE LUDE

Auberge des Îles *moderate*
This traditional restaurant near the château has a riverside terrace.
8 rue des Ponts, 72800; 02 43 94 63 25; closed Tue dinner, Wed

BOURGUEIL

Le Moulin Bleu
inexpensive–moderate
Occupying a 15th-century mill with a terrace looking out over vineyards, this pretty restaurant serves up enjoyable Touraine specialities – pork, duck and excellent wines.
7 route du Moulin Bleu, 37140; 02 47 97 73 13; closed Tue dinner, Wed, Sun dinner Nov–Mar

Eat and Drink: inexpensive, under €20; moderate, €20–€40; expensive, over €40

Above View of the grand château at Amboise
Below Picture-book village of Montrésor

WHERE TO STAY

LOCHES

Le Logis de Bief *moderate*
This splendid 16th–17th-century house has three *chambre d'hôtes* rooms and a suite that has been elegantly refurbished.
21 rue Quintefol, 37600; 02 47 91 66 02; www.logisloches.com

MONTRÉSOR

Le Moulin de Montrésor *inexpensive*
Montrésor's 19th-century mill now contains four charming rooms.
Montrésor, 37460; 02 47 92 68 20; www.moulindemontresor.fr

CHENONCEAUX

La Renaudière *moderate*
This 18th-century house with garden has a nicely relaxed feel.
24 rue de Docteur Bretonneau, 37150; 02 47 23 90 04; www.renaudiere.com

AMBOISE

Manoir Les Minimes
moderate–expensive
Rooms are luxurious in this elegantly restored 18th-century mansion.
34 quai Charles Guinot, 37400; 02 47 30 40 40; www.manoirlesminimes. com; closed mid-Nov–Dec

CHAUMONT-SUR-LOIRE

Hostellerie du Château *inexpensive*
This is a pleasant traditional Logis hotel.
2 rue Maréchal de Lattre de Tassigny, 41150; 02 54 20 98 04; www. hostellerie-du-chateau.com

⑪ Loches

Indre-et-Loire, Centre; 37600
A gem of a small town, Loches has a remarkable history. Its château *(open daily)* is one of the Loire valley's oldest, begun by Foulques Nerra, first Count of Anjou, around 988, and its ruined keep has the dramatic feel of a warrior fortress. It later became a prison and the cages in which famous prisoners were kept are another highlight. The keep and the 15th-century **Logis Royal** are at either end of a lovely walled hilltop old town, the **Cité Royale**, which also contains the superb Romanesque and Gothic church of **St-Ours**.

🚗 *From below the old town follow signs for Beaulieu-les-Loches and then Montrésor on the D760.*

⑫ Montrésor

Indre-et-Loire, Centre; 37460
The gorgeous village of Montrésor has a stately **château** *(open daily Apr–Oct, Sat–Sun Nov–Mar)* which was founded in 1005 by Foulques Nerra of Anjou. It was rebuilt in the Renaissance style around 1500. In the 19th century it was bought by the exiled Polish count, Xavier Branicki. The château still retains the opulent Second Empire decor he installed, and an unusual art collection reflecting the eclectic interests of his family. The village also has a refined Gothic church and there is a beautiful

walk by the Indrois river with a marvellous view of the château.

🚗 *Take the D10 to Genillé and turn right on the D764 Blois road for Montpoupon and its château.*

⑬ Château de Montpoupon

Indre-et-Loire, Centre; 37460
A spectacular approach on the road from Loches sets the scene for this gracious château, built in early Renaissance style around 1480 but comprehensively renovated in the 18th and 19th centuries *(open daily Apr–Sep; Sat–Sun Feb–Mar, Oct–Dec)*. It is privately owned and sumptuously decorated, with luxurious bedrooms and a splendid kitchen, intimately evoking country-house life in the early 20th century. The impressive stables contain a museum, the **Musée du Veneur**, on horses and hunting.

🚗 *Follow the D764 towards Blois and Montrichard.*

⑭ Montrichard

Loir-et-Cher, Centre; 41400
Visitors experience another spectacular approach when they cross the stone bridge on the Cher river to Montrichard. The small town is laid out in the classic way of Loire valley towns, with old streets winding beneath the imposing keep or **donjon** of its 11th-century castle. Partly restored, the castle contains museums on local

history and archaeology *(open daily Apr–Sep)*. Beside it is the Romanesque church of **Ste-Croix**, originally the castle chapel.

🚗 *Turn left after crossing the Cher river onto the D176 for Chenonceaux.*

⑮ Chenonceaux

Indre-et-Loire, Centre; 37150
Chenonceaux is a popular destination because of the grand **Château de Chenonceau** *(open daily)*. Unlike other Loire châteaux, this one was created according to the wishes of powerful women, notably King Henri II's mistress Diane de Poitiers and his widow, Cathérine de Médicis. The wooded approach to the park, and the famous gallery across the Cher river, create an impression of matchless grandeur. Its rooms include the bedchambers of many queens and royal mistresses.

🚗 *Turn left out of the château towards Tours. In Civray-de-Touraine turn right onto the D81 for Amboise, through the Forêt d'Amboise. Follow signs for the château and park beside the Loire.*

⑯ Amboise

Indre-et-Loire, Centre; 37530
The grand **château** *(open daily)* in the old town of Amboise is a delight to visit. The favourite residence of King Charles VIII, this was the first royal château on the Loire to be converted from a medieval fortress into a Gothic palace, with later monarchs adding Italian Renaissance architecture. In 1516, King François I enticed Leonardo da Vinci to France and gave him the nearby **Clos Lucé** manor house *(open daily)*, where the artist died in 1519.

🚗 *Drive on past the château on the D751 along the south bank of the Loire to Chaumont.*

⑰ Chaumont-sur-Loire

Loir-et-Cher, Centre; 41150
Chaumont is known for its picture-book castle, the **Château de Chaumont** *(open daily)*, whose massive pinnacle-roofed turrets soar up on a bluff above the Loire. It was built for the Dukes of Amboise between 1465 and 1510. In 1560, it was bought by Queen Cathérine de Médicis, who installed her rival Diane de Poitiers here. Diane's bedchamber is one of its most attractive rooms.

Every year the Château de Chaumont hosts a dazzling **Festival International des Jardins** *(late-Apr–mid-Oct)*, when different designers are invited to create inventive gardens.

🚗 *Continue on the D751 road to Candé-sur-Beuvron. Turn right on the D7 to Les Montils. At Les Montils, take the D77 in the direction of Seur. At Seur, take the right turn onto the D61 towards Chitenay/Contres. At Chitenay, take the C9, and then the D956 towards Cormeray. Two kilometres (1 mile) after Cormeray, take the left turn for Cour Cheverny onto the D52 road and then the D102.*

Diane and Catherine

Diane de Poitiers (1499–1566) was one of the most influential figures at the court of Henri II. Twenty years older than Henri, she was appointed to teach the young prince manners, but later became the king's mistress. He adored her, and as king even consulted her on official business. Chenonceau was given to her as a personal residence. This was predictably resented by his Italian queen Cathérine de Médicis (1519–89), and when Henri was killed while jousting, she wasted no time in seizing Chenonceau for herself and expelling Diane to Chaumont.

Above Celebrated royal château of Chenonceaux **Below** Giant turrets of Château de Chaumont

EAT AND DRINK

LOCHES

Le Presbytère *inexpensive–moderate*
A likeably unfussy modern terrace restaurant with excellent light meals.
1 rue Thomas Pactius, 37600; 02 47 59 65 25; www.ancien-presbytere.fr; open mid-May–Oct; closed Tue

MONTRÉSOR

Café de la Ville *inexpensive–moderate*
This bar-restaurant has a fine view of the castle, and a menu that is a mix of traditional and modern.
28 Grande Rue, 37460; 02 47 92 75 31; open Fri, Sat, Mon–Thu lunch

MONTRICHARD

Le Bellevue *moderate–expensive*
This comfortable restaurant offers a great riverside view and refined food.
16 quai du Cher, 41400; 02 54 32 06 17; www.hotel-le-bellevue41.com; closed Fri, Oct–Apr

CHENONCEAUX

Le Relais Chenonceaux
inexpensive–moderate
This friendly restaurant has a relaxed approach, and good crêpes and salads.
10 rue du Dr Bretonneau, 37150; 02 47 23 98 11; www.relais-chenonceaux.fr; closed Dec–mid-Feb

AMBOISE

Chez Bruno *inexpensive*
An enjoyable terrace restaurant, this place serves tasty salads and larger dishes to go with its very fine wine selection.
40 place Michel Debré, 37400; 02 47 57 73 49; closed Sun dinner, Mon, Jan

Above Façade of Château de Cheverny
Below Pont Jacques-Gabriel bridge across the Loire at Blois

VISITING BLOIS

Tourist information
23 place du Château, 41006; 02 54 90 41 41; www.bloispaysde chambord.com

WHERE TO STAY

CHEVERNY

Château du Breuil *moderate–expensive*
With its pepperpot-towers this mansion looks like a smaller version of the royal châteaux.
Route de Fougères, 41700; 02 54 44 20 20; www.chateau-du-breuil.fr

BLOIS

La Petite Fugue *moderate*
Style and tranquillity are the keynotes at this beautifully renovated old townhouse on the river quay in Blois, with four rooms in subtly understated colour schemes, two with river views.
9 quai du Foix, 41000; 02 54 78 42 95; www.lapetitefugue.com

⑱ Cheverny
Loir-et-Cher, Centre; 41700

Cheverny stands out among the Renaissance châteaux nearby because of its elegant Louis XIII style. It is opulently furnished throughout. The house *(open daily)* was also the inspiration for the Château de Moulinsart in the Tintin cartoons, and there is an interesting Tintin exhibition in the grounds. The area also has two *appellations contrôlées*, Cheverny and Cour-Cheverny, known for their beautifully crisp white wines.

🚗 *Turn left out of the château and drive through Cour-Cheverny onto the D102 to Bracieux. Turn left to approach Chambord along the Grande Allée through its immense woodland park.*

⑲ Chambord
Loir-et-Cher, Centre; 41250

The largest and most awe-inspiring of all the Loire châteaux, Chambord *(open daily)* was begun in 1519 for King François I. It is believed that parts of it were designed by Leonardo da Vinci, especially the remarkable double-spiral staircase. Everything is on a giant scale, from the chambers to the fantastic roofline of windows and chimneys. The vast estate, the **Domaine de Chambord**, has lovely walks and cycle paths.

🚗 *From the château car park turn right and then left following signs for St-Dyé-sur-Loire. Once there, turn left to drive into Blois on the D951.*

⑳ Blois
Loir-et-Cher, Centre; 41000

Compact Blois is perhaps the ideal Loire valley town. King Louis XII brought his court here in 1498, making it a virtual "second capital". Royal patronage attracted the nobility, wealthy merchants and fine craftsmen, leaving the town with a special mix of historic architecture.

A two-hour walking tour

Leave the car in the large car park beneath Place Valin de la Vaissière, and walk up into pretty **Place Louis XII** ①. Turn left to leave the square below a raised row of old houses and enter Rue St-Lubin, a charming old street, now housing snug restaurants and trendy jewellery, fashion and crafts shops. Continue beyond Place Gaudet until the street meets the steeply-climbing stairway of the Rampe des Fossés du Châteaux, on the right, but rather than climbing up immediately, turn left and then right for a look at the tranquil 12th-century **Église**

St-Nicolas ②. Leaving the church turn right up Rue des Trois Marchands to return to the stairway.

Walk up the stairway beneath the towers of the Château de Blois, and at the top take another set of steps up to the **Jardins de Lys et Fleurs Royales** ③ and across to the Bastion du Roi for a superb view of the château. Then walk down the ramp below the bastion and up another on the right to enter Place du Château. The **Château Royal de Blois** ④ *(open daily)* has a magnificent entrance on the square, topped by a statue of King Louis XII on horseback. The château has three separate wings: the late Gothic one of Louis XII, a Renaissance-style one added by François I and another in Classical style added by Gaston d'Orléans, brother of Louis XIV.

After exploring the château, leave the square by the same route, but turn right from the ramp to the **Jardins Augustin Thierry** ⑤, backed by the Baroque **Église St-Vincent** ⑥. The park crosses the top of Rue de la Porte du Côté, with a fine view across the town to the cathedral. Head down this street, but turn left down Rue Chemonton, and right up Rue du

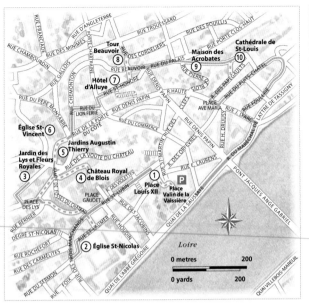

EAT AND DRINK

BLOIS

Les Banquettes Rouges *inexpensive–moderate*
A hip but laidback style and the architecture of old Blois meet up in this warm, snug little bistro. Local favourites like goats' cheese salads, herby soups and creamy desserts feature on the menu, and there is plenty to choose from.
126 rue des Trois Marchands, 41000; 02 54 78 74 92; www.relaisdebracieux. com; closed Mon, Sun

Le Castelet *inexpensive–moderate*
This atmospheric bar-bistro in a splendid 16th-century building has become a local institution for the good value of its menus, which include vegetarian choices.
40 rue St-Lubin, 41000; 02 54 74 66 09; www.le-castelet.eu; closed Sun, Wed

Below Château de Chambord with the Cosson river in the foreground

Lion Ferré, with several 16th-century houses. Turn left again on the shopping street of Porte Chartraine, and right on Rue St-Honoré, to continue uphill. At no. 8 is the **Hôtel d'Alluye** ⑦, built in 1508 for Louis XII's treasurer. Part way up, turn up the steps on the left to cross Rue Beauvoir and find the **Tour Beauvoir** ⑧, a remnant of Blois' 11th-century fortifications. Return to Rue Beauvoir and turn left to cross the top of Rue Denis Papin, a stairway with a fantastic view of the river. From here Rue du Palais leads to the cathedral. Below it is one of the most characterful *quartiers* of old

Blois. At the top of Rue Pierre de Blois, look out for the **Maison des Acrobates** ⑨ on the corner, so-called because of the little carved figures on its façade. Explore the Gothic-style **Cathédrale de St-Louis** ⑩, then take the Grand Degrés St-Louis steps on the left to meet Rue des Papegaults. Continue to Place Ave Maria before turning left again into Rue du Puits-Châtel, which has some impressive Renaissance houses. Continue to Rue Foulerie to see the 1510 Hôtel Sardini and then on to Rue Jeanne d'Arc. Turn right towards the Loire for a walk along the *quais* back to Place Valin.

DAY TRIP OPTIONS

There are four good ways to divide the complete drive in this region. To get directly to the Loir valley from the Paris area, take the A10 and leave at exit 14, outside Orléans, for Vendôme. To begin a tour at Blois and the grand châteaux, stay on the A10.

Grand cathedral
Visit the majestic cathedral at Chartres ① and the charming old town. Continue to Illiers-Combray ② and Châteaudun ③.

From Châteaudun, take the N10 back to Chartres.

Along the Loir
Spend a peaceful day discovering the countryside of the Loir valley from Vendôme ④ to Le Lude ⑦ – kids, especially, are fascinated by its cave houses.

From Le Lude turn back towards Château-du-Loir to join the A28 for Paris via Le Mans, or south via Tours.

Wines and tranquility
Wine lovers and those who wish to avoid the crowds can truly enjoy themselves by visiting the small vineyards around Bourgueil ⑧ and Chinon ⑨, and then cut across to

Loches ⑪ to end the day in one of the region's most atmospheric towns.

Follow the A85 from Tours and leave at exit 5 for Bourgueil. From Chinon, take the D760 directly to Loches.

Pure grandeur
Give a day over to the greatest of the Loire's châteaux in a circuit from Blois ⑳ to Chambord ⑲, taking in Montrichard ⑭, Chenonceaux ⑮, Amboise ⑯, Chaumont ⑰, and Cheverny ⑱.

From Blois take the D764 road to Montrichard, and take up the main itinerary from there.

Eat and Drink: inexpensive, under €20; moderate, €20–€40; expensive, over €40

Slopes of Gold

Beaune to Nolay

Highlights

- **Rolling vineyards**
  Wander around the *sentiers viticoles* of the Côte de Beaune which produce some of the finest and most renowned red and white wines of Burgundy

- **Canals and châteaux**
  Follow the course of the Canal de Bourgogne, punctuated by beautiful castles and abbeys

- **Forests and lakes**
  Visit the green lungs of Burgundy, the Parc Naturel Régional du Morvan

- **Yonne villages**
  Relax in the medieval villages of Vézelay and Noyers, buffered with forest and valleys

Canal de Bourgogne set against the backdrop of lush countryside

Slopes of Gold

In 1790, during the French Revolution, the Duchy of Bourgogne was divided into the four departments which exist today – the Nièvre, Saône-et-Loire, Yonne and Côte d'Or. The Côte d'Or is said to bear the greatest resemblance to ancient Bourgogne, where vines and Romans arrived on the scene in the 1st century. Its name, "slope of gold", comes from the sun glistening on the vine leaves. The vineyards have bounced back from several disasters – nearly 90 per cent were wiped out by the phylloxera pest in the 1870s. From the wine routes, the Côte d'Or spreads north to historic Cistercian abbeys, Gallo-Roman battlefields and riverside medieval villages, and west to feudal châteaux, canals and the Parc Naturel Régional du Morvan. The Morvan park wraps itself like a large green cloak around 117 towns and villages in Burgundy, offering lakes and mountains, and farm fresh produce.

Above Tractor tracks through fields near Châteauneuf-en-Auxois, see p133

ACTIVITIES

Try a variety of wines at Beaune's *bars à vins*

Stroll among Beaune's eco-friendly, award-winning gardens

Cycle alongside the Canal de Bourgogne between Châteauneuf-en-Auxois and Pouilly-en-Auxois

Attend a concert at the Abbaye de Fontenay

Treasure hunt for old jewels and knick-knacks in Burgundy's village *brocantes*, or antiques shops

Dine on Charolais beef and other rural gastronomy in Saulieu

Kayak, fish or windsurf on the Lac des Settons

Admire Gallo-Romaine vestiges and religious art at the Musée Rolin in Autun

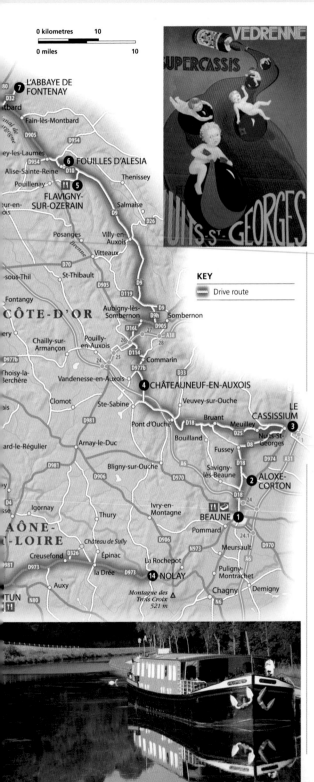

Left Vintage poster of a famous *crème de cassis* producer at Le Cassissium, *see p132* **Below** Canal de Bourgogne near Noyers, *see p134*

PLAN YOUR DRIVE

Start/finish: Beaune to Nolay.

Number of days: 4, including a day to cover the vineyards and villages of the Côtes de Beaune, a day in the Morvan park region and half a day between Vézelay and the château of Bazoches.

Distance: 360 km (225 miles).

Road conditions: In the *départements* of Yonne and Nièvre some roads are of poor quality; however, there are warnings of very sharp corners and unstable road edges. In the Morvan park there are many potholes on smaller roads.

When to go: Burgundy summers are very hot, and winters are long and wet. The area of the Morvan park is especially to be avoided then. Autumn is the best time to visit.

Opening hours: Most sights and national museums usually close on Monday. Municipal museums close on Tuesday.

Main market days: Beaune: Wed, Sat; Saulieu: Thu, Sat; **Autun**: Wed, Fri; Nolay: Mon.

Shopping: After ordering bottles of post-home wines from the cellar doors in Beaune and its wine growing region, head to the villages to buy artisan picnic and gardening baskets, made from willow, wicker and wire.

Major festivals: Beaune: Festival Cours Eau Jardins, Jul–Sep; Jazz à Beaune, Sep; **Vézelay:** Rencontres Musicales de Vézelay, Aug; **Saulieu:** Fête du Charolais and Nuits Cajun and Zydeco, Aug; **Autun:** Fete du Livre, Apr.

DAY TRIP OPTIONS

Parts of the itinerary make perfect day trips. **Wine enthusiasts** can visit the Côte de Beaune vineyards; **castle and countryside lovers** will like the area around Châteauneuf-en-Auxois; **families** will enjoy the Lac des Settons and the activities it offers. For more details, *see p137*.

Above Cafés in a square in Beaune **Above right** Vineyard of the Côte de Beaune **Below** Houses with the Châteauneuf-en-Auxois in the background

WHERE TO STAY

BEAUNE

Hôtel Grillon inexpensive–moderate
Housed in a 19th-century home, with a pool and large gardens, this has 17 comfortable, well-fitted rooms.
21 route de Seurre, 21200; 03 80 22 44 25; www.hotel-grillon.fr

Hotel de la Poste
moderate–expensive
The hotel has an old-world façade with a suave interior. It has 36 rooms including three lavish suites around an internal garden. There is also a formal restaurant and a casual bistro.
3–5 boulevard Clémenceau, 21200 ; 03 80 22 08 11; www.hoteldelapostebeaune.com

Le Cep expensive
A hotel since the 16th century, this is an amalgam of ancient 14th- and 15th- century dwellings. Today it is known for its sheer historic luxury.
27 rue Maufoux, 21200; 03 80 22 35 48; www.hotel-cep-beaune.com

① Beaune

Côte d'Or, Bourgogne; 21200
A hive of historic streets and squares, ramparts, chapels and gardens, Beaune is much more than its historic *hospices civils* – the civil infirmaries – recognized worldwide by the multicoloured tile roofs of the **Hôtel-Dieu**, a 15th-century convent-turned-hospital for the poor. The **Couvent des Ursulines** now houses the town hall. From here a well-marked trail leads to the residence of the former dukes, **Hôtel des Ducs**, and its Musée du Vin; the fine arts museum, **Musée des Beaux-Arts** in the Porte Marie de Bourgogne; the medieval market **Place de la Halle**; and the **Square des Lions**, a lovely garden located within the ruins of a 17th-century fortress.

🚗 *Take the D18 from Beaune towards Savigny-lès-Beaune; turn right onto the D115D.*

Advertisement for a Beaune winemaker

② Aloxe-Corton

Côte d'Or, Bourgogne; 21420
The Route Touristique des Grands Crus de Bourgogne is a signed drive through some of Burgundy's best vineyards in Côtes de Beaune and Hautes-Côtes de Beaune. The village of Aloxe-Corton lies within the largest zone of *grands crus* and is known for its *appellation contrôlée* – Corton is Côte de Beaune's only *grand cru* red wine appellation. In the valley behind Aloxe-Corton is **Savigny-lès-Beaune**. The château here has an eclectic collection of fighter planes and red Abarth racing cars.

🚗 *Return to the D18, turn right, continue to Fussey; turn right onto the D8 and arrive in Nuits-St-Georges. Le Cassissium is in the industrial zone. Go into the centre of Nuits-St-Georges and follow directions for the autoroute. Le Cassissium can be seen from here. It is well signposted from here on.*

③ Le Cassissium

Côte d'Or, Bourgogne; 21700
Set within the Verdenne fruit liqueur factory on Burgundy's blackcurrant route, this multimedia museum (open daily Apr–Nov, Tue–Sat Nov–Mar) presents a walk-through audiovisual guide around the history, botany and production process of *crème de cassis*. The visit includes a film and visit to the distillation room and finishes with a taste of the liqueur.

🚗 *Turn left out of the road where Le Cassissium is situated, follow directions for Dijon and then continue to Bruant. From here turn into the D18. Pass Pont d'Ouche and turn off to the right at the sign for Châteauneuf.*

Wine Auction

For over five centuries the *Hospices Civils de Beaune* have been involved in winemaking. The hospices' vineyards produce many *grands crus* and premier wines. The sale of these wines is a central part of its charity and fundraising activities, and the annual auction is a major event that has been taking place over 150 years as part of the Trois Glorieuses festival at Beaune in November.

④ Châteauneuf-en-Auxois
Côte d'Or, Bourgogne; 21320

Looming over the countryside from a rocky outcrop, the feudal castle which gives its name to the village is a natural stronghold. Visit its dungeons, frescoed chapel and residences. Then stroll up the steep main street to the **Église Saint-Jacques**. Follow the signs to the Belvedere for views over the countryside of Châteauneuf, and the lake, **Réservoir de Panthier**, in the neighbouring village of Vandenesse-en-Auxois.

From the bottom of the village turn right onto the D977bis, pass through Commarin, turn left onto the D114 then right onto the D108M and right again onto the D16L after driving underneath the motorway. Pass through Aubigny-lès-Sombernon, and take the D905, turn left onto the D9H and left again onto the D9 all the way to Flavigny-sur-Ozerain.

⑤ Flavigny-sur-Ozerain
Côte d'Or, Bourgogne; 21150

Julius Caesar camped on this site in 52 BC during the siege of Alesia, which took place on the other side of the Ozerain river. The town was named after the feudal landowner, Flavinius. Enter through the 15th-century gate, the Porte du Bourg, and walk to the Benedictine **Abbaye Saint-Pierre**, which has an 8th-century Carolingian crypt. The village's houses and shops were a backdrop for the 2000 film *Chocolat*. The true town sweet, however, is the *anis* first made by Benedictine monks for Pope John VIII

in AD 873. Traditionally available only in aniseed flavour, the candy now comes in many varieties, including organic ones.

Continue along the D9, and turn left onto the D10, towards Alise-Sainte-Reine. Follow the sign via Chemin des Fouilles to the excavation on the hilltop.

⑥ Fouilles d'Alesia
Côte d'Or, Bourgogne; 21150

Excavations of the Gallo-Roman settlement of Alesia on the top of Mont-Auxois show evidence of 2,000 years of settlement from prehistory through to Julius Caesar's times. The *oppidum*, the elevated fortress, was one of the largest in Western Europe. On the standard unguided visit *(open daily Feb–mid-Nov)* wander at will around the vestiges of the 1st–4th century town. It is here that the siege of Alesia took place and children will love the special visits with actors playing characters such as Vercingétorix, the Gallic tribal chief who led the revolt against Caesar. The **Muséo Parc**, an interpretation centre, discovery trail and archaeological museum, will open progressively throughout 2010–11.

Leave Alise-Sainte-Reine on Rue Vercingétorix and turn left onto the D954, pass through Venarey-les-Laumes, and take the D905. Turn right before Montbard onto the D32.

Hospital Riches
An inventory of 5,000 objects in Beaune's Hôtel-Dieu includes furniture, tapestries, paintings, pharmacy jars and sculptures. It was drawn up in 1501 by Nicolas Rolin, Chancellor to the Duke of Beaune. Hôtel-Dieu literally means "God's Hall" and is the old French word for hospital.

Above Multicoloured tile roofs of the Hôtel-Dieu in Beaune **Left** Pretty town of Flavigny-sur-Ozerain **Below** Bottles of *grands crus* on display in Aloxe-Corton

EAT AND DRINK

BEAUNE

Le Bistrot Bourguignon *inexpensive*
This traditional *bar à vins* has an extensive list of local wines. It also serves regional food and is the venue for Saturday night jazz concerts.
8 rue Monge, 21200; 03 80 22 23 24; www.restaurant-lebistrotbourguignon.com; closed Sun

La Beaun'Franquette
inexpensive–moderate
High quality, good value fish and meat dishes, salads, children's menus and regional specialities are served here.
3 avenue République, 21200; 03 80 22 41 35; closed Tue, Wed

L'Oiseau des Vignes
moderate–expensive
French country staples are served in a warm bistro ambience; this is also an incredible place for wine tasting.
27 rue Maufoux, 21200; 03 80 24 12 06; www.hotel-cep-beaune.com; closed Sun, Mon and Feb

FLAVIGNY-SUR-OZERAIN

La Grange de Flavigny *inexpensive*
Sample the produce of a dozen local farmers in this old stone barn.
Place de l'Eglise, 21150; 03 80 96 20 62; open Tue–Sun lunch Jul–Aug, Sun lunch Sep–Jun

Eat and Drink: inexpensive, under €20; moderate, €20–€40; expensive, over €40

Above left Choir of the Basilique Sainte-Marie Madeleine, Vézelay **Above right** Romanesque Abbaye de Fontenay **Below right** Town of Vézelay seen from a distance

VISITING VÉZELAY

Tourist information
Rue Saint-Etienne, 89450; 03 86 33 23 69; www.vezelaytourisme.com; open daily Jun-Sep.

Parking
There are two to three paid car parks near the city walls.

WHERE TO STAY

VÉZELAY

Le Compostelle *inexpensive*
This two-star small, simple hotel has wonderful valley views, 18 attic and garden rooms, a terrace on the main town square, and offers free Wi-Fi.
Place du Champ de Foire, 89450; 03 86 33 28 63; www.lecompostellevezelay.com

L'Esperance Marc Meneau *expensive*
In this intimate, personal hotel, 2 km (1 mile) east of Vézelay, fine china meets contemporary art. There is an English salon-library, a private bar and exquisite gardens. The classical and modern rooms and suites are scattered between the main building and the old mill.
Route de Vézelay, Saint-Père, 89450; 03 86 33 39 10; www.marc-meneau-esperance.com; closed mid-Jan–mid-Mar

AROUND VÉZELAY

Les Deux Ponts *inexpensive*
Seven simple but pleasant rooms are located in this handsome Burgundy stone hotel with a restaurant, in the pretty village of Vauban.
1 route de Vézelay, Vauban 89450; 03 86 32 31 31; www.lesdeuxponts.free.fr

❼ L'Abbaye de Fontenay
Côte d'Or, Bourgogne; 21500

One of Europe's oldest surviving Cistercian monasteries, this Romanesque abbey was founded by St Bernard in 1118 in a marshy valley just outside Montbard. The monastery has an impeccably preserved church, cloister, council room, forge and monks' dormitory, which offer insights into the Cistercian way of life. Listed as a UNESCO World Heritage Site in 1981, the abbey was a backdrop for scenes in the 1990 Gérard Depardieu film *Cyrano de Bergerac*. Its French and English gardens were redesigned by the British landscape architect Peter Holmes in 2004. The abbey is open daily year round and there are hour-long guided tours, special themed visits for adults and children, and many concerts and cultural events held here.

🚗 *Head back to the D905 and turn right to pass through Montbard and then left onto the D956 to Noyers.*

❽ Noyers
Yonne, Bourgogne; 89310

This medieval village encircled by the Serein river is a delightful stop. Stroll between its evocatively named squares – from Place de la Petite Étape au Vin to Place du Marché au Blé where the wheat market was held. Also of interest is the craftsmen's guild house, the **Maison du Compagnonnage**, with its Gothic pinnacles and carved pillar-tops. Visitors will also enjoy a trip to the town hall on Place de l'Hôtel de Ville and the salt loft and salt tax collector's house on Place du Grenier à Sel. Finally leave the old city gates and take a walk around the 2-m (7-ft) thick ramparts from tower to tower.

🚗 *Take the D86, pass through Massangis and turn right onto the D11. At Joux-la-Ville take the D32 then the D9 and pass Voutenay-sur-Cure. Continue on the D606 and turn right for Vézelay onto the D951 and park on the Route de Saint-Père.*

⑨ Vézelay

Yonne, Bourgogne; 89450

Much of Vézelay's World Heritage glory comes down to the cultural and religious history linked with its role as the holy *colline éternelle* (eternal hill). The town, stretched out on a rocky plateau, is packed with Renaissance, Romanesque and Gothic treasures. The surrounding countryside is like a large checked tablecloth of crops, fields and forested valleys. Vézelay is to be visited strictly on foot.

A 90-minute walking tour

Set out from the car park on the Route de Saint-Père, which is a short walk from the main gateway, the **Porte du Barle et Citerne** ①. Go up Rue Sainte-Étienne and on the right is the tourist office where a small but clearly marked map can be picked up. Further up there is a fork of two narrow streets: take Rue Saint-Pére, which leads past the **Hôtel de Ville** ② (signposted Marie), now a library with a Gothic interior, and the turret and clock of Tourelle Gaillon.

At the crest of the hill is the **Basilique Sainte-Marie Madeleine** ③, dominating the hilltop Place de la Basilique. Built between the 9th and 12th centuries, the cathedral is considered a masterpiece of Romanesque art and architecture. It is a mass of stone spires, carved figurines and pillars engraved with biblical scenes. Damaged by successive battles and on the verge of collapse, the basillica was restored by architect Eugene Viollet-le-Duc in the mid-19th century. The **Musée de l'Oeuvre**

Viollet-le-Duc ④, located alongside the basilica in a former monk's dormitory, has exhibits explaining the restoration process.

Behind the Place de la Basilique are the old city walls, with an incredible view over the surrounding countryside from the **Terrasse de l'Ancien Château** ⑤. Return to the Place de la Basilique, and continue past the cathedral to the **Ancien Couvent des Ursulines** ⑥. From here, descend the Chemin de la Cordelle to reach **Porte Sainte-Croix** ⑦, the gateway on the northern ramparts. Turn right onto the rampart pathway and stroll back around the city walls to the southern ramparts passing under the tower, **Tour des Colombs** ⑧. Stop and take in the views over the valley and the Cure river before heading back to the car park on Route de Saint-Père.

🚗 *Take the D957 to reach Saint-Père. Here turn right onto the D958. Pass Domecy-sur-Cure, and follow the signs for the turn off to the Château de Bazoches, which is on the left.*

Above Ancient fortified gateway, Vézelay

EAT AND DRINK

VÉZELAY

Le Dent Creuse
inexpensive–moderate
Grills, salads, pizzas, local produce are the highlights here.
Place du Champ de Foire, 89450; 03 86 33 36 33; www.vezelaytour.net

Marc Menau *expensive*
Marc Menau is a *grand chef cuisinier* and culinary author. The menu focuses on natural food and its innate flavours.
Route de Vézelay, Saint-Père, 89450; 03 86 33 39 10; www.marc-meneau-esperance.com; closed Tue, Mon and Wed lunch, mid-Jan–mid-Mar

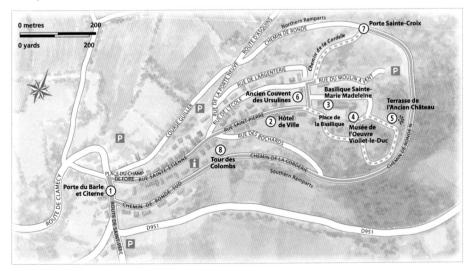

Eat and Drink: inexpensive, under €20; moderate, €20–€40; expensive, over €40

Above Grand and imposing Château de Bazoches **Below** Beautiful Place du Terreau in Autun

WHERE TO STAY

SAULIEU

Hostellerie La Tour d'Auxois
moderate
This friendly establishment has plain, pleasant rooms and suites. There is a bistro, a restaurant, a piano bar and a swimming pool.
Square Alexandre Dumaine, 2210; 03 80 64 36 19; www.tourdauxois.com

AUTUN

Les Ursulines *moderate*
Between the cathedral and forested surrounds, this ivy-covered hotel-restaurant is situated on a gardened swathe of old city walls. The decor of the rooms and suites combines medieval with modern. The restaurant menu features Burgundy dishes and French classics.
14 rue Rivault, 71400; 03 85 86 58 58; www.hotelursulines.fr

🔟 Château de Bazoches
Nièvre, Bourgogne; 58190
From a wooded hilltop, the château with its multiturreted roof has commanding views over the countryside as far as Vézelay, over which it was designed to watch. The overwhelmingly handsome structure is composed around four towers with two matching sides. The superb landscaped gardens, on the site of an old Roman camp, unfurl into paddocks and forest. The bedrooms, salons, study, armour displays, internal court and sundial of the château provide a rare glimpse into the life of Maréchal Vauban whose family still owns the château. Check for concerts and events held here *(open daily Mar–Nov)*.

🚗 *Continue on the D958, then left onto the D128. In the centre of Chalaux bear off to the right onto the D286, continue on the D210, then back onto the D286 through to Dun-les-Places. Turn left and take the D6 then the D26A and finally the D977bis to Saulieu.*

🔟 Saulieu
Côte d'Or, Bourgogne; 21210
This pretty town is surrounded by farmland, forest and lakes. Saulieu's ancient name Sedelocum – a stopover – comes from its situation as a historic passage between the north and south of France and as the gateway to the Morvan. The **Basilique St-Andoche** is a masterpiece of Romanesque art, notably in the intricate granite features on its façade and elaborately carved chancel, or choir and altar area. The gargoyle-spouted fountain on the church square adds to the claim of its being one of the prettiest Romanesque churches in Burgundy. Head to the **Musée François Pompon**, named after a famous local sculptor (1856–1933), to see the history of sacred art, local gastronomy and folklore. For living history, take a seat at the **Café Parisien** which has graced the Rue du Marché since 1832.

🚗 *There are adjacent signs pointing in two different directions from Saulieu to the Lac des Settons – take the Chemin des Plaines and turn right onto the D977bis. At Montsauche-les-Settons turn left and take the D193. The road leads to a crossroads with signs pointing to Lac des Settons rive gauche or rive droite (left or right bank).*

🔟 Lac des Settons
Nièvre, Bourgogne; 58230
The Lac des Settons is the biggest of three artificial lakes in the depths of the Morvan forest area. Its *rive droite*, or right bank, is the lake resort, densely dotted with paddle boats and windsurfers, and with restaurant terraces, old lakeside hotels and camping grounds around its banks. Nautical centres for boat rides and yacht and windsurf hire are also concentrated here, near the huge dam. Visitors can easily continue on the loop road around the lake to the other side, or take to one of the walking trails, which are also great for joggers.

Of the other Morvan lakes, the **Lac de Pannecière** is 24 km (15 miles) further west from Settons, through Montsauche-les-Settons. From there take the D977bis, turn left onto the D301 and right into the D303. Pannecière is a rustic place, ideal for fishing and enjoying nature. This lake saved Paris from being regularly flooded by the rising water levels of the Seine river. The **Lac de Saint Agnan** is more rural, bordered by meadows and grazing cattle. To reach the lake from Saulieu, head west on the D977bis, continue on the D106 and the D225; then turn left onto the D226.

🚗 *Take the D193 and pass by Moux-en-Morvan. Then take the D302, turn right onto the D20, then the D149 and continue straight through on the D980. Follow the signs to the city centre. There are car parks near the tourist office on Place du Champ-de-Mars.*

⑬ Autun
Saône-et-Loire, Bourgogne; 71400
Founded at the end of the 1st century BC at the behest of Emperor Augustus, the town of Autun was originally known as Augustodunum. From its hillock, the old city dominates the Morvan mountains and forests, and the river-plains of the Saône-et-Loire. Among its many Gallo-Roman relics are the Roman **amphitheatre**, the biggest of its time, seating 20,000 people; two monumental gateways, the **Porte Saint-André** and **Porte d'Arroux**; vestiges of the once 6-km (4-mile) long city wall; and, across the Arroux river, the remains of the Roman **Temple of Janus**. On the Place du Terrau, the elaborately decorated, late Gothic **Cathédrale St-Lazare** has what is considered one of the finest examples of Romanesque tympana, with its mass of carved stone relief. The **Musée Rolin** next door displays a collection of religious artworks,

including Gallo-Roman mosaics. Soak up the ambience of Latin antiquity on an evening stroll – in July and August the **tourist office** *(13 rue Général Demetz , 03 85 86 80 38)* organizes guided night-time tours.

🚗 *Exit town via the N80 then turn onto the D973 through to Nolay. A worthwhile detour along the way is the Château de Sully – take the D326 to the left near Creusefond and follow the signs to the château.*

⑭ Nolay
Côte d'Or, Bourgogne; 21340
The centrepiece of this medieval market town is its open-sided **Halles** or covered market, whose solid wooden pillars support a roof made of paving stones. From the **Hôtel de Ville** on Rue de la Républuse, seek out Medieval *échoppes*, stores and carpenters' workshops with stone cellars and wood-panelled façades. The Rue Saint Querin has several *colombage* houses, the legacy of a strong trade in carpentry until Henri IV banned such buildings because of the frequent fires. The chapel in the quarter of Saint-Pierre is one of just three that remain from the village's original 15.

Above left Elaborate clock of the Cathédrale St-Lazare in Autun *Above right* Tourist boats moored near the Lac des Settons *Below left* Vineyard near Nolay

EAT AND DRINK

SAULIEU

Café Parisien *inexpensive*
This iconic café with a marble and stone façade has a menu consisting of soups, salads, sweets and *plats du jour*. *Rue du Marché, 21210; 03 80 64 26 56; www.cafeparisien.net*

Le Relais Bernard Loiseau Hôtel-Restaurant *expensive*
This restaurant offers classic dishes in elegant surroundings. *2 rue d'Argentine, 21210; 03 80 90 53 53; www.bernard-loiseau.com; closed Tue, Wed, lunch Oct–Mar*

AUTUN
Relais des Ursulines *inexpensive*
This buzzing restaurant is known for its pastas, pizzas, and salads. *2 rue Dufraigne, 71400; 03 85 52 26 22; www.lerelaisdesursulines.com, closed Sat lunch, Sun*

Le Chalet Bleu *moderate–expensive*
Housed in a colourful blue window-shuttered cottage, the restaurant serves traditional French cuisine. *3 rue Jeannin, 71400; 03 85 86 27 30; www.lechaletbleu.com; closed Sun and Mon dinner, Tue*

DAY TRIP OPTIONS
The following day trips are best undertaken from Beaune, Vézelay and the Morvan region (either Autun or Saulieu) respectively.

Wine country
Amateurs as well as professionals can expand their knowledge of wine during a day's visit to the biggest zone of *grands crus* in Burgundy, centred on Aloxe-Corton ❷.

For Aloxe-Corton take the D18 from

Beaune towards Savigny-les-Beaune and then turn right onto the D115D.

Castles and canals
The Canal de Bourgogne between Châteauneuf-en-Auxois ❹, Veuvey-sur-Ouche and La Bussière-sur-Ouche is perfect for boating.

The canal borders the D18 from Veuvey-sur-Ouche to the turn-off to Châteauneuf-en-Auxois. From Veuvey-sur-Ouche it heads towards La Bussière-sur-Ouche via the D33.

Rural lakes
Water sports and activities rule on the right bank of the Lac des Settons ⑫ – swimming, canoeing and fishing. However, the lakeside also has several hidden corners ideal for picnicking.

For those based in Saulieu, follow the itinerary. If you are in Autun, head north on the D980, turn left on the D149, continue on the D20 and turn left onto the D302, pass through Moux-en-Morvan and take the D193 to Lac des Settons.

Eat and Drink: inexpensive, under €20; moderate €20–€40; expensive, over €40

The Heart of France

Cluny to Romanèche-Thorins

Highlights

- **Abbey of Cluny**
  Marvel at the astounding religious and architectural heritage within this Benedictine abbey

- **Wine route**
  Drive through the Route des Vins Mâconnais-Beaujolais, crisscrossing hidden countryside between Roman vestiges, monasteries and châteaux

- **Beaujolais villages**
  Along the wine route, admire the delightful *villages de charme* from Fuissé to Saint-Amour-Bellevue

- **Mighty rocks**
  Explore the landmark rock formations that dominate the countryside

View of the towers and steeple of the Abbey of Cluny

The Heart of France

The Route des Vins Mâconnais-Beaujolais was established by winemakers in 1986 and explores the landscape and legacy of southern Burgundy in all its variety. The first grapes were planted by the Romans and tended by the monks at Cluny in the Middle Ages. Along this route visitors will cross the rolling countryside of the Mâconnais area and the vineyards and villages of Beaujolais.

Above Vast tracts of vineyards extend along the Route des Vins Mâconnais-Beaujolais, s

PLAN YOUR DRIVE

Start/finish: Cluny to Romanèche-Thorins.

Number of days: 1–2.

Distance: 90 km (56 miles).

Road conditions: Good and well-signed; parts of the wine route are circuitous, with very narrow roads.

When to go: June to August has the best weather; late September to early October is the time to see the grape harvest in progress.

Opening hours: Most sites are closed on Mondays and on public holidays.

Main market days: Cluny: Sat; Juliénas: Mon; Romanèche-Thorins: Sat.

Major festivals: Cluny: Les Grandes Heures de Cluny, Jul–Aug; Juliénas: Fête des Vins, Nov.

Above Statue in the Hameau du Vin, Romanèche-Thorins, *see p143*

KEY

⟶ Drive route

① Cluny

Saône-et-Loire, Bourgogne; 71250

A cradle of Christendom in medieval Europe, the famous Benedictine **Abbey of Cluny** was the largest religious building in the world before the completion of Rome's St Peter's Basilica. Built in AD 910, it ruled over a monastic empire of 10,000 monks. An independent or guided tour of the abbey explores the pillars and arches of its various monastic buildings, Gothic churches, courtyards and gardens, ending at the Abbey's Museum of Art and Archaeology. Other highlights of the town include the honeycomb of medieval and Romanesque houses in the old city, the **Tour des Fromages** and the **Hôtel-Dieu** (town hospital) and its chapel. Horse-lovers can take a guided visit of the **Haras National** (national stud) established by Napoleon I as a military equestrian centre.

🚗 *Leave Cluny via the D15 and D980, turn left into the D17 towards La Roche-Vineuse on D85 with a possible detour on the D220 to Berzé-la-Ville.*

Beaujolais

Beaujolais is the collective name given to 12 appellations including the world famous Beaujolais Nouveau. Each appellation is linked with a different terroir. Saint Amour, Juliénas, Chénas, and Moulin à Vent are among the region's ten jewels – the Beaujolais Crus. The launch of the latest Beaujolais vintage is celebrated every November to cries of "the Beaujolais Nouveau has arrived!"

② Route des Vins Mâconnais-Beaujolais

Saône-et-Loire, Bourgogne; 71000

The wine route weaves its way through the valley northwest of Mâcon known as Val Lamartinien. It passes by the imposing château of Berzé-le-Châtel and neighbouring town of Berzé-la-Ville – an offshoot of Cluny – whose **Chapelle des Moines** has prized Byzantine frescoes. The circuit from Berzé-la-Ville and La Roche-Vineuse towards Verzé, Igé and Hurigny is particularly picturesque with its undulating mix of crops and countryside, forest, vales, vines and villages. Each hamlet has its Roman church, Renaissance

houses and communal washing places called *lavoirs*. Visit the **Musée de la Vigne** *(open Mon–Sat)* in the Château de la Greffiere at La Roche-Vineuse and the 11th-century Benedictine chapel in Igé.

🚗 *Continue on the D85 to Marigny, Verzé and Igé, then right into the D134, then D82 towards Hurigny. From there take the D194 to Chevagny-les-Chevrières and Prissé, the D45 to Bussières, the D45/D177 to Vergisson and Davayé.*

Pouilly-Fuissé

Saône-et-Loire, Bourgogne; 71960

The vineyards which lay claim to the renowned Pouilly-Fuissé wine label exist on a narrow strip of land 10 km (6 miles) west of Mâcon. Since the appellation was created in 1936, its borders have been irrevocably fixed around the four villages of Chaintré, Fuissé, Solutré-Pouilly and Vergisson. Between Romanesque fountains and churches, the villages have vaulted wine cellars, some of them in châteaux. On the village square of Solutré, the **Atrium** *(open Tue–Sun)* is a showcase and tasting room for the Pouilly-Fuissé Growers Association.

🚗 *From Davayé take the D209 to Pouilly, then to Fuissé, then the D172/D31 to Solutré-Pouilly. From Solutré-Pouilly, the D54 leads to the Roche de Solutré behind the village – there are parking zones alongside the D54. An option is to leave the car in the village and start the walk from there along a marked pathway via the cemetery.*

Above Steeple of the Abbey of Cluny surrounded by the lush green countryside

WHERE TO STAY

CLUNY

Hostellerie Le Potin Gourmand
inexpensive
The hotel's themed rooms include Potters, Gardeners and Byzantine.
4 Champ de Foire, 71250; 03 85 59 02 06; www.potingourmand.com

Hôtel Restaurant de Bourgogne
moderate
This is a 1817 house that is furnished with antiques and has a restaurant.
Place de l'Abbaye, 71250; 03 85 59 00 58; www.hotel-cluny.com

POUILLY-FUISSÉ

Domaine la Source des Fées
moderate
This 16th-century stone building houses a serene guesthouse on a wine estate.
Le Bourg route de Chaintré, 71960; 03 85 35 67 02; www.lasourcedesfees.com

EAT AND DRINK

CLUNY

La Halte de l'Abbaye *inexpensive*
This is a mix of café, bar, brasserie and restaurant, with snacks, salads, meat dishes, crêpes and desserts.
3 rue Porte-des-Prés, 71250; 03 85 59 28 49; open Thu–Mon lunch only

AROUND POUILLY-FUISSÉ

La Courtille de Solutré *inexpensive*
The restaurant, 9 km (6 miles) west of the village, is known for traditional French and Burgundian dishes.
Le Bourg, 71960; 03 85 35 80 73; closed Sun night and Mon

Above Cross stands by the road in Solutré-Pouilly as vineyards stretch to the horizon

Eat and Drink: inexpensive, under €20; moderate, €20–€40; expensive, over €40

Above Limestone escarpment of Roche de Solutré

VISITING ROCHE DE SOLUTRÉ

Tourist Information
The Tourist Information office is in the complex of the Musée Départemental de la Préhistoire de Solutré.
Solutré-Pouilly, 71960; 03 85 35 85 24

Parking
There are parking zones alongside the D54.

WHERE TO STAY

SAINT-AMOUR-BELLEVUE

Auberge du Paradis
moderate–expensive
This old stone hotel has been rendered fresh and fashionable while retaining some retro artifacts. It has eight rooms with creative names such as Gingembre, Muscade and Cumin. They are painted in warm tones and come with luxury fittings. Delicious home-made produce is used for breakfast, this is served in the pretty courtyard.
Plâtre Durand, 71570; 03 85 37 10 26; www.aubergeduparadis.fr; closed Jan

ROMANÈCHE-THORINS

Les Maritonnes Hôtel-Restaurant
moderate
This is a family-run Beaujolais country house with 25 rooms, period furniture, bar, pool and park. The restaurant serves regional cuisine and French favourites and the menu covers a wide range of prices.
Route de Fleurie, 71570; 03 85 35 51 70; www.maritonnes.com; restaurant closed for weekday lunches

❹ Roche de Solutré
Saône-et-Loire, Bourgogne; 71960

Surging up from the slopes of vines above the village of Solutré-Pouilly, the Roche de Solutré is a striking limestone escarpment which has a profile likened to the Sphinx.

A 45-minute walking tour

The main car park is just off the D54 at the foothills of the Roche de Solutré. From here a path leads to Crot-du-Charnier, a prehistoric mass grave. Near it is the subterranean **Musée Départemental de la Préhistoire de Solutré** ① *(closed Dec)*, showcasing the site's history and the archaeological excavations that have been carried out here since the 1860s. The escarpment, aside from being a geological phenomenon, also holds great archaeological interest as the site of a prehistoric hunting ground. Excavations have found animal bones, stone tools and other flint artifacts showing evidence of occupation 15,000 or more years ago. The hunting site is preserved in the **Parc Archéologique et Botanique** ② run by the museum. From here, the Sentier Pedestre trail – marked with yellow signs – leads to the 493-m (1,617-ft) **summit** ③. After about 100 m (328 ft) the trail forks;

the path to the left is shorter but also much steeper; the main trail is gently sloped. The 3-km (2-mile) return walk is graded easy, and it takes about 20 minutes to reach the top. The trail leads through cliffs and vineyards to an enclosed paddock. The path forks again here from where the summit trail is clearly marked.

The trail has a few viewpoints, and 360-degree views are on offer at the summit: the Saône valley can be seen to the east, and on a clear day the Jura mountains and the Mont Blanc chain; to the north is Vergisson village with its own distinctive ochre-hued Roche de Vergisson; to the south is the village of Solutré-Pouilly. Visitors can extend their walk to Solutré-Pouilly by taking the path from the base of the rock or retrace their steps to the car park.

🚗 *Head back to the D54, then the D31 and then turn left at La Grange du Bois onto the D627 to reach the Col.*

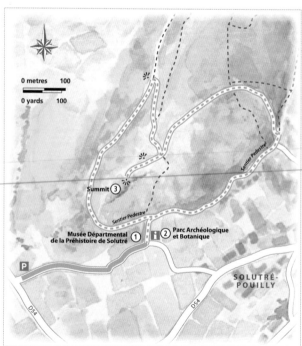

⑤ Col de Gerbey
Rhône, Rhône-Alpes; 69840

Pass through the small hamlet of La Grange du Bois, but not without stopping to take in the wonderful perspectives over the landmark rocks of Solutré and Vergisson. Continue on a forested road through pine trees up to the Col de Gerbey (613 m/ 2,010 ft) for a sharp contrast between the vineyards of lower Beaujolais and the arid highland prairies of Haut-Beaujolais. One place here is called the Paradise of Goats and visitors will see many of these animals grazing along with cows.

🚗 *Take the D137 and follow signs in the direction Juliénas.*

⑥ Juliénas
Rhône, Rhône-Alpes; 69840

At the heart of an undulating collage of villages, vineyards, mountain foothills and streams is the town of Juliénas, which owes its name to Julius Caesar. It has been growing vines now for over 2,000 years. The commune produces two appellations – Juliénas and Beaujolais-Villages – and roadside signs will direct vacationers to small private cellars. The **Château du Bois de la Salle**, on the other hand, is much larger and home to the cooperative cellar of 100 Juliénas vignerons. This 17th-century priory was built by Charrier de la Roche, chaplain of Napoleon I.

🚗 *Take the D17E and then the D169; pass through the village and take the D486T. Turn left at Plâtre-Durand to reach Saint-Amour-Bellevue.*

⑦ Saint-Amour-Bellevue
Saône-et-Loire, Bourgogne; 71570

The lovely sounding village of Saint-Amour-Bellevue welcomes visitors with a flourish of red hearts attached to signposts, trees, streetlights and stores. Bucolic stone homes and travellers inns, flowery restaurant terraces and love-heart decorated craft shops line the **Avenue Plâtre Durand**. However, the village's real love affair is with its *grand cru* wine. Visitors should visit the private cellars perched between the village square and almost immediate countryside.

🚗 *Retrace the route to Plâtre-Durand and take the D186. Turn left into the D95, pass through Les Paquelets, turn right onto the D186 then right again onto D166. Pass Les Deschamps, take the D68, then turn left into the D266.*

⑧ Romanèche-Thorins
Saône-et-Loire, Bourgogne; 71570

At the heart of Beaujolais and *cassis* (blackcurrant) countryside, Romanèche-Thorins is the place where visitors will discover tasting rooms for wine and liqueurs behind Romanesque façades. The **Hameau du Vin** *(open daily)*, an initiative of noted *vigneron* George Duboeuf, tells the history of winemaking through various interactive displays and exhibits. It also has a beautiful Beaujolais garden. Another curiosity for visitors is the **Musée du Compagnonnage** *(open daily Jan–mid-Dec)* – a museum that showcases the special French associations for the carpentry, stone masonry and joinery trades.

Above Scenic slopes of the villages and vineyards of Juliénas **Below** Church at Romanèche-Thorins with vineyards in the foreground

---

EAT AND DRINK

SAINT-AMOUR-BELLEVUE

Auberge du Paradis
moderate–expensive
Chef Cyril Laugier's renowned fusion of spicy spontaneity, farm-fresh produce and attention to detail makes the Auberge du Paradis a special restaurant. The decor of white stone and linen and red love heart lights lends the place a romantic atmosphere. *Plâtre Durand, 71570; 03 85 37 10 26; www.aubergeduparadis.fr; closed Sun dinner, Mon, Tue and Fri lunch, Jan*

ROMANÈCHE-THORINS

La Maison Blanche
inexpensive–moderate
The restaurant specializes in traditional cooking and regional food. It also serves *à la carte* and seasonal menus. *RN6, 71570; 03 85 35 50 53; closed Sun dinner, Mon, Jan*

Valleys and Mountains

Villard-de-Lans to Clelles-en-Trièves

Highlights

- **Vercors Massif**
  Explore the extensive subalpine plateau of the Vercors, its gorges and forests

- **The great outdoors**
  Go skiing, hiking or horse-riding in the breathtaking mountain setting of the Vercors and the Alps

- **Farmers' markets**
  Shop at the local *marchés paysans* for the freshest of produce – from sparkling wine to walnuts and honey

- **Mountain passes**
  Cross the spectacular passes which link the Vercors valley and villages to the Isère on the other side

Grey peak of Tête de l'Obiou between the Vercors and the Dévoluy mountain chains

Valleys and Mountains

The Vercors is a massive pre-Alpine range composed of limestone valleys, gorges and extensive tablelands that separate the Alps from Provence. Its high plateaus form a long silvery wall which sweeps by the villages of the Parc du Vercors. One of France's largest natural parks, it stretches over 1,860 sq km (718 sq miles) through seven natural regions, including the Vercors Drômois, the Diois and the Trièves, at the crossroads of mountain and Mediterranean climates; snow-capped peaks glisten under deep blue winter skies and lavender permeates the alpine air in summer. The Vercors Central, radiating out from Villard-de-Lans, is a mixed landscape of alpine pastures, chalet-filled ski villages, rivers and ravines. The Diois is the heart of sunny Drôme Provençale. In the adjacent valley, Le Trièves is a dairy farming region in a huge alpine basin.

ACTIVITIES

Enjoy skiing at Villard-de-Lans

Climb aboard a horse-drawn carriage in Villard-de-Lans

Go canyoning, caving or climbing in the Vercors

Take in the stunning landscape while paragliding across the Vercors

Learn about organic gardening at Terre Vivante

Go swimming in the Lac du Sautet

Below Tête de l'Obiou showing white glaciation marks, *see p151*

Above Rolling fields of the Clelles countryside, *see p153*

PLAN YOUR DRIVE

Start/finish: Villard-de-Lans to Clelles-en-Trièves.

Number of days: 4–5, allowing at least a day in the Parc du Vercors area and another day in the Trièves.

Distances: 210 km (130 miles).

Road conditions: There is a risk of rock-fall on the mountain roads through the Gorges de la Borne and along the alpine passes, Col de Menée and Col de Grimone. Some of the roads have hairpin bends. Cliff-faces are contained along some stretches with rock nets. Following a series of rock falls in the gorge the authorities decided to embark on a long-term maintenance scheme. Currently the plan necessitates the road to be closed during certain times of the year. Please contact Bison Futé for details *(see p18)*.

When to go: For spring flowers visit from May to June; from July to August for long hot summer days. Autumn is good for the colours; and winters are great for winter sports (don't forget snow tyres or chains).

Opening hours: Sights are generally open from 10am to 5pm. National museums and sights are closed on Mondays and public holidays. Check with the tourist office before visiting.

Main market days: Villard-de-Lans: Wed, Sun; **La Chapelle-en-Vercors:** Thu; **Mens:** Wed (Jul–Aug), Sat.

Shopping: Take home local and farm produce of the Vercors: cheeses, cured meats, walnuts, jams and wine.

Major festivals: Saint-Martin-en-Vercors: Fête du Tilleul, late-Jul–Aug; **La Chapelle-en-Vercors:** Fête du Bleu, Aug; **Die:** Velorizons Mountain-bike Festival, Jun.

DAY TRIP OPTIONS

The drive can be broken up into various day trips: Villard-de-Lans offers **family-friendly** skiing resorts; **gardening enthusiasts** should head to Terre Vivante in Le Trièves; the Lac du Sautet provides leisure as well as adventures for **mountain lovers**. For details, *see p153*.

Map

0 kilometres 5
0 miles 5

Vif
D1075
St-Théoffrey
Pierre-Châtel
Avignonet
D1075
Nantes-en-Ratier
D529
Roucac
Susville
Le Sénépy △ 1,769 m
La Mure
Siévoz
D26
Valbonnais
D26
D526
Bonne
Monestier-de-Clermont
Ponsonnas
Prunières
D526
St-Pierre-de-Méaroz
Roissard
ISÈRE
Drac
St-Jean-d'Hérans
St-Sébastien
N85
Ste-Luce
Lavars
D34
St-Martin-de-Clelles
Cornillon-en-trièves
Cordéac
LAC DU SAUTET
D66
D66
14 D526 Sandon
D526
CLELLES-EN-TRIÈVES
10 **MENS**
La Croix-de-la-Pigne
D526
Las Moras
11 Corps
Les Oncs
Le Monestier-du-Percy
D216
TERRE VIVANTE **13**
11
l'Aiguille △ 2,037 m
D66A
Pellafol
Prebois
St-Baudille-et-Pipet
La Posterle
D537
St-Maurice-en-Trièves
Ebron
D66
Tête de l'Obiou △ 2,789 m
12
Lalley
Mt de Ménis △ 1,514 m
Tréminis
SOURCES DES GILLARDES
Soloise
t Barral △ 1,903 m
Le Château-Bas
Tête de l'Aupet △ 2,627 m
St-Disdier
e de Jocou △ 2,051 m △
Rognon △ 1,851 m
D1075
Col de la Croix Haute
Grand Ferrand △ 2,758 m
D117
Tête de Lauzon △ 2,278 m
D937
D539
Buëch
Grimone lage
9
COL DE GRIMONE
D1075
La Jarjatte
Lunel

KEY

▭▭ Drive route

Right La Maison du Patrimoine on Place de la Libération, Villard-de-Lans **Below** Dramatic cliffs of the Gorges de la Bourne

WHERE TO STAY

VILLARD-DE-LANS

La Taiga *inexpensive*
This ten-bedroom forest chalet is loved by families for its personal welcome, attentive owners, alpine panoramas, comfortable rooms and home cooking. From Villard-de-Lans take the Route de la Baumette in and turn left into the Rue des Jeux Olympiques.
150 rue des Jeux Olympiques, La Balmette, 38250; 04 76 95 15 40; www. lataiga.com

AROUND VILLARD-DE-LANS

Col de l'Arc Hôtel-Restaurant *inexpensive*
This 2-star hotel, 9 km (6 miles) north of Villard-de-Lans, has ski slopes on its doorstep. There are 25 cosy rooms with balconies. The hotel has its own library, bar and restaurant.
Lans-en-Vercors, 38250; 04 76 95 40 08; www.hotelcoldelarc.com

Hôtel du Golf *moderate–expensive*
Five kilometres (3 miles) from Villard-de-Lans, Hôtel du Golf was once a simple mountain bistro. It has now been converted into a contemporary chalet hotel with a warm local stone, wood and leather interior. The floor-to-ceiling windows in the restaurant look over the Vercors landscape. The spa has a sauna and Jacuzzi. Take the Route de la Baumette south of Villard-de-Lans; continue on the Route du Corrençon to Corrençon-en-Vercors.
Le Bois Fleuri, Corrençon-en-Vercors, 38250; 04 76 95 84 84; www.hotel-du-golf-vercors.fr

① Villard-de-Lans
Isère, Rhône-Alpes; 38250

An epitome of the French alpine village with its geranium decorated chalets and lively mountain hamlet ambience, Villard-de-Lans is the capital of the Parc du Vercors. Tourism boomed in the 1920s when the Grenoble bourgeoisie discovered the health benefits of its climate. Take a draught horse-ride around its mountainous streets or stroll between lovely café-crowded squares; explore local history at **La Maison du Patrimoine** *(Wed–Mon Jul–Aug, Fri–Sat May–Jun and Sep–Dec)* on Place de la Libération; at Place de l'Ours see the statue of the emblematic bear last seen in the Alps in the Vercors Park in 1937. On certain Fridays the village hosts an animated farmers market, the *marché paysan*.

🚗 *Take the D531 towards the Gorges de la Bourne.*

Flora and Fauna
The Rhône-Alps has the greatest biodiversity in France. The Vercors is home to a wide range of wildlife such as deer, wolves, chamois, lynx, marmot, ibex, vultures, falcons, and robins. The wide range of climate and terrain has allowed various kinds of flowers to flourish, including crocus, mountain lilies, violets, delphiniums and carnations.

② Gorges de la Bourne
Drôme, Rhône-Alpes; 26420

The thrilling drive along the edge of the alpine gorges of the Bourne river can be hair-raising: parts of the road are virtually enveloped by the cliff-face and the large containing nets and warning signs make no bones about the dangers of rock-falls. Gushing down from the 2,000-m (6,500-ft) summits of the Vercors, the river has carved out a 20-km (12-mile) long corridor through the pre-Alps from Villard-de-Lans down to Pont-en-Royans. At the eerily named bridge, Pont de la Goule Noir (Black Ghoul), the road forks along both sides of the chasm. There are several spectacular viewing points over the ravine, but the bridge is the easiest and most secure place to get out and take in the views.

🚗 *At the fork near the Pont de la Goule Noir, turn left, pass through the tunnel and continue on the D103. Continue along the D103 to reach Saint-Martin- en-Vercors; some of the bends around the gorges are very sharp.*

③ Saint-Martin-en-Vercors
Drôme, Rhône-Alpes; 26420

In a long valley at the heart of the Parc du Vercors, the little village of Saint-Martin-en-Vercors is set within an overwhelmingly grand alpine landscape. The valley is rimmed all the way along by the ridges of the Vercors, like a huge rocky wall mural, its lower parts coloured by crops, and the tractors and cows in the fields reduced to dots against the surroundings. Sit at a café under the 400-year-old lime tree on the Place du Village of Saint-Martin, try some morel-filled *ravioles*, the Drôme version of ravioli, and take in the stunning views. Gazing at the sunset, visitors might see the Vierge du Vercors – an optical illusion of a saintly virgin etched into the cliffs dominating the Val de Saint-Martin.

🚗 *Continue on the D103; turn left onto the D103A and then right onto the D611 for La Chapelle-en-Vercors.*

Linden Tree Reforestation
Around the beginning of the 17th century, King Henri IV rewarded people for planting linden trees, *tilleuls de Sully* (named after his finance minister), as he deemed France's forests overexploited. A sacred tree since the Middle Ages, the linden was used to sculpt many church statues. Its flowers also make a sleep-enhancing herbal tea.

④ La Chapelle-en-Vercors
Drôme, Rhône-Alpes; 26420

The prettily named village, snuggled at an altitude of 945 m (3,100 ft) within long silvery arms of the rocky Vercors plateau, harbours many wartime horror stories. It is hard to believe that this incredible alpine setting turned into a violent war zone during World War II. The Vercors villages, based in the natural citadel of the Vercors mountains, were strategic points for the Resistance and hence prime targets of the Nazis. In July 1944 La Chapelle-en-Vercors was bombarded by Luftwaffe planes and a quarter of the houses were destroyed. While some villagers managed to hide in the surrounding forests, many were captured by the Nazis and held at the local school. The Nazis later set the village on fire. This was not before massacring 16 hostages in a farmyard, **La Cour des Fusilles**, which is now a memorial and a museum. On the forested

edges of town, the Parc de la Draye Blanche is an immense stalactite-filled grotto, with guided palaeontology visits focusing on the site's prehistoric geology and fauna which included buffalo, bears and wolves.

🚗 *Take the D178 towards Vassieux-en-Vercors; approaching the town drive straight onto the D76.*

⑤ Vassieux-en-Vercors
Drôme, Rhône-Alpes; 26420

A peaceful place with a hellish history, the village was obliterated by the Nazis in 1944. It was later rebuilt. The **Memorial de la Resistance and Muséographie** *(open daily, closed mid-Nov–mid-Dec)* includes an audiovisual presentation on the war, the occupation of the Vercors by the Nazis, and its liberation, with witness stories and a short film. As visitors exit the memorial there is a panoramic view over the 11-km (7-mile) long Vassieux Plain.

🚗 *Continue on the D76 to climb the Col de St-Alexis through a few sharp bends. From here follow the signs to the Col du Rousset, which will proceed along the D518.*

ACTIVITIES IN VILLARD-DE-LANS

DRAUGHT HORSE-RIDES AND SKIING
Tourist Information
101 place Mure-Ravaud, 38250; 04 76 95 10 38; www.villarddelans.com

PARAGLIDING
Vercors Aventure
www.vercors-aventure.com

CAVING, CLIMBING AND CANYONING
Bureau des Moniteur
www.speleo-canyon.com

EAT AND DRINK

VILLARD-DE-LANS

La Grange du Pere Jules *moderate*
Lovers of country flavours and rustic decoration should head to this café-restaurant and gift store. The grange has rustic tables, a carved wooden bear standing guardian at the door and a large menu with tarts, goat's cheese salads and meat and fish dishes.
41 rue des Pionniers, 38250; 04 76 94 91 89; closed Sun and Wed dinner, Mon

AROUND VILLARD-DE-LANS

L'Auberge de Malaterre *moderate*
People walk, or go by snowshoes or cross-country ski to reach this 1904 forest cabin, 5 km (3 miles) from Villard-de-Lans, its menu includes mushroom, wild strawberry tart and gratins.
Route Forestière Grand-Allée, Bois-Barbu, 38250; 04 76 95 04 34; www.fermeboisbarbu.com; open daily mid-Dec–mid-Mar, Jul–Aug, rest of the year only on Sun

Above Mural in the village of Vassieux-en-Vercors **Below left** Spectacular scenery of the Drôme countryside **Below right** Stone houses line an avenue in La Chapelle-en-Vercors

Right Tiled roofs of houses in the town of Die
Below Aerial view of the large artificial Lac du Sautet

WHERE TO STAY

CHÂTILLON-EN-DIOIS

Hotel du Dauphiné *inexpensive*
Housed in a brightly shuttered Diois stone house in the heart of the village, this hotel has a sun-terrace, a petite bar and eight light-filled rooms with white linen, iron beds and retro furnishings.
Place Pierre Dévoluy, 26410; 04 75 21 13 13

AROUND CHÂTILLON-EN-DIOIS

Le Mont Barral *inexpensive*
This 20-room hotel, 14 km (8 miles) north of Châtillon-en-Diois, has a park, pool and a good regional restaurant.
Les Nonières, Treschenu-Creyers, 26410; 04 75 21 12 21; www. hotelmontbarral-vercors.com

Le Sareymond *inexpensive*
This bed-and-breakfast offers bright rooms with mountain views. There is a hot tub and Wi-Fi services are offered. Evening meals are served if desired.
Hameau de Menee, Treschenu-Creyers, 26410; 04 75 21 73 66; www.lesareymond.com

⑥ Col de Rousset
Drôme, Rhône-Alpes; 26420
After a series of sweeping bends around the sides of a huge alpine valley, the swerves concertina and culminate in the Col de Rousset. The area is a winter ski playground dotted with ski lifts; its forests are prime habitats for ibex, beavers, rock partridge and the griffon vulture. The Col de Rousset ends in a road tunnel. After the tunnel, the scenery changes distinctively in the Vercors Diois region. Dominated by the Glandasse massif, the Drôme river and its tributaries run through the valley nourishing lavender crops and vineyards, source of the sparkling wine *Clairette de Die*.

🚗 *Continue on the D518 to Die, following the signs to "Centre Ville" or Gap. There is a large car park near the tourist office and another at the cathedral square.*

⑦ Die
Drôme, Rhône-Alpes; 26150
With its brightly shuttered houses, squares bordered by cafés and courtyards with villagers playing petanque, Die reminds visitors of Provence. The steep cobblestoned streets are lined with bars and stores full of the aromas of local produce: lavender, honey, *picodon* (goat cheese), *agneau de la Drôme* (lamb) and *carré de pic* (prosciutto-like smoked ham). Climb up the narrow streets around the ramparts; see the valley view from the old stone bridge; and visit the **cathedral**. Ask the **tourist office** *(open Mon–Sat, Sun Apr–Sep)* for details of the

outdoor activities nearby and cellars such as the **Cave de Die Jaillance** where guests can taste the sparkling wines, *Crémant* and *Clairette de Die*. On the edge of town, along the Route de Gap, the **Jardin des Découvertes Hydroponique** *(open daily May–Aug)* is a butterfly discovery centre with hundreds of colourful and exotic species.

🚗 *Take the D93 and turn left at Pont de Quart to take the D539 and follow the signs to Châtillon-en-Diois. There is a large car park to the left at the foot of the village.*

⑧ Châtillon-en-Diois
Drôme, Rhône-Alpes; 26410
On the foothills of the 2,041-m (6,696-ft) Glandasse mountain, this sun-drenched village lies among the most southern cliffs of the Vercors and is much more Mediterranean than alpine in temperament. Explore the ancient artery Rue des Rostangs and the cobbled side alleyways with their gaily painted window shutters and pretty ironwork. As well as medieval vestiges, there are 17 fountains with stone basins and a distinctive 18th-century church clocktower, the **Tour de l'Horloge**. Walk to the crumbling arches and passageways near the belfry tower, which is adjacent to the lively little hub of cafés on Place du Reviron. Garden enthusiasts may wish to see the 150 species of climbing plants in the botanical garden *(open daily)*.

🚗 *Continue on the D539 towards Col de Grimone. Pass through Glandage and Grimone. Check fuel and water levels before tackling these passes.*

Left Stone fountain near Col de Grimone
Right Église de Notre-Dame in Mens
Below Road tunnel where Col du Rousset culminates

EAT AND DRINK

DIE

La Petite Auberge *moderate*
The locals regard this restaurant as one of the best in town. Although the building is nothing to look at from the outside, the dishes are well presented and refined and the staff are friendly. Try the duck basted with hazelnuts followed by the pineapple *carpaccio* with a nougat glacé. If you're staying at the attached hotel, ask for a room at the back, where it is quieter.
13 Avenue Sadi-Carnot, 26150; 04 75 22 05 91; closed Sun evening, Mon

Le Saint-Domingue
inexpensive–moderate
The restaurant serves generous helpings of local food including raviolis, smoked ham and fish dishes plus excellent mixed salads. The terrace, with a view over the roofs of Die, is a great refuge from the summer heat and crowds.
44 rue Camille-Buffardel, 26150; 04 75 22 03 08; www.hotelsaint dominique.com; closed Sun dinner, Mon

MENS

Café des Sports *inexpensive*
This café is housed in a typical Trièves village stone house painted pale pink with burgundy shutters. Local dairy products, meat and vegetables, including organic produce, are used in cooking. The place serves generous portions of home-style *cuisine familiale* in an amiable atmosphere. There are *apéro-concerts* – live music and an aperitif – on some Sundays.
Rue du Breuil, 38710; 04 76 34 60 37; closed Mon

⑨ Col de Grimone
Drôme, Rhône-Alpes; 26410

The spectacular mountain pass of **Col de Grimone** (1,318 m/4,324 ft) bridges the deeply carved Jurassic-era valleys of the Drôme and the Drac. From the lavender-coated hills of the Drôme, the passage towards the Col de Grimone rises up gradually, becoming incredibly narrow around the Gorges des Gats. Continuing on the D539, turn left onto the D1075 towards the 1,179-m (3,927-ft) **Col de la Croix Haute**, the final mountain pass before the descent to the Trièves. Here the entire region unfolds to reveal the ridges and peaks of the mountains of the Diois and Trièves Alps: Mont Aiguille, Tête de Lauzon and Grand Ferrand.

🚗 *From the Col de la Croix Haute, proceed along the N75. Turn right onto the D66 towards Lalley. Pass through Lalley and continue on the D66 following the signs to Mens.*

⑩ Mens
Isère, Rhône-Alpes; 38710

During the 16th-century religious wars, Mens was a fief of Protestant faith and remains a major mountain centre of the Reform Church. Every street here ends in a mountain, rising above the houses with their splintered stone roof tiles. **Tête de l'Obiou**, a grey peak rippled with white glaciation marks, is nearest to the village. Head to the Place de la Halle to see the medieval market hall. On the same square is the **Église de Notre-Dame** with a fine sundial, and the **Musée du Trièves** *(open Tue–Sun May–Sep, Sat–Sun Apr and Oct–Nov)*, with exhibits on local history. Mens has several examples of the Trièves hexagonal stone fountains.

🚗 *From Mens take the D66 towards Cordéac. Pass through La Croix-de-la-Pigne and Les Moras and descend towards the lake. Turn left to the dam and there is a car park on the right.*

⑪ Lac du Sautet
Isère, Rhône-Alpes; 38970

The turquoise waters of this large artificial lake are cupped in the valley at the base of Tête de l'Obiou. The barrage was created in 1935, at the confluence of the Drac and Souloise rivers. Along the lakeside near the village of Corps, there is a nautical resort offering various activities.

🚗 *Return to the junction near the lake and go straight on along the D537 to the right (do not cross the bridge), past Pellafol and La Posterle. Do not cross the Souloise river; turn into the Gillardes car park on the left.*

Eat and Drink: inexpensive, under €20; moderate, €20–€40; expensive, over €40

Above Water gushing up between the rocks at the Sources des Gillardes

⑫ Sources des Gillardes

Near Pellafol, Isère, Rhône-Alpes; 38970

Deep in the forest on the border of the Isère and Haute-Alpes region, the Souloise springs up from the mountainous ridges of the Col de Rabou, and runs down along the valley and into the Lac du Sautet. There are many walks and picnic spots along its banks. Along its course it passes gaping calcareous (chalky) canyons and the surging waters of the Sources des Gillardes.

A 30–90 minute walking tour

The walk is ideal for dry, sunny days. It must be avoided during periods of snow or frost. At the end of the bridge over the Souloise river there is the car park. Next to this is the riverside forest **picnic area** ①, a glorious place to sit, stroll and picnic. After lunch, cross the road from the picnic area towards the forested banks of the Souloise river. Several marked walking trails start out from here through the Souloise valley. By the road is an initial sign for the Sentier de Découverte. Up a gentle slope there is a cluster of signs which point in various directions. Take the direction of the arrow pointing to Pellafol la Posterle, Les Gillardes and Les Gorges de l'Infernet, all of which are along the same trail. Within a short distance the trail leads to the **Sources des Gillardes** ②. Described as a Vauclusian spring, the water resurges under pressure from the bedrock through deep passageways to form a swelling surface pool. The

area is hemmed in by the limestone cliffs of the Grand Bréchon, woodland and pine forest. A panel in French explains how the landscape was shaped by water: the Pellafol plateau was once covered in an immense glacial lake; waters from the melting ice eroded the plateau, creating a giant trough along the sides of the Souloise.

Ramble around the sides of the river to see the Gillardes, the river and forest from different angles. The forest is composed mostly of black and Scots pines and beech trees. The fauna is particularly diverse: there are many birds, including the rare Aigle Royale, peregrine falcons and the crow-like alpine chough. Game animals include chamois, red deer and roe deer. Return from here, along either side of the river, or continue along the left bank of the river to the **Canyon de l'Infernet** ③, a section of the Souloise where its turquoise waters are set in a deep, narrow ravine. From here, take the

WHERE TO STAY

AROUND SOURCES DES GILLARDES

Les Gachets Chambres d'hôtes
inexpensive
Natural Danish design meets French provincial in this farmhouse, 6 km (4 miles) after Cordéac, of wood and stone, colour-washed walls and iron furniture. Breakfast on home-made breads, buns and jams. The hosts, on request, will organize a full *table d'hôte*. Solar-heated water adds to the very strong eco-bent. Reservations essential.
Cordéac, 38710; 04 76 34 90 91; www.gachets-trieves.fr

AROUND CLELLES-EN-TRIÈVES

Hôtel Au Gai Soleil du Mont Aiguille
inexpensive
Loved by the hiking crowd, this welcoming hotel, 6 km (4 miles) west of Clelles-en-Trièves, occupies an incredible location right at the foot of Mont Aiguille, at the tiny hamlet of la Richardière – an offshoot of the village of Chichilianne. The rooms are spic and span, and comfortable. The restaurant serves seasonal specialties of the Trièves, and the Vercors: home-made *foie gras*, Dauphiné ravioles and chicken with shrimp.
La Richardière, Chichilianne, 38930; 04 76 34 41 71; www.hotelgaisoleil.com

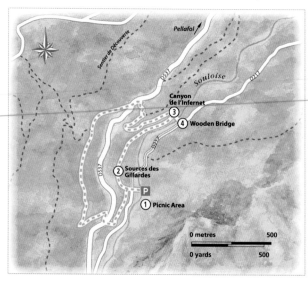

small **wooden bridge** ④ across the river and return to the picnic area along the right bank to reach the car park.

The walk can be extended along the banks following the signs for Pellafol-par-la-Souloise. The ghost town of Pellafol occupies a geological site shaped by water erosion and gullying, which also created several fascinating landforms, including "les Ruines", a reference not to the abandoned village but to the startling rock forms.

🚗 *Return along the D537, pass Pellafol and turn left into the D66A. Continue on the D66 to Mens. From there take the D526 in the direction of Clelles. About midway between Mens and Clelles, turn off to the left onto the D216 in the direction of Prebois, and then almost immediately again to the left, there is a signposted road into the Terre Vivante ecological centre.*

⑬ Terre Vivante
Isère, Rhône-Alpes; 38710
Founded 30 years ago by French engineer-ecologist Claude Aubert, Terre Vivante *(open daily May–late-Oct)*, is a practical ecology centre which exhibits and teaches organic gardening techniques, composting, green living and ecological house construction in a lively, interactive manner. Once an abandoned farm, the terrain was converted into an enchanting garden surrounded by the mountain peaks of the Trièves. Wander at will along different circuits and through the gardens and ethnically varied ecological houses. There are also guided visits at 2pm and gardening workshops at 4pm plus many special weekend events and workshops.
🚗 *Descend back down to the D526. Turn left and continue to Clelles.*

⑭ Clelles-en-Trièves
Isère, Rhône-Alpes; 38930
Nineteenth-century French writer Jean Giono was in awe of the "cloister of mountains" around the village. The vision of Mont Aiguille is incredible, especially as a sunlit silhouette. Drive down the main street of Clelles to the fountain on Place de la Mairie, past the small wooden cinema sign strung between the church steeple and a wooden bucket of flowers. There are many walks in the immediate area, village and countryside strolls. Drop by the tourist office at the Place de la Mairie for more information. All climbs in the vicinity of Mont Aiguille start from the hamlet of La Richardière near neighbouring Chichilianne.

Top Church steeple standing tall above the roofline of Clelles-en-Trièves **Above** Organic garden at Terre Vivante **Left** Exhibits within Terre Vivante

EAT AND DRINK

CLELLES-EN-TRIÈVES

Le Meli-Melo *inexpensive*
This restaurant-bar serves traditional food, and *plats du jour* at lunchtime. *Le Bourg, 38930; 04 76 34 42 31; closed Wed dinner*

AROUND CLELLES-EN-TRIÈVES

Café de la Page *inexpensive*
A local village café, with regional fare. *Percy, 38930; 04 76 34 31 61*

DAY TRIP OPTIONS
The first day trip is best undertaken from Villard-de-Lans. Trièves and Lac du Sautet respectively are ideal bases for the last two day trips.

Dramatic ravines
Head to the dramatic Vercors ravines of the Gorges de la Bourne ❷, from Villard-de-Lans ❶. On the way back drive up to Corrençon-en-Vercors, a plateau-top ski station.

Take the D531 from Villard-de-Lans to the Gorges de la Bourne. Corrençon-en-Vercors can be reached via the D215C.

Ecology and gardening
While outdoor enthusiasts may want to tackle Mont Aiguille, a softer day-trip option is the ecological and gardening center Terre Vivante ⑬. Ideal for children, it also has a lot on offer for adults. Visit the gardens, picnic and participate in organic gardening demonstrations.

To reach Mont Aiguille from Clelles, cross the D1075 and take the D7 towards Chichilianne. Then follow the signs to the La Richardière from where the walk "Pas de l'Aiguille" begins. Follow the directions in the itinerary for Terre Vivante.

Lakes and parks
In the lakeside camping area in Corps, families can boat, swim and sun. At Lac du Sautet's ⑪ nautical centre visitors can hire canoes, paddle boats and kayaks. There is also a picnic area and children's park with an aquatic playground. The adventurous can set out on the *Via Ferrata*, a mountain route equipped with fixed cables 5 minutes from the lake.

Follow the directions as per the itinerary. From the lake and Barrage du Sautet, cross the Pont du Sautet and take the D537 to reach Corps.

Eat and Drink: inexpensive, under €20; moderate, €20–€40; expensive, over €40

Volcanoes of the Auvergne

Clermont-Ferrand to Salers

Highlights

- **Spectacular summit**
  Get an overview of the volcanic mountains from the Puy de Dôme

- **Pas de Peyrol and Puy Mary**
  Drive up to France's highest road pass and climb the steps to the summit

- **Renaissance town**
  Stroll around the handsome mountain town of Salers

- **Cheeses galore**
  Taste and buy Cantal and the Auvergne's many other cheeses

View of the eroded volcanic Roche Tuilière and Roche Sanadoire from the Col de Guéry

Volcanoes of the Auvergne

Reminders of the Auvergne's turbulent geological past are everywhere along this route which travels north to south through Parc Naturel Régional des Volcans d'Auvergne. Near the beginning and the end of the itinerary there are spectacular ascents to the summits of Puy de Dôme and Puy Mary. In between, the route climbs over several mountain passes and runs past crags of solidified lava and glassy crater lakes. The natural landscape is enlivened by medieval towns and villages characterized by their castles and churches. When visitors stop for lunch, Cantal cheese, for which the Auvergne is renowned, is sure to be on the menu.

0 kilometres 10

0 miles 10

Above Breathtaking view of the summit of Puy Mary, *see p160* **Below right** Doorway of the church in Salers, *see p161* **Below far right** Fontaine d'Amboise in Clermont-Ferrand, *see p158*

ACTIVITIES

Put on tough boots and go hiking; there are well-marked trails at all levels of difficulty

Savour the renowned cheeses from the Cantal, and other parts of the Auvergne

Explore the region's heritage of exquisite Romanesque churches

Take a trial hang-gliding flight from the top of a volcano

Go wildflower-spotting at high altitudes

Spend a day in Vulcania theme park and have fun while learning about volcanoes

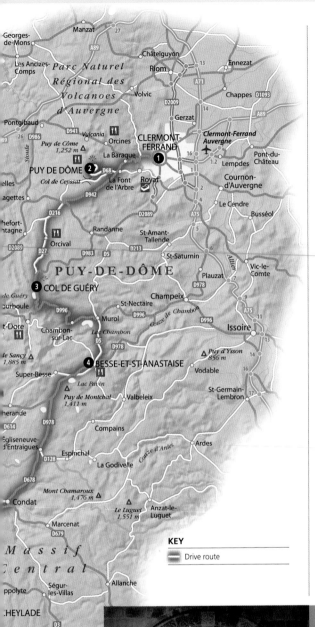

PLAN YOUR DRIVE

Start/finish: Clermont-Ferrand to Salers.

Number of days: 3, allowing time to walk around the Puy de Dôme's summit and climb to the top of Puy Mary.

Distances: 190 km (120 miles).

Road conditions: There are several *cols* (passes) on the route and the higher ones may be blocked by snow in winter. A sign on the approach road will tell whether it is *ouvert* (open to traffic) or *fermé* (closed). The Pas de Peyrol is closed between October and April.

When to go: May to October.

Opening hours: Monuments and museums are generally open from 10am to 6pm. Most sights close on Monday or Tuesday and on public holidays.

Main market days: Besse-et-St-Anastaise: Mon; **Salers:** Wed.

Shopping: The Auvergne's most popular purchases are edible: cheese, honey, home-made cakes and Riom-ès-Montagne's gentian liqueur. Also shop for enamelwork, pottery and carved stone or wooden objects.

Major festivals: Clermont-Ferrand: International Short Film Festival, late-Jan/early-Feb. Salers: Fête de la Vache et du Fromage (cheese festival), Aug.

DAY TRIP OPTIONS

Families will enjoy a day out in Vulcania; **mountain lovers** will admire the view from the Puy de Dôme; **keen drivers** will enjoy the drive through Pas de Peyrol. For details, *see p161*.

Above Detail of a stained-glass window in the cathedral at Clermont-Ferrand **Below** Ruins of the Gallo-Roman Temple de Mercure, Puy de Dôme

❶ Clermont-Ferrand
Puy-de-Dôme, Auvergne; 63000

Clermont is one of the oldest cities of France. It was one of the largest towns of Roman Gaul, and became an episcopal seat in the 5th century. In 1095 Pope Urban II proclaimed the First Crusade here. In 1630 the town was allied with neighbouring Montferrand, which belonged to the Counts of Auvergne. Together they evolved into today's conurbation which surrounds a volcanic mound on which stands the distinctive Cathédrale Nôtre-Dame-de-l'Assomption, built entirely of black lava. Nearby is the town's oldest fountain, the 16th-century Fontaine d'Amboise, while downhill stands the Romanesque church of **Nôtre-Dame-du-Port**, another architectural treasure.

🚗 *Follow signs for Limoges on Rue Fontgiève and Avenue Raymond Bergougnan, then signs for Puy de Dôme on the D941. At the crossroads in La Baraque, drive straight onto the D942. At La Font de l'Arbre, turn right onto the D68 to reach the Puy de Dôme.*

❷ Puy de Dôme
Puy-de-Dôme, Auvergne; 63870

This unmistakeable volcanic hump looming over Clermont-Ferrand was formed 11,000 years ago by three volcanic eruptions, the last two spewing viscous flows of lava that filled in the crater caused by the first and rounding off the mountain. The views from the top on a clear day takes in around 100 nearby volcanoes. Choose the day and time carefully as it is not worth ascending in low cloud or fog.

A one-hour walking tour

A road sign indicating steepness

Visitors can park their car and walk up the old Roman road, the Chemin des Muletiers, to the summit. It takes about 45 minutes to climb the 350-m (1,150-ft) track. Alternatively, a 15-minute train journey transports visitors to the entrance, where the **Visitor Centre** ① houses an information area, ticket office, restaurant, multi-media room and a shopping area. From the summit an arc of gentle, wooded volcanic hills curves away. These are the southern peaks of the Chaine des Puys. Puy de Dôme also belongs to this range. Turn left (west) and follow the *chemin de ronde* (circuit path), to circle the summit clockwise. The Monts-Dore to the southwest soon come into view. Standing out from them is the Puy de Sancy, (1,885 m/6,185 ft), the highest mountain in the Massif Central. Far behind the Puy de Sancy are the Monts du Cantal. Keep going clockwise around the western rim of the summit. The next viewpoint is to the northwest. Beyond the wooded Puy de Côme (1,252 m/4,108 ft), the artificial volcanic cone of Vulcania theme park *(see p161)* is visible. A little further round, (north to north-east) look down upon Puy de Pariou (1,189 m/3,900 ft), a perfect cinder cone with a crater.

The path now goes around the summit of the Puy de Dôme on which stands a **meterological observatory** ②. The site is scientifically symbolic as it was here, in 1648, that polymath Blaise Pascal sent his brother-in-law to take measurements to prove how atmospheric pressure changed with altitude. A **television mast** ③ next to the observatory adds 89 m (292 ft) to the natural height of the mountain (1,465 m/4,806 ft).

The last view from the summit, to the east, is over Clermont-Ferrand with its black-stone cathedral standing proud. A little ahead are the excavated ruins of the Gallo-Roman **Temple de Mercure** ④, which was built in the early 2nd century AD. On 7 March 1911, aviator Eugène Renaux made history by landing a plane on top of the Puy de Dôme after flying for 5 hours from Paris. He did it in response to a challenge by the Michelin brothers, tyre manufacturers of Clermont-Ferrand. From the temple, retrace the route on the Chemin de Ronde.

🚗 *Retrace the route to the D942 and turn right for Mont-Dore. Take the third exit at the roundabout onto the D216, then the D27 for Orcival. At the next junction, turn* *right onto the D983 and look for signs for Col de Guéry.*

③ Col de Guéry
Puy-de-Dôme, Auvergne; 63240

From the Col de Guéry there is a stunning view of two volcanic outcrops. The Roche Tuilière, on the left, is composed of trachyte columns from the chimney of a ruined volcano. The Roche Sanadoire, on the right, is the remnant of a volcanic cone. A castle stood on its summit until destroyed by an earthquake in 1477.

🚗 *Continue on the D983 along the woods beside the Lac de Guéry. Turn left at the next junction onto the D996 passing Chambon-sur-Lac, with its Romanesque chapel, on the left. At Murol, turn right onto the D5 following signs for Besse.*

Above left Salers cow in lush Auvergne pastures **Above right** Romanesque chapel in Chambon-sur-Lac

---

Map

CHEMIN DE RONDE

Television Mast ③

② Meteorological Observatory

④ Temple de Mercure

CHEMIN DE RONDE

CHEMIN DE RONDE

🚂 Train Station

Visitor Centre ①

CHEMIN DES MULETIERS

P

| 0 metres | 100 |
| 0 yards | 100 |

ACTIVITIES IN THE AUVERGNE

Hiking and hang-gliding
www.auvergne-tourisme.info

WHERE TO EAT

PUY DE DÔME

Mont-Fraternité *moderate*
This restaurant with brasserie is located on top of the Puy de Dôme and offers great views. Regional specialities are served.
Orcines, 63870; 04 73 62 23 00; closed Mon & mid-Nov–mid-Apr

AROUND COL DE GUÉRY

Nôtre Dame *inexpensive*
This is a simple place to eat in Orcival, 9 km (6 miles) north of Col de Guéry. Specialities include trout and *tarte de myrtille* (bilberry pie) for dessert.
Orcival, 63210; 04 73 65 82 02; open daily; closed Jan & Dec

Eat and Drink: inexpensive, under €20; moderate, €20–€40; expensive, over €40

Above left Handsome buildings lining narrow streets in Besse-et-St-Anastaise
Above right Hanging baskets of flowers on a wooden door in Besse-et-St-Anastaise
Below Medieval Église St-Léger in the town of Cheylade

ACTIVITIES

Vulcania Theme Park
08 20 82 78 28; www.vulcania.com; open daily mid-Mar–mid-Nov; closed mid-Nov–mid-Mar, Mon and Tue Sep–Oct

WHERE TO STAY

AROUND CHEYLADE

St-Georges inexpensive
Thirteen kilometres (8 miles) north of Cheylade, this hotel is housed in a modernized 19th-century building in the middle of town. It also has a restaurant; a children's menu is available.
5 rue du Capitaine Chevalier, Riom-ès-Montagnes, 15400; 04 71 78 00 15; www.hotel-saint-georges.com

SALERS

Saluces inexpensive–moderate
This is the most charming of Salers' hotels with eight tastefully decorated rooms. Two chambres d'hôtes are available in an annexe across the street at a slightly cheaper price. The owner is extremely knowledgeable about the local area. Breakfast and teas are served but there is no restaurant.
Rue de la Martille, 15140; 04 71 40 70 82; www.hotel-salers.fr

AROUND SALERS

Hostellerie de la Maronne expensive
This is a hotel and restaurant (Les Jardins de Revel) in a quiet location, 6 km (3 miles) below Salers. Rooms have flat-screen TVs and Internet access. There is also a garden and swimming pool.
Le Theil, 15140; 04 71 69 20 33; www.maronne.com

④ Besse-et-St-Anastaise
Puy de Dôme, Auvergne; 63610
Built from a uniform grey volcanic stone on a solidified flow of lava, Besse-et-St-Anastaise (also sometimes known by its previous name of Besse-en-Chandesse) is a compact town of medieval and Renaissance houses standing on narrow, sloping streets. Its most significant buildings are a small château, a fortified gateway crowned by an octagonal belfry and a house where Marguerite de Valois supposedly stayed while fleeing from her husband, King Henry IV. Leave Besse on the D978 and at the roundabout which serves the ski resort of Super-Besse, make a short detour to the left to see **Lac Pavin**, a circular crater lake shrouded by trees, which can be easily circumnavigated in an hour's stroll. Furthur down the D978 is Égliseneuve-d'Entraigues, which has a Maison de la Fromage (cheese centre) that is open only in summer.

🚗 Continue on the D978. At Condat, turn right onto the D678 towards Riom-ès-Montagnes. Leave Riom on the D3. At the roundabout take the third exit onto the D49 and drive past the ruins of the Château d'Apchon and through St-Hippolyte to reach Cheylade.

⑤ Cheylade
Cantal, Auvergne; 15400
Stop at this little village to visit the Église St-Léger. Look up to see three vaults panelled with Naïve polychromatic paintings of flowers and mythological beasts. The church was rebuilt in the 15th century after having being ruined in the Hundred Years' War between the House of Valois and the House of Plantagenet. The stunning ceiling paintings are, however, a 17th-century addition.

🚗 Turn right from Cheylade onto the D62 towards Salers and Puy Mary. After Le Claux this road climbs to the head of the valley, through woods, to the Col de Serre (1,364 m/4,475 ft). Turn right here onto the D680 for the Pas de Peyrol and Salers. On reaching the Pas de Peyrol, turn right towards Salers and park in the space provided on the downward slope.

Volcanic France

The last volcanic eruption in the Auvergne, in the Chaine des Puys, was 7,000 years ago but many of the volcanoes are considered dormant rather than extinct. That is, another eruption at some point of time is "not improbable". No one can be more specific than that: where, when or how powerful it might be is anyone's guess.

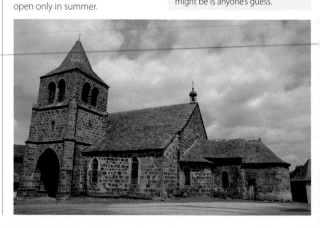

⑥ Pas de Peyrol

Cantal, Auvergne; 15400

The Pas de Peyrol is a cramped three-way crossroads with barely enough space to accommodate a Visitor Centre and a bar-restaurant. A flight of broad concrete steps sets off from here to the summit of Puy de Mary above. Allow 20–30 minutes to get to the top, where there are cairns and a viewing table.

🚗 *From the pass continue on the D680, through forests, with occasional views on the right. Fork left, uphill, still on the D680, for Salers. The trees eventually clear before the Col de Neronne (1,242 m/4,075 ft) emerges. Continue straight on, high above the Maronne valley to the left, to reach the next stop, Salers.*

⑦ Salers

Cantal, Auvergne; 15140

In 1550, the modest town of Salers was chosen to be the seat of the bailiff – the official charged with the dispensation of justice on behalf of the king – for the Auvergne mountains. This act transformed the town's fortunes as it attracted well-off families to settle here. They built themselves houses out of the dark volcanic stone. The bailiwick disappeared with the French Revolution of 1789, but Salers has managed to survive as a harmonious collection of vernacular Renaissance architecture superimposed on a medieval street plan. The town's church has exquisite polychromatic tombs dating back to 1495.

Above Calm waters of Lac Pavin, surrounded by lush green vegetation **Below** Pas de Peyrol and the summit of Puy de Mary

WHERE TO EAT

BESSE-ET-ST-ANASTAISE

Hotel de la Providence et de la Poste *inexpensive*
Restaurant with a shady terrace where Auvergne specialities are served.
2 rue de l'Abbé Blot, 63610; 04 73 79 51 49; www.hotel-providence-besse.com

AROUND CHEYLADE

Le Chalet du Puy Mary
inexpensive–moderate
Located down the D62, 6 km (4 miles) from Cheylade, this place offers an inexpensive daily menu.
Le Claux, 15400; 04 71 20 82 81; www.lepuymary.com; open May–Nov

SALERS

Templiers *inexpensive–moderate*
The most popular restaurant in Salers with Cantal cheese specialities on the menu.
Rue de Couvent, 15140; 04 71 40 71 35

DAY TRIP OPTIONS

Clermont-Ferrand (on the A71) and Salers (take the D680 from the D922) are the best bases for day trips in southwestern Auvergne.

Volcanic theme park
Devote the better part of the day to visiting Vulcania. As well as being an educational family outing, this is also a useful wet-weather option since most of the displays are indoors. Visitors can just enjoy the rides and activities or use it to understand the formation of the landscapes.

Leave Clermont-Ferrand as for the tour but turn right at the crossroads

in Orcines onto the 941. Vulcania is signposted off this road. Retrace the route to return to the city.

Amazing volcanoes
Ascend the Puy de Dôme ② for an incomparable view and then visit Orcival and Murol.

Using Clermont-Ferrand as a base, follow the tour route out of the city and up the Puy de Dôme. Continue on the route as far as Murol. Return to Clermont-Ferrand by the D5 (north) and turn right on the D2089.

Valleys and mountains
The town of Salers ⑦ makes a good base for touring the mountains and

valleys of the Cantal. Drive to the Pas de Peyrol ⑥ and then climb up to the Puy de Mary for great views.

Check the weather forecast with the tourist information office in Salers, and if the skies are clear drive the route in reverse up to the top of the Pas de Peyrol and walk to the summit of Puy Mary. Descend from the Pas de Peyrol into the Vallée de Mandailles on the D17. Turn off right on the D246. Turn right on the D35 and follow this road, becoming the D60, to Tournemire Take the D160 to meet the D922. Then turn right and right again on the D680 to return to Salers.

Eat and Drink: inexpensive, under €20; moderate, €20–€40; expensive, over €40

The Dordogne: Source to Sea

Puy de Sancy to Bourg-sur-Gironde

Highlights

- **Dramatic gorges**
  Explore the *cingles* and the gorges of the Dordogne

- **Romanesque and Gothic buildings**
  See the superb abbeys and churches of Beaulieu-sur-Dordogne, Mauriac and Souillac

- **Riverside villages and castles**
  Visit gloriously preserved riverside châteaux and medieval villages

- **Fine vineyards**
  Sample the wines from Bergerac and St-Émilion

Traditional *gabare* floats by on the Dordogne river at La Roque-Gageac

The Dordogne: Source to Sea

To many, the region around the Dordogne river offers an ideal image of summers spent walking through lush green hills, bathing in clear rivers, visiting châteaux and vineyards, and eating *confit de canard* (preserved duck), *foie gras* and truffles. However, the Dordogne is first and foremost a river. For centuries it was the only means of communication between mountains and sea, a busy waterway with trade in wine and wood, salt and spices. Following the course of the river brings the region's history and geography to life. Along the way visitors pass through some of France's finest wine regions, and can sample some of its best cuisine.

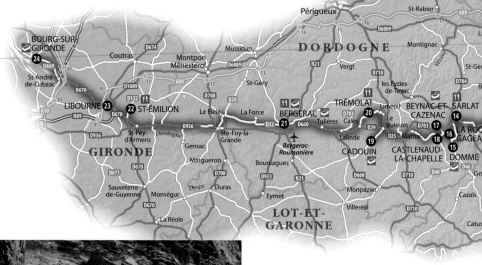

ACTIVITIES

Take a cure at the thermal spa of Le Mont-Dore

Ride in a *gabare*, a traditional river boat, from Argentat or La Roque-Gageac

Admire the Romanesque carving of the Église Abbatiale St-Pierre in Beaulieu-sur-Dordogne

Visit the châteaux of Beynac and Castelnaud

Canoe or swim in the gorges of the Dordogne river

Above Gothic cloisters of the monastery in Cadouin, *see p173* **Left** Golden-hued houses along the cliffside in La Roque-Gageac, *see p172* **Right** Aerial view of the château at Beynac-et-Cazenac by the Dordogne river, *see p172*

PUY-DE-DÔME

Puy de Dôme
1,464 m

St-Sauves-d'Auvergne
Les Gannes
Avèze
La
Bourboule
LE MONT-DORE ②
PUY DE SANCY ①
Super-Besse

Meymac
Ussel
Tauves
Trémouille-St-Loup
Picherande
Condat

Lestards
Egletons
CHÂTEAU DE VAL ③
Le Péage
BORT-LES-ORGUES ④
Champagnac

CORRÈZE
Seilhac
St-Merd-de-Lapleau
Pont de St-Projet
Saignes
Tulle

SPONTOUR-SUR-DORDOGNE ⑦
BASSIGNAC-LE-HAUT ⑧
⑥
MAURIAC ⑤
Cheylade

Brive-la-Gaillarde
Barrage du Chastang
Darazac
BARRAGE D'AIGLE
Saint Martin Valmeroux

ARGENTAT ⑨
Meyssac
Mercoeur
Montvert
CANTAL

BEAULIEU-SUR-DORDOGNE ⑩
Calviac
Aurillac

CARENNAC ⑫
CHÂTEAU DE CASTELNAU-BRETENOUX ⑪
Bretenoux
Cayrols

JILLAC
Gramat
Latronquière
Maurs

LOT
Le Bourg
Livernon

Labastide-Murat

0 kilometres 20

0 miles 20

KEY

Drive route

PLAN YOUR DRIVE

Start/finish: Puy de Sancy to Bourg-sur-Gironde.

Number of days: 6–7, allowing half a day to climb Puy de Sancy.

Distance: 500 km (300 miles).

Road conditions: Well maintained and signposted, with some steep winding roads around the gorges.

When to go: The best time is autumn or spring, since popular areas can be very busy in summer. However, in the upper reaches of the river, quiet spots can be found even in August.

Opening hours: Shops, churches and monuments are generally open from 10am to 6pm. National museums and sights are normally closed on Tuesdays. Always check the opening hours for private museums.

Main market days: Sarlat: Wed, Sat; Cadouin: Wed; Domme: Thu; Bergerac: Wed, Sat; Trémolat: Tue; St-Émilion: Sun; Libourne: Tue, Fri, Sun.

Shopping: Wine and luxury food like truffles, *foie gras*, cheese, walnuts and mushrooms are available.

Major festivals: Souillac: Souillac en Jazz, Jul; Sarlat: Festival des Jeux du Théâtre de Sarlat, Jul–Aug; Bergerac: Fêtes des Vendanges, Oct.

DAY TRIP OPTIONS

Nature lovers can visit the Puy de Sancy and Mauriac, while **wine lovers** can visit the vineyards along the Dordogne. For details, see p175.

Above Rocky ravine where the Dore and Dogne meet

Tourist Information
*Place de la Bourse, Clermont-Ferrand,
63038; 04 73 42 22 50; www.sancy.com*

Parking
Drive south on the D983 from Le
Mont-Dore and park at the foot of the
Station du Téléphérique.

WHERE TO STAY

LE MONT-DORE

Le Puy Ferrand *moderate*
Located below the Puy de Sancy,
this mountain hotel offers panoramic
views, wood fires and an indoor
swimming pool.
*Le Mont-Dore, 63240; 04 73 65 18 99;
www.hotel-puy-ferrand.com*

AROUND LE MONT-DORE

La Lauzeraie *moderate*
A cosy, friendly *chambre d'hotes*
outside La Bourboule, 7 km (4 miles)
west of Le Mont-Dore, this hotel offers
home-made produce.
*577 chemin de la Suchères, La
Bourboule, 63150; 04 73 81 15 70 ;
www.lalauzeraie.net*

➊ Puy de Sancy

Puy-de-Dôme, Auvergne; 63240

A cable car and a half-hour walk will bring visitors to the Puy de Sancy, the highest summit in central France at 1,885 m (6,184 ft) with a terrific panoramic view over the Massif Central. In a ravine down below, at an altitude of 1,350 m (4,429 ft), two little springs appear – the Dore and Dogne. They are soon joined by other tributaries and give rise to a new river, the Dordogne. The northern and southern slopes of the Puy de Sancy offer excellent winter sports opportunities drawing in many enthusiasts every year.

A one-hour walking tour

Climbing the Puy de Sancy has been a favourite excursion since the 19th century. The visitors who flocked to the Mont-Dore spa to take the curative waters revelled in the romantic experience of towering mountains. French novelist George Sand was one such visitor, describing the quest for the "profound harmony and solitude of nature". But even back then it was often too crowded in summer and Sand preferred spring or autumn, "when the damp grass smells good, the flowers are scattered with diamonds of water, and the cows gleam in the sun, like a Dutch painting." Today's visitors would do well to pay heed to her advice.

Formerly, visitors walked or rode on mules to the foot of the mountain. Now it is possible to ascend using the *téléphérique* (cable car), one of the first to be installed in France in the 1930s for the newly popular sport of skiing. From the **Station du Téléphérique** ➀ the cable car operates all year round, every day. In 10 minutes it ascends to an altitude of 1,780 m (6,126 ft) – a dramatic ride as visitors swing up the hillside with tiny goats and cows snoozing below.

Near where the cable car drops visitors off, there is a **restaurant** ➁ offering drinks and brasserie food with fine views from the terrace. From the restaurant, a further half-hour walk will bring walkers to the **summit** ➂. The path is well marked, and wooden steps make the going easy. From the summit they can enjoy the magnificent view over the volcanic cones, icy lakes and deep wooded valleys of the Auvergne. The orientation table

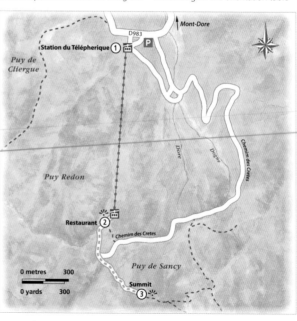

will help with the area's geography. On a clear day it is possible to see as far as the Alps. The Puy de Sancy is part of an ancient dormant volcano, once much higher than it is today. The mountain is part of what is now the Parc Naturel Régional des Volcans d'Auvergne *(see pp156–61)*, an area popular for walking, paragliding, climbing, and in winter, skiing. Visitors can return on the *téléphérique* or descend on foot on the well-indicated Chemin des Crêtes, which will take 2 hours. It is here on the northern slopes of the Puy de Sancy that the Dordogne rises. Seek out the rocky ravine at the foot of the peak, where two little springs appear, neatly labelled Dore, which means "water" in old Celtic, and Dogne. They trickle together over mossy stones and, fed by tributaries, the new river soon flows briskly down through the spa towns of Le Mont-Dore and La Bourboule.

🚗 *Follow the D983 north through Les Egravats to reach Le Mont-Dore.*

2 Le Mont-Dore
Puy-de-Dôme, Auvergne; 63240

Located on the right bank of the Dordogne river, Le Mont-Dore has been a spa since Roman times, revived during the Belle Époque when taking the waters was very fashionable. Now it can seem rather grim, all grey granite and white shutters. This perception changes, however, once visitors see the grand interior of the **Thermes** *(open Apr to Oct, closed Sun)* with its colonnades, Byzantine tiles and monumental staircase. From Le Mont-Dore, visitors can take a funicular railway (dating from 1898) to the Capucin plateau for walks and picnics. In winter, a blanket of snow transforms the Sancy area, which is popular for both downhill and cross-country skiing. The neighbouring spa of **La Bourboule** has ornate pink bridges and Art Nouveau flourishes to add a touch of frivolity to the granite.

🚗 *Leave Le Mont-Dore through La Bourboule, on the D130. At La Bourboule take the D996; at the junction before St-Sauves-d'Auvergne, turn left onto the D922 to Tauves. Then, for a first glimpse of the Dordogne gorges, turn right onto the D987 towards Avèze. At Les Gannes turn left onto the D73. Follow this winding route*

south until the D922, turning right after Trémouille-St-Loup. Turn right after 7 km (3 miles) at Le Péage to reach Château de Val.

3 Château de Val
Puy-de-Dôme, Auvergne; 15270

Château de Val with its six pepperpot towers is a romantic sight beside the lake, less so when visitors realize the lake was once a river and there are several drowned villages under the water. A photographic exhibition shows the progress of the building of the Bort-les-Orgues dam, and remnants of the villages, revealed when the lake was drained for maintenance. The château *(open Apr–mid-Oct, closed Tue)* is delightful, with Renaissance fireplaces, fine tapestries, and attics full of tools and old bedsteads.

🚗 *Drive back to the D922. Turn right and drive straight to Bort-les-Orgues.*

Above left Typical stone house in Le Mont-Dore **Above right** Château de Val with the lake below it **Below** Scenic spa town of La Bourboule near Le Mont-Dore

EAT AND DRINK

LE MONT-DORE

Le Bougnat *moderate*
Authentic hearty Auvergnat cuisine is served in the rustic interior of this restored shepherd's dwelling.
23 rue Georges Clemenceau; 04 73 65 28 19

AROUND LE MONT-DORE

Auberge Champêtre du Vergne-Noir *moderate*
This rustic restaurant in a converted farm outside La Bourboule, 7 km (4 miles) west of Le Mont-Dore, is well known for hearty terrines, local cheese and Auvergne wine.
La Bourboule, 63150; 04 73 65 28 19; closed Tue & Wed

Eat and Drink: inexpensive, under €20; moderate, €20–€40; expensive, over €40

Above Wooded gorges of the Dordogne near Bort-les-Orgues **Below** Houses built on the banks of the Dordogne river in Argentat

WHERE TO STAY

AROUND BORT-LES-ORGUES

Chateau de Bassignac *moderate*
About 9 km (5.5 miles) south of Bort-les-Ourges, this comfortable bed-and-breakfast is housed in a 16th-century slate-roofed manor house. It has a *ferme-auberge* next door.
Saignes,15240; 04 71 40 82 82; www. chateau-de-bassignac.fr; closed Nov–Apr

AROUND BASSIGNAC-LE-HAUT

Rendezvous des Pêcheurs *inexpensive*
Located 14 km (9 miles) north of Bassignac-le-Haut, this is a wonderful small hotel under shady trees right by the riverside. Excellent regional cuisine is served in the restaurant. The hotel is accessible by a winding route on the right bank via St-Merd-de-Lapleau following the D978 and the D13.
Pont du Chambon, St-Merd-de-Lapleau, 19320 ; 05 55 27 88 39; closed Nov–Feb

ARGENTAT

Hotel Fouillade *inexpensive*
A traditional family hotel in a19th-century mansion, with a cosy restaurant (with a fireplace in winter) that serves local delicacies such as *escargot* (snails) and ceps stuffed with sorrel.
Place Gambetta, 19400; 05 55 28 10 17; www.fouillade.com; closed Dec

④ Bort-les-Orgues
Corrèze, Limousin; 19110
The largest of the Dordogne dams, Bort-les-Orgues is a dramatic sight. It is 120 m (394 ft) high with a reservoir 21 km (13 miles) long. The dam controls the flow of water and generates enough hydroelectricity to supply power to over 77,000 homes. Visitors can see the huge lake, the amphitheatre of the dam and the drop to the gorge below. Located in the valley at the foot of the dam is the small town that lends its name to the dam. The river now carves its way down in a huge curve through the deep ravines of the Dordogne gorges.

🚗 *Follow the D922 out of town and turn right onto the D15. Drive through Chassagne and cross the river at Pont de Vernéjoux; once on the right bank of the river, turn left onto the D168. Join the D982 (which becomes the D682 accross the river), and cross the river at Pont de St-Projet. Turn left onto the D678 for Mauriac.*

⑤ Mauriac
Cantal, Limousin; 15200
Mauriac was a pilgrimage town in the Middle Ages, and the remains of its 11th-century Benedictine **Monastère St-Pierre** can still be seen. The **Basilique Nôtre-Dame-des-Miracles** *(open daily)* is a huge Romanesque church with a 12th-century octagonal belltower, superb carvings on the tympanum and a beautiful carved font inside. The town is home to many other handsome old buildings, including the **Hôtel d'Orcet**, built between the 15th and 18th centuries. Mauriac is also famous for its cattle market, trading mainly Salers cows, whose milk produces the renowned Fourme de Cantal and Salers cheeses.

🚗 *Retrace the route to the D682. Take the D105 at the next junction and then turn right onto the D16 to cross the Barrage d'Aigle.*

⑥ Barrage d'Aigle
Cantal, Limousin; 15200
The Aigle dam, spanning a dizzying drop deep in the river ravine, is also known as the Resistance Dam. It was begun in 1938, but French Resistance efforts slowed down its construction and hence the Nazis were unable to use its power. The dam did not start operations until 1945. A footpath along the gorge offers spectacular views. From Aigle there is a narrow road which closely follows the river, glimpsed tantalizingly between the chestnut trees that line the banks.

🚗 *Retrace the route to the D105 and turn right on the D678 which becomes the D978. Cross the river into Spontour.*

Where to Stay: inexpensive, under €70; moderate, €70–€150; expensive, over €150

7 Spontour-sur-Dordogne
Corrèze, Limousin; 19550

Until the dams were built, Spontour-sur-Dordogne was a major river port. The Dordogne provided an important means of transport. Trees were cut from the surrounding forests and taken down to the lower Dordogne to make stakes for the vines. It was here that the *gabares* were constructed, flat-bottomed boats which were skillfully manouevred down the river. Today the town, with its stone roofed houses and church spire, sleeps quietly beside the Dordogne; nostalgic *gabare* trips are all that is left of its once vital role in river life.

🚗 *Drive back across the river onto the D978, then a sharp right onto the D75. Continue to Darazac, then turn right onto the D13 to Bassignac-le-Haut.*

8 Bassignac-le-Haut
Corrèze, Limousin; 19220

The D13 abandons the river gorges near the little village of Bassignac-le-Haut, zigzagging to the uplands above. Around here, visitors will find small, self-contained villages, limestone replacing the granite of the Auvergne, but still with steeply pitched roofs of lauze stones and surrounded by rich pastures roamed by well-fed cows. Stop at the tiny village of Bassignac-le-Haut to see a remarkable Romanesque sculpture, a 16th-century limestone cross outside the church. The cross has deeply incised carvings of scenes from the life of Christ, endearing in their naivety, and astonishingly preserved from any damage.

🚗 *From the village follow the D13, then turn right onto the D75 at*

Darazac. Further down the road turn right onto the D29, to the Barrage du Chastang, for a splendid view of the dam and the river. From Chastang turn right onto the D129 which runs alongside the river, until it widens out at Argentat.

9 Argentat
Corrèze, Limousin; 19400

The town of Argentat is situated at the junction of three regions: Midi-Pyrénées, Limousin and Auvergne. This was once a key river port, where boats went downstream with wood, chestnuts, butter, cheese and skins, and returned with oil, wine, walnuts and salt. Visitors can still see the cobbled quays and houses built right next to the river; note the *maisons à bolet*, riverside houses with a roofed balcony connected with the garden at the back of the house. The first bridge was built here in 1829; before that, the Dordogne river could only be crossed by wading through it or by ferry. It is a delightful town to wander around, with its maze of streets. There is still evidence all around town of the coopers, carpenters and tanners who once made their living here. Now there are cafés and restaurants on the quays and *gabare* river trips available. Argentat has also emerged as a great destination for sports and outdoor activities, including golf, paragliding, rock-climbing and watersports.

🚗 *Take the D116 out of town. Turn right onto the D940 and cross the river to Beaulieu-sur-Dordogne.*

Above Water gushing out of the massive Barrage d'Aigle on the Dordogne **Left** Sixteenth-century limestone carving in Bassignac-le-Haut **Below** Dordogne river flows between the slopes, Bort-les-Orgues

ACTIVITIES IN ARGENTAT

Office de Tourisme d'Argentat
Place da Maïa,19400; 05 55 28 16 05; www.tourisme-argentat.com

EAT AND DRINK

MAURIAC

Ecu de France *moderate*
Originally a post house built in the 1880s, this hotel-restaurant has retained the building's charm and typical Auvergne style. A varied menu of superb quality is available.
6 avenue Charles Périé, 15200; 04 71 67 36 77; closed Mon lunch

Above Charming house in Beaulieu-sur-Dordogne **Below** Busy market scene in front of Église Sainte-Marie, Sarlat

WHERE TO STAY

BEAULIEU-SUR-DORDOGNE

Les Charmilles *inexpensive*
This is a hotel with a terrace restaurant on the banks of the Dordogne.
20 boulevard Saint Rodolphe; 05 55 91 29 29; www.auberge-charmilles.com

Manoir de Beaulieu *moderate*
A recently renovated traditional hotel on the main square, this has antique furniture, an open wood fire in the bar, a restaurant and a swimming pool.
4 place Champs de Mars ; 05 55 91 01 34; www.manoirdebeaulieu.com

AROUND CARENNAC

La Farga *moderate*
This bed-and-breakfast is located in the village of Carennac, next to the river. It has a magnificent terrace, garden and heated swimming pool. A *table d'hote* is available every day.
Le Bourg, 46110; 05 65 33 18 97; www.lafarga.wordpress.com

Moulin du Goth *moderate*
On the route between Carennac and Souillac, Moulin du Goth is housed in a restored 13th-century watermill. It has a large pond and a garden.
Creysse, 46600; 05 65 32 26 04; www.moulindugoth.com

AROUND SOUILLAC

Château de la Treyne *expensive*
About 7 km (4 miles) from Souillac, this magnificent white château is set in parkland above the river. Tennis and canoeing facilities are available.
Lacave, 46200; 05 65 27 60 60; www.chateaudelatreyne.com

Le Pont de l'Ouysse *expensive*
Located 11 km (7 miles) from Souillac, Le Pont de l'Ouysse is not far from the caves of Lacave. Enjoy an atmosphere of casual luxury and superb food.
Lacave, 46200; 05 65 37 87 04; www.lepontdelouysse.fr

⑩ Beaulieu-sur-Dordogne
Corrèze, Limousin; 19120

The Dordogne river is broader and more stately here, winding across limestone country to the alluvial plain, and fields of strawberries, maize and the first vines. Beaulieu is a fine town, with two strawberry crops a year (the thin *gariguette* in spring, and the fragrant *maras de bois* later in the year), and a magnificent abbey. The town nestles in a loop of the river, here running shallow over gravel. Visitors can see the walls of the original monastery, fine stone buildings and wood-framed houses with overhanging eaves.

Beaulieu was on the pilgrimage route of Santiago de Compostela, and the Romanesque Gothic **Église Abbatiale St-Pierre** still has relics from those days. There is a fantastically carved doorway. The tympanum depicts the Last Judgment, complete with the dead lifting the stones of their tombs. The supporting columns are carved with figures bent under the weight of the tympanum, their bodies elegantly elongated to fit the space.

🚗 *Cross the river again and follow the D940 southwards to Bretenoux.*

Carved church column, Beaulieu

Then take the D14 further south to Castelnau-Bretenoux.

⑪ Château de Castelnau-Bretenoux
Lot, Limousin; 46130

The Château de Castelnau-Bretenoux *(open daily Apr–Sep; closed Tue Oct–Mar)*, an imposing keep of dramatic red limestone that dominates the skyline, is surrounded by an immaculately restored village with houses of the same red stone. The castle was originally built during the 13th century with three main buildings around an internal courtyard and was remodelled in the 15th century. It is filled with medieval sculptures and a huge variety of furniture and *objets d'art*.

🚗 *Continue on the D14 until arriving at a junction. Turn right onto the D30 which becomes the D20; fork right onto the D43 for the next stop, Carennac.*

⑫ Carennac
Lot, Limousin; 46110

Carennac, a monastic village on the riverside which grew up around a 12th-century priory, has been quite

Where to Stay: inexpensive, under €70; moderate, €70–€150; expensive, over €150

beautifully restored, and is a favourite location for weddings. Within its walls of soft ochre limestone is an extraordinary ensemble of rooftops, the slate of the mountains now giving way to terracotta tiles. Stop by the fine 16th-century **Château des Doyens** and the **Église St-Pierre** with a superbly carved tympanum. There are Romanesque and Gothic cloisters, and a chapter house with a collection of 15th-century statuary.

🚗 *Follow the D43, then turn right onto the D840 to cross the river at Gluges, where there are views from Belvédère de Copeyre. Once across the river, turn left onto the D43, then left onto the D23, which becomes the D14 after Creysse. Turn right onto the D15, left onto the D96 to Pinsac and then right onto the D43 to reach Souillac.*

Disposable Boats

From the Middle Ages onwards there was a huge demand for timber from the upper Dordogne, in particular for the oak casks required for wine. Floating the timber down, however, was hazardous and damaging to the wood, so an ingenious idea arose: boats, named *courpets*, were built to carry the cask wood, and then they were simply broken up and sold for firewood at the journey's end, or reused for building houses. The crew then returned home on foot.

⑬ Souillac
Lot, Limousin; 46200

Souillac is situated in the Périgord, where the river makes great shining loops through a rich green land, with fairy-tale châteaux dominating the limestone cliffs above and poplars shading the banks. Souillac is worth a visit for its very special **Église Abbatiale Sainte-Marie** with its three enormous cupolas visible against the skyline. Much restoration work has been done here, after the depredations of the Wars of Religion in the 16th century. A notable example is the entrance door, now protected inside the church, with its superb Romanesque bas-reliefs. Look especially at the carvings of Abraham, Isaac and Isaiah on the pillars.

🚗 *Take the D804, then the D703. Then turn right onto the D704 to Sarlat.*

⑭ Sarlat
Corrèze, Limousin; 24200

One of the first towns in France to be protected for its architecture, Sarlat is a gorgeous ensemble of Renaissance and medieval buildings where visitors can really get a feel of the past. Discover the narrow lanes, arched passages and fine town houses of richly carved ochre stone, the **Place de la Liberté**, the **Cathédrale St-Sacerdos** and the **Bishops' Palace**. Sarlat is famous for its markets and shopping. Make sure not to miss the **Église Sainte-Marie**, renovated in 2001 by architect Jean Nouvel. Now used as a marketplace, it is one of the best places to buy *foie gras*, the local delicacy.

🚗 *Take the D46 southwards and cross the river at Vitrac, to Domme.*

Above left Cascading petunias adding colour to a medieval building in Sarlat **Above right** Gothic cloisters of the Église St-Pierre in Carennac **Below** Red limestone house in Castelnau-Bretenoux

EAT AND DRINK

SOUILLAC

La Vieille Auberge *moderate*
This is an old riverside inn serving local delicacies such as truffles and artichokes stuffed with *foie gras*.
1 rue de la Récège, 46200; 05 65 32 79 43; www.la-vieille-auberge.com; closed mid-Nov–mid-Feb

SARLAT

La Madeleine *moderate*
One of Sarlat's best hotel-restaurants, La Madeleine is housed in a fine 19th-century building in the old town. It serves top-notch regional cuisine.
1 place de Petite Rigaudie, 24200; 05 53 59 10 41; www.plaza-madeleine.fr; closed Jan–mid-Mar

Eat and Drink: inexpensive, under €20; moderate, €20–€40; expensive, over €40

15 Domme

Dordogne, Aquitaine; 24250

The fortified village of Domme offers a wonderful panorama of the Dordogne from its clifftop position. Founded in 1281, the town saw many upheavals through the Hundred Years' War and later the Wars of Religion. It retains its defensive structure with the two stone towers of the **Porte des Tours** guarding the town's entrance. Domme is a classic *bastide* (fortified town) with streets in a geometric pattern round the market square and little alleys between the houses. The cliff beneath the village is riddled with caves which can be visited. During World War II, the caves provided hiding places for members of the Resistance.

🚗 *Leave the village on the D46 and cross the river and turn left onto the D703 to reach La Roque-Gageac.*

16 La Roque-Gageac

Dordogne, Aquitaine; 24250

La Roque-Gageac is a village strung along the cliffside, appearing as if it has simply morphed out of the stone. The golden-hued houses of this sleepy little village are reflected serenely in the water, but it was once an important port bustling with boatmen and merchants. Visitors can still see the riverside houses with their ground floor cellars constructed for storage of goods waiting to be transported downriver. Today, pleasure trips are offered in traditional *gabares*.

🚗 *Continue along the D703 to arrive at Beynac-et-Cazenac.*

Above Row of houses in La Roque-Gageac
Above right Ornate windows of a house in Domme **Below** Grand and majestic château at Beynac-et-Cazenac

WHERE TO STAY

DOMME

L'Esplanade *moderate*
Ask for a room with a view in this fabulous hotel overlooking the Dordogne. Enjoy the vistas, too, from the dining room, where diners can try all the rich local delicacies of the region, including lamb and *foie gras*.
2 rue Pontcarral, Le Bourg, 24250; 05 53 28 31 41; http://esplanade-perigord.com

BEYNAC-ET-CAZENAC

Manoir de la Malatrie *moderate*
This elegant manor house hotel, decorated in typical 19th-century French style, has views of the Dordogne river from the terrace. Excellent breakfasts are available.
Vézac, 24220; 05 53 29 03 51; www.chambresdhotes-lamalatrie.com

CADOUIN

Manoir de Bellerive *expensive*
This hotel is housed in a splendid manor house built by Napoleon III, with a galleried entrance and huge staircase. Rooms are luxurious and service is attentive. There is a restaurant with specialities such as Quercy lamb.
Route de Siorac, Le Buisson de Cadouin, 24480; 05 53 22 16 16; www.bellerivehotel.com

17 Beynac-et-Cazenac

Dordogne, Aquitaine; 24220

A little further downstream is Beynac-et-Cazenac, a fortified village clinging to a precipice above the river, and clustered around the **Château de Beynac** (*open daily*). It was in 1827 that the communes of Beynac and Cazenac were merged to form this village. The château is a favourite film set; it was used for Luc Besson's 1999 *The Messenger: The Story of Joan of Arc*. It has an atmospheric interior, with its great halls, towers and frescoed chapel, lit with torches and furnished with great wooden chests. The ongoing restoration work is equally authentic; young men hammer stones into mortar, a method unchanged since the château was built.

🚗 *Retrace the route on the D703 until the right turn onto the D57 to cross the river. Turn right onto the D53 to visit the two very special châteaux at Castelnaud.*

Where to Stay: inexpensive, under €70; moderate, €70–€150; expensive, over €150

⑱ Castelnaud-la-Chapelle
Dordogne, Aquitaine; 24250
The medieval village is so steeply stacked around the **Château de Castelnaud** that one of the tiled roofs bears a notice: "This is a roof. Please do not sit on it." The château passed back and forth between the French and English during the Hundred Years' War, and was finally yielded to the French after a siege in 1442, for 400 gold ecus. It houses the **Museum of Medieval Warfare** (open daily), which has an amazing collection of armour and weaponry, with real cannon at the windows and reconstructions of siege catapults on the battlements. The museum also exhibits furniture from the period. Models and videos explain the various methods in which the building was protected over the years. There are panoramic views of the river from the château.

From Castelnaud follow the D53 along the river for 6 km (4 miles) to the beautiful **Château des Milandes** (closed Sat Apr–Jun and Sep, Oct–Mar). François de Caumont, Lord of Castelnaud, built it in 1489 for his wife. After the French Revolution, the estate passed through the hands of several owners. In 1947, dancer and vaudeville star Josephine Baker bought the property to house her rainbow tribe of adopted children from all over the world. The château has been stunningly restored; visitors can see her magnificent salon and dining rooms, bedrooms and six bathrooms, two of which featured the same colours as her favourite perfumes. There is a terrific collection of memorabilia, dresses, letters, photographs, and even her famous banana skirt. Baker spent extravagantly on the château and its surrounding properties, but eventually went broke. A poignant photograph shows her locked outside the kitchen, barefoot in her dressing-gown, after she was finally thrown out. The new chatelaine, Angelique de St-Exupéry, is committed to honouring the memory of Josephine Baker, and projects are underway to raise a statue to her, and also to fund a village for orphaned children and widows in Rwanda.

🚗 **Continue along the D53 and at the junction turn right onto the D50. After** crossing Marnac, turn left onto the D703. At the crossroads, drive straight across, onto the D25 to Le Buisson-de-Cadouin and Cadouin.

⑲ Cadouin
Dordogne, Aquitaine; 24480
The Cistercian monastery of Cadouin was long one of the Périgord's most famous pilgrimage sites, with devotees flocking to see the relic of Christ's shroud. After the shroud was definitively deemed inauthentic in 1934 the pilgrimages stopped, but contemporary visitors can still enjoy the austere calm of the church and the intricately carved capitals of the Gothic cloisters.

🚗 **Retrace the route to Le Buisson-de-Cadouin. Turn left onto the D51 and cross the river twice to reach Limeuil. Turn left onto the D31 that goes around the Cirque de Trémolat to Trémolat.**

Dams on the Dordogne
Several huge dams have tamed the Dordogne river since they were constructed in the 1940s and 50s. They control water flow, function as reservoirs and supply electricity. In fact, these dams are one of the largest concentrations of hydro-electric power in France. Specially designed elevators lift migratory fish like shad, lamprey, salmon and trout out of the river and release them upstream. These amazing engineering projects, a staircase of barrages, can be admired from various vantage points and belvédères.

Above Arched passage to the Château de Castelnaud in the medieval town of Castelnaud
Below Aerial view of the Château des Milandes and its grounds

EAT AND DRINK

LA ROQUE GAGEAC

La Belle Étoile moderate
Watch the river go by from the dining room or shady terrace of this restaurant, and enjoy a deft mix of local cuisine with modern touches. Rooms are also available.
Le Bourg, 24250; 05 53 29 51 44; www.hotel-belle-etoile-dordogne.fr; closed Mon, Wed lunch, Nov–Mar

Eat and Drink: inexpensive, under €20; moderate, €20–€40; expensive, over €40

Above Façade of the 16th-century Maison des Vins in Bergerac **Below** Dordogne river looping past fields near Trémolat

ACTIVITIES IN TRÉMOLAT

Mairie de Trémolat
*Le Bourg, 24510; 05 53 22 80 17; www.
pays-de-bergerac.com/mairie/tremolat*

WINE TASTING IN BERGERAC AND ST-ÉMILION

Maison des Vins (Conseil Interprofessionnel des Vins de la Région de Bergerac)
*1 rue des Récollets, Bergerac, 24100;
05 53 63 57 57; www.vins-bergerac.fr*

Tourist Office of St-Émilion Jurisdiction
*Le Doyenné, Place des Créneaux,
St-Émilion, 33330; 05 57 55 28 28*

WHERE TO STAY

BERGERAC

La Flambée *moderate*
Set in parkland, this peaceful hotel
has tasteful bedrooms.
*Route de Périgueux, 49 Avenue
Marceau-Fevry, 24100; 05 53 57 52 33;
www.laflambee.com*

AROUND BERGERAC

Château des Merles *expensive*
Housed in a 19th-century château,
12 km (7 miles) east of Bergerac, the
rooms are stylishly decorated.
*Tulières, Mouleydier, 24520; 05 53 63
13 42; www.lesmerles.com*

BOURG-SUR-GIRONDE

Château de la Grave *expensive*
This is a luxurious bed-and-breakfast
in a turreted 16th-century château.
*Bourg-sur-Gironde, 33710; 05 57 68 41
49; www.chateaudelagrave.com*

⑳ Trémolat
Dordogne, Aquitaine; 24558
Head to Trémolat for a superb view of
the Dordogne, and the great loops,
known as *cingles*, for which the river
is famous. There are various viewpoints from which to enjoy them; the
Rocamadou *belvédère* is among the
most popular. The *cingles* can be
seen clearly from here, curving around
fields planted in wedges like a giant
brown-and-green dartboard. The little
village of Trémolat has a Romanesque
church, the **Église Saint-Nicholas**,
which has restored frescoes. Trémolat
has many leisure and sporting activities to offer such as mountain-
biking and canoeing. From Trémolat,
the Dordogne continues towards the
sea, widening out between banks of
fruit and walnut trees and vines.

🚗 *Cross the river on the D31, and
then take the D28 to Calès. Turn right
onto the D29 at Calès. Recross the river
at Lalinde, turn left onto the D703, then
take the D660 to Bergerac.*

㉑ Bergerac
Dordogne, Aquitaine; 24100
Bergerac, which was under English
rule during the Hundred Years' War,
was one of the main destinations for
river traffic in the past, and is now
the centre of a thriving wine region.
Visitors can still see the boatmen's
houses in the narrow medieval streets
of this charming old town. Explore
the quiet, shady squares and visit the
Musée de Batellerie *(open Tue–Sun
mid-Mar–mid-Nov, Tue–Fri mid-Nov–mid-
Mar)* which houses a whole range of
exhibits, including photographs,
explaining the various types of river
boats and how they were constructed.
On the quayside is the 16th-century
cloister which now houses the
Maison des Vins, and where barrels
of wine were once stored for ship-
ping. Note the flood measurements
in the wall. Visitors can easily
understand why the riverside houses
needed steep roofs to store essentials
when the river was in flood. Today,
the cloister plays host to exhibitions
and concerts during summer. After
Bergerac, the Dordogne heads to the
sea, growing even wider as it
approaches the estuary.

🚗 *Take the D32 out of town and at Le
Fleix, turn left onto the D20 for Ste-
Foy-la-Grande. Cross the river to enter
Ste-Foy. Turn right onto the D936 and
at Ste-Pey-d'Armens turn right onto
the D670 and then turn right onto the
D122 to St-Émilion.*

㉒ St-Émilion
Gironde, Aquitaine; 33330
This is wine-country now, and the
names become even more legendary. St-Émilion should not be missed,
a wonderful place for lunch, to

sample wine, or simply stroll around its streets, in places paved with slabs of granite said to have come from Cornwall as ballast for ships that had transported wine. Medieval houses still line the narrow streets of the town. The golden limestone crown of St-Émilion seems almost to shine with light. The great architectural treasure here is Europe's largest monolithic church, the **Église de Saint-Émilion**, a huge underground carved chamber and a 14th-century portal, hewn from soft limestone. There are great views of the vineyards from the top of the belltower. **Retrace the route to the D670, turn right and continue to Libourne.**

23 Libourne
Gironde, Aquitaine; 33500

Libourne is the next port along the river. It was built as a *bastide* by the English, and evidence of this can still be seen in its town gates and arcaded streets. It was an important wine-trading port; from here the wines of the region were shipped all over northern Europe and especially

to Britain. The quays are lively with cafés, worth visiting especially on market days.
Continue along the D670 and at St-André-de-Cubzac take the D669 to Bourg-sur-Gironde.

24 Bourg-sur-Gironde
Gironde, Aquitaine; 33710

Bourg-sur-Gironde was once located on the estuary of Gironde, but now alluvial deposits have extended the spit of land between the Garonne and the Dordogne and the town is now actually on the Dordogne. Bourg is a quiet little place with a big quayside, a park around the citadel and lots of artists' galleries. Continue a little further following signs to **Château d'Yquem** to see the end of the river at Bec d'Ambes, the tip of the promontory known to wine lovers as Entre-deux-Mers. Here the Dordogne meets the Garonne to form the Gironde estuary. The river is wide and glittering, the light is dazzling, and if the smell of ripe grapes were not so strong visitors might even smell the sea.

Above Boats in the harbour of Bourg-sur-Gironde
Below Charming rooftops of St-Émilion

EAT AND DRINK

TRÉMOLAT

Bistrot d'en Face *inexpensive*
Hearty bistro fare such as sausages and *confit de canard* is available in this rustic bistro where Claude Chabrol filmed his classic, *Le Boucher* (1970).
Trémolat, 24510; 05 53 22 80 69; closed Mon, Tue between Oct–Apr.

BERGERAC

L'Imparfait *moderate*
This is an intimate, friendly restaurant housed in 12th-century cloisters in the old town of Bergerac. Regional classics are served with the best Bergerac wine.
8 rue Fontaines, 24100; 05 53 57 47 92; www.imparfait.com; open daily

ST-ÉMILION

L'Envers du Décor *inexpensive*
Sample a great selection of St-Émilion and other local wines in this central wine bar and restaurant, and try local dishes or simple omelettes and salads.
11 rue du Clocher, 33330; 05 57 74 48 31

DAY TRIP OPTIONS
With Le Mont-Dore (on the D983), Mauriac (on the D678) and Bergerac (on the D660) as bases, the drive can be divided into sections.

Breathtaking views
Enjoy views of the Auvergne from the Puy de Sancy ❶. Then head along the D983 to Le Mont-Dore ❷ or La Bourboule, where visitors can relax and indulge in a spa treatment.

From Le Mont-Dore take the D983 to Puy de Sancy.

Mauriac and the gorges
Mauriac ❺ is a good base to explore some of the amazing gorges of the Dordogne and admire its famous dams, such as Bort-les-Orgues ❹ and the Barrage d'Aigle ❻.

From Mauriac take the D678 and D105 to the Pont de St-Projet and follow the Route des Ajustants to Bort-les-Orgues.

Riverside vineyards
From Bergerac ㉑ to the mouth of the Dordogne river there are many vineyards to explore and numerous wine tastings on offer. Consult the Maison des Vins in Bergerac for tours and visit the numerous caves and surrounding vineyards of St-Émilion.

From Bergerac take the D936 to St-Foy-le-Grande continuing along the D936 and the D670 to St-Émilion.

Eat and Drink: inexpensive, under €20; moderate, €20–€40; expensive, over €40

Lazy Rivers and Unspoilt Villages

Albi to Rocamadour

Highlights

- **Historic city of Albi**
  Visit this beautiful city, once the home of the celebrated artist Toulouse-Lautrec

- **Arts and crafts mecca**
  Explore the restored medieval village of Cordes-sur-Ciel, filled with arts and crafts shops

- **Perfectly preserved village**
  Stroll through the narrow alleys and the medieval houses in St-Cirq-Lapopie

- **Legendary Rocamadour**
  Discover one of France's biggest pilgrimage sites

Village of St-Cirq-Lapopie perched high above the Lot river

Lazy Rivers and Unspoilt Villages

Two of the most beautiful natural regions of southwest France, the Tarn and the Lot blend into each other. This route explores the best of both, taking in green flowing rivers, verdant landscapes and unspoilt medieval villages. The itinerary begins in the historic town of Albi on the Tarn, birthplace of the artist Toulouse-Lautrec (1864–1901), and meanders northwards crossing the Aveyron river and a limestone plateau before dropping down into the Lot valley. The goal at the end, further northwards just south of the Dordogne, is the sacred shrine of Rocamadour, breathtakingly situated on the side of a steep valley.

Top right Village of Penne perched on top of a rock outcrop, *see p181*
Above Massive 13th–15th-century château at Lacapell-Marival, *see p183*

ACTIVITIES

Soak up the art of Toulouse-Lautrec in Albi's dedicated museum

Stroll around atmospheric villages such as Cordes-sur-Ciel or St-Cirq-Lapopie

Marvel at the prehistoric paintings of mammoths and horses in the cave at Pech-Merle

Descend to the depths of a huge crater, the Gouffre de Padirac

KEY

▱ Drive route

PLAN YOUR DRIVE

Start/finish: Albi to Rocamadour.

Number of days: 3, allowing half a day for Albi.

Distances: 240 km (150 miles).

Road conditions: The roads are good and easy to drive, but take care on the narrow roads along the Lot and Célé valleys.

When to go: Any time of the year. The countryside is particularly beautiful in spring and early summer.

Opening hours: Monuments and museums are generally open from 10am to 6pm. Most sights close one day a week, most commonly Monday. Smaller sights may close over lunch from noon to 2pm. Most sights will be closed on public holidays. It is advisable to confirm times with the local tourist office prior to visiting.

Main market days: St Antonin-Noble-Val: Sun; **St-Cirq-Lapopie:** Wed Jul–Aug.

Shopping: Among the rich variety of food and drink produced in the Lot, truffles, chestnuts and walnuts are the most easily transportable. Cahors is famous for its red wine. Rocamadour is known for its goats' milk cheese. Crafts are made all over the Lot and Tarn but the best place to shop for them is Cordes-sur-Ciel.

Major festivals: Albi: Carnival, Feb/Mar; **Cordes-sur-Ciel:** Fêtes Médiévales du Grand Fauconnier (medieval festival), Jul; **Rocamadour:** Cheese festival, Jun; Les Eclectiques, Jul; Sacred Music Festival, Aug.

DAY TRIP OPTIONS

The drive can easily be broken down into separate day trips. **Lovers of the countryside** will have plenty to do around the Lot. The sights around Tarn have a lot of **rustic charm** in addition to **historic villages**. For details, *see p183.*

Below Market hall in Cordes-sur-Ciel

❶ Albi

Tarn, Midi-Pyrénées; 81000

Most visitors come to Albi to see two sights: the massive cathedral and the episcopal palace that now houses a museum dedicated to the artist Toulouse-Lautrec who was born in the city. The rest of the city centre is a compact labyrinth of narrow streets on which stand many 15th- and 16th-century mansions.

A 90-minute walking tour

Start from the Parking de la Cathédrale next to the Boulevard du Général Sibille. Turn right into the Rue de la Maîtrise to find the gates of the 13th-century **Palais de la Berbie** ①, the former bishops' castle-palace. This building now houses the Musée Toulouse-Lautrec (*open daily Apr–Sep, Wed–Mon Oct–Mar*), an outstanding collection of the artist's work. Go around the building and down the steps to see the formal gardens which give views over the Tarn, then return to the Rue de la Maîtrise.

Now walk up Rue des Fargues and turn left along Rue de la Souque and turn right past the **Hôtel de Gorsse** ② (not open to the public), one of a number of private mansions built in the city during the 15th and 16th centuries. Go around the covered market, a reconstructed version of the 1900s original, along the Rue des Foissants and Rue Saint-Julien. Turn left up Rue Sainte-Cécile and left to go around the Romanesque and Gothic **La Collégiale Saint-Salvy** ③. The southern gallery of its 13th-century cloister is still standing. Turn

right along Rue Mariès and fork right along Rue Timbal. The **Pharmacie des Penitents** ④ on the right has a magnificent 16th-century façade of crisscross timbering and brick. Further up the street, on the left, is the **Hôtel de Reynès** ⑤, a Renaissance mansion of brick and stone. At the end of Rue Timbal turn right along the Place du Vigan and right again down Rue de l'Hôtel de Ville which runs past the **Hôtel de Ville** ⑥, made up of two 17th-century mansions. Turn left into the Rue de Saunal to come to a crossroads where the Rue Sainte-Cécile meets the Rue de Verdusse. Turn left and almost immediately right into the Rue Toulouse-Lautrec. The artist was

Toulouse-Lautrec

Henri de Toulouse-Lautrec was born into a noble Albi family in 1864. Afflicted by a bone disease, he was unable to live the life of a country squire and was drawn instead to art. After his death in 1901, his mother offered his works to the Louvre but they were refused and so the collection came to be installed in Albi.

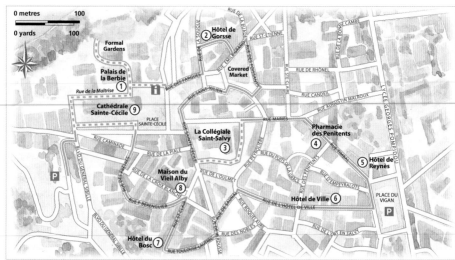

ALBI

Auberge du Pont Vieux *moderate*
The inventive menu has an emphasis on modern cooking using locally grown produce; try the duck *tartare* with *foie gras* or the excellent fish selection. The terrace has great views over the river Tarn.
98 Rue Porta, 81000; 05 63 77 61 73; closed Tue evening, Wed & Sat lunch

L'Epicurien *moderate–expensive*
Gourmet restaurant run with passion. If diners are not sure about what to choose, they can ask for the *menu dégustation*: any six dishes, with apéritif and wines included.
42 place Jean-Jaurès, 81000; 05 63 53 10 70; www.restaurantlepicurien.com; closed Sun, Mon

CORDES-SUR-CIEL

Bistrot Tonin'Ty *moderate–expensive*
The restaurant of the Hostellerie du Vieux Cordes, located just above the church, is part of the Cordes-based catering chain owned by master chef Yves Thuriès. The menu is based around salmon and duck. There is a terrace for summer eating.
Haut de la Cité, 81170; 05 63 53 79 20; www.thuries.fr; closed Mon, Tue lunch, Sun dinner, Jan–mid-Feb

born in the large brick house on the left, the **Hôtel du Bosc** ⑦. Next door is the home of Jean-François Galaup de Lapérouse, who was sent on an expedition to circumnavigate the earth by Louis XVI in 1785, but disappeared in the Pacific in 1788. At the end of the street is **Maison du Vieil Alby** ⑧ a brick and *colombage* house that is now an exhibition centre on local heritage. Turn left up Rue Puech Bérenguier and turn right down Rue des Prêtres to cross Rue de la Piale and head straight to reach the Place Sainte-Cécile with the entrance to the **Cathédrale Sainte-Cécile** ⑨ on the left. The world's largest brick cathedral is a masterpiece of French Gothic architecture. From the cathedral walk down to the car park across Boulevard du Général Sibille.

🚗 *Leave Albi by crossing the modern bridge and forking left on Avenue Dembourg for Cordes. This becomes the D600. In Cordes park beside the road at the base of the hill.*

② Cordes-sur-Ciel
Tarn, Midi-Pyrénées; 81170
The hilltop town of Cordes-sur-Ciel was founded in 1222. In the 14th century, it grew prosperous from craftworking and trade but subsequently fell into decline. It was restored in the 20th century and is once again filled with craft workshops. It is easy to find the way around as there is one main street with gateways at either end and handsomely carved stone buildings in the middle. The **Église St-Michel** and market hall are just off this street.

🚗 *Continue on the D600 towards St-Antonin-Noble-Val. After Vindrac turn left for Vaour on the D91, then left*

onto the D33 towards Vaour. On the left there is a detour to the ruined château Commanderie des Templiers. At Vaour, turn left onto the D15 and right at the second sign again onto the D33 and then the D133 for Penne.

③ Penne
Tarn, Midi-Pyrénées; 81140
Dramatically sited on a rock outcrop overhanging the gorge of the Aveyron river below, and overlooked by the jagged stump of its ruined 13th-century castle, this small village is worth a brief stop and stroll. There are some picturesque *colombage* houses, some of them incorporating stones from the castle above.

🚗 *Descend the hill to the valley and turn right on the D115 for St-Antonin. Before crossing the river, there is a good view of the town on the opposite bank. Cross the bridge and turn left at the end. Follow the road to the Caylus turn-off. Park here and walk down Rue de la Pélisserie to the town.*

Above Albi's cathedral standing tall above the Tarn river **Below left** Medieval building in Cordes-sur-Ciel **Below right** Distant view of the hilltop town of Cordes-sur-Ciel

Above left Baskets of flowers adorning the walls of the town hall in St-Antonin-Noble-Val **Above right** Stately château of Cenevières, Lot valley **Below** Pretty town of St-Antonin-Noble-Val by the Lot river

VISITING ROCAMADOUR

Parking
The layout of Rocamadour is complicated. There are essentially three parts: the village at the bottom, the shrines (sanctuaries) in the middle and the buildings that stand above the shrines, the château and the service centre of L'Hospitalet. Park in L'Hospitalet.

Tourist Information
L'Hospitalet, 46500; 05 65 33 22 00; www.rocamadour.com

WHERE TO STAY

ST-CIRQ-LAPOPIE

Mas de Redoules *inexpensive*
This restored farmhouse offers beautifully decorated rooms in what was the farmhouse, former barn and stable. Walking, riding and cycling excursions in the surrounding area are on offer. *Nougayrac, 46330; 06 31 79 63 86; www.masderedoules.com*

AROUND ROCAMADOUR

Le Pagès *inexpensive–moderate*
A hotel-restaurant 14 km (9 miles) west of Rocamadour, Le Pagès stands in its own extensive grounds. *Calès, 46350; 05 65 37 95 87; www.hotel-lepages.com*

Moulin de Fresquet
inexpensive–moderate
This is a converted mill 11 km (6 miles) southeast of Rocamadour offering bed-and-breakfast and a candlelit dinner (no dinners on Thursdays). The rooms are decorated with antiques and tapestries. *Gramat, 46500; 05 65 38 70 60; www.moulindefresquet.com*

4 St-Antonin-Noble-Val
Tarn, Midi-Pyrénées; 82140
St-Antonin's oldest and finest building, the **Maison Romane** on the central square, Place de la Halle, is also claimed to be the oldest civic building in France. Above it is a stout belfry. In the narrow medieval streets of the town are several other buildings worth seeing, including the town hall next to the church and the **Maison de l'Amour** on Rue Droite, where a 15th-century stone carving shows the heads of a man and a woman turned towards each other in what seems to be an immortal kiss. Leaving St-Antonin on the D19, a short detour after 7 km (4 miles) takes visitors to the restored Château de Cas, once a Templar possession and open to visitors since its restoration.

Leave St-Antonin on the D19 for Caylus, where it is worth stopping for a moment to see the house opposite the tourist information office, the Maison des Loups, which carries snarling stone beasts lunging out of its façade. Go over the crossroads in Caylus onto the D19 for Lacapelle and St-Projet, marked Route des Causses de Quercy.

5 Causse de Limogne
Tarn-et-Garonne and Lot, Midi-Pyrénées; 46260
The deep river valleys of southwest France are separated by limestone plateaux or *causses*. At the entrance to Lacapelle-Livron, turn right for a detour to the little chapel of **Nôtre-Dame des Grâces**. About 2 km (1 mile) further on the D19 is **St-Projet**, home to a 13th-century château. Continue on the D19 towards Limogne-en-Quercy. About 5 km (3 miles) further on is **Beauregard** which surrounds a 14th-century stone market hall. Turn off left on the D53 for Limogne and cross it in a dogleg to pick up the D24 which meanders down to **Cénevières** in the Lot valley. Outside this village is a renowned château, a stately Renaissance home.

Follow the road through the village of Cénevières towards the Lot river but do not cross the bridge – just before it turn left onto the D8 for Crégols, after which turn right for St-Cirq-Lapopie. Turn left at the end of the road. Park either above or below the village and take the footpath.

6 St-Cirq-Lapopie
Lot, Midi-Pyrénées; 46330
One of France's most beautiful villages, St-Cirq enjoys a spectacular site high above the Lot river. Its steep streets have fine houses. The founding theorist of Surrealism, André Breton, chose this as his home in the 1950s.

Continue past St-Cirq, turning right above the village for Bouzies into a small road that runs high above the valley. At Bouzies, cross the river by the narrow bridge. Turn right towards Cajarc and left for Cabrerets on the D41. Keep on this road all the way up the Vallée du Célé.

⑦ Vallée du Célé

Lot, Midi-Pyrénées; 46320

There are three stops worth making as visitors wind their way up the valley. Above Cabrerets, **Grotte du Pech-Merle** has extraordinary prehistoric cave paintings of mammoths and horses. At **Marcilhac-sur-Célé** there is a ruined 11th–16th-century Benedictine abbey. Finally, the church at **Espagnac-Ste-Eulalie** across the river has a photogenic belltower.

🚗 *From Espagnac, backtrack down the D41 and turn right onto the D38 to Grèzes. After the village turn right on the D653 and go through Livernon to Assier; beyond it, turn left onto the D840 and then right onto the D940 to Lacapelle-Marival and Aynac. After Aynac follow signs for St-Céré to the D807 and turn right onto it. At the roundabout at the bottom of the hill, turn right for St-Céré. A right turn off this road leads to the Château de Montal. Return to the roundabout, go over it, and turn left onto the D38.*

⑧ Autoire

Lot, Midi-Pyrénées; 46400, 46130

The village of Autoire is a harmonious cluster of stone houses sprouting turrets. At the entrance to the village (opposite the cemetery) fork right and climb to **Loubressac**, a pretty village on the crest of a hill from which it enjoys magnificent views over the Dordogne valley.

🚗 *From Loubressac take the D118 towards Rocamadour. Turn left at the crossroads onto the D14 and then turn right on the D673. In Padirac turn left onto the D673, or detour right to visit the famous Gouffre de Padirac crater. The D673 leads into L'Hospitalet. Park here to visit Rocamadour.*

⑨ Rocamadour

Lot, Midi-Pyrénées; 46500

Rocamadour is France's second most important medieval shrine after Mont-St-Michel *(see p95)*. A good way to visit the place is to continue past L'Hospitalet to the **château**, from the ramparts of which there is a view down over the valley. Then walk or take the lift down to the village and climb the monumental staircase to the **shrine complex**.

Above Panoramic view of the village of Rocamadour **Below** Stone houses with turrets in the village of Autoire

EAT AND DRINK

ST-CIRQ-LAPOPIE

Le Gourmet Quercynois *moderate*
A 17th-century house that serves traditional regional cuisine.
Rue de la Peyrolerie, 46330; 05 65 31 21 20; closed Jan

VALLÉE DU CÉLÉ

Des Grottes *inexpensive–moderate*
Hotel-restaurant at the southern end of the valley, with a shady riverside terrace.
Route Grotte du Pech-Merle, Cabrerets, 46330; 05 65 31 26 62; www. hoteldesgrottes.com; closed Nov–May

AUTOIRE

Auberge de la Fontaine
inexpensive–moderate
Family-run hotel-restaurant serving trout, *foie gras*, and *confits*.
Le Bourg, 46400; 05 65 10 85 40; www. auberge-de-la-fontaine.com; closed Sun dinner, Mon

ROCAMADOUR

Les Vieilles Tours *moderate*
This stone-built hotel-restaurant serves Quercynois specialities.
Lafage, 46500; 05 65 33 68 01; open daily dinner only; closed Nov–Mar

---

DAY TRIP OPTIONS

The first day trip around the Tarn is ideal for those based in Albi (A68 from Toulouse) while the second around the northern region of Lot is most easily done from Rocamadour (just off A20 from Toulouse).

Historic towns and pretty villages

The handsome historic towns of Cordes-sur-Ciel ② and St-Antonin-Noble-Val ④ can be combined in an easy day out which includes a stop at the impressively sighted village of Penne ③ and a drive down the Aveyron gorge.

Start from Albi and follow to Cordes then continue to St-Antonin-Noble-Val. Keep on the D15 along the Aveyron valley and turn right on the D600 to return to Albi.

Abbey and crater

Based in Rocamadour ⑨, visitors can spend the morning visiting the abbey and the afternoon exploring the crater Gouffre de Padirac and the charming village of Autoire ⑧.

From L'Hospitalet above Rocamadour follow the route in reverse through Alvignac to Padirac (making a detour from here to see the crater). Resume the route (still in reverse) to Loubressac and then Autoire. Then head towards St-Céré. From the roundabout before the town, take the D807 and turn right on to the D673 to get back to Rocamadour.

Eat and Drink: inexpensive, under €20; moderate, €20–€40; expensive, over €40

• Paris • Metz

Rennes •

F R A N C E

Clermont-
Ferrand •
• Lyon

• Bordeaux

Toulouse •
• Nice
• Marseille

Wine and Water

Bordeaux to Rochefort

Highlights

- **Wine city**
  Walk around Bordeaux, the
  handsome 18th-century wine city

- **Châteaux of the Médoc**
  Visit a string of famed wine-producing
  châteaux and taste fine wines

- **Historic charm**
  Take a stroll around the estuary-side
  Talmont-sur-Gironde built around a
  picturesque Romanesque church

- **Legendary naval base**
  Explore Rochefort on the Atlantic
  coast with its harbours, riverbanks
  and royal rope-making factory

Stately 19th-century Neo-Classical
Château Margaux

Wine and Water

Bordeaux could claim to be the wine capital of France, if not the world. The first part of this route explores a prime part of its hinterland, the Médoc peninsula. An isosceles triangle, the peninsula is bordered by the Atlantic and the Gironde estuary where world-famous claret-producing châteaux preside over immaculate vineyards. The route then crosses the Gironde by means of a short ferry ride and meanders up the picturesque right bank through the Saintonge, an area best known for its Romanesque churches. The end point of the route is the historic seafaring town of Rochefort.

Above Vineyard alongside the château in Margaux, *see p189*

ACTIVITIES

See how wines are made, taste them and buy on the spot in the wine towns of Margaux and Paulliac

Take a boat trip along the Gironde estuary

Go bird-watching in the marshes of the Gironde estuary

Visit the Romanesque churches of the Saintonge

0 kilometres 10

0 miles 10

KEY

Drive route

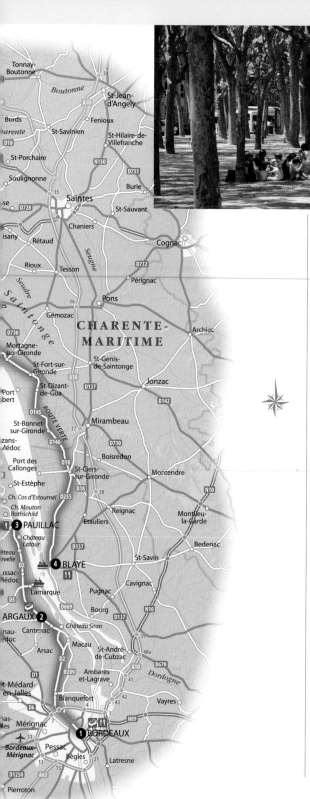

Above Picnicking in the shade beside Esplanade des Quinconces in Bordeaux, *see p188*

PLAN YOUR DRIVE

Start/finish: Bordeaux to Rochefort.

Number of days: 2, allowing half a day to explore Bordeaux.

Distances: 258 km (160 miles).

Road conditions: The roads are in good condition. The route includes a ferry crossing from Lamarque to Blaye. Blaye can also be reached by road from Bourdeaux via Bourg.

When to go: This is an all-season trip but the vineyards look best as the grapes mature in late summer.

Opening hours: Most sights and museums generally open from 10am to 6pm. Smaller sights may close over lunch from noon to 2pm. Confirm times with the local tourist office.

Main market days: Bordeaux: daily, except Tue; **Pauillac:** Sat; **Rochefort:** Tue, Thu and Sat.

Shopping: Wine is the obvious item to buy on this tour. The first part of the tour goes through many prestigious chateaux where visitors can try and buy vintages from the producers.

Major festivals: Bordeaux: Fête le Vin, Jun; **Blaye:** Wine market, Mar; **Pauillac:** Fête de l'Agneau et du Vin, May.

DAY TRIP OPTIONS

Wine enthusiasts can dedicate a day to visit the famous wine chateaux of the Médoc peninsula north of Bordeaux. **Families** will have fun at the Saintonge. For details, *see p191*.

❶ Bordeaux

Gironde, Aquitaine; 33000

Its name synonymous with wine, Bordeaux has long prospered from trade in its world-famous product. Its accumulation of wealth can be seen in the handsome collection of architecture, most of which dates from the 18th century. The city has been declared a UNESCO World Heritage Site under the name "Port of the Moon", referring to the city's position on a crescent-shaped bend of the Garonne river.

A two-hour walking tour

Start the walk from the car park at Place Jean-Jaurès, and take the Quai de la Douane. Walk to the Esplanade des Quinconces and across it to the **Monument aux Girondins** ①. This is a fountain around a column that stands at the end of the broad esplanade furthest from the river bank. This extravagant work of art was built under the Third Republic (1870–1940) to commemorate the members of parliament from Bordeaux who fell victim to the Terror during the Revolution. A statue of Liberty looks down on Bordeaux from the top of her 50-m (160-ft) column.

Go down Cours du 30 Juillet, to the south of the monument. The tourist information office is on the left. The sharply triangular building opposite is the **Maison du Vin** ②, home of Bordeaux wine's regulatory authority and a wine bar in which visitors can taste a selection of fine wines.

After reaching the **Grand Theatre** ③ on Place de la Comedie, turn right down Cours de l'Intendance. Just off this to the right on Place du Chapelet is the Classical-Baroque **Église Nôtre-Dame** ④.

Continue along Cours de l'Intendance a little further and turn left down Rue Vital Carles to reach Place Pey-Berland, on which stands the **Cathédrale Saint-André** ⑤ and the town hall, **Palais Rohan** ⑥. Behind the cathedral is a flamboyant Gothic tower, **Tour Pey-Berland** ⑦. From beneath the tower, take the Rue Duffour-Dubergier to the **Musée d'Aquitaine** ⑧, a museum of

VISITING BORDEAUX

Tourist Information
12 cours du 30 Juillet 33080; 05 56 00 66 00; www.bordeaux-tourisme.com

Parking
The most convenient car park for central Bordeaux and for the walking tour is the subterranean multistorey in Place Jean-Jaurès, which is just off the Quai de la Douane (along the river bank) and a street away from the start and end of the walk in the Esplanade des Quinconces.

WHERE TO STAY

BORDEAUX

La Maison Bord'Eaux *expensive*
A small boutique hotel in which the rooms look on to a garden where breakfast and meals are served. The owners can arrange wine-tasting visits to châteaux. Parking available.
113 rue Albert Barraud, 33000; 05 56 44 00 45; www.lamaisonbordeaux.com

MARGAUX

Le Pavillon de Margaux *moderate*
The hotel has 14 rooms and has a smart restaurant that also serves three-course bistro-style lunches on weekdays.
3 rue Georges Mandel, 33460; 05578 87754; www.pavillonmargaux.com

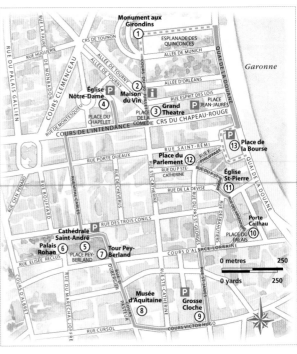

regional archaeology and history, and turn left down Cours Victor Hugo to reach the **Grosse Cloche** ⑨, a 15th-century gateway which was the belltower of the former town hall. Turn left here down Rue St-James and right down Cours d'Alsace-Lorraine. Cross the road and take the little fork to the left to enter Place du Palais, presided over by the **Porte Cailhau** ⑩, another 15th-century gateway.

Facing the gateway, take the road to the left, the Rue des Argentiers, to the square outside the **Église St-Pierre** ⑪, cross it and continue in roughly the same direction along Rue du Parlement St-Pierre into the **Place du Parlement** ⑫, with its bars and cafés. Turn right here down Rue Fernand Philippart into the grandiose **Place de la Bourse** ⑬. In the middle of the square is a fountain of the Three Graces. Across the road on the river bank is another fountain, this one strikingly contemporary: the Miroir d'Eau (Water Mirror) which has a computer-controlled display. Turn left along the Quai de la Douane which follows the river bank to come alongside Place Jean-Jaurès and the car park.

🚗 *From Place Jean-Jaurès in the centre of Bordeaux make for the quais by the river to pick up the signs to the Rocade (ring road), Rue Fondaudège. Cross the Rocade and take the right turn for Blanquefort and Pauillac on the D2. Go right through Blanquefort. All the famous Médoc châteaux stand on or near the D2 after Macau, beginning with Château Siran, just off the road (right), and Château d'Issan outside Cantenac. Château Palmer, on the right, announces the arrival in the village of Margaux.*

Wines of the Médoc

Many of the world's most famous (and expensive) red wines, including four ranked as *premier cru*, come from the Médoc (Middle Country) region. The vineyards begin at the town of Blanquefort and stretch northwards, inland from the banks of the estuary, in a narrow strip of immaculately tended gravelly land never more than 5 to 8 km (3 to 5 miles) wide. A thousand wine producers here call themselves "chateaux" but only a few actually have premises to match the name.

② Margaux
Gironde, Aquitaine; 33460

There are over 60 wine châteaux in the vicinity of Margaux village, which gives its name to an *appellation d'origine controlée* (AOC). **Château Margaux** itself, a 19th-century Neo-Classical mansion *(open Mon–Fri by appointment only, closed Aug)*, is just outside the village, behind gates at the end of a long drive. The estate, which stretches over 262 ha (650 acres) produces one of the most expensive wines in the world. The **Maison du Vin et du Tourisme** in Margaux will tell visitors all they need to know about wine visits in the area.

🚗 *Leave Margaux still heading north on the D2. Visitors who have seen enough vineyards can turn into Lamarque on the D5, passing the tall, domed belltower and heading for the port to take the ferry across the estuary. Otherwise, make a detour to Pauillac by continuing on the D2.*

Above Monument aux Girondins, Bordeaux
Below left Place du Parlement in Bordeaux
Below right Vineyards at Château Margaux

VISITING THE VINEYARDS

Many of the Médoc's wine-producing châteaux can be visited. Ask for details at the Maison du Vin et du Tourisme (Wine Information Centre) either in Margaux or Pauillac.

Margaux
7 place de la Trémoille, 33460; 05 57 88 70 82

Pauillac
La Verrerie, 33250; 05 56 59 03 08; www.pauillac-medoc.com

EAT AND DRINK

BORDEAUX

Baud et Millet *inexpensive*
This restaurant specializes in wine (950 vintages) and cheeses (200 varieties) served with home-made bread.
19 rue Huguerie, 33000; 05 56 79 05 77; www.baudetmillet.fr; closed Sun

Eat and Drink: inexpensive, under €20; moderate, €20–€40; expensive, over €40

Above Impressive 17th-century fortress at Blaye **Below** Grand Château Pichon-Longueville in Pauillac

CROSSING THE ESTUARY

There are nine sailings a day in high season in both directions between Lamarque and Blaye, from 7:30am to 7:30pm. Timetables are given on a leaflet available from local tourist information offices. The crossing takes about 20 minutes.
05 57 42 04 49; www.CG33.fr

WHERE TO STAY

AROUND TALMONT-SUR-GIRONDE

Les Chambres d'hôtes d'Ana *moderate*
Rooms are sunny and tastefully decorated. Breakfasts, with home-made cakes and jams (such as wild plum, orange and strawberry), can be taken in the garden in summer.
3 rue de l'Amiénois, 17120; 05 46 91 16 66

Le Moulin de Châlons *moderate*
About 28 km (17 miles) north of Talmont, en route to the Château de St-Jean-d'Angle, this renovated 18th-century mill has comfortable rooms and a restaurant with a riverside terrace.
2 rue du Bassin, La Gua, 17600; 05 46 22 82 72; www.moulin-de-chalons.com

ROCHEFORT

La Corderie Royale *moderate*
Hotel-restaurant between the yacht harbour, the Charente river and the adjacent royal rope-making factory, this is an ideal base for visiting the historic core of Rochefort or as a lunch stop while sightseeing.
Rue Audebert, 17300; 05 46 99 35 35; www.corderieroyale-hotel.com

❸ Pauillac
Gironde, Aquitaine; 33250
The commune of Pauillac consists of only 12 sq km (4.5 sq miles) of vineyards, but produces three of Bordeaux's five *premier cru* wines: Latour, Lafite Rothschild and Mouton Rothschild. There are several prestigious châteaux on or near the D2 around the small riverside town of Pauillac. Starting with **Beychevelle**, the route passes **Beaucaillou** and **Latour** to the right, and **Pichon-Longueville** and **Lanessan**, with its horse museum, to the left. A short way beyond the town on the left are **Lafite Rothschild** and **Mouton Rothschild**, which uses leading artists to create its wine labels and has a small museum of paintings on wine themes from all over the world. The unique Oriental structure of **Château Cos d'Estournel** stands on the right.
After visiting the Paulliac area return down the D2 to Lamarque. From Lamarque turn onto the D5, passing the tall, domed belltower again and heading for the port to take the ferry across the estuary to reach Blaye.

❹ Blaye
Gironde, Aquitaine; 33390
The squat fortress which watches over Blaye was built in the 17th century by Vauban under the orders of Louis XIV. It formed part of the defences of the port of Bordeaux against the English. The fortress was complemented by **Fort Médoc**, facing it from the other bank of the estuary, and **Fort Paté** on an island

off Blaye. From the outside it is a complex of inclined walls, gateways, bastions, watchtowers and powder stores. Inside the walls there is a hotel, restaurant, museum and a few bars and shops.
Take the D255 northwards to St-Ciers-sur-Gironde. From here take the D145, the "Route Verte" (Green Route), which winds up and down through low hills. On the way are pleasant villages and outlying vineyards of the Cognac brandy region. In St-Dizant-de-Gua stop to look at the 15th-century Château de Beaulon. After reaching Talmont, park in the area provided as cars are excluded from the village.

❺ Talmont-sur-Gironde
Charente-Maritime, Poitou-Charentes; 17120
The most picturesque sight on the Gironde estuary is the 12th-century Romanesque church built by Benedictine monks on a low cliff at Talmont. The village was added in 1284 by Edward I of England, who reigned over this part of France. It was conceived as a model medieval community with streets and alleys laid out on a grid pattern and protected by walls. Today the village is extremely well cared for by its inhabitants and filled with flowers.
Take the D114 to Cozes and from there the D17 to Saujon. Follow signs around or through Saujon onto the D117 for Sablonceux, where you may want to stop and see the Cistercian abbey. Continue north through Nancras to Pont-l'Abbé-d'Arnoult. Turn left at the entrance to the town

Where to Stay: inexpensive, under €70; moderate, €70–€150; expensive, over €150

on the D18 towards the Île d'Oloron. Champagne has a rebuilt Romanesque church. Turn left after Champagne, still onto the D18, which leads into St-Jean-d'Angle. In the middle of the village, turn right for Oloron, still the D18. Look out for the discreet entrance to the château on the right.

6 Château de St-Jean-d'Angle
Charente-Maritime, Poitou-Charentes; 17620

This charming moated château-fort, easily missed by anyone driving past unawares, was built in 1180 by Guillaume de Lusignan to safeguard the revenue from the salt works on the marshes below the town. The castle fell into ruin after the Revolution but has been restored in recent years.

🚗 *Leave the village on the D18 and go through St-Just-Luzac. At the round-about after the village turn right for Oloron on the D728. This busy road bypasses Marennes, which styles itself* as France's oyster capital, and heads for the Île d'Oloron. Turn right for Hiers-Brouage on the D3 and go through it to reach Brouage itself.

7 Brouage
Charente-Maritime, Poitou-Charentes; 17320

When the town of Brouage was founded in 1555 it stood on the sea. It was an important place of commerce, and as such was solidly fortified. Cardinal Richelieu had his fortress here which he used as his base during the Siege of La Rochelle (1627–8). As the marshes were reclaimed and the sea retreated during the 18th century, Brouage was left stranded and redundant with its ramparts intact and picturesquely overgrown at places.

🚗 *Continue on the D3 to Moëze and then Soubise. In Soubise follow the signs for Rochefort which lead to the southern end of the modern bridge across the Charente river. While crossing it, there is a view of the transporter bridge below to the right.*

8 Rochefort
Charente-Maritime, Poitou-Charentes; 17300

During the 17th century, France's navy began to swell in power, and in 1666, Louis XIV ordered the construction of an arsenal at Rochefort. The arsenal closed in 1927 and since then the site, extending along the bank of the Charente, has been restored for visitors. The main building is the elongated Corderie Royale, the royal rope-making works. Next to it is a dry dock where a replica of the *Hermione*, an 18th-century wooden frigate, is being constructed according to its original plans *(open daily, closed Jan).*

Above Romanesque church at Talmont-sur-Gironde **Left** Brightly painted door and window of a house in Talmont-sur-Gironde

EAT AND DRINK

PAUILLAC

Hotel de France et d'Angleterre *moderate expensive*
The hotel-restaurant offers both gourmet and bistro meals.
3 quai Albert Pichon, 33250; 05 56 59 01 20; closed Sun, Dec & Jan

BLAYE

Auberge du Porche *inexpensive–moderate*
Restaurant serving seafood and meat accompanied by local Blaye wines.
5 rue Ernest Régnier, 33390; 05 57 42 22 69; www.auberge-du-porche.com; closed Wed, Sun dinner

TALMONT-SUR-GIRONDE

L'Estuaire *inexpensive–moderate*
Restaurant with a menu strong on seafood. Also has a bar and tearoom.
1 avenue de l'Estuaire, 17120; 05 46 90 43 85; www.hotellestuaire.com

BROUAGE

Le Brouage *inexpensive*
Oysters from Marennes, eels and fish are among the items on the menu.
Rue de Quebec,17320; 05 46 85 03 06; www.le-brouage.com; closed Thu

---

DAY TRIP OPTIONS

Bordeaux (on the A10) and Rochefort (from Paris turn off the A10 onto the N248, then take the N11 and D911) are the best bases for exploring the Médoc and the western Saintonge.

Wine chateaux
Visit the famous wine chateaux of the Médoc peninsula north of Bordeaux ❶ which are mainly concentrated around Margaux ❷ and Pauillac ❸ then cross the Garonne estuary to Blaye ❹ to see the imposing squat fortress there. Then return to Bordeaux on the other bank.

Follow the route as far as Pauillac. Double back (still following the route) to Lamarque and take the ferry across the estuary to Blaye. Take the D937/D137 to meet the A10. Take this back to Bordeaux.

The Saintonge
Explore the coast and hinterland south of Rochefort ❽ including the fortified village of Brouage ❼ and the castle at St-Jean-d'Angle ❻. In between are marshes rich in birdlife.

After visiting the town, follow the route in reverse through Brouage as far as St-Jean-d'Angle. After St-Jean-d'Angle turn left on the D733 to return to Rochefort.

Eat and Drink: inexpensive, under €20; moderate, €20–€40; expensive, over €40

The Pyrenees: End to End

Collioure to St-Jean-de-Luz

Highlights

- **Panorama of the highest peaks**
  Take a cable car ride to Pic du Midi's observatory for some stunning views

- **Stupendous Cirque de Gavarnie**
  Admire this natural rock amphitheatre containing Europe's highest waterfall

- **Cols of the Tour de France**
  Take on some of the high mountain passes made famous by the world's most celebrated bicycle race

- **Basque country**
  Discover one of the prettiest corners of France with picturesque villages galore

Road winds up through the beautiful
Col d'Aspin past a little village

The Pyrenees: End to End

The mountains of the Pyrenees form a neat line across southern France, limited to the east and west by the Mediterranean and Atlantic coasts respectively. This drive runs the length of the chain, from shore to shore, from French Catalonia to the Pays Basque, staying as close to the highest mountains as possible. In doing so, it climbs over many passes, most offering spectacular views. Innumerable detours are possible on the way, ranging from stiff upland walks to more leisurely explorations of the towns and villages of the foothills.

L'Esprit du ChemiN

Above Stone doorway in St-Jean-Pied-de-Port, *see p203* **Below** Horse-drawn cart on the streets of Arreau, *see p199*

KEY

Drive route

ACTIVITIES

Swap the car for a bike for a gentle lowland tour or a rigorous Tour de France mountain pass

Go for a hike along the marked routes in the Pyrenees

Take a cable car ride up to the heights, the most sensational being the one to the top of the Pic du Midi

Enjoy a scenic, high-altitude train ride in Catalonia or up La Rhune in the Basque Country

Relax on the beach at Collioure at the start of the tour, or St-Jean-de-Luz at the end

Discover the variety of food and drink, particularly cheeses, along the way

PLAN YOUR DRIVE

Start/finish: Collioure to St-Jean-de-Luz.

Distance: 800 km (500 miles).

Number of days: 7, allowing half a day to explore the Pont d'Espagne.

Road conditions: Mostly good, but be prepared for some stretches of narrow, winding mountain roads.

When to go: From mid-May to October, the route is passable but check before ascending. In winter, higher passes may be closed by snow.

Opening hours: Monuments and museums are generally open from 10am to 6pm. Most sights close one day a week, most commonly Monday, and on public holidays.

Main market days: Collioure: Wed, Sun; **Céret:** Sat; **Arreau:** Thu; **St-Jean-Pied-de-Port:** Mon; **Espelette:** Wed, Sat in Jul & Aug.

Above Former monastery just outside the village of Mosset near Villefranche-de-Conflent, see p197 **Below** Church in the village of St-Savin, see p202

Shopping: Pick up a pair of handmade traditional clogs on the way down the Bethmale valley in the Ariège.

Major festivals: Céret: Fête de la Cérise, May; Festival Pablo Casals, Jul–Aug; **Espelette:** Fête du Piment, Oct.

DAY TRIP OPTIONS

Those interested in **Catalan culture** can spend a day in Catalonia; **mountain lovers** will enjoy a day out in the Hautes-Pyrénées; the Béarn is perfect for those who like **nature** and the Basque Country for those who **love the coast**. For details, see p205.

Above left Narrow road winding through lush vegetation with the Mediterranean in the distance Above middle Cross near Vernet-les-Bains Above right Picturesque Romanesque church in Axiat

VISITING COLLIOURE

Tourist Information
Place 18 Juillet, 66190; 04 68 82 15 47; www.collioure.com

Parking
Collioure can get very crowded in the summer season, and the main town car park around the château may be full. An alternative is to park outside the town and take a shuttle service.

WHERE TO STAY

COLLIOURE

Les Templiers *moderate*
On the quayside of Collioure, this hotel has rooms overlooking the harbour. It also has a traditional bar full of art, and a good restaurant.
Quai de l'Amirauté, 66190; 04 68 98 31 10; www.hotel-templiers.com

Casa Païral *moderate*
This hotel is housed in a 19th-century Catalan villa tucked away in the old town with shady gardens and a swimming pool.
Impasse des Palmiers, 66190; 04 68 82 05 81; www.hotel-casa-pairal.com

CÉRET

Del Bisbe *inexpensive*
This funky little Catalan hotel on a tiny square in Céret serves hearty regional dishes, such as *escalivada* (Catalan vegetable stew) and rabbit with aioli.
4 place Soutine, 66400; 04 68 87 00 85

① Collioure
Pyrénées-Orientales, Languedoc-Roussillon; 66190
The Côte Vermeille is where the Pyrenees meet the Mediterranean, a coastline of secluded coves and rocky headlands. Collioure is the gem of the coast, a fishing port dominated by the **Château Royal** *(open daily)*, a massive fortress first established by the Templars in the 13th century and reinforced in 1669 by military engineer Vauban. The château offers views of the port, with its cobbled streets, its beaches and the 17th-century church, **Nôtre-Dames-des-Anges**. South of the town is the **Musée d'Art Moderne** *(open daily, except Tue Oct–May)*.
🚗 *From Collioure take the D114 towards Argelès, then the D914 towards Perpignan. At junction 11 turn right onto the D618, towards Le Boulou. Follow Le Perthuson to the D900, take the D618 towards Maureillas, for Céret. Follow directions to "Centre Ville" where there is a free car park.*

② Céret
Pyrénées-Orientales, Languedoc-Roussillon; 66400
The town of Céret in the Vallespir, the valley of the Tech river, is famous for its 14th-century bridge, the **Pont du Diable**. Céret's shady squares, loggias, stuccoed walls and bullfighting arena give it a vibrant Spanish feel. Picasso and other artists worked here and the splendid **Musée d'Art Moderne** celebrates their art *(open daily, except Tue Oct–Apr)*.
🚗 *Take the D618 onto the D115 to Amélie-les-Bains-Palalda and turn left*

onto the D618 again towards Palada and St Marsal. Drive past Prunet-et-Belpuig and signs for Boule d'Amont, and turn left onto the D84 to Serrabone.

③ Prieuré de Serrabone
Pyrénées-Orientales, Languedoc-Roussillon; 66130
Commanding a spectacular view of the surrounding peaks, the priory of Serrabonne is one of several Romanesque abbeys in the Canigou Massif. The 12th-century abbey *(open daily)* is built of local pink-veined marble, with a single cloister arcade overlooking the hills. Inside it has columns with carved capitals and a tribune embellished with carved flowers, animals and human faces.
🚗 *Return to the D618 and continue to Bouleternère and turn left onto the N116. At Prades, at the roundabout continue straight and then turn left onto the D27 towards Abbaye St-Michel-de-Cuxà.*

Carved pillar in Villefranche-de-Conflent

④ Abbaye St-Michel-de-Cuxà
Pyrénées-Orientales, Languedoc-Roussillon; 66500
This ancient abbey *(closed Sun morning and religious holidays)* is a superb setting for the annual Pablo Casals festival of chamber music held between July and August. Founded in 878 by the Benedictines, the abbey is a rare example of pre-Romanesque architecture in France, with one great square tower remaining, a huge stone barrel vault and a palm vaulted crypt. The highlight is the 12th-century cloisters of pink marble columns and Romanesque

capitals, carved with various mythical animals and local flora.

Continue on the D27 which winds its way through the villages of Taurinya and Fillols, arriving at Vernet-les-Bains.

5 Vernet-les-Bains

Pyrénées-Orientales, Languedoc-Roussillon; 66820

With a gentle, sheltered climate and wonderful views of Mont Canigou, Vernet-les-Bains is a tranquil spa town. In its heyday, Vernet hosted several famous visitors, including writers Rudyard Kipling and Hans Christian Andersen. The town is one of the starting points for climbs of Mont Canigou, the focus of Catalan devotion, with a great iron cross perched on the summit and extensive views of sea and mountains. Take the D116 south of Vernet to Casteil to reach the **Abbaye de St-Martin-du-Canigou** (open daily, closed Jan, Mon Oct–May, guided tours only). From the village of Casteil, a 40-minute walk leads to the abbey perched on a craggy rock. It was founded in the early 11th-century by Guilfred, Count of Cerdagne. Visitors can see the tiny tomb he carved for himself, as well as the 11th-century cloisters.

Once back at Casteil take the D116 north through Vernet-les-Bains to Villefranche-de-Conflent.

6 Villefranche-de-Conflent

Pyrénées-Orientales, Languedoc-Roussillon; 66500

This town of stone ramparts guarding the narrowest point of the Têt valley has been a fortress since the Middle Ages, reinforced by Vauban in the 17th century. It is now a UNESCO

World Heritage Site, with pink marble paths, beautifully restored dwellings and shops selling leather and pottery. The 12th-century **Église de St-Jacques** has fine carved capitals and a 13th-century oak door embellished with intricate ironwork. An underground passage of 1,000 steps leads to **Fort Libéria** high above the gorge. Nearby are the **Grottes des Canalettes**, a labyrinth of stalactites and stalagmites. Visitors can take the Petit Train Jaune from here up to the Cerdagne mountain plateau.

Take the N116 to Prades, the D619 to Catllar, then the D14 towards Mosset. Then follow the D84 towards Roquefort; take the D17 towards Axat and turn left onto the D118 and then the D25 towards Le Puech and Le Pla. Follow signs to Mijanes and Ax-les-Thermes. After Ascou, turn right on the D613 for the Col du Chioula and the Col de Marmare and turn left onto the D20, the Route des Corniches.

7 Route des Corniches

Ariège, Midi-Pyrénées; 09250

The D20 provides a scenic drive to Tarascon. Soon after Bestiac, the road passes under the cable car linking the world's largest talc quarry to the valley below at Luzenac. Shortly after comes the ruined **Château de Lordat**. After crossing the Gérul river, which makes a pretty waterfall, visitors reach Axiat which has a Romanesque church.

Pass over the top of Bompas to reach a T-junction with the D618. Turn left into Tarascon and park near the bridge to explore the old town.

EAT AND DRINK

COLLIOURE

Le Neptune *expensive*
A wonderfully positioned restaurant on rocks overlooking the sea, Le Neptune is known for its gourmet treatment of local specialities such as lobster and Collioure's own anchovies. *Route Port Vendres, 66190; 04 68 82 02 27; www.leneptune-collioure.com; closed Tue, Wed (low season)*

AROUND ABBAYE ST-MICHEL-DE-CUXÀ

Casa de l'Olivier *inexpensive*
Located 7 km (4 miles) from St-Michel-de-Cuxà, Casa de l'Olivier stands in the small village of Catllar, just outside Prades. This small restaurant has a big terrace and serves tapas, steaks and seafood, all fresh, home-made and locally sourced. There is also jazz on summer nights. *Place République, Catllar 66500; 04 68 05 72 81; closed Mon, Sun dinner*

VILLEFRANCHE-DE-CONFLENT

Auberge St Paul *expensive*
This chic restaurant in a converted 13th-century chapel in the centre of the town has its own terrace and serves local specialities with a modern, eclectic twist. It also offers a good choice of wine. *7 place Eglise, 66500; 04 68 96 30 95; closed Mon, Sun dinner, Tue (low season)*

Below Relaxed café in a village square near Vernet-les-Bains

Above Waterside cottage in Arreau **Below** Picturesque rolling hills of the Col d'Aspin between Arreau and La Mongie

VISITING NIAUX

Reservations
05 61 05 10 10

WHERE TO STAY

ARREAU

Hotel d'Angleterre *moderate*
This old coaching inn, which was a favourite stopover for the 19th-century pioneer mountaineer Henry Russell, is now a modernized hotel-restaurant run by the Aubiban family. It has 17 rooms and Gascon and Pyrenean dishes on the menu.
Route de Luchon, 65240; 05 62 98 63 30; www.hotel-angleterre-arreau.com

PIC DU MIDI DE BIGORRE

Pic du Midi *expensive*
A night spent in the observatory at the top of the Pic du Midi can be an unforgettable part of a visit to the Pyrenees. The cable car ride, dinner and a guided tour of one of the telescope domes are all part of the overnight package but the highlight is to watch the sunrise in the morning. The rooms are very simple, none *en suite* but all have stunning views. An unbeatable treat which needs to be reserved well in advance.
Rue Pierre Lamy de la Chapelle, La Mongie, 65200; 08 25 00 28 77; www. picdumidi.com; open on specific days of the year only

⑧ Tarascon-sur-Ariège

Ariège, Midi-Pyrénées; 09400
There is not much left of the old quarter of Tarascon but enough to justify an hour's stroll up the Rue du Barri and Rue Naugé to the **Place Garrigou** where a square tower remains from the 14th-century **Église St-Michel**. Another lonely tower, the 18th-century belfry, presides picturesquely over the town.

🚗 *Leave Tarascon southwards on the D618Y. Turn left at the roundabout towards Andorre and right at the second roundabout for Niaux onto the D8. Turn left at the end of Niaux and follow the road uphill to visit the caves.*

⑨ Niaux

Ariège, Midi-Pyrénées; 09400
Niaux has some of the finest prehistoric cave art in France and is carefully managed to allow as many visitors as possible to see it, although daily numbers are limited and advance reservation is essential. The striking black-outlined paintings of bison and horses in the Salon Noir are estimated to be 13,000 years old. The nearby Park of Prehistoric Art displays replicas of these paintings.

🚗 *From Niaux, continue driving on the D8 to Vicdessos. Cross the river and turn right onto the D18 towards Aulus-les-Bains. Ascend to the Port de Lers (1,517 m/4,977 ft) and then climb over the Col d'Agnes (1,570 m/5,151 ft). Turn left at the T-junction onto the D8F that leads to Aulus.*

⑩ Couserans

Midi-Pyrénées, Ariège; 09140
The southern Ariège, a group of 18 valleys collectively known as the Couserans, includes some of the remotest, most densely wooded and most sparsely populated landscapes in France. There is not a single pass over the Pyrenees to the south for almost 50 km (30 miles) in either direction. The region's flora includes chestnut, oak, hazel, beech and fir.

The spa of **Aulus** is one of the main towns of the Upper Couserans. The town has several walking routes. At the roundabout in Aulus turn left and follow the D8 down the Vallée d'Ustou to **Seix**, a popular spot for outdoor activities. Turn left across the river and take the D17 for the **Port de la Core** (1,395 m/4,577 ft). Descend into the Bethmale valley, passing the scenic **Étang de Bethmale** lake. The road bypasses Aret but visitors may want to follow the signs to the workshop of one of the Ariège's last traditional *sabotiers* (clog makers). At the end of the valley turn right onto the D4 towards St-Girons, go through Castillon-en-Couserans, and turn left onto the D618. Cross St-Lary, a popular ski resort, and continue on the D618 to cross the **Col de Portet d'Aspet** pass (1,069 m/3,507 ft), often part of the Tour de France cycle race.

🚗 *From the Col de Portet d'Aspet turn left onto the D85; go straight onto the D44 and cross Col de Menté (1,349m/4,427 ft) to descend into St-Béat.*

⑪ St-Béat

Haute-Garonne, Midi-Pyrénées; 31440
White marble has been carved out of the sides of the valley at St-Béat since Roman times. The ancient quarries are still plainly visible on the right just before visitors reach the town. St-Béat is worth a brief stop to see the castle and the Romanesque church, both of which date from the 12th century. There are also several old houses picturesquely overhanging the Garonne river.

🚗 *Cross the bridge in St-Béat, turn right down the main street and follow the D44. Go through Marignac and turn left at the roundabout at Cierp-Gaud onto the D125 to Luchon.*

⑫ Bagnères-de-Luchon

Haute-Garonne, Midi-Pyrénées; 31110
The Romans were the first to make use of Luchon's thermal waters, which gush out of the ground at around 65–72° C (150–160° F) and are rich in sodium sulphate. The first spa of modern times was built in the late 18th century by the Baron d'Etigny, after whom the main street is named, but most of Luchon's handsome civic architecture dates from the town's heyday under the Second Empire (1852–70).

🚗 *Leave Luchon on the D618 towards Col de Pèyresourde (1,569 m/5,148 ft). Admire views over the Vallée de Louron on the way to Arreau.*

⑬ Arreau

Hautes-Pyrénées; 65240
One of the prettiest towns in the Pyrenees, Arreau stands at the confluence of the Aure and Louron rivers and visitors are never far from the

sound of rushing water. The most conspicuous building is the **town hall** with a covered marketplace underneath. Beside it is the magnificent 16th-century **Maison de Lys**, with a façade ornamented with *fleur-de-lys* motifs.

🚗 *Go straight through Arreau on the D618 and turn left to cross the bridge over the Neste river. Follow signs onto the D929 towards Lannémazan. Turn left onto the D918 for the Col d'Aspin (1,490 m/4,889 ft). On the other side of the Col d'Aspin come down to Ste-Marie-de-Campan. Turn left, still on the D918, towards La Mongie and the Col du Tourmalet. Park in the middle of the ski resort of La Mongie to take the cable car up to the Pic du Midi de Bigorre.*

⑭ Pic du Midi de Bigorre

Hautes-Pyrénées, Midi-Pyrénées; 65200
At 2,877 m (9,439 ft), this is one of the most accessible peaks of the Pyrenees. There has been an observatory on its summit since the late 19th century and this is now reached from the ski-resort of La Mongie by a cable car. At the top there is a shop, restaurant and astronomy museum. The view from the various terraces gives a good overall impression of the highest part of the Pyrenees.

🚗 *Come back to La Mongie on the cable car. Continue on the D918 from La Mongie and cross the Col de Tourmalet (2,115 m/6,939 ft). On the way down there is a botanic garden growing Pyrenean species. Go through the ski resort of Barèges to reach Luz-St-Sauveur. Turn left onto the D921 and drive up the valley towards the Cirque de Gavarnie via Pont Napoléon.*

Above left Flowers adding colour to buildings in Tarascon **Above right** *Colombage* town hall and marketplace in Arreau **Below** View of the château and church of St-Béat

EAT AND DRINK

TARASCON-SUR-ARIÈGE

Hostellerie de la Poste *inexpensive–moderate*
A restaurant with a shady terrace on the riverbank. Specialities include *azinat*, the typical stew of the Ariège, *cassoulet* and *foie gras*.
16 avenue Victor Pilhes, 09400; 05 61 05 60 41; www.hostellerieposte.com; closed Mon and Tue lunch

BAGNÈRES-DE-LUCHON

Les Caprices d'Etigny *inexpensive*
One of several restaurants on Luchon's main street; this serves good desserts.
30 bis Allees d'Etigny, 31110; 05 61 94 31 05; closed Mon, Thu & Sun dinner

Above Azure waters of the stunningly beautiful Lac de Gaube with Vignemale in the distance *Below* Ruined castle of Luz-St-Sauveur perched high on a hilltop

⑯ Cirque de Gavarnie
Hautes-Pyrénées, Midi-Pyrénées; 65120
This glaciated *cirque* (spectacular natural rock amphitheatre) is one of the most visited spots in the Pyrenees. It is reached by an easy hour's walk from Gavarnie village. Alternatively, visitors can get there by donkey or on horseback. The curving wall of rock, nearly 1,500 m (4,900 ft) high, is punctuated by the highest waterfall in France, the **Grande Cascade de Gavarnie** (422 m/1,384 ft). Above the *cirque* are high peaks and the **Brèche de Roland**, an unnatural-looking gap in the cliffs on the border with Spain. The gap is at an altitude of 2,804 m (9, 200 ft) and is 100 m (328 ft) high and 40 m (131 ft) wide.

🚗 *Return to Luz-St-Sauveur and turn left on the D921 towards Lourdes. At the roundabout where the valley opens up, go straight for Soulom, still on the D921. In the middle of Soulom, turn left onto the D920 for Cauterets. Drive through Cauterets, passing the superb waterfalls of Cascade du Lutour and Cascade de Cerisey, until the Pont d'Espagne car park barrier.*

⑮ Pont Napoléon
Hautes-Pyrénées, Midi-Pyrénées; 65120
This high stone bridge across a wooded gorge is named in honour of Napoleon III. He ordered its construction in 1859 while he and the Empress Eugenie were staying at the spa of **Luz-St-Sauveur**. The emperor himself chose the site of the bridge, which is 68 m (223 ft) long and 63 m (207 ft) above the river.

🚗 *Continue up the D921 to Cirque de Gavarnie.*

⑰ Pont d'Espagne
Hautes-Pyrénées, Midi-Pyrénées; 65110
The impressive Pont d'Espagne has always been one of the most popular places to visit in the Pyrenees because it offers easy access to the high mountains. This classic short excursion to a beautiful lake yields clear air and great views for relatively little effort. It makes use of a chairlift which operates between May and September.

A three-hour walking tour
From the top of the car park, follow the path to the **Pont d'Espagne** ① itself. The "Bridge of Spain" does not stand on or anywhere near the present-day frontier but its name

VISITING PONT D'ESPAGNE

Tourist Information
*Place Foch, Cauterets, 65110;
05 62 92 50 50; www.cauterets.com*

Parking
There is a paid car park a short distance before the Pont d'Espagne from where a trail leads to the bridge.

WHERE TO STAY

PONT D'ESPAGNE

Hôtellerie du Pont d'Espagne *inexpensive*
A modest hotel of ten bedrooms in an incomparable setting right next to the Pont d'Espagne, this has a terrace for drinks and meals overlooking the waterfalls.
Quartier Pont d'Espagne, Cauterets, 65110; 05 62 92 54 10; www.hotel-du-pont-despagne.fr; closed mid-Oct–mid-Dec

AROUND PONT D'ESPAGNE

Lion d'Or *moderate*
Located in Cauterets, about 8 km (5 miles) north of the bridge, this hotel aims to re-create the atmosphere of a 19th-century hotel while providing modern comforts.
12 rue Richelieu, Cauterets, 65110; 05 62 92 52 87; www.liondor.eu; closed 4h–16th May, mid-Oct–Nov

Where to Stay: inexpensive, under €70; moderate, €70–€150; expensive, over €150

recalls the days when mule tracks would take this route between Gascony and Aragón across an ill-defined border. The bridge stands at the confluence of two rushing mountain streams – the Gave de Gaube and the Gave de Marcadau – that plunge into dizzying waterfalls here.

Cross the bridge to the Hôtellerie du Pont d'Espagne and then another bridge to take the path to the **Télésiège de Gaube** ②. This is the bottom station of a chairlift on the Plateau de Clots. Take the 12-minute chairlift ride up to the viewpoint **Belvédère de Gaube** ③. The viewpoint can also be reached by a path that zigzags up to it.

From the viewpoint it is an easy walk across the slope and down to the **Lac de Gaube** ④ (1,725 m/5,660 ft), a glaciated lake. A bar-restaurant stands on the northern shore of the lake and its terrace provides a magnificent view. A short way beyond the bar offers an even better view. From here gaze up at the the north face of the pyramidal Vignemale (3,298 m/10,820 ft), which stands on the border with Spain, and is the highest summit in the French Pyrenees. This mountain was the life-long fascination of the 19th-century Irish-French Pyrenean mountaineering pioneer Henry Russell. One night he

had himself buried (to keep out the cold) on the summit by his guides – leaving only his head exposed – for the experience of seeing the sunrise at such an altitude.

The walk can be extended by taking the path that follows the west side of the lake to the Refuge de Oulettes (2,151 m/7,057 ft), below Vignemale. However, note that it is at least a 3-hour round trip from the lake.

Behind the restaurant, the lake drains away through a delta as a fast, clear-flowing stream, the Gave de Gaube. Take the path that follows the course of this stream. This is a section of the GR10, the long-distance footpath running all the way along the Pyrenees from the Mediterranean to the Atlantic. The path winds downhill to meet the road from the car park to the Pont d'Espagne. Turn right to return to the starting point. An alternative to taking the GR10 down is to retrace the route back from the lake to the Belvédère de Gaube and take the chairlift down to the valley. From the Télésiège de Gaube head back to the car park.

🚗 *From the Pont d'Espagne, return via Cauterets to Soulom and turn left at the red light onto the D921. In Pierrefite turn left onto the D13 for St-Savin.*

Above Pont Napoléon, the stone bridge across the Gave de Pau

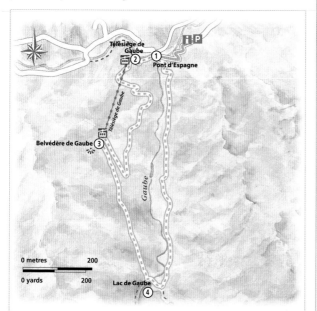

EAT AND DRINK

AROUND PONT NAPOLÉON

Templiers *inexpensive*
This crêperie, about 2 km (1 mile) from Pont Napoléon, has an 11-room hotel attached to it. *Galettes* (savoury pancakes made with buckwheat) and sweet crêpes are on the menu, of course, but there is much else besides, changing with the seasons, including main courses of trout, pheasant and salmon and a choice of salads.
6 place de la Comporte, Luz-St-Sauveur, 65120; 05 62 92 81 52; www.hotellestempliers.com; open daily mid-Jun–Sep

Eat and Drink: inexpensive, under €20; moderate, €20–€40; expensive, over €40

Above Isolated house at the foot of a hill on the outskirts of Ste-Engrâce **Below** Romanesque Église de Ste-Engrâce

⑱ St-Savin

Hautes-Pyrénées, Midi-Pyrénées; 65400
The 12th-century Romanesque **Église de St-Savin** and chapter house at the heart of this Pyrenean village are all that remains of a Benedictine monastery. The church was built to house the relics of the 9th-century hermit St-Savin. It still preserves a number of valuable works of sacred art, including a 14th-century ciborium (a cup with an arched cover) and 15th-century paintings of the life of the saint.

A short walk south of the centre of town is the pretty, isolated **Chapelle de Piétat** with its distinctive belltower. Built in the late 15th century, the chapel was greatly expanded during the 18th century. Dedicated to Our Lady of Mercy, it stands in an elevated position above the **Vallée d'Argelès** and its balcony offers lovely views.

🚗 *Take the slope down beside the Église de St-Savin towards Argelès-Gazost on the D101. At the roundabout in Argelès turn left onto the D918 towards Col d'Aubisque to drive through the Vallée d'Ossau.*

⑲ Vallée d'Ossau

Pyrénées-Atlantiques, Aquitaine; 64440
The route from Argelès through the Vallée d'Ossau, which encompasses 18 communes and is one of the Béarn's three major valleys, is a spectacular one. It goes over two passes, first the **Col de Soulour** (1,474 m/ 4,836 ft) and then the **Col d'Aubisque** (1,709 m/ 5,607 ft), a popular winter sports destination and part of the Tour de France, before descending via the ski resort of **Gourette** and the spa town of **Eaux-Bonnes** into the valley itself. At the junction of the D918 and D934, turn right into **Laruns**, home to the Château d'Espalungue, made famous in *The Three Musketeers* – it is where the musketeer Aramis is said to have died. Turning left here, make a detour to Fabrèges to take a breathtaking ride in the narrow-gauge Petit Train d'Artouste, which runs along a winding ledge at a height of 2,000 m (6,500 ft). Back in Laruns turn right onto the D240 for **Béost**, cross the bridge and turn left, still on the D240, towards **Aste-Béon**. In Béon turn left onto the D290, passing the Falaise aux Vautours, a vulture observatory. Cross the bridge and go over the roundabout onto the D934 for **Bielle**, home to the 15th–16th-century church of St-Vivien. Drive through Bielle, then turn left onto the D294 for **Bilhères**. Go through it, climbing steeply, towards the Col de Marie-Blanque. The road curves around the Chapelle de Houndas. Cross the Col de Marie-Blanque, a popular pass with cyclists, leaving the Vallée d'Ossau behind.

🚗 *Descend to Escot and turn left on the D238 towards Sarrance. Reaching the main road turn left on the N134. At Sarrance, turn off right onto the D241 for Lourdios-Ichère and continue through it to reach a three-way cross-roads. Go straight over onto a road marked "Col de Labays, Accès Pierre St Martin". At the T-junction turn right onto the D441 for Arette-Pierre-St-Martin. At the Col de Labays turn left*

AROUND ÉGLISE DE STE-ENGRÂCE

Auberge Elichalt *inexpensive*
Directly opposite Ste-Engrâce's Romanesque church is this simple inn run by the Burguburu family. It has four bed-and-breakfast rooms and more beds in a dormitory. As well as full meals, sandwiches and home-made cakes are also available.
Ste-Engrâce, 64560; 05 59 28 61 63; www.gites-burguburu.com

Left Horses grazing near the Col de Soulour mountain pass **Top** Chapelle de Piétat above the Vallée d'Argelès **Above** Spa town of Eaux-Bonnes

for Arette-Pierre-St-Martin on the D132. At the Col du Soudet just before Arette-Pierre-St-Martin, turn right onto the D113 for Ste-Engrâce.

⑳ Église de Ste-Engrâce
Pyrénées-Atlantiques, Aquitaine; 64560
The small 11th-century Romanesque church of Ste-Engrâce has a carved portal and carved capitals inside. In the cemetery are some ancient discoid Basque gravestones. Behind the church, the valley side is sliced by a white gorge, the Gorges du Ehujarré. Down the road there is another, smaller, more accessible gorge, the Gorges de Kakouetta, a managed beauty spot.

🚗 Continue on the D113 from Ste-Engrâce and the Gorges de Kakouetta to meet the D26. Turn left for Larrau. After passing through Larrau, turn right onto the D19 towards St-Jean-Pied-de-Port. This goes over the wooded Col de Bagargui at 1,327 m (4,354 ft), colonized by Les Chalets d'Iraty, a rural and ski resort built of huts shaped like upturned boats. After meeting the D18 next to a lake, turn right for St-Jean-Pied-de-Port, crossing over the Col de Burdinkurutcheta (1,135 m/3,724 ft). In St-Jean-le-Vieux, turn left on to the D933 for St-Jean-Pied-de-Port.

㉑ St-Jean-Pied-de-Port
Pyrénées-Atlantiques, Aquitaine; 64220
The name, translated literally "St-Jean-Below-the-Pass", explains the function of the town: it was founded by the kings of Navarra in the 12th century as a frontier town. Nowadays, as it was then, it is busy with pilgrims following the **Chemin de Saint-Jacques** – the route to the shrine of Santiago de Compostela – who stop here for the night before crossing the Pyrenees into Spain. The scallop-shell symbol of the pilgrimage can be seen everywhere in the town.

🚗 Leave St-Jean on the D918, towards Bayonne. Turn off left (Km 37) for Itxassou and follow the signs for Espelette on the left.

Cols of the Tour de France
The arduous climbs to the high mountain passes (cols) of the Pyrenees provide some of the most popular stages of the legendary Tour de France cycle race. The most challenging cols – all on the route of this drive – include Pèyresourde, Portet d'Aspet, Aspin, Tourmalet and Aubisque. Many amateur cyclists relish the challenge of getting to the top of these cols where they get a "passport" stamped to commemorate their achievement.

EAT AND DRINK

ST-SAVIN
Los Viscos moderate–expensive
A celebrated restaurant with rooms in this charming village, Los Viscos's menu is built around the cuisine of the southwest, particularly the local region of Bigorre. Choice ingredients include black pork, Trebons onions, foie gras confit and fresh mountain herbs.
1 rue Lamarque, 65400; 05 62 97 02 28; www.chateauxhotels.com/viscos; closed Sun dinner and Mon; Jan

ST-JEAN-PIED-DE-PORT
Le Relais de la Nive
inexpensive–moderate
Picturesquely overhanging the river between the new bridge and the old, this brasserie serves meals, crêpes and sandwiches.
2 place du Général de Gaulle, 64220; 05 59 37 04 22

Eat and Drink: inexpensive, under €20; moderate, €20–€40; expensive, over €40

Above Small château in Espelette
Below left Brightly-painted balcony of a Basque house in Ainhoa **Below right** Lively beach in St-Jean-de-Luz

LA RHUNE RAILWAY

Departures every 35 minutes or so between 9:30–11:30am and 2–4pm depending on number of passengers. *Col de Saint Ignace; 05 59 54 20 26; www.rhune.com; open Mar–Nov*

WHERE TO STAY

AROUND ESPELETTE

Domaine de Silencenia *inexpensive*
Just off the road at Louhossoa, 11 km (7 miles) east of Espelette, this bed-and-breakfast has a swimming pool and a small lake in its grounds. There are five cosy bedrooms, each individually decorated and equipped with a four-poster bed.
Louhossoa, 64250; 05 59 93 35 60; www.domaine-silencenia.com

AROUND AINHOA

Ttakoinenborda *inexpensive*
This is a traditional 17th-century farmhouse with four guest bedrooms in the fields and woods near the lovely town of Sare, about 9 km (5.5 miles) west of Ainhoa. Basque specialities are served at dinner accompanied by home-made bread.
Sare, 64310; 05 59 47 51 42; www.chambredhotebasque.fr

㉒ Espelette
Pyrénées-Atlantiques; 64250
Espelette is synonymous with the pepper it produces and many of the house façades in this attractive Basque town are adorned with red peppers hanging to dry in the sun. The *piment d'Espelette* has been grown in the area since the 17th century and is protected by its own *appellation d'origine contrôlée*. It is mildly hot and can be used judiciously as a substitute for black pepper. Espelette's 14th-century **château** now houses the town hall and the tourist office. Archaeological excavations around it have revealed vestiges of a fortress dating from the end of the Middle Ages. Another highlight is the 16th-century **Église**

Ste-Etienne, with three rows of galleries in typical Basque style and an altarpiece showing the stoning of Ste-Etienne. Its cemetery has traditional Basque discoid tombstones.

🚗 *From Espelette follow the signs back onto the D918 and continue towards Ainhoa. Turn left onto the D20 for Ainhoa.*

㉓ Ainhoa
Pyrénées-Atlantiques; 64250
Little more than a single street, Ainhoa is nonetheless a delight to walk around. The town was founded during the 12th century as a stop on the pilgrims' route to Santiago de Compostela in Spain, but much of it dates from the 17th and 18th centuries, having being rebuilt after the Thirty Years' War. Its stout, well-kept, *colombage* Basque houses are all orientated east-southeast and many have their date of construction and the name of their first inhabitant embossed on the lintel. Ainhoa, like Espelette, has a Basque-style galleried church.

🚗 *Go back to the roundabout at the entrance of Ainhoa and turn left towards Sare on the D305. Next, turn right on D4. Cross the river and turn left, still on the D4, for Sare, which, like Ainhoa, is a pleasant town to stop and stroll in. Follow the signs from Sare towards St-Jean-de-Luz, continuing on the D4. The winding road will take visitors up to the Col de St-Ignace and to the next stop at La Rhune.*

Where to Stay: inexpensive, under €70; moderate, €70–€150; expensive, over €150

㉔ La Rhune

Col de Saint Ignace; 64310

Located at the western end of the Pyrenees, La Rhune is right on the border between France and Spain. The wooden coaches of a cog railway, the **Petit Train de la Rhune**, ascend from this low saddle to the summit of Massif de la Rhune, a 900-m (2,952-ft) mountain overlooking the Basque coast. Once the train reaches the top of the mountain, visitors step out from it and in a few paces are over the border in Spain where *ventas* (inns) await. La Rhune is also known for its several hiking trails and the adventurous can reach the summit on foot.

Descend from the Col de St-Ignace to Ascain and follow the signs through the town to St-Jean-de-Luz.

㉕ St-Jean-de-Luz

Pyrénées-Atlantiques; 64500

Together with Ciboure, its neighbour, St-Jean-de-Luz is one of the prettiest and liveliest resorts on the Basque coast, with an excellent long, sandy beach. Almost swallowed by the bars and souvenir shops on the main street of the town is the church, the **Église St-Jean-Baptiste**, in which the Sun King Louis XIV married the Spanish Infanta Marie-Thérèse in 1660 in order to cement a trans-Pyrenean treaty. The door by which the couple left was immediately and forever blocked up. This galleried church, with a stunning 17th-century altarpiece, can still be visited today. Also visit the **Maison Louis XIV** *(open Apr–Oct; closed Tue)* where the king stayed in 1660.

Above Bright blue door and windows adding colour to a stone house in Ainhoa **Left** Hikers climbing up the rugged Massif de la Rhune

EAT AND DRINK

ESPELETTE

Hotel Euzkadi *inexpensive*
This restaurant serves Basque specialities flavoured with Espelette pepper, including *axoa*, made with veal, green peppers and garlic, and *pipérade*, made with ham, tomatoes and green peppers.
Espelette, 64250; 05 59 93 91 88; www.hotel-restaurant-euzkadi.com; closed Mon, Tue, Nov–Jan

AINHOA

Ithurria *moderate–expensive*
This is a 17th-century house converted into a restaurant and hotel. The menu includes Basque dishes.
Ainhoa, 64280; 05 59 29 92 11; www. ithurria.com; closed Wed, Thu except Jul–Aug, Nov–Apr

---

DAY TRIP OPTIONS

The following day trips are best done from Céret (on the D115), Lourdes (on the N21), Pau (on the A64) and St-Jean-de-Luz (on the A63) respectively.

Catalan France
Use Céret ② as a base to visit the priory at Serrabone ③ before continuing to Prades and the abbey of St-Michel-de-Cuxà ④. Continue to the spa of Vernet-les-Bains ⑤ and Villefranche-de-Conflent ⑥.

From Céret, follow the itinerary but on reaching Prades for the second time stay on the N116 and follow the route in reverse to return to Céret.

Mountain heights
The city of Lourdes is an ideal base for a day's circuit of the highest parts of the Pyrenees including a cable car trip to the Pic du Midi ⑭ and a visit either to the Cirque de Gavarnie ⑯ or the Pont d'Espagne ⑰.

From Lourdes take the D937 and D935 to Bagnères-de-Bigorre and turn right on the D935 joining the route at Ste-Marie-de-Campan. Follow the route to Argelès-Gazost and continue down the valley back to Lourdes on the D821.

Impressive mountain passes
From Pau, drive through the Béarn's spectacular Col du Soulor, Col

d'Aubisque and Vallée d'Ossau ⑲.

Leave Pau on the D937 towards Lourdes. Turn right on the D35 and left on to the D126 for Col du Soulor. Turn right to follow the itinerary but stay on the D934 at Bielle to return to Pau.

Amazing coastline
St-Jean-de-Luz makes ㉕ the best base for exploring the pretty French Basque Country including the towns of Sare, Ainhoa ㉓, Espelette ㉒ and St-Jean-Pied-de-Port ㉑.

From St-Jean-de-Luz drive the route in reverse to St-Jean-Pied-de-Port. Return in the direction of the route but stay on the D918 for a more direct route back.

Eat and Drink: inexpensive, under €20; moderate, €20–€40; expensive, over €40

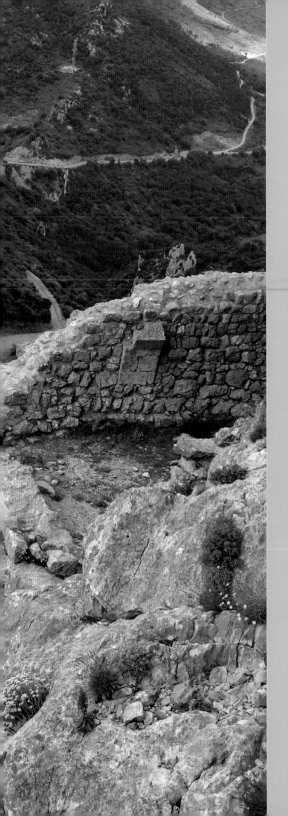

The Cathar Trail

Carcassonne to Montségur

Highlights

- **Historic citadel**
  Discover the history of the medieval citadel of Carcassonne

- **Lofty castles**
  Explore the great windswept castles of the Corbières

- **Dramatic gorges**
  Drive through the thrilling gorges of Galamus and Pierre Lys

- **The last stand of the Cathars**
  Climb to the summit of Montségur, the Cathars' last stronghold

Winding path that leads up to Quéribus, with a stunning backdrop

The Cathar Trail

The Cathar Trail combines a remote and beautiful region of France with a rich variety of historical sights. Castles, perched on seemingly inaccessible summits, are framed by wild herb-scented *garrigue*, vineyards, deep gorges and tumbling rivers. Originally built as defences against the Spanish, these castles sheltered the Cathars in the 13th century. A Christian sect that rebelled against corruption in the church, the Cathars flourished at first, but then Pope Gregory IX and the king of France joined forces in the cruelest crusade of the Middle Ages, resulting in terrible sieges and massacres.

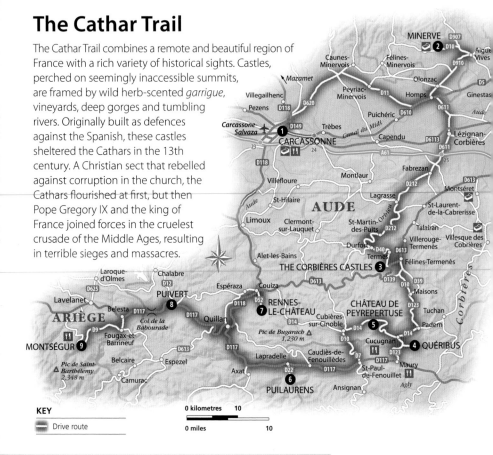

KEY

🚗 Drive route

0 kilometres 10
0 miles 10

Above Imposing citadel of Carcassonne, restored by Viollet-le-Duc, *see p209*

PLAN YOUR DRIVE

Start/finish: Carcassonne to Montségur.

Distance: 295 km (180 miles).

Number of Days: 2, allowing half a day to explore Carcassonne.

Road conditions: Usually good roads with some steep approaches to castles and gorges.

When to go: Any time of year.

Opening hours: Most sights stay open from 10am to 6pm and close on either Mondays or Tuesdays.

Main market days: Carcassonne: Tue, Thu and Sat.

Major festivals: Carcassonne: Festival de la Cité, Jul; Conilhac-Corbières: Jazz festival, Nov.

❶ Carcassonne
Aude, Languedoc-Roussillon; 11000

Carcassonne's citadel (La Cité) of pepperpot towers has been a strategic site for over 2,000 years. It is a dramatic sight on a rocky outcrop above the Aude river – a medieval town encircled by a double wall of fortifications punctuated by massive towers. It was restored in the 19th century by the Gothic revivalist Viollet-le-Duc.

Evidence of settlement dates from the 6th century BC, and Carcassonne became a key part of Roman colonization. Parts of the inner walls and towers date from the Roman period, including the Avar Postern Gate. By the 12th century the town was one of the great powers of the south.

During the crusade against the Cathars, Carcassonne was on the frontline and finally fell after a siege led by Simon de Montfort in 1226. The citadel was then reinforced with a second ring of ramparts and towers. However, La Cité lost its role of frontier guard once the Treaty of the Pyrenees moved the border in 1659. The citadel fell into decline until Viollet-le-Duc stepped in.

Enter the castle through the twin sandstone towers of the Narbonne Gate. Between the ramparts are the *lices*, a further defensible space, once used for jousting and now the best place to walk round to get a good sense of the defences. Inside the citadel is a maze of well-restored medieval houses and winding streets. The **Château Comtal** *(open daily)* dominates the centre. Visitors can see the watchtowers, posterns, covered wooden walkways and machicolations here. Do not miss the **Basilique**

St-Nazaire-et-St-Celse *(open daily)* with its lovely medieval stained glass and the famous Siege Stone depicting the death of Simon de Montfort.

🚗 *From La Cité follow signs to Mazamet on the D149 and turn right onto the D620. Then turn right onto the D11 to cross the Canal du Midi and join the D610. Turn left and at Homps take the D910 to Olonzac; continue on the D910 to Aigues-Vives. Turn left onto the D907, then take the D10 to Minerve.*

❷ Minerve
Hérault, Languedoc-Roussillon; 34210

In the bleached hills of the Minervois wine country, Minerve sits perched on its rocky spur at the confluence of the Cesse and Brian rivers. It is defended by the Candela, the octagonal tower that is all that remains of the original château. In 1210 this little village resisted a seven-week siege which ended with the immolation of 140 Cathars. Walk along the Rue des Martyrs to the 12th-century church of **St-Etienne**, with its 5th-century marble altar table.

🚗 *Return to Homps on the D910. Turn left onto the D610 then right onto the D611 towards Lézignan-Corbières. Continue to Fabrezan, then take the D212 to Durfort.*

Above Pepperpot tower of the citadel in Carcassonne **Below left** Bridge across the gorge to Minerve **Below right** Minerve's Rue des Martyrs lined with medieval houses

VISITING CARCASSONNE

Tourist Information
28 rue de Verdun, 11890; 04 68 10 24 30.

Parking
The main parking spaces are Parking André Chénier, Parking des Jacobins and Parking Gambetta. No cars are permitted in La Cité itself.

WHERE TO STAY

CARCASSONNE

Hotel de La Cité *expensive*
Grand hotel in the ramparts of La Cité with celebrated restaurant, La Barbacane, serving all the luxuries of the region from *foie gras* to truffles.
Place Auguste-Pierre Pont, 11000; 04 68 71 98 71; www.hoteldelacite.com

MINERVE

Relais Chantovent *inexpensive*
Simple accommodation in the village with views over the gorge and a restaurant serving local classics.
17 Grand Rue, 34210; 04 68 91 14 18; www.relaischantovent-minerve.com

EAT AND DRINK

CARCASSONNE

Jardins de la Tour *inexpensive*
Pretty, idiosyncratic restaurant with garden dining and authentic regional dishes such as *cassoulet* and good fresh fish.
11 rue Porte d'Aude, 11000; 04 68 25 71 24; www.jardindelatour.fr; closed Sun, Mon

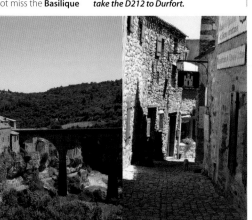

Eat and Drink: inexpensive, under €20; moderate, €20–€40; expensive, over €40

Above Stunning Gorge de Pierre Lys on the way from Puilaurens to Quillan **Below left** Fourteenth-century Château de Puivert **Below middle** Cathar cross in Montségur **Below right** Keep of the Château de Montségur, a Cathar stronghold

WHERE TO STAY

AROUND THE CORBIÈRES CASTLES

Domaine Haut Gléon *inexpensive*
This wine estate, 25 km (15 miles) from Villerouge-Termenès, has rustic accommodation in a renovated stable wing, and fine wine to taste.
Durban 11360; 04 68 48 85 95; www.hautgleon.com

Domaine Saint-Marie des Ollieux *inexpensive*
Stay in one of three rooms available at this family-run vineyard, and enjoy an aperitif in the wonderful gardens surrounding the domaine. Breakfast is available on request.
Montséret, 11200; 04 68 43 59 20; www.likhom.com

③ The Corbières Castles
Aude, Languedoc-Roussillon; 11330
The Corbières, the Pyrenean foothills southeast of Carcassonne, were one of the main centres of Cathar resistance. Much of the land is untamed *garrigue*. Here, visitors can discover several castles, spectacularly perched sanctuaries on craggy peaks that made ideal sites for hilltop fortresses. At **Durfort** is a ruined château. From here turn left onto the D40 to **Termes** to see its castle, which suffered a four-month siege in 1210. Turn left from here onto the D613 to reach the **Château de Villerouge-Termenès** *(closed Jan, Mon–Fri, Mar and mid-Oct–Dec)*, where the last known Cathar was burned alive in 1321.

🚗 *From Villerouge-Termenès backtrack to turn left onto the D39 then right onto the D139. Turn left on the D10 and again left on the D410. Next turn right on the D123 for Padern. After Padern turn right onto the D14 to Cucugnan and then left onto the D123 to Quéribus. Turn right at sign to Quéribus and continue up the steep hill to the main (second) parking place.*

④ Quéribus
Aude, Languedoc-Roussillon; 11350
The one remaining keep of Quéribus, perched on its peak at a height of 728 m (2,388 ft), dominates the plain of Roussillon below and has spectacular views *(open daily, closed Jan)*. It is well preserved, with a complex of stairways, tunnels, dungeons and a vaulted central hall, which was perhaps originally a chapel. Quéribus sheltered a few remaining Cathars after the fall of Montségur and was finally besieged only in 1255.

🚗 *Return to the D14 and head in the direction of Peyrepertuse. The access road is a left turn from Duilhac.*

⑤ Château de Peyrepertuse
Aude, Languedoc-Roussillon; 11350
The most vertiginous castle of all at 800 m (2,625 ft), rising out of a craggy barrier of rock, Peyrepertuse can only be reached via a long and winding road, and is a climb of at least half an hour. The site is so narrow that the castle *(open daily, closed Jan)* is only a few yards wide in parts and accessible by only one narrow entrance. It is still a formidable fortress, with two towers, and a Romanesque chapel in the keep of St-Georges. The wind takes the breath away, as do the views to the sea, to the void below and to the far peaks of the Pyrenees.

🚗 *After Peyrepertuse continue along the D14 to Cubières-sur-Cinoble and take the D10 through the dramatic but tortuous Gorges de Galamus. Then follow the D7 to St-Paul-de-Fenouillet, and turn right onto the D117, until arriving at Lapradelle. Look out for a sign to Puilaurens, requiring a left turn in the village onto the D22.*

⑥ Puilaurens
Aude, Languedoc-Roussillon; 11140
Puilaurens is one of the best examples of the amazing refuges of the Cathars, perched at nearly 700 m (2,300 ft). Visitors can drive nearly all the way up so only a modest 10-minute climb is required. A single steep stone stairway zigzags its way to the top of the ramparts. The architecture of the castle *(open daily, closed Nov–Jan)* offers a fine illustration of medieval defence methods with its walled courtyard, slanted arrow slits and chutes.

🚗 *Return to and continue on the D117 to Quillan, via the Gorge de Pierre Lys. Turn right onto the D118 to Couiza, and right again on the D52 to reach Rennes-le-Château.*

Where to Stay: inexpensive under €70; moderate €70–€150; expensive over €150

❼ Rennes-le-Château
Aude, Languedoc-Roussillon; 11190
This tiny village has become a great attraction for those in search of the occult. The mystery behind the priest, Abbé Saunière, suddenly growing rich in the late 19th century has never been satisfactorily explained and the legend of hidden treasure draws many visitors every year. It has inspired bestsellers such as *The Da Vinci Code*. Sights to visit are Saunière's church and his house and garden with its library tower, now a museum *(open daily)*.

🚗 *Return to Quillan; turn right onto the D117 to Puivert.*

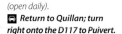
Tapestry in the museum at Puivert

❽ Puivert
Aude, Languedoc-Roussillon; 11230
The 14th-century private château *(open daily, closed 15 Nov–15 Dec)*, constructed round a courtyard with six towers, has a beautifully restored chapel. Known as the troubadour's castle, it has a minstrels' room with sculpted capitals of musicians. Some of their instruments are displayed in the town's museum *(open daily Mar–mid-Nov, Sun–Fri mid-Dec–Apr, closed mid-Nov–mid-Dec)*.

🚗 *Continue on the D117 to Belesta. Turn left onto the D5 for Fougax-et-Barrineuf and then turn right onto the D9 to reach Montségur.*

Above Saunière's majestic library tower in Rennes-le-Château

---

❾ Montségur
Ariège, Midi-Pyrénées; 09300
The approach to Montségur is part of the experience. Catching glimpses of the stone remains of the castle, it is possible to imagine the last band of Cathars fleeing here to seek refuge in this remote place.

A one-hour walking tour
From the car park access to the **Château de Montségur** ① is a few turns of the steep road upwards. The walk to the top (1,216 m/3,990 ft) is clearly indicated. It is a short but steep climb up the rocky path and there are several points along the way where visitors can pause to get their breath back and look at the view of the mountains around.

Eventually the path brings walkers to the rocky summit and the base of the castle ramparts. One large keep remains, its great stone walls pierced only by two arched doorways and narrow arrow slits. This was to be the last stronghold of the Cathars. Many sympathisers and pilgrims fearing persecution fled here and for ten years about 500 people lived within the ramparts or the village that huddled round them.

In 1242 the Cathars despatched a band of soldiers who assassinated 11 Inquisitors trying their fellows in Avignonet. In retaliation King Louis IX sent an army of 6,000 to besiege Montségur. After ten months of siege through a hard Pyrenean winter, they were given a stark choice: renounce their faith or die.

More than 200 chose to die, and hurled themselves into the flames of a vast pyre. When visitors descend again they will see a Cathar cross at the foot of the mountain, marking the spot where they died. The castle dominates the small village, which is worth visiting afterwards for lunch and a trip to the small **museum** ②, which has information about the Cathars *(open daily, closed Jan)*. Retrace the route to the car park.

EAT AND DRINK

AROUND QUÉRIBUS
L'Auberge du Vigneron *moderate*
About 4 km (2 miles) from Quéribus, this restaurant in an auberge wine-cellar is known for regional specialties such as rib of wild boar with ceps.
2 Rue Achille Mir, Cucugnan, 11350; 04 68 45 03 00; closed Mon

Pascal Borrell *moderate*
This lively restaurant, 7 km (4 miles) from Quéribus, uses local wines for cooking, especially the sweet dessert Maury wine.
La Maison du Terroir, Avenue Jean-Jaurès, Maury, 66460; 04 68 86 28 28

MONTSÉGUR
Auberge de Montségur *moderate*
At the foot of Montségur, in the heart of the village, is this small cosy hotel-restaurant with comfortable rooms.
52 le Village, 09300; 05 61 01 10 24

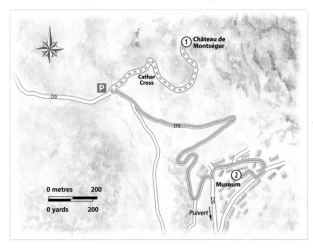

Eat and Drink: inexpensive under €20; moderate €20–€40; expensive over €40

Two Thousand Years of Bridges

Pont du Gard to La Couvertoirade

Highlights

- **Roman aqueduct**
  Marvel at the 2,000-year-old Pont du Gard stretching across the Gardon river

- **Dense wilderness**
  Explore some of the thickest forests of France in the Cévennes

- **Dramatic gorges**
  Stop and admire the plunging gorges of the Tarn

- **Modern bridge**
  Wonder at the Viaduc de Millau, a 21st-century triumph of art and engineering

Viaduc de Millau, one of the greatest achievements of modern architecture

Two Thousand Years of Bridges

This tour begins at the 2,000-year-old Pont du Gard, the highest bridge ever built by the Romans, and ends beyond the amazing new viaduct spanning the Tarn gorge at Millau. It includes the ancient Roman city of Nîmes and the exquisite town of Uzès. Between the two bridges lies magnificent scenery, the wild uplands and shady chestnut forests of the Cévennes and the deep canyons of the Gorges du Tarn. The culinary journey ranges from the wine and olives of the Mediterranean to the earthy cuisine of the mountains.

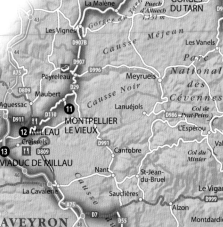

Above Musée des Vallées Cévénoles, St-Jean-du-Gard, *see p219*. **Top right** Town of Millau, *see p220*. **Below right** Pont du Gard, the Roman bridge that has survived two millennia, *see p216*

ACTIVITIES

Canoe in the Gardon river below the Pont du Gard

Taste the finest wines of the Costières vineyards in Nîmes

Explore the bamboo garden at La Bambouseraie de Prafrance

Investigate the history of silk-making in St-Jean-du-Gard

Swap the car for a donkey on the Robert Louis Stevenson trail

Try river rafting in the Gorges du Tarn

Enjoy canyoning from St-Enimie in the Gorges du Tarn

KEY

Drive route

PLAN YOUR DRIVE

Start/finish: Pont du Gard to La Couvertoirade.

Number of Days: 3-4, allowing half a day to explore Nîmes.

Distances: 290 km (180 miles).

Road conditions: Well-made and signposted roads, but some narrow winding ones in the gorges, with steep hills and hairpin bends. At times there can be flooding around Nîmes and the Gardon river; in winter higher altitudes may receive snowfall.

When to go: Good any time of year but more crowded in the summer. Spring can be rainy, and winter is generally clear, though occasionally snow is possible in the mountains.

Opening hours: Most sights are generally open from 10am to 6pm. Some close either on Mondays or on Tuesdays, and on major public holidays.

Main market days: Nîmes: daily Uzès: Wed, Sat, Sun; St Jean du Gard: Tue (May–Oct: also Wed & Sat) Florac: Thu; Millau: Wed, Fri.

Major Festivals:: Nîmes: Feria, May and Sep; Uzès: Music Festival, Jul; St Jean du Gard: Walking Festival, May; Millau: Dance and Jazz Festival, Jul.

DAY TRIP OPTIONS

The entire route can be broken into three day trips. **History enthusiasts** can visit Nîmes and the Pont du Gard in a day. **Nature lovers** will enjoy a day's visit to the Cevennes *corniches*. The Gorges du Tarn will make an excellent day trip for **adventure seekers**. For more details, *see p221*.

Above Three-tiered Pont du Gard, a Roman engineering marvel **Below left** Massive stone columns of Les Arènes, Nîmes **Below right** Imposing and historic Maison Carré, Nîmes

VISITING THE PONT DU GARD

Tourist Information
www.ot-pontdugard.com

Parking
There are paid car parks on both banks of the Gardon. For the Rive Gauche take the D19; for the Rive Droite (right bank), turn off from the D981.

WHERE TO STAY

NÎMES

Le Royal Hotel *inexpensive*
This arty small hotel has a popular tapas bar and a huge dining terrace.
3 boulevard Alphonse Daudet, 30020; 04 66 58 28 27; www.royalhotel-nimes.com

La Magne *moderate*
Rooms are well-decorated and there is a swimming pool in the garden.
296D Impasse des Troénes, 30900; 04 66 23 70 86; www.chambres-la-magne.com

① Pont du Gard

Gard, Languedoc-Roussillon; 30210
The first sight of the 2,000-year-old Pont du Gard, near the village of Remoulins, is astonishing. A stupendous feat of engineering still unsurpassed, it has resisted both tampering and the erosion of time and floods. The three great storeys of golden limestone arches span the Gardon river to a height of 49 m (160 ft). Built from enormous blocks of stone hauled into place by slaves using pulleys and wheels, the aqueduct originally carried water 50 km (30 miles) from the springs at Uzès to Nîmes, sometimes through underground channels dug out of solid rock. The Visitor Centre on the Rive Gauche offers guided walks across the bridge and has a **museum** *(open daily)* detailing its history. In the summer, canoes can be hired to explore the river around the bridge.

🚗 *Drive to Nîmes on the D6086, following directions to "Centre Ville" and the "Office du Tourisme", and then park on Boulevard Jean-Jaurès.*

② Nîmes

Gard, Languedoc-Roussillon; 30000
The ancient city of Nîmes has been a crossroads since Roman times, and is renowned for its Roman antiquities, especially its magnificent amphitheatre. At its heart is a medieval warren of streets full of shops and lively cafés. Recently, imaginative architectural projects, particularly the glittering arts museum opposite Nîmes' celebrated Roman temple, have pulled the city into the future. This colourful southern city is vibrant with outdoor life, most of all during its famous *féria*.

A two-hour walking tour

From the car park, walk up Boulevard Jean-Jaurès to the **Jardins de la Fontaine** ① *(open daily)*. These 18th-century formal gardens were constructed around a spring discovered by the Romans, now a network of pools, stone terraces and marble nymphs and cupids. Among the chestnut trees is the ruined **Temple de Diane** ②, a Roman fragment whose original purpose remains a mystery. High on Mont Cavalier above the garden is the octagonal ruin of the Tour Magne *(open daily)*, once a key component of the original Roman walls and now a fine place for an overview of Nîmes. Head into the city from the Quai de la Fontaine, turning right along Boulevard Alphonse Daudet, to find the **Maison Carré** ③ *(open daily except public holidays)*, a beautiful, symmetrical Roman temple from the 1st century BC. It has a great flight of stone steps leading to finely fluted Corinthian columns. The museum of contemporary art, the **Carré d'Art** ④ *(closed Mon)*, designed by British architect Norman Foster, is a glass and steel reflection of the Maison Carré opposite, a modern temple complete with steps and columns. A huge atrium incorporates a library and art galleries focusing on modern French art and Mediterranean artists. Pause in the

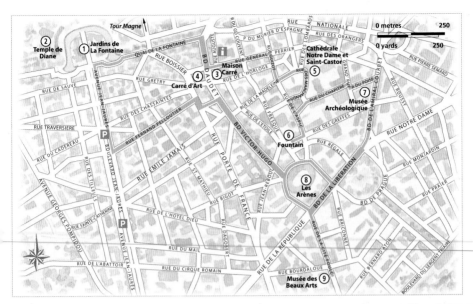

roof terrace restaurant for a drink and a superb view of the Roman temple. Next head along Rue Général Perrier, past the Halles, the market hall, great for regional food specialities. Turn right on Rue Guizot and Place de l'Horloge into the old town, turning left along Rue de la Madeline to reach Place aux Herbes. Here is the Romanesque **Cathédrale Notre-Dame et St Castor** ⑤, badly damaged during the Wars of Religion (1562–98), although the remains of a Romanesque sculpted frieze can still be seen on the façade. Much of the old town is well preserved, with narrow streets and intimate little squares. To see some fine buildings walk from Place aux Herbes down Rue des Marchands then take the right fork into Rue Auguste Pelet to Rue de l'Aspic. Turn right into Place du Marché, where artist Martial Raysse designed the **fountain** ⑥, a modern version of Nîmes' emblem, a crocodile tied to a palm tree. Its origin is attributed to Roman legionnaires, veterans of the Egyptian campaign. Return to Rue de l'Aspic and turn left back up the road, then right into Plan de l'Aspic and into Rue du Chapitre. Turn right into the Grand'Rue then left into Rue du Poise to Boulevard de l'Amiral

An intricate metal postbox

Courbet. Turn right to the **Musée Archéologique** ⑦ *(closed Mon)* in a former Jesuit monastery. It has a splendid collection of Roman statues, sarcophagi, entablature, glass, coins and mosaics. From the museum continue down Boulevard de l'Amiral Courbet and Boulevard de la Libération to the amphitheatre, **Les Arènes** ⑧ *(open daily except for public holidays and performances)*, built at the end of the 1st century BC. It can seat 20,000 spectators and is used for music and opera performances. To fully appreciate the massive structure with its vast oval arena and tiers of seats, explore the echoing stone arcades that encircle it or climb round the top tier. Cross Boulevard de la Libération and walk down Rue de la Cité Foulc to the beautiful **Musée des Beaux Arts** ⑨ *(closed Mon)*. It houses a collection of paintings by French, Italian and Dutch masters. From here return to the Arènes and head up Boulevard Victor Hugo, turning left at Place Questel and right onto Rue Fernand Pelloutier, at the end of which is the car park.

🚗 *From Nîmes take the D979 towards Uzès, crossing Pont St-Nicolas, pausing for a look at the winding Gorges du Gardon. Drive uphill to Uzès. Park just below the Tour Fenestrelle.*

Above Quiet and charming Quai de la Fontaine, Nîmes

VISITING NÎMES

Tourist Information
6 rue Auguste, Nîmes, 30020; 04 66 58 38 00; www.ot-nimes.fr

Parking
There is parking on Boulevard Jean-Jaurès.

EAT AND DRINK

NÎMES

Vintage Café *inexpensive*
Friendly little café in the old town, serving drinks and a Provençal menu.
7 rue de Bernis, 30020; 04 66 21 04 45; closed Sun, Mon

Le Lisita *moderate*
This excellent restaurant has a large shady dining terrace. Specialities include pigeon with wild mushrooms.
2 boulevard des Arènes, 30000; 04 66 67 29 15; closed Sun, Mon

Eat and Drink: inexpensive, under €20; moderate, €20–€40; expensive, over €40

Top left Herd of sheep on a remote farm in the Cévennes **Top right** Tableau of Camisard chief Roland in front of the Musée du Désert, Mas Soubeyran **Above** View of the rolling hills of the Cévennes **Below** Medieval square of Uzès

SHOPPING

Bamboo artifacts
Intriguing bamboo-inspired artworks add to the experience at La Bambouseraie, and a shop offers a wealth of items and plants.

WHERE TO STAY

UZÈS

Hotel du Général d'Entraigues *expensive*
This gorgeous 17th-century townhouse has rooms full of antiques.
Place de l'Eveche, 30700; 04 66 22 32 68; www.hoteldentraigues.com

AROUND ST-JEAN-DU-GARD

La Porte des Cevennes *moderate*
A quiet hotel, 14 km (9 miles) south of the town, this place has views of the Gardon valley from its terrace.
Route St-Jean-du-Gard, Anduze, 30140 ; 04 66 61 99 44; www.hotel-restaurant-porte-cevennes.com

La Ferme de Cornadel *moderate*
This is a rustic Cevennes farmhouse with comfortable rooms. The cuisine is based on local produce such as sausages and sheep's cheese.
Route de Générargues, Anduze, 30140; 04 66 61 79 44; www.cornadel.fr

③ Uzès
Gard, Languedoc-Roussillon; 30700
At the heart of Uzès is the medieval square of Place aux Herbes, with shady arcades full of cafés around a central fountain. There is also a delightful medieval garden in the Old Town, full of herbs and medicinal plants. The **Tour Fenestrelle** *(not open to visitors)* dominates the town with its 12th-century arcaded bell tower, all that remains of the Romanesque cathedral. Do not miss the privately owned palace, **Le Duché d'Uzès** *(open daily)*, with its 12th-century tower, Renaissance façade and Burgundian-tiled chapel. The 17th-century **Cathédrale St-Theodorit** is the main location for the Uzès music festival in July.

🚗 Take the D982 to Moussac. From Moussac turn left (signposted Nîmes) and then right towards La Reglisserie, then turn left onto the D8 towards Aigremont. Turn right onto the D907 before entering the village of Aigremont. At Lédignan follow signs to Anduze. Now follow signs to La Bambouseraie, turning right onto the D129.

④ La Bambouseraie de Prafrance
Gard, Languedoc-Roussillon; 30140
A vast exotic garden, established in 1856 by French botanist Eugene Mazel, La Bambouseraie *(open daily Mar–mid-Nov)* is now the largest bamboo forest in Europe. Wander round the shady green avenues of many varieties of bamboo, some reaching a height of 27 m (88 ft), and admire other exotic species such as japonica, palms, sequoia and ginkgo biloba. The park also includes a Laotian village, constructed entirely of bamboo, with an enclosure of Vietnamese pigs, a tranquil Zen garden, water gardens, bonsai and a labyrinth.

🚗 Continue along the D129 into the village of Générargues and turn left onto the D50 to reach Mas Soubeyran.

⑤ Mas Soubeyran
Gard, Languedoc-Roussillon; 30140
One of the most important sites of French Protestantism, Mas Soubeyran is a sombre, inspiring memorial to the oppression of Huguenots (French Protestants) during the religious wars of the 17th and 18th centuries. The hills of the Cévennes provided sanctuary for the rebellious Camisards

(the "white shirts"). This remote hamlet was where Camisard chief Roland was born, and today is home to the **Musée du Désert** *(open daily Mar–Nov)* which offers a moving testimony to the faith of the persecuted Huguenots.

🚗 *From the D50 turn left following signs to St-Jean-du-Gard. Park in the car park at the centre of the village.*

6 St-Jean-du-Gard

Gard, Languedoc-Roussillon; 30270
This small unpretentious town on the banks of the Gardon river, with its ancient bridge and 12th-century clock tower, is the gateway to the Cévennes. It was famous for its silk-making tradition until the last mill closed in 1965. The best way to appreciate the town and its history is to visit the **Musée des Vallées Cévénoles** *(open daily, Apr–Oct, Tue, Thu, Sun, Nov–Mar)* located in a 17th-century inn. It offers a survey of every aspect of Cévenol rural life.

🚗 *From St-Jean-du-Gard take the D907 and then the D260 signposted to Corniche des Cévennes (D9).*

7 Corniche des Cévennes

Gard, Languedoc-Roussillon; 30270
A fine way to appreciate the Cévennes landscape is to drive along the ridge road that was built by the Romans and improved by Louis XIV. Ascend through the chestnut forests to the limestone plateaux or *causses*, riddled with extraordinary caves and gorges and scattered with remote farms.

From the Col de Pierre there is a glimpse of Mont Aigoual and its observatory. Parc National des Cévennes, now a UNESCO Biosphere Reserve, is a strictly-controlled environment, balancing agriculture and forestry with ecological concerns. Rare flora, such as orchids and adonis, and fauna, including otters, vultures and red deer, have proliferated or been reintroduced.

🚗 *Continue along the Corniche de Cévennes (D9) to the Col du Rey where it becomes the D983, which then joins the D907 at Baraques de la Fontaine. Here turn right to Florac.*

The Stevenson Trail

In 1878, Robert Louis Stevenson walked 220 km (137 miles) from Le Monastier to St-Jean-du-Gard with his truculent donkey, Modestine, sleeping under the stars or in rudimentary inns. In his *Travels with a Donkey in the Cévennes* he captures perfectly the rugged beauty of the region. The trail he took is now very popular with walkers.

8 Florac

Lozère, Languedoc-Roussillon; 48400
This charming little town, nestling at the foot of rocky cliffs, is a Cévenne crossroads and gateway to the Gorges du Tarn. The old town of narrow winding streets and quiet shady squares clusters around the Fontaine des Dives, a refreshing pool and waterfall. The 17th-century château, centre of information for the Parc National des Cévennes *(open daily Easter–Sep, Mon–Fri rest of the year)* has an exhibition space devoted to the landscape and flora and fauna.

🚗 *From Florac follow signs to Gorges du Tarn. First take the N106, then D9078 signposted to Ispagnac and Quézac.*

Above Inside the exotic garden of La Bambouseraie de Prafrance **Below** Wicker baskets on display at a shop in Uzès **Left** Fontaine des Dives in the delightful little town of Florac

EAT AND DRINK

ST-JEAN-DU-GARD

La Chanterelle *moderate*
Simple, friendly restaurant for Cevenol specialities, *sole meunières*, and imaginative salads.
79 Grand Rue, 30270; 04 66 85 38 50; open lunch only, except Sat dinner; closed Fri

FLORAC

La Source de Pecher *moderate*
With a picturesque terrace overlooking the river and waterfall, this place is known for local specialities such as duck with bilberry sauce, Lozère trout and chestnut cake.
Rue Remuret, 48400; 04 66 45 03 01

AROUND FLORAC

La Lozerette *inexpensive*
One of author Robert Louis Stevenson's stops, outside Florac (4 km/2 miles east on D998), this rustic *auberge* with a garden offers meals of regional specialities like Aubrac beef, washed down with good local wines.
Cocures, 48400; 04 66 45 06 04; closed Tue, Wed, Nov–Apr

Eat and Drink: inexpensive, under €20; moderate, €20–€40; expensive, over €40

Above Schist- and terracotta-tiled roofs of St-Enimie Right Medieval village near the Gorges du Tarn Below Dramatic gorges of the Tarn

ACTIVITIES IN GORGES DU TARN

CANOEING AND KAYAKING

Canoë Canyon
St-Enimie, 48210; 04 66 48 50 52

WHERE TO STAY

AROUND ST-ENIMIE

Manoir de Montesquiou *moderate*
This beautiful 15th-century manor house, 10 km (6 miles) south of St-Enimie, has wonderful views, an inner courtyard for summer dining, rooms in the turret and four-poster beds.
La Malène, 48210; 04 66 48 51 12; www.manoir-montesquiou.com

AROUND MONTPELLIER LE VIEUX

Grand Hotel de la Muse et du Rozier *moderate*
Beautifully renovated, the Grand Hotel stands on the banks of the Tarn, 12 km (7 miles) north of Montpellier. It has a sleek modern restaurant, gardens for al fresco meals, and a fabulous pool.
La Muse, Peyreleau, 12270; 05 65 62 60 01; www.hotel-delamuse.fr

⑨ Gorges du Tarn
Lozère, Languedoc-Roussillon; 48210
Often referred to as the Grand Canyon of Europe, the Gorges du Tarn is a great fissure slashed through the limestone plateaux by the Tarn river. There are amazing views as the road snakes along the side of the gorge from Ispagnac to Peyreleau, dominated by craggy cliffs of rock. Below are stunning views of the emerald waters. It is a superb location for walking, canoeing and bird-watching. Along the way are the cascades of tributary rivers and spectacular rock formations. Medieval villages, ruined towers and châteaux cling to the canyon walls.
🚗 Follow the D907B to St-Enimie.

⑩ St-Enimie
Lozère, Languedoc-Roussillon; 48210
This beautiful village with its schist-tiled roofs stacked against the steep slopes of the gorge is a centre for outdoor activity in the region. Explore the twisting stone streets to visit the remains of a monastery, the 12th-century church and the Place au Beurre at the heart of the village. **Le Vieux Logis** *(closed Tue, Sat)* is a museum devoted to local traditions.
🚗 Continue along the D907B to beyond Les Vignes towards Peyreleau; here the road changes to D907. Approaching Peyreleau turn left onto the D996. Drive into the village and take the D29 right. Climb up a narrow winding road and turn right onto the D110 then left again to Montpellier le Vieux.

⑪ Montpellier le Vieux
Aveyron, Midi-Pyrénées; 12750
This extraordinary natural chaos of rock formations high up on the

windswept Causse Noir was hidden by an impenetrable forest until 1870. It was believed to be an ancient ruined city by local peasants. Weirdly contorted rocks form columns, arches, and all manner of shapes, named the "Sphinx", the "Arc de Triomphe", even "Queen Victoria's head". A choice of signposted trails let visitors wander at will, breathe the pure air of the forest and admire far-reaching views across the *causses*. A small train *(daily Mar–Nov)* offers an easier ride to the heart of the site.
🚗 Leaving Montpellier le Vieux take the D110 signposted to Millau. Look out for the first sight of the viaduct while descending the hill into the town.

⑫ Millau
Aveyron, Midi-Pyrénées; 12700
Millau has always been a crossroads between east and west, north and south. It was famous for its tanning, in particular glove-making, and the surviving *ateliers* can be still be visited on Rue de la Paulèle. Start with the **Office de Tourisme**, on Place du Beffroi, located in a restored 17th-century building behind the market hall and near the imposing octagonal belltower. Visit the local museum in a fine 18th-century mansion, **Hôtel de Pégayrolles** *(open daily, closed Sun Oct–May)*, to learn about leather and glove production. Today Millau has another reason for fame. It was notorious for its traffic bottleneck, as vehicles struggled up and down the steep sides of the Gorges du Tarn. But there

now stands the magnificent bridge which has reduced the crossing to a matter of minutes, and completes the direct A75 motorway link between Paris and the Mediterranean.

🚗 *Drive north of Millau on the D911, following signs to Cahors and the A75. Then follow signs to Montpellier (junction 45) on the A75. Go through the péage (toll) and take the exit to Aire de Viaduc where there is ample parking and a short walk up to a viewpoint of the bridge.*

⑬ Viaduc de Millau
Aveyron, Midi-Pyrénées; 12700
The Viaduc de Millau was a tourist attraction even before it was finished in 2004 as people came to marvel at the inspired engineering that has created one of the world's highest bridges – the tallest pier is 340 m (1,115 ft), higher than the Eiffel Tower. This suspension bridge spans the gorge created by the Tarn river on a series of delicately soaring concrete

pillars over a distance of 2.5 km (1.5 miles), a work of art of astonishing beauty. Designed by British architect Lord Norman Foster and structural engineer Michel Virlogeux, and built by a French engineering company, Eiffage, it can be admired from below, or from several viewing points around Millau. Foster described the ultimate experience of crosssing the viaduct as "flying by car."

🚗 *After crossing the Viaduc de Millau stay on the A75, and head for La Couvertoirade. Take exit 48, follow the D7 east and turn right onto the D55.*

⑭ La Couvertoirade
Aveyron, Midi-Pyrénées; 12230
Built as a retreat by the Knights Templar during the 15th century, La Couvertoirade is a superbly preserved and renovated walled town with tur-reted towers, ramparts, a church and stone houses. It was built around a 13th-century château. Many of the streets are still unpaved.

EAT AND DRINK

MILLAU

Château de Creissels *moderate*
Located in a 12th-century château with lovely gardens and a view of the viaduct, this gourmet restaurant creates imaginative dishes from local produce, such as the lamb of Lozère. *Route de Saint-Affrique, 12100; 05 65 60 16 59; www.chateau-de-creissels.com ; closed Sun lunch, Mon dinner (low season), Nov–Mar*

La Mangeoire *moderate*
A favourite with locals, this cosy restaurant has an open grill for hearty steaks and sausages, to savour with *aligot*, the Aveyron speciality of mashed potato and cheese. *8 boulevard de la Capelle 12100; 05 65 60 13 16; closed Mon, Jan*

DAY TRIP OPTIONS
This route can be easily broken down into separate parts, to suit those who have less time to spare or with particular interests. The bases can be Nîmes, St-Jean-du-Gard and Florac.

Legacies of the Roman Empire
For any visitor interested in history, a day trip to Nîmes ❷ and the Pont du Gard ❶ provides the perfect opportunity to explore the rich Roman legacy of the region. Spend a morning strolling round the fine old city of Nîmes and then visit the Pont du Gard in the afternoon. Admire the astonishing monument, walk across

the bridge itself to see the view of the river and even take a dip from the little beach below.

From Nîmes take the D6086 to the Pont du Gard.

Cévennes history
The Corniche de Cévennes ❼ and then Florac ❽ can be enjoyed in a day's drive, starting with the gardens of La Bambouseraie de Prafrance ❹, the Protestant museum – Musée du Désert – in Mas Soubeyran ❺, and the museum of Cévennes life in St-Jean-du-Gard ❻.

From La Bambouseraie take the D129 and turn left on the D50 for Mas Soubeyran. Then turn left and follow

signs to St-Jean-du-Gard. From here take the D907 and then the D260 to Corniche des Cévennes. Continue on the D9 to Col du Rey. Then take the D983 and the D907 to reach Florac.

Natural wonders and châteaux
The Gorges du Tarn ❾, starting from Florac ❽ and ending at Peyreleau, offers a wealth of experiences, from the stunning natural wonders of the river, waterfalls, and rock formations to medieval villages and romantic châteaux. Visitors can hike or hire canoes to fully appreciate the beautiful landscape.

From Florac take the N106, then the D31and drive along the D907B.

Eat and Drink: inexpensive, under €20; moderate, €20–€40; expensive, over €40

Gardens and Glamour

Menton to Nice

Highlights

- **A driver's dream**
  Enjoy spectacular views while navigating the South of France's most breathtaking road, the Grande Corniche

- **Fame and fortune**
  Visit the former residences and favourite restaurants of some of the most high profile visitors to the French Riviera

- **Lush landscapes**
  Admire the Côte d'Azur's gardens which range from rustic groves of ancient olive trees to manicured visions of paradise

Colourful, flower-filled Stone Garden at Villa Ephrussi de Rothschild, Cap-Ferrat

Gardens and Glamour

Synonymous with extravagance, wealth and royalty, the Côte d'Azur is France's effervescent playground. From the mid-19th century onwards, northern Europeans spent long winters in the mild yet invigorating seaside climate of the South of France. The 1920s and 30s saw summer take precedence as the most popular season to visit. One of the great legacies of this golden age is the penchant for elaborate gardens. Many of these enchanting oases are open to the public today. Going from Menton on the Italian border to the Riviera's self-proclaimed capital of Nice, this driving tour winds its way past the haunts of Europe's glitterati, taking in all three *corniches* – parallel coastal roads, each higher up and further from the sea than the next – along the way.

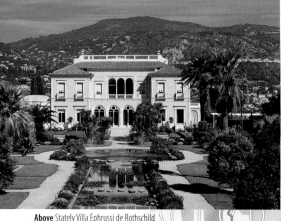

Above Stately Villa Ephrussi de Rothschild on Cap-Ferrat, *see p229*

ACTIVITIES

Take a private tour of the modern architectural masterpiece, Cabanon Le Corbusier in Roquebrune-Cap-Martin

Try to break the bank at Monaco's Le Casino de Monte-Carlo

Wander the nine exotically themed gardens at the Villa Ephrussi de Rothschild in Cap-Ferrat

Spend a lazy day dipping in and out of the waves from the golden sand of Villefranche-sur-Mer's beach

Pick up ripe seasonal produce or bouquets of Provençal wildflowers from local farmers at Nice's markets

KEY

 Drive route

PLAN YOUR DRIVE

Start/finish: Menton to Nice.

Number of days: 2 to 3, allowing half a day to explore Cap-Martin and Promenade Le Corbusier.

Distances: 55 km (35 miles).

Road conditions: Generally good, with clear signposting; some narrow roads with tight turns. Between July and August traffic is very heavy, particularly along the Basse Corniche, the D6098.

When to go: Between April and June, before holidaymakers fill the French Riviera, or from September to October, when rates drop but the weather is still pleasant.

Opening hours: Most shops are open from 10am until around 7pm (some with a lunch break between noon and 2pm), while major sights tend to close an hour or two earlier. Restaurants are often closed one or two days a week, usually Sunday and/or Monday. During the low season be sure to telephone ahead for opening hours.

Main market days: Menton: daily (antiques on Fri); **Monaco:** daily (antiques on Sat); **Beaulieu-sur-Mer:** Mon, Tue, Sat; **Villefranche-sur-Mer:** Sat, Sun; **Nice:** Tue–Sun (antiques on Mon).

Shopping: Shop for top designer labels in Monaco and 1950s Italian furniture at Nice's Marché à la Brocante, an antiques and flea market (Mondays), at the Cours saleya.

Major festivals: Menton: Fête du Citron, Feb; **Monaco:** Formula One Grand Prix, May; **Cap-Ferrat:** Les Azuriales Opera Festival, Aug; **Nice:** Carnival, Feb–Mar; Jazz Festival, Jul.

DAY TRIP OPTIONS

Nature lovers can walk Cap-Ferrat's 3-hour coastal path, while drivers with a **head for heights** should head to the Grand Corniche, which offers stunning views over the Mediterranean coastline. For details, see p229.

Below left Doorway in the old town in Villefranche-sur-Mer, *see p229* **Below right** Cafés in a crowded square in Nice, *see p229*

Above Chemin des Douaniers, the coastal pathway around Cap-Martin

WHERE TO STAY

ROQUEBRUNE-CAP-MARTIN

Hôtel Les Deux Frères *moderate*
The ten rooms at this 18th-century former schoolhouse offer stunning views. Restaurant Les Deux Frères is renowned in its own right. Stop by at lunch for chef Samuel Foret's fixed-price three-course menu that comes with half a bottle of wine.
1 place des Deux Frères, 06190; 04 93 28 99 00; www.lesdeuxfreres.com; restaurant closed Mon, Sun dinner, Tue lunch

① Menton

Alpes-Maritimes, Provence-Alpes-Côte d'Azur; 06500

From its pasta-filled menus to its Old Town's architecture, Italian culture has had a profound influence on this little French town, located less than 2 km (1 mile) from the border. Its appeal is not just multicultural – the town is also home to lovely gardens and a superb collection of 20th-century fine art. Writer and artist Jean Cocteau selected Menton for his **Musée Jean-Cocteau** *(open Wed–Mon)*, housed in a restored 17th-century bastion on the seafront.

🚶 *Head west along the seafront, taking the promenade in the direction of Cap-Martin. Turn left onto Avenue Winston Churchill, following the signs for Promenade Le Corbusier, to reach the car park at the tip of Cap-Martin.*

Menton's Gardens

The temperature rarely dips below 5° C (41° F) in Menton, making this the ideal climate for no less than seven stunning gardens. Spend a sunny afternoon exploring the magnificent flora, including lotus and hibiscus, at the exotic **Val Rahmeh** *(open Wed–Mon)*, or examine Europe's largest citrus garden, **Le Jardin d'Agrumes at Palais Carnolès** *(open Wed–Mon)*, the former summer residence of the Prince of Monaco.

② Roquebrune-Cap-Martin

Alpes-Maritimes, Provence-Alpes-Côte d'Azur; 06190

Austere yet romantic Roquebrune is perched at 300 m (984 ft), a fortified medieval village overlooking lush Cap-Martin jutting into the Mediterranean below. Just outside Roquebrune on Chemin de Menton, the *olivier millénaire* (1,000-year-old olive tree) is a great attraction for amateur botanists. Fashionistas can seek out a glimpse of Villa Egerton, Coco Chanel's villa. Down on Cap-Martin, Promenade Le Corbusier skirts the sea, suspended between the peninsula's man-made luxury and the clear blue water of the Mediterranean.

A 75-minute walking tour

The Côte d'Azur's answer to the Hollywood Hills, the lanes that thread Cap-Martin are lined with luxurious mega-mansions, set well back from the roads and framed with bougainvillea. With a mix of pleasure palaces and permanent homes, it has long been favoured by some of the Riviera's wealthiest residents. Start the walk at the parking at the Cap's tip next to Avenue Winston Churchill's southernmost turn, which marks the beginning of Promenade Le Corbusier. Turn left and take the pedestrianized coastal walkway, passing sculptor Arlette Somazzi's bust of Charles Edouard Jeanneret,

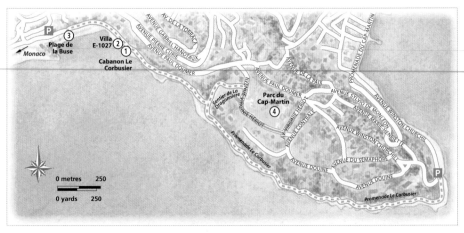

Where to Stay: inexpensive, under €70; moderate, €70–€150; expensive, over €150

better known as Le Corbusier. The Cap's coastal path, formerly Chemin des Douaniers (customs officers' path) was later renamed in his honour. As visitors amble along, tiny *sentiers* (trails) dip down on the left. With the exception of weekend days during summer's peak, they will be able to find their own rocky outcrop for private swimming and sunbathing.

Rounding the Cap's southwest corner, pause to enjoy the view of Monaco. Visitors will soon pass two of the walk's highlights, shortly before the path's end. In 1952, Le Corbusier planned and built **Cabanon Le Corbusier** ①, his seaside getaway on Cap-Martin. The tiny modular cabin is normally closed to the public, but on Tuesday and Friday mornings guided tours can be booked through the tourist office. Nearby, designer Eileen Gray's 1929 **Villa E-1027** ② is considered one of the Côte d'Azur's most architecturally innovative buildings for its use of space and its flexible, open design. The villa is now being restored. Cool off with a quick swim at **Plage de la Buse** ③ at the path's end. Then retrace the route around the Cap until the left turn into Sentier de la Dragonniere. Walk uphill, then right into Avenue Virginie Hériot which leads to **Parc du Cap-Martin** ④ *(open daylight hours)*, filled with centuries-old olive trees. Retrace the route to the car park on Avenue Winston Churchill.

🚗 *Continue on Avenue Winston Churchill then turn left onto the D52 to join the D6007. Follow signs to Beausoleil until the next roundabout*

and take the D6098 to Place du Casino, Monte-Carlo. Park in the square's underground car park.

③ Monaco
Alpes-Maritimes, Provence-Alpes-Côte d'Azur; 98000

Ruling Monaco for over 700 years, the Grimaldi family has flourished in its own international spotlight. However, it was not until 1865, when Charles III established **Le Casino de Monte-Carlo** *(open daily)*, and 1868, when all taxes were abolished, that playboys and bigwigs really began to arrive. In 1956, American actress Grace Kelly married Prince Rainier, putting a fairy-tale icing onto the principality's cake. Visitors can spoil themselves at the city's exclusive boutiques, or witness the changing of the guards at the **Palais Princier** *(daily at 11.55am)*.

🚗 *Exit the car park and turn left towards the port. Head west on Avenue de Monte-Carlo which becomes Rue Grimaldi. Follow the D6098 to Cap d'Ail; there is a car park on the right, just off Avenue du 3 Septembre.*

Above left Ancient olive trees in Parc du Cap-Martin **Above right** Terracotta rooftops of the medieval village of Roquebrune **Below** Le Casino de Monte-Carlo, Monaco

VISITING ROQUEBRUNE-CAP-MARTIN

Tourist Information
218 Aristide Briand, 06190 ; 04 93 35 62 87; www.roquebrune-cap-martin.com

EAT AND DRINK

MONACO
Café de Paris *moderate–expensive*
This brasserie and cocktail bar, located next to Le Casino de Monte-Carlo, is renowned for celebrity spotting.
Place du Casino, Monte-Carlo, 98000; 377 98 06 76 23; www.montecarloresort.com

AROUND MONACO
La Salière *moderate*
The Italian-run La Salière, 9 km (6 miles) from the city centre serves oversized salads and delectable home-made pastas.
14 quai Jean-Charles Rey, Fontvieille, 98000; 377 92 05 25 82

Above Narrow cobblestoned streets in the village of Eze Below Lovely Stone Garden at Villa Ephrussi de Rothschild, Cap-Ferrat

④ Basse Corniche

Alpes-Maritimes, Provence-Alpes-Côte d'Azur; 06320

One of the French Riviera's three *corniches*, the Basse Corniche (D6098) rambles along the coast, alternatively soaring above the sea or dipping down just above the Mediterranean. Clamber down to pretty **Plage Mala** from Cap d'Ail. From there take the coastal footpath eastwards, passing **Villa The Rock**, where actress Greta Garbo often came to spend a holiday, and **Villa Capponcina**, the mansion formerly owned by UK press baron Lord Beaverbrook. Travellers can also explore the coastal strip of **Eze-sur-Mer**, home to U2 singer Bono.

🚗 *Head west out of Cap d'Ail on the D6098. Take a quick sharp right for Eze onto the D45, and then continue on the Moyenne Corniche (D6007) to Eze. There is a car park at the foot of the town in Place du Général de Gaulle.*

⑤ Eze

Alpes-Maritimes, Provence-Alpes-Côte d'Azur; 06360

At 400 m (1,312 ft) above sea level, Eze is the archetypal *village perché* (hilltop village). A century ago, as Nietzsche climbed its steep path, Eze's golden cobblestones were familiar ground only to local donkeys, used to haul up provisions. Between 1923 and 1953, Sweden's Prince William and his family wintered at what is now Château Eza. Visit **Le Jardin d'Eze** *(open daily)* and Château Balsan, where director Alfred Hitchcock shot his 1955 film *To Catch a Thief*, for views over Cap-Ferrat.

🚗 *Take the D46 north, then the Grande Corniche (D2564), following signs for Nice. Turn left onto the D33, right onto the D6007, then a quick left onto Avenue Léopold II (D33), towards Villefranche-sur-Mer. At the crossroads turn left onto Boulevard Edouard VII (D133) to Beaulieu-sur-Mer. There are car parks in Place Clemenceau and near the Port de Plaisance.*

⑥ Beaulieu-sur-Mer

Alpes-Maritimes, Provence-Alpes-Côte d'Azur; 06310

The sleepy Art Deco environs of Beaulieu-sur-Mer carry a regal air. Delve into the town's history, and it is apparent that its early 20th-century residents – royalty from Italy, Britain, Portugal, Belgium, Sweden and Russia – have all left their mark. Gustave Eiffel, architect of the Eiffel Tower in Paris, lived here, as did Théodore Reinach, creator of **Villa Kerylos** *(open daily)*, a replica 2nd-century BC Greek villa built between 1902 and 1908. The town is also home to the **Grand Casino** where Winston Churchill gambled away many an evening.

🚗 *Drive west along the seafront, following directions for Cap-Ferrat on the D125. Turn left at the Pont Saint-Jean intersection. Follow signs to Saint-Jean and park in Place Clemenceau.*

⑦ Cap-Ferrat

Alpes-Maritimes, Provence-Alpes-Côte d'Azur; 06230

Formerly the grazing grounds for local livestock, Cap-Ferrat is now one of the wealthiest spits of land in the world. During the early 20th century, King Leopold II of Belgium purchased much of the Cap, from his private villa

Iberia near Plage Passable to the lighthouse at the southern tip. Baroness Beatrice Ephrussi de Rothschild designed Île-de-France, her dream villa, in 1905. Now known as **Villa Ephrussi de Rothschild** *(open daily)*, it boasts nine themed gardens. Since the 1950s, vacationing glitterati have included Edith Piaf, Elizabeth Taylor, Roger Moore, and recently, Bill Clinton. Actors Charlie Chaplin and later David Niven owned the villa **Lo Scoglietto**, and British author Somerset Maugham hosted the Marx brothers and the Aga Khan at his home, **La Mauresque**.

🚗 *Drive back to the Pont Saint-Jean intersection and turn left onto the D6098. At Carrefour de la Libération, before the Jardin Francois Binon (tourist office), take a sharp left onto the Avenue Sadi Carnot. Head downhill to the car park at Place Wilson.*

8 Villefranche-sur-Mer
Alpes-Maritimes, Provence-Alpes-Côte d'Azur; 06230
Arrive in this miniature paradise and it is hard to believe that Nice's metropolis is just 6 km (4 miles) away. The town sits peacefully on the west side of a bay, flanked by Cap-Ferrat to the east. Pastel buildings cluster along the waterfront, nestling between a 16th-century citadel and the town's golden sweep of beach. Nearby, the Rolling Stones recorded *Exile On Main Street* at **Villa Nellcote**, where guitarist Keith Richards played host at some of the Riviera's wildest parties. Visit **Chapelle Saint-Pierre** *(opening time varies)*, its façade and interior vividly decorated with Jean Cocteau's murals of Saint Peter, patron saint of fishermen.

🚗 *Retrace Avenue Sadi Carnot back to the D6098. Turn left onto the D6098, also known as Boulevard Princesse Grace de Monaco, for Nice. Park in the port's car park to the left, or continue up Rue Cassini to the car park on Avenue Félix Faure.*

9 Nice
Alpes-Maritimes, Provence-Alpes-Côte d'Azur; 06000
Nice has been the French Riviera's most popular tourist destination for over a century *(see also pp234–5)*. From artist Marc Chagall who celebrated his 80th birthday party at the Palais de la Méditerranée in 1967 to film stars Brad Pitt and Angelina Jolie who had their twins here at the Lenval Hospital in 2008, illustrious visitors fill the city year-round. Get a sense of the local action at the **Cours Saleya's markets**, or order a *café crème* at one of the old town's pavement cafés. Head up to the **Parc du Château** *(open daily)* for views over the Promenade des Anglais and the Cap d'Antibes beyond.

Above left Seaside Villa Kerylos, Beaulieu-sur-Mer *Above right* Seafront promenade and restaurants, Villefranche-sur-Mer

EAT AND DRINK

EZE

Château Eza *expensive*
Cuisine and stupendous views are best enjoyed on the restaurant's terrace. *Rue de la Pise, 06360; 04 93 41 12 24; www.chateauezarestaurant.com; closed Mon, Tue (low season), Nov & Dec*

BEAULIEU-SUR-MER

African Queen *moderate–expensive*
A celeb favourite, it is renowned for its crispy pizzas, fresh fish and lobster. *Port de Plaisance, 06310; 04 93 01 10 85*

VILLEFRANCHE-SUR-MER

Cosmo *moderate*
Contemporary French cuisine is served on a patio overlooking the bay. *11 place Amélie Pollonais, 06230; 04 93 01 84 05*

NICE

Castel Plage *moderate–expensive*
This is the town's best beachside bar. *8 quai des États-Unis, 06000; 04 93 85 22 66; closed mid-Sep–mid-Mar*

DAY TRIP OPTIONS
Although the main roads between Menton and Nice can be busy during high season, if visitors opt for the heights of the Moyenne (D6007) or Grande Corniches (D2564), they can cover the distance between both ends of the drive with ease.

Panoramic pleasures
For cooler breezes and sweeping vistas, head to the hills. The quiet Grande Corniche (D2564) leaves the crowded seaside as it climbs ever

higher. Spend the afternoon exploring pretty Roquebrune-Cap-Martin **2**, then head over to the Riviera's favourite perched village, Eze **5**. Outdoor enthusiasts can descend to Eze's beach, Eze-sur-Mer, by hiking along the Nietzsche Path (approximately an hour's trek).

Take D2564 east from Roquebrune-Cap-Martin. Turn left onto D46, which heads downhill to Eze. D6007 will lead back to Roquebrune-Cap-Martin.

Coastal walk
Drive to Saint-Jean-Cap-Ferrat or park the car in Beaulieu-sur-Mer **6** and take a walk along the well-signposted rocky coastal path at Cap-Ferrat **7**. Finish at the beach at Villefranche-sur-Mer **8**.

D6098 connects Beaulieu-sur-Mer and Villefranche-sur-Mer along the base of Cap-Ferrat, and can be easily accessed from any of the stops along this driving tour. Parking is available by Beaulieu-sur-Mer's casino.

Eat and Drink: inexpensive, under €20; moderate, €20–€40; expensive, over €40

The Riviera Artists' Trail

Nice to Mougins

Highlights

- **Live like an artist**
  Sleep in Matisse's former home, dine in Modigliani's ex-studio or order a *café crème* at Chagall's favourite breakfast spot

- **Mediterranean inspiration**
  Revel in the verdant landscapes, turquoise seas and rosy sunsets that inspired Monet, Renoir and Picasso to make the Côte d'Azur their home

- **Artisan crafts**
  Get an insider's view of the methods used to create traditional artisan crafts, from Biot's open "bubble" glass workshops to artists spinning potters' wheels on the streets of Vallauris

Famous Promenade des Anglais along the Mediterranean coast, Nice

The Riviera Artists' Trail

Whether it is the quality of the light, the blue Mediterranean sea or simply the clarity of the Provençal air, the Côte d'Azur has long attracted the world's most renowned artists. Impressionists Claude Monet and Pierre-Auguste Renoir were the first to make the French Riviera their base. Other artists, catching word of the region's unique, vibrant light, soon followed. Henri Matisse first visited Nice in 1917, and for the next 35 years he divided his days between Nice and Vence. Pablo Picasso, smitten by the coast after visiting in the 1930s, spent the next four decades in Golfe Juan, Vallauris, Antibes and Mougins. Marc Chagall moved to Provence in the 1940s, eventually settling in Saint-Paul-de-Vence with his wife; the village is now a shrine to modern art. Today, in spite of the various popularity swings and style changes, the Riviera continues to boast one of the most prolific outpourings of creativity in the world.

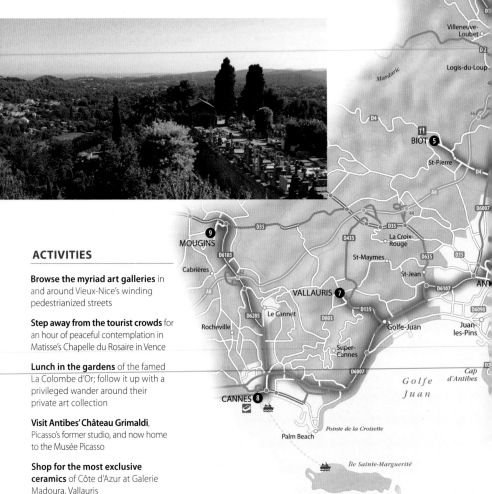

ACTIVITIES

Browse the myriad art galleries in and around Vieux-Nice's winding pedestrianized streets

Step away from the tourist crowds for an hour of peaceful contemplation in Matisse's Chapelle du Rosaire in Vence

Lunch in the gardens of the famed La Colombe d'Or; follow it up with a privileged wander around their private art collection

Visit Antibes' Château Grimaldi, Picasso's former studio, and now home to the Musée Picasso

Shop for the most exclusive ceramics of Côte d'Azur at Galerie Madoura, Vallauris

Swim in the surf of the star-studded beach in Cannes

Église
St-Nicolas
La Madeleine
St-Antoine
Magnan
Ste-
Marguerite
PROMENADE
DES ANGLAIS
1 NICE
Les
Pugets
Ste-Hélène
St-Laurent-
du-Var
La Californie
Musée Renoir
2 CAGNES-SUR-MER
Nice Côte-
d'Azur
Cros- de Cagnes
Bouches-du-Loup
Baie des
Anges
na Baie des Anges
neuve-
bet-Plage

0 kilometres 2

0 miles 2

KEY

Drive route

Above left Panoramic view of the landscape and the Mediterranean, Saint-Paul-de-Vence, *see p236* **Below left** Musée Picasso in Antibes, *see p236* **Below right** Ancienne Cathédrale de la Nativité de Notre-Dame in Vence, *see p235*

PLAN YOUR DRIVE

Start/finish: Nice to Mougins.

Number of days: 2 to 3, allowing half a day to explore Vieux-Nice.

Distance: 90 km (55 miles).

Road conditions: Generally very good, with clear signposting.

When to go: Between April and June, before holidaymakers fill the French Riviera, or between September and October, when rates drop.

Opening hours: Shops and churches are usually open from 10am to 5pm. Many museums and major sights close on Mondays and/or Tuesdays, as well as public holidays.

Main market days: Nice: Tue–Sun (antiques on Mon); **Vence:** Tue–Sun; Biot: Tue; Antibes: Tue–Sun.

Shopping: Shop for glassware in Biot and pottery in Vallauris.

Major festivals: Nice: Carnival, Feb–Mar; Jazz Festival, Jul; **Cagnes-sur-Mer:** Fête de l'Olivier, Mar; **Vence:** Fête des Fontaines, May; Festival des Nuits du Sud, Jul.

DAY TRIP OPTIONS

Those who want a taste of times past can pay a visit to enduringly popular Antibes, while **artists** seeking inspiration should spend the morning in Mougins. For more details, *see p237.*

Above Matisse's former home on the Cours Saleya, Nice

VISITING NICE

Tourist Information
5 promenade des Anglais, 06000; 08 92 70 74 07; www.nicetourism.com; closed Sun Oct–May

Parking
Parking Saleya, Parking Port de Nice and Parking Palais de Justice are all centrally located. Car parks can fill up early in the day during high season.

WHERE TO STAY

NICE

Hôtel Windsor *moderate–expensive*
Rooms at this chic hotel have been decorated by 20 contemporary artists.
11 rue Dalpozzo, 06000; 04 93 88 59 35; www.hotelwindsornice.com

Hôtel et Plage Beau Rivage *expensive*
Home to Matisse during 1917–18, this classy seafront hotel was renovated by famed architect Jean-Michel Wilmotte.
24 rue Saint François de Paule, 06300; 04 92 47 82 82; www.hotelnice beaurivage.com

❶ Nice

Alpes-Maritimes, Provence-Alpes-Côte d'Azur; 06000

For centuries Nice bounced back and forth between French and Italian ownership, but architecturally, Vieux-Nice, the city's Old Town, exemplifies the historical Italian influence. Narrow streets slip between buildings soaked in deep pastel hues. Picturesque squares form the perfect backdrop for pavement cafés. Nice's pedestrianized Old Town is at its most breathtaking early in the morning, when visitors will have the streets to themselves, or at dusk, when the Mediterranean sunset steeps the city in a golden hue.

A 90-minute walking tour

From Parking Saleya, follow Rue St-François de Paule to the pedestrianized **Cours Saleya** ①. This street has been home to Nice's produce market for well over a century. Matisse lived on the third and fourth floors of 1 place Charles Félix, at the eastern end of this boulevard, from 1921 to 1938. The imposing saffron-coloured building is closed to the public, but it is easy to see how the views over the Old Town, Colline du Château and Mediterranean sea inspired the artist.

Head through **Place Gautier** ②, packed with stalls selling primarily organic produce. Turn right into Rue Alexandre Mari, left into Rue St-Gaétan, then right into Rue de la Préfecture. Cross the road and step into **Galerie Sainte-Réparate** ③ (*open Tue–Sat*), which hosts some of the finest contemporary art and photography exhibitions in the city. Walk north along Rue Ste-Réparate to Place Rossetti. On the left, the **Cathédrale Ste-Réparate** ④ provides an ornate, 17th-century contrast to

Galerie Sainte-Réparate. Cross Place Rossetti (stopping in at Fenocchio to have some of the finest ice cream), follow Rue Rossetti uphill and turn left into Rue Droite. A host of galleries like **Galerie du Château** ⑤, **Galerie Renoir** ⑥ and **Atelier Phobé** ⑦ line Rue Droite, Rue de la Loge and Rue Benoît Bunico. After browsing the art on display, then walk up Rue St-François to the town's **fish market** ⑧. Follow Rue St-François as it veers left, turning left again into Boulevard Jean-Jaurès. Cross the road to Avenue St-Jean Baptiste and weave right around **Lycée Félix Faure** ⑨, Nice's prettiest secondary school. Turn left into Rue Désiré Niel and enter **L'Atelier Soardi** ⑩ (*open Tue–Sat*), an art gallery and framing shop, formerly Matisse's studio in 1930–31 where he created his enormous mural, *La Danse*. Retrace the route to Avenue Félix Faure, ambling down to the restored **Place Massena** ⑪, an open-air art gallery. Continue on Avenue de Verdun. Turn left and stroll down the famous Promenade des

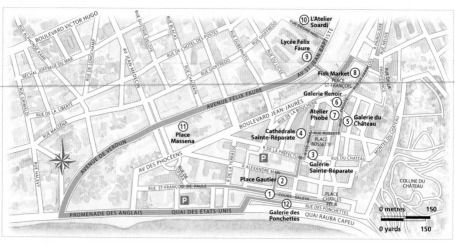

Anglais and the Quai des États-Unis to visit **Galerie des Ponchettes** ⑫ *(open Tue–Sun)*, where Matisse held his first exhibition in Nice. Retrace the route to the car park at the Quai des États-Unis.

🚗 *Follow the voie rapide west to the airport, where it becomes D6007, into Cagnes-sur-Mer. At the fork bear right onto Avenue Cyrille Besset (D36), then right again onto Ave des Tuillieres, then a quick left onto Chemin des Collettes following brown signs for Musée Renoir. Park in the car park.*

Voie Rapide

An elevated motorway, Nice's *voie rapide* connects the city's port neighbourhood with the airport. The expressway provides one of the finest driving experiences in an urban area. Travelling from east to west, look out for the multicoloured onion domes of Russian Orthodox Église St-Nicolas on the right.

② Cagnes-sur-Mer
Alpes-Maritimes, Provence-Alpes-Côte d'Azur; 06800
Pierre-Auguste Renoir spent the last 12 years of his life in this resort town in a house that is now the **Musée Renoir** *(open Wed–Mon)*. Rather than a comprehensive collection of paintings, the museum offers a peek at the artist's home, original furnishings, possessions and ten of his paintings. Visit Renoir's studio, as he left it, or admire the view to medieval Haut-de-Cagnes from the garden of citrus and 500-year-old olive trees.

🚗 *Head back down Chemin de Collettes and turn right for Avenue des*

Tuillieres, which becomes Ave Renoir *(D36). Continue on the D36 to Vence, passing Saint-Paul-de-Vence on the left. Follow signs to Vieux-Vence and on reaching the Old Town turn left at the junction and follow the road into Place du Grand Jardin, where there is a car park (to gain entry into the car park it is necessary to take the first left after crossing the square into a one way system).*

③ Vence
Alpes-Maritimes, Provence-Alpes-Côte d'Azur; 06140
A well-signposted 15-minute walk northwest of Vence's town centre is the joyful **Chapelle du Rosaire** *(open Mon–Thu and Sat, closed mid-Nov–mid-Dec)*. It was designed by Henri Matisse as an act of gratitude to his former nurse, Dominican nun Sister Jacques-Marie. It is located across the road from Villa Le Rêve, Matisse's residence in Vence from 1943 to 1949. In the Old Town, the **Ancienne Cathédrale de la Nativité de Notre-Dame** houses Marc Chagall's mosaic, *Moses Saved from the Waters*. The paintings, now located in Nice's Musée Marc Chagall, were originally created to adorn the walls of this cathedral; the final location had to be changed due to the high humidity within the church.

🚗 *On exiting the car park, take Avenue de la Résistance west to Place Maréchal Juin. At the roundabout, take the third exit onto Avenue Emile Hugues (D236), which leads south to Route de Saint-Paul (D2). At the edge of Saint-Paul-de-Vence, park in Parking Sainte-Clare, on the left.*

Above View to Haut-de-Cagnes from the gardens of Musée Renoir, Cagnes-sur-Mer **Below** Russian Orthodox Église Saint-Nicolas near Nice

WHERE TO STAY

SAINT-PAUL-DE-VENCE

Hostellerie Les Remparts
inexpensive–moderate
The hotel is located in the heart of pedestrianized Saint-Paul-de-Vence and has pretty Provençal rooms.
72 rue Grande, 06570; 04 93 24 10 47

ANTIBES

Le Bastide de la Brague
moderate–expensive
Situated only a 10-minute drive from Antibes port, this family-run bed-and-breakfast has double rooms and a friendly atmosphere. Enjoy an excellent dinner eaten with your hosts.
55 Avenue No 6, Antibes, 06600; 04 93 65 73 78; www.bbchambreantibes.com

CANNES

Hotel 3.14 *expensive*
Each of this hotel's five floors has a different continent as its theme. Guests can lounge at the ultra-cool 3.14 beach club, or beside the rooftop pool.
5 rue François Einesy, 06400; 04 92 99 72 00; www.3-14hotel.com

Above Sun-dappled corner in Biot's Old Town
Below Saint-Paul-de-Vence perched on a hilltop

④ Saint-Paul-de-Vence

Alpes-Maritimes, Provence-Alpes-Côte d'Azur; 06570
Picture-perfect on a hilltop and ringed by ramparts, Saint-Paul-de-Vence has long been a magnet for both artists and visitors to the French Riviera. Marc Chagall is buried in the pretty cemetery. Just west of town, **Fondation Maeght** *(open daily)* was set up by art dealers Marguerite and Aimé Maeght in 1964. Its permanent collection (partially in storage during annual summer exhibitions) includes works by Pierre Bonnard, Alberto Giacometti and a garden labyrinth by Joan Miró.

🚗 *From the car park take the D7, then the D336 to Cagnes-sur-Mer. Turn right onto the D136 which merges with the D6007, passing behind Marina Baie des Anges, an iconic apartment complex. Turn right onto the D4 and park at one of Biot's signposted car parks.*

⑤ Biot

Alpes-Maritimes, Provence-Alpes-Côte d'Azur; 06410
Sleepy, even during summer's peak, medieval Biot is renowned for its "bubble" glass. To see glassblowers in action, pick up a Chemin des Verriers leaflet and map of the town's workshops from the tourist office. Just south of town is the **Musée Fernand Léger** *(open Wed–Mon)*. The bright white space makes a striking contrast with Léger's colourful paintings, while the garden café is an idyllic lunch spot.

🚗 *Take the D4 back to the D6098. Head south to Antibes, keeping left to reach the port's many car parks.*

⑥ Antibes

Alpes-Maritimes, Provence-Alpes-Côte d'Azur; 06600
These days Antibes' Port Vauban may boast a strip of moorings known as Billionaire's Quay, but the fishing village's first superstar resident was Impressionist artist Claude Monet in 1888. Nearly 60 years later, in 1946, Pablo Picasso set up studio in the nearby Château Grimaldi. Now the **Musée Picasso** *(open Tue–Sun)*, it is home to a collection of the artist's paintings, drawings and ceramics.

🚗 *Follow signs for the Antibes railway station then follow the signs to Cannes on the D6107. At Golfe-Juan, turn right for Route de Vallauris (on the D135), which leads to Vallauris' town centre.*

⑦ Vallauris

Alpes-Maritimes, Provence-Alpes-Côte d'Azur; 06220
Vallauris is famous for artisan pottery. Its ceramic industry was revitalized in the early 1950s, primarily due to Picasso's passion. **Galerie Madoura** *(open Mon–Fri)*, where Picasso created the bulk of his ceramics, has pieces for sale, as well as photographs of Picasso and Chagall working side-by-side. On Place Paul Isnard stands Picasso's bronze *L'Homme au Mouton*, depicting a shepherd carrying a sheep. On the adjoining Place de la Libération is the Château-Musée de Vallauris, home to the **Musée National Picasso La Guerre et La Paix** *(open Wed–Mon)*. Picasso's last major political artwork, the 1952 *La Guerre et La Paix* (War and Peace), is installed in the château's 12th-century Romanesque chapel.

🚗 *Retrace the D135 to Golfe-Juan, and head west on the D6007 to*

casino that now hosts contemporary art exhibitions. The promenade runs alongside one of the finest beaches of France.

🔄 *Retrace the route to Place du 18 Juin. Drive straight down, across the square, following signs for Le Cannet and Grasse, on Boulevard Sadi Carnot (D6285). Follow signs for Grasse (ignore signs for Mougins on the N85) until arriving at a large roundabout (over the A8). Take the second exit off the roundabout, signposted for Grasse, onto the dual carriageway, the D6185, and exit at Mougins. The car park is at the foot of the town.*

⑨ Mougins
Alpes-Maritimes, Provence-Alpes-Côte d'Azur; 06250

This picturesque medieval village offers sweeping views over Cannes and the Mediterranean below. Spend an afternoon wandering around its cobbled alleys, or stop at the **Musée de la Photographie André Villers** (*open daily, closed Nov*). Villers' black-and-white photos of Picasso chronicle the last 15 years of the artist's life, which he spent in Mougins.

Cannes. On approaching Cannes, turn right at the roundabout following signs for Le Cannet. At Place du 18 Juin, take the second left onto the narrow road to Boulevard de la Croisette. Turn right at the T-junction, following signs for the old port, where Parking Laubeuf is situated on the western quay.*

⑧ Cannes
Alpes-Maritimes, Provence-Alpes-Côte d'Azur; 06400

One of the top Mediterranean resort towns, Cannes has been attracting the world's most famous visitors for over a century. The **Palais des Festivals et des Congrès**, where the Cannes Film Festival takes place every year in May, was built in its present form between 1979 and 1982. Cruise along the **Promenade de la Croisette**, on which stands the town's landmark **Hotel Carlton**, a 1911 Belle-Époque wonder. It is also home to the **Musée de la Malmaison** (*closed Tue*), a former

Left Popular beach in Cannes during the peak season **Below** Ceramics in vibrant colours on sale in Vallauris

EAT AND DRINK

SAINT-PAUL-DE-VENCE

Café de la Place
inexpensive–moderate
Marc Chagall's preferred breakfast spot, this café is placed alongside a sun-dappled *petanque* (French boules) pitch. *Place Général de Gaulle, 06570; 04 93 32 80 03; closed Nov–mid Dec*

La Colombe d'Or *expensive*
Paul Roux, the venue's original owner, was a passionate collector of art, who encouraged artists to trade artworks in lieu of payment. Treasures by Picasso, Raoul Dufy and Georges Braque, among many others, now pack the guesthouse and restaurant's public spaces. *Place Général de Gaulle, 06570; 04 93 32 80 02; www.la-colombe-dor.com; closed Nov–mid Dec*

BIOT

Le Jarrier *moderate–expensive*
Highly acclaimed, this restaurant is located in Biot's medieval centre. Pride of place is given to the seasonal menu, which changes each fortnight: find cherry tomato and strawberry soup in June, and sea bream with figs in September. *30 passage La Bourgade, 06410; 04 93 95 93 21; closed Sun, Mon*

DAY TRIP OPTIONS

The Côte d'Azur is packed with museums and arty hotspots. No matter where visitors are based, the D6007 provides easy access to both of the following day trips.

Antibes and the Cap
Its Old Town ringed by amber-hued stone walls, Antibes ⑥ has been a popular seaside destination for close to a century. Wander its colourful flowery lanes, or visit the newly renovated Musée Picasso. Around the corner, Cap d'Antibes is where Coco Chanel made suntans fashionable, water-skiing was

invented and F. Scott Fitzgerald's *Tender is the Night* was set. Nearby Juan-les-Pins also hosts Europe's oldest jazz festival every July – Charles Mingus, Miles Davis, Ray Charles, Ella Fitzgerald and Herbie Hancock have all performed here.

The D6098 connects Antibes to the D2559, which runs around the Cap d'Antibes.

Art and nature
Spend the morning in the picturesque medieval village of Mougins ⑨, exploring its cobble-stoned alleys. Aspiring artists will

find themselves drawn to the simple yet enchanting Musée de la Photographie André Villers, as well as the town's incredible vistas over Cannes ⑧ and the Mediterranean Sea. In the afternoon, head downhill to take in Cannes' busy shops and light smattering of galleries. Visitors should pack their paints – both Mougins and Cannes offer plenty of inspiration to artists.

Head west along the D6007 to Cannes. Turn right onto the D6185, following signs for Mougins. The public car park is on the left at the base of the town.

Eat and Drink: inexpensive, under €20; moderate, €20–€40; expensive, over €40

Vineyards of Provence

Saint-Tropez to Cassis

Highlights

- **Crisp whites, fruity rosés, ruby reds**
  Discover the different vineyards that line the roads between the Saint-Tropez peninsula and the lush green valleys east of Marseilles

- **Star-spotting**
  Keep an eye open for A-list celebrities while wandering the pretty streets of Saint-Tropez

- **Medieval hilltop villages**
  Explore Ramatuelle, Gassin, Bormes-les-Mimosas and Le Castellet and marvel at the magnificent sea views each offers

- **Sun-drenched beaches**
  Spend lazy days swimming, sunning and snorkelling at the beaches dotted all along the Mediterranean coast

Visitors enjoying themselves at the beach near Rayol-Canadel-sur-Mer

Vineyards of Provence

With a varied topography that could easily be considered France's finest, Provence boasts golden beaches, valleys and the fjord-like Calanques. This driving tour makes its way slowly along the region's prettiest roads, from the glitzy bling of Saint-Tropez to the rugged beauty of Cassis's towering Calanques, passing resort towns that saw their heyday in the 1920s and verdant countryside full of vineyards. Vines thrive and grapes ripen slowly in the nurturing Mediterranean climate – it is sunny most of the year, sea breezes keep the air fresh and what little rainfall there is makes for intense flavours.

Above Exterior of La Citadelle, Saint-Tropez, *see p242*

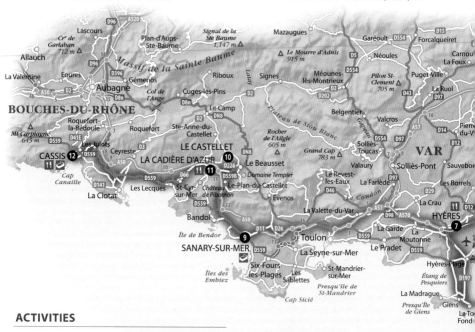

ACTIVITIES

Kick back with a glass of wine or a cocktail and spot celebrities at a swanky beach club on Plage de Pampelonne

Snorkel the *sentier marin* underwater route at Rayol-Canadel-sur-Mer's Domaine du Rayol

Drive round the Cap de Brégançon, home to the French presidential retreat and packed with vineyards

Explore Hyères' Villa Noialles and gardens, a favourite 1920s haunt for artists, now showcasing contemporary exhibitions

Rent a bike and cycle to a secluded beach on the Île de Porquerolles

Pick up a map from the tourist office and hike Cassis's vineyards, following the *Vin et Terroir* route

0 kilometres 8

0 miles 8

KEY

 Drive route

Left Vineyards of Cassis, *see p247*
Below left Place de l'Ormeau, Saint-Tropez, *see p243* **Below right** Gigaro beach, Saint-Tropez peninsula, *see p242*

PLAN YOUR DRIVE

Start/finish: Saint-Tropez to Cassis.

Number of days: 4, allowing half a day to explore Saint-Tropez and a day on the Île de Porquerolles.

Distance: 201 km (125 miles).

Road conditions: Generally good, with clear signposting; some steep, narrow roads with tight turns. In July and August traffic is heavier.

When to go: Between May and June, before peak season is in full swing, or in September, as the vineyards begin to harvest their grapes.

Opening hours: Most businesses are open from 10am to 7pm. Museums and major sights tend to close on Mondays and/or Tuesdays, while restaurants are often closed on Sundays and /or Mondays.

Main market days: Saint-Tropez: Tue–Sun, Sat; **Ramatuelle:** Thu, Sun; **Rayol-Canadel-sur-Mer:** Fri (Apr–Sep); **Bormes-les-Mimosas:** Wed; **Hyères:** Tue, Sat; **Sanary-sur-Mer:** Tue, Fri; **Cassis:** Wed, Fri.

Shopping: The boutique-lined streets of Saint Tropez have designer bargains, while wholesale wine, direct from the vineyards, can be picked up at a fraction of its retail price.

Major festivals: Saint-Tropez: Voiles de Saint-Tropez Regatta, Sep–Oct; **Ramatuelle:** Jazz Festival, Aug; **Bormes-les-Mimosas:** Santo Coupo Food and Wine Festival, Sep; **Cassis:** Quai des Artistes, Jun–Aug; Traditional Wine Festival, Sep.

DAY TRIP OPTIONS

Outdoors enthusiasts will enjoy hiking or kayaking Cassis's Calanques, while **wine lovers** will enjoy visiting the vineyards around Ramatuelle, Gassin and Bormes-les-Mimosas. **Families** will enjoy a day at the beaches of Île de Porquerolles. For details, *see p247*.

Above View over Saint-Tropez town and its bay

❶ Saint-Tropez

Var, Provence-Alpes-Côte d'Azur; 83990

Boasting a reputation that precedes it by a mile, Saint-Tropez could easily be shrugged off as the exclusive stomping ground of the über-rich and ultra-famous. However, at heart it is a picturesque fishing village which packs in surprises and activities for all its visitors. Spend a day roaming its enchanting alleys and it will be difficult not to succumb to Saint-Tropez's small-town charms.

A 90-minute walking tour

For those visiting this pretty seaside town mid-summer, it pays to start strolling before *le jet-set* deem it time to roll out of bed. Park at the western end of the charming **Place des Lices** ❶ and walk through the square, turning left into Rue Gambetta and then right into Rue Miséricorde. Immediately past the entrance to **Chapelle de la Miséricorde** ❷, Rue Miséricorde twists uphill, passing under the church's three 17th-century archways. Follow the road's left fork into Rue Aire du Chemin, lined with touristy restaurants, making a right at the ever-popular Restaurant de la Citadelle.

Across Place Forbin, scramble up the long, diagonal staircase to **La Citadelle** ❸ (open daily). A massive defence system built during the early 17th century, it was last occupied by the Axis powers in World War II. The ramparts afford spectacular views over Saint-Tropez's bay. After exploring the creepy dungeon cells, amble downhill along Montée de la Citadelle. At the road's first kink, step off onto the dirt trail that skirts the citadel's outer walls. Head around the corner for a breathtaking panorama east over the town's seaside cemetery, where film director Roger Vadim, of *And God Created Woman* fame, is buried. Down below is the delightful **Plage des Graniers** ❹.

Retrace the route to Montée de la Citadelle. Just before Place Forbin, make a sharp right onto Avenue Antoine de Saint-Exupéry, named after the famed author of *The Little Prince*. A small plaque, dated 29 June 2000, honours the 100th anniversary of Saint-Exupéry's birth.

A dirt path cuts left downhill, running alongside an old stone wall

WHERE TO STAY

SAINT-TROPEZ

Le Colombier *inexpensive–moderate*
Located in a private cul-de-sac, this tiny hotel is one of the town's best-kept secrets. Book well in advance to snag one of their pretty pastel rooms. In summer, breakfast in the flower-filled garden is a must.
Impasse des Conquêtes, 83990; 04 94 97 05 31; closed mid-Nov–Feb

Pastis *expensive*
Owned by a pair of British former designers, Pastis's nine rooms meld antique furniture and avant-garde artworks. The result is a serene oasis 5 minutes from the harbourside glitz. It has its own private pool and there is free parking.
61 avenue du Général Leclerc, 83990; 04 98 12 56 50; www.pastis-st-tropez.com

PLAGE DE PAMPELONNE

Tiki Hutte *inexpensive–expensive*
Simple seafront *cabanas* near the Plage de Pampelonne's trendiest beach clubs. The area quiets down in the evening, but hanging out on an exclusive patch of sand after a day of indulgence is divine. Minimum stay of one week.
Plage de Pampelonne, Ramatuelle, 83350; 04 94 55 96 96; www.tiki-hutte.com; closed Nov–Mar

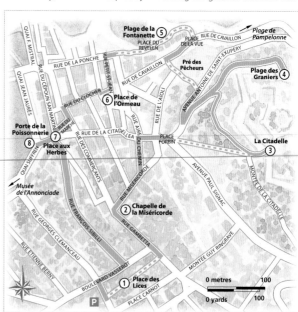

Where to Stay: inexpensive, under €70; moderate, €70–€150; expensive, over €150

across the open field of Pré des Pêcheurs. Swing right to check out Place de la Vue, a popular spot for artists who set up their easels and paint the seascape beyond. The energetic can continue east along Rue de Cavaillon's footpath, tracing the 12 km (7 miles) around Saint-Tropez's *cap* to trendy Plage de Pampelonne. Take Place de la Vue's small set of stairs down to **Plage de la Fontanette** ⑤. Visitors can get into their swimsuit and cool off with a quick dip in the Mediterranean.

Rested and refreshed, follow the coastline westwards to Port des Pêcheurs, tucking back inland at the bustling Place du Revelen. Go through the arched walkway beneath Porte du Revelen, taking Rue Petit St-Jean along to **Place de l'Ormeau** ⑥, a serene square. Exit the square at its northwest corner, where quiet Rue du Clocher leads to the buzz of Rue des Commerçants, lined with bakeries, cafés and shops.

Rue du Marché, the first right turn, will lead to **Place aux Herbes** ⑦ which hosts a tiny but vibrant flower and produce market (*Tue–Sun mornings*), stocked with artisan cheeses, lavender honey and plump olives. Between the square and the town's Vieux Port (Old Port), the **Porte de la Poissonnerie** ⑧ is brimming with the day's catch. Each morning, fishermen ply mounds of red mullet, sea bream and octopus to local residents and top chefs alike.

Art lovers can take a detour to the far side of the Vieux Port to the former chapel that is now the Musée de l'Annonciade (*open Mon–Wed, closed Nov*). It houses treasures by Bonnard, Dufy, Signac and Derain. Walk down Rue François Sibilli back to the car park at Place des Lices and grab a table at Le Café. Order a pastis, and try Provence's favourite pastime, *pétanque* – a set of *boules* can be borrowed from the café for free.

🚗 *Exit via Avenue du Général de Gaulle (runs east of the port), which becomes Avenue du 15 Aout 1944. Turn left onto the D93, known as Route des Plages, and head south until reaching a left-turn indication onto Chemin des Moulins. Drive through the vineyards to reach the car parks that line the Plage de Pampelonne.*

② Plage de Pampelonne
Var, Provence-Alpes-Côte d'Azur; 83350
Turquoise waters gently lap the 5 km (3 miles) of white sandy beach here. Although it may appear a paradise today, Plage de Pampelonne witnessed drama with the Allied landings in August 1944.

The first beach bar, the trendy **Tahiti Plage**, opened two years later and Pampelonne soon became a popular naturist spot. Strip down and dive in (Le Liberty and Neptune are naturist beaches), or follow the celebrities to the famous **Le Club 55**. Pampelonne's 27 beach clubs are the places to be seen in, attracting over 30,000 daily visitors in summer.

🚗 *Take Chemin des Moulins back to Route des Plages (D93). Turn left, heading south along the D93 until the first roundabout. Drive straight onto D61 following signs for Ramatuelle.*

Above Charming Plage de Pampelonne on the Saint-Tropez peninsula **Below** Passageway in the citadel of Saint-Tropez

VISITING SAINT-TROPEZ

Tourist Information
Quai Jean Jaurès, 83990; 08 92 68 48 28; www.ot-saint-tropez.com

Parking
There are two large car parks to the west of the port, the aptly named Parking du Port and Parking du Nouveau Port. There is an additional car park in Place des Lices. All are within easy walking distance of the town centre. However, finding parking during the high season is very difficult.

EAT AND DRINK

SAINT-TROPEZ

Le Café *inexpensive–moderate*
The café offers classic southern French dishes, including the town's sweet-tooth speciality, *tarte tropézienne*. Le Café's passion is *pétanque*.
Place des Lices, 83990; 04 94 97 44 69; www.lecafe.fr

La Ponche *moderate–expensive*
Traditional Mediterranean recipes mingle with playful, high-end gastronomy at La Ponche, just steps away from the sandy stretch of Plage de la Ponche.
3 rue des Remparts, 83990; 04 94 97 09 29; www.laponche.com; closed Nov–mid-Feb

Eat and Drink: inexpensive, under €20; moderate, €20–€40; expensive, over €40

here annually. The village is also where Gérard Philipe (1922–59), a leading young French actor of the 1950s, is buried.

🚗 *Head north on the D61, following signs for La Foux and Saint-Tropez. After around 3 km (2 miles), look out for a left turn indicating Château Minuty – it is easy to miss. Turn left at Château Minuty. The road continues uphill to Gassin where there are car parks on the edge of the town.*

4 Gassin

Var, Provence-Alpes-Côte d'Azur; 83580
Saint-Tropez's peninsula is blessed with copious rolling vineyards. **Château Minuty** *(open daily Jul–Aug, Mon–Sat Apr–Jun, Mon–Fri Sep–Mar)* is one of the area's finest and has a pretty chapel and 19th-century mansion. Sample and stock up on *Cru Classé* Côtes de Provence (visitors are expected to make a minimum purchase post-tasting). Afterwards, go up to the heights of Gassin, one of France's most beautiful villages, to see the 360-degree vistas.

🚗 *Edging along Gassin's ramparts, follow signs to La Croix-Valmer. At La Croix, head west to Rayol-Canadel-sur-Mer on the D559, in the direction of Le Lavandou. Turn left at the Rayol tourist office; signs clearly mark the downhill drive to Domaine du Rayol.*

5 Rayol-Canadel-sur-Mer

Var, Provence-Alpes-Côte d'Azur; 83820
Its shimmering beaches may resemble those of a Caribbean lagoon, but Rayol-Canadel's true

Top left View over the Cap de Brégançon from Bormes-les-Mimosas **Top right** Colourful window of a café in the Domaine du Rayol botanical gardens, Rayol-Candel-sur-Mer **Above** Vineyards around Château Minuty with the hilltop town of Gassin in the distance

3 Ramatuelle

Var, Provence-Alpes-Côte d'Azur; 83350
Located on a hilltop, this attractive village is enclosed by wooded slopes and vineyards. The village was called Rahmatu'llah (God's Gift) by the Saracens. Today, visitors can send their senses into overdrive by visiting this medieval village on market day. Stalls line the streets of the pedestrianized town centre, selling ripe produce, wicker baskets, linen and a smattering of eccentric art. Grab a newspaper and relax out on the sun-dappled terrace of **Café de l'Ormeau** to take in Provençal life at its finest. Theatre and jazz festivals take place

WHERE TO STAY

AROUND RAMATUELLE

Château de Valmer *expensive*
About 7 km (4 miles) from Ramatuelle is the gorgeous Château de Valmer. A palm-lined path connects this 19th-century *mas* with a white sand beach. Opt for one of the romantic rooms, or book La Cabane Perchée, a treehouse located in the hotel's vineyards. *Gigaro, La Croix Valmer, 83420; 04 94 55 15 15; www.chateauvalmer.com; closed mid-Oct–mid-Apr*

AROUND BORMES-LES-MIMOSAS

Les Plumbagos *moderate*
This lovely bed-and-breakfast has air-conditioned rooms with amazing views over the nearby hills towards the sea. There is also a huge swimming pool and terrace with sun loungers. *Le Mont des Roses, 88 Impasse du Pin, 83230; 06 09 82 42 86; www.bormeslesmimosas.com*

Above Paintings and other wares on display in a roadside shop, Ramatuelle

Where to Stay: inexpensive, under €70; moderate, €70–€150; expensive, over €150

pride is its massive botanical gardens, **Domaine du Rayol** (*open daily*). With its Visitor Centre housed in an old Art-Deco hotel, the *domaine* is peppered with Chinese bamboo, Chilean wine palm groves and Californian Joshua trees. Book in advance to visit the *sentier marin* (sea garden) for a guided snorkelling trip that explores the Baie du Figuier.

🚌 *Take the D559 west. Just past Le Lavandou, turn right onto the D41, following signs north to Bormes-les-Mimosas. At the T-junction take the left fork of the D41 going south to Bormes-les-Mimosas.*

⑥ Bormes-les-Mimosas

Var, Provence-Alpes-Côte d'Azur; 83230

A striking *village perché* (perched village), Bormes-les-Mimosas is thick with climbing bougainvillea. It offers cool breezes, as well as splendid views over Cap de Brégançon and its fort, an official French presidential retreat. Leave the village on the Route de Cabasson, going south to Fort Brégançon. The winding road goes past vineyards interspersed with poplars, palms and olive trees, making this the area's most picturesque drive. Turn right, along Route de Léoube, and sample the fine AOC Côtes de Provence at **Château de Brégançon** (*open Mon–Sat*) or **Domaine de Léoube** (*open daily, closed Sun during low season*).

🚌 *Continue along the Route de Léoube. Follow it west to La Londe-les-Maures, turn left onto the D559, then follow signs for Hyères. At the roundabout, take the D98 to Hyères. Take the second city centre indication, turning right onto Rue Ambroise Thomas. This passes the tourist office and leads straight into town, where various car parks are signposted.*

⑦ Hyères

Var, Provence-Alpes-Côte d'Azur; 83400

Hyères is the oldest winter resort established in the south of France. Today it may have lost some of its Belle-Époque glamour but it is well worth hunting down the Neo-Moorish buildings designed by 19th-century architect Pierre Chapoulard, which are dotted around the city. A must-see is the stunning **Villa Noialles** (*closed Tue Jul–Sep; closed Mon–Tue Oct–Jun*), perched

above the pedestrianized old town. A great attraction for 20th-century artists, the beautiful villa was where Man Ray filmed *Les Mystères du Château de Dé*; it has also hosted the likes of Dalí, Miró and Picasso.

Place de la République in the centre of town has one of Hyères main churches, the Romanesque and Provençal-Gothic St-Louis.

In 1867, a palm-growing industry was established in Hyères. It soon became the largest of its kind in Europe and still functions as an important industry. Hundreds of palms still line the boulevards of the town.

🚌 *Head south along Avenue Gambetta. The road forks; bear left on the D197 for Presqu'île de Giens, passing the airport, following the old seaside railway. Continue south to La Tour Fondue: there is parking at the ferry terminal.*

Above View from ruins of the old Château d'Hyères **Below** Domaine du Rayol botanical gardens, Rayol-Canadel-sur-Mer

EAT AND DRINK

RAMATUELLE

L'Ecurie du Castellas *expensive*
The menu offers local Mediterranean-style dishes, served on a terrace with lovely views over the village. The desserts are wonderful, particularly the coconut *bavarois* with pineapple and a piña colada sauce. There's a very reasonably priced set menu at lunchtime on weekdays. Reservations essential.
Route des Moulins de Paillas Saint Tropez, 83350; 04 94 79 20 67; www. lecurieducastellas.com; closed Sun and Mon dinner

AROUND BORMES-LES-MIMOSAS

L'Instant *moderate*
A small, lively restaurant on Le Lavandou's main square serving fresh, local food cooked in the regional style. The home-made *foie gras* is delicious, as is their platter of cold Corsican meats. Servings are generous and it offers excellent value for money as well as friendly service.
2 Quai Gabriel Péri, Le Levandau 83980; 06 71 61 42 43; www. restaurantlinstant.sitew.com; closed Mon, Tue, mid-Oct–Feb

HYÈRES

Bistrot de Marius
inexpensive–moderate
The cuisine here is modern Provençal and seafood: start with seafood and fresh coriander salad, or order the octopus *daube*, a slow-cooked stew served with polenta.
1 place Massillon, 83400; 04 94 35 88 38; closed Mon, Tue and mid-Nov–mid-Dec

VISITING THE ÎLE DE
PORQUEROLLES

Ferry Information
Frequent ferries ply the 20-minute
route between La Tour Fondue and Île
de Porquerolles. Ferries also serve the
nearby Levant and Port Cros islands.
*Gare Maritime, La Tour Fondue,
Presqu'île de Giens, 83400; 04 94 58
21 81; www.tlv-tvm.com*

Parking
Park on the mainland at La Tour Fondue.
For those planning to leave their car
overnight during high season, it is best
to reserve a parking spot in advance.

WHERE TO STAY

ÎLE DE PORQUEROLLES

Le Mas du Langoustier *expensive*
This place is a tropical paradise,
complete with secluded beaches and
a Michelin-starred restaurant.
*Île de Porquerolles, 83400; 04 94 58 30
09; www.langoustier.com*

SANARY-SUR-MER

Hôtel de la Tour *moderate*
The second floor rooms at this portside
hotel offer floor-to-ceiling sea views.
*24 quai du Général de Gaulle, Port de
Sanary, 83110; 04 94 74 10 10; www.
sanary-hoteldelatour.com*

CASSIS

Maison°9 *moderate–expensive*
Set amid vineyards, this 18th-century
country home is now an elegant bed-
and-breakfast.
*9 rue du Docteur Yves Bourde, 13260;
04 42 01 26 39; www.maison9.net*

Château de Cassis *expensive*
This restored 8th-century castle offers
the finest views over Cassis.
*Traverse du Château, 13260; 04 42 01
63 20; www.chateaudecassis.com*

Above Fishing boats with Château de Cassis
perched on the hill above **Below** La Tour Fondue,
where ferries depart for Île de Porquerolles

⑧ Île de Porquerolles
Var, Provence-Alpes-Côte d'Azur; 83400
One of the three Îles d'Or, or Golden
Islands, Île de Porquerolles was
bought by the French state in 1971
in a move to protect the island from
rampant industrial development.
Since then it has remained a blissful
haven. Vehicles are banned; rent a
bike or stroll the dirt paths to secluded beaches, such as the pristine
Plage de Nôtre-Dame. The island also
boasts several wine estates, including
the all-organic **Domaine de La
Courtade** *(open Mon–Fri)*, which
began operations in 1983 .

🚗 *Drive back from the port along the
D197. Then either take La Route du
Sel which leads north between the sea
and salt marshes or continue on the
D197 through Hyères to take the A570
west to the A57, merging with the A50,
which goes through a long tunnel at
Toulon, the quickest way through
congested Toulon. Exit at junction 13,
taking the D26, which leads to the
D11 south to Sanary-sur-Mer.*

⑨ Sanary-sur-Mer
Var, Provence-Alpes-Côte d'Azur; 83110
Formerly a provincial port, tiny
Sanary-sur-Mer rose to international
stardom in the 1930s. Refugees from
Nazi Germany, including playwright
Bertold Brecht and novelist Thomas
Mann, chose to adopt this town as
their home. Sanary-sur-Mer was also
home to Aldous Huxley, influential
author of the futuristic novel *Brave
New World*. These days, the colourful
fishing boats, pastel façades and
sandy beaches make the town a
pleasant stop.

🚗 *Take the D559 west. Just past the
left turn for Bandol city centre, bear*

right onto the D559B, heading north.
Make a left turn onto the D226, which
leads directly to the car parks at the
base of Le Castellet.

⑩ Le Castellet
Var, Provence-Alpes-Côte d'Azur; 83330
The backdrop for director Marcel
Pagnol's 1938 film *La Femme du
Boulanger*, Le Castellet is incredibly
picturesque with its pale stones and
12th-century medieval streets. Peek
through **Le Trou de Madame**, a portal
in the ancient walls, for uninterrupted
views over the Bandol vineyards
below. Stop for a glass of rosé, or pick
up craft items, such as handmade
olive oil soap or wooden toys, from
the local artisans.

🚗 *Go back down to the D559B and
head south. Make a right turn onto
the D66, crossing over the A50 and
following signs for La Cadière d'Azur.
There is a car park to the right just
before the village entrance.*

⑪ La Cadière d'Azur
Var; 83740
From Le Castellet to the coast,
AOC Bandol vineyards form a golden
ripple against the azure horizon.
To sip the sweetest local produce, visit
the prestigious **Château de Pibarnon**
(open Mon–Sat) or **Domaine Tempier**
(open Mon–Fri). If pressed for time, **La
Cadierenne Coopérative** *(open Mon–
Sat)*, just off the A50 at junction 11,
sells the wares of scores of local
producers. After finishing shopping for

the day, relax at one of charming La Cadière's pavement cafés.

🚗 *Continue west on the D66, passing through St-Cyr-sur-Mer. Take the D559 west to La Ciotat and then Cassis. Descending from the roundabout near junction 8 of the A50, take the first right, marked "Les Julots", through the vineyards to reach the town centre.*

⑫ Cassis

Bouches-du-Rhône, Provence-Alpes-Côte d'Azur; 13260

Hemmed in by the white cliffs of the Calanques to the west and the precipitous Route des Crêtes to the east, Cassis is a lively little port and a great tourist destination for families. Restaurants line the quays, and sunny days see holidaymakers crowd Plage de la Grand Mer. A dozen *domaines* encircle the town, boasting renowned AOC Cassis whites; visit **Le Clos Sainte Magdeleine** *(open Mon–Fri)*, where vineyards cling to the steep cliffs of Cap Canaille, and hike through the

vineyards on the *Vin et Terroir* route. Cassis was an important trading port before the Nazis almost wiped out its entire fleet during World War II. Much of the town's history can be discovered at the charming **Musée Municipal Méditerranéen** *(open Wed–Sun)* which has many interesting exhibits, some recovered from the seabed, dating back to the Greeks.

The Calanques

A great limestone cliff that spans the 20 km (12 miles) between Marseilles and Cassis, the Massif des Calanques forms one of France's most breathtaking stretches of coastline. Peaks rise over 500 m (1,640 ft), while the shore below harbours miniscule white sand inlets; hike, kayak or cycle across the rugged natural landscape. The Calanques is a protected area, and may be closed on hot summer days due to the risk of forest fire. Be sure to check with the Cassis tourist office *(www.ot-cassis.com)* before setting off.

*Above left Tranquil beach in Île de Porquerolles **Above right** Boats moored at the Old Port in Sanary-sur-Mer*

EAT AND DRINK

ÎLE DE PORQUEROLLES

L'Arche de Noé *moderate–expensive*
Mouth-watering *bouillabaisse* and *bourride* grace the menu here.
Place d'Armes, 83400; 04 94 58 33 71; www.larcheporquerolles.com; closed Tue Apr–Jun Sep–Oct, all of Nov–Mar

LA CADIÈRE D'AZUR

Hostellerie Bérard
moderate–expensive
Father and son team René and Jean-François Bérard pair seasonal ingredients with locally sourced wines.
La Cadière d'Azur, 83740; 04 94 90 11 43; www.hotel-berard.com; closed Mon, Tue lunch May–Oct, Jan–mid-Feb

CASSIS

Le Bistrot *inexpensive–moderate*
Excellent daily specials and tasty Neapolitan-style pizza are served here.
Place du Grand Carnot, 13260; 04 42 01 07 59

DAY TRIP OPTIONS

Visitors should base themselves either between Cassis and Bandol, or in Saint-Tropez, where the D559 provides easy access to the following day trips.

Breathtaking coastline

Explore the cliffs and coves that surround Cassis ⑫. Hop on one of many boats departing from the port. On mornings from July to August, disembark at the Calanque En-Vau and hike back to town. For those who have an aversion to exercise, opt for a clifftop drive from Cassis to La Ciotat along the Route des Crêtes.

The Route des Crêtes (D141) is clearly signposted from the centre of Cassis;

alternately, take Avenue Marechal Foch, which becomes Avenue Pierre Imbert. Turn right onto the Route des Crêtes. Hikers can follow the same route up Avenue du Revestel. The Calanques to the west of Cassis can only be accessed by boat or kayak from the port, or on foot.

Vineyard tour

Spend the morning looping through the vineyards around the hilltop village of Ramatuelle ③. Next visit the Château Minuty and the village of Gassin ④, with rolling vineyards on either side, to taste some of the wines of this region. Spend the afternoon at Bormes-les-Mimosas ⑥ and follow the Route de Léoube to

sample some fine wines at the Château de Brégançon.

From Saint-Tropez take the D93 along the coast, straight to Ramatuelle. From here take the D61 to Gassin and then the D559 to Bormes-les-Mimosas.

Resort town and beaches

Stroll around the streets of the resort town of Hyères ⑦, before heading to La Tour Fondue from where visitors can take a ferry ride to the Île de Porquerolles ⑧. Spend the rest of the day on its pristine beaches.

The D559 provides easy access to Hyères. From Hyères, take the D197 to La Tour Fondue and then a ferry to the island.

Eat and Drink: inexpensive, under €20; moderate, €20–€40; expensive, over €40

DRIVE **24**

Ancient Ports and Deserted Beaches

Erbalunga to Calvi

Highlights

- **Turquoise seas**
  Stake out your own piece of paradise on the Désert des Agriates coastline of white sand beaches and crystal-clear waters

- **Traditional crafts**
  From sandstone ceramics to wooden music boxes, discover the island's most curious souvenirs at artisans' hilltop workshops along the Strada di l'Artigiani

- **A sumptuous feast**
  Sample Corsica's unique cuisine, trying each town's speciality or settling in for a Corsican feast

Calm waters of the harbour near Erbalunga's Old Town

Ancient Ports and Deserted Beaches

Northern Corsica is a world apart from the ritzy high-life of the French Riviera. Frequent ferries ply the route between Nice and Bastia or Calvi: visitors can drive their vehicles on board and whizz out on the open road at the other end. The roads between Erbalunga, on Cap Corse, and Calvi, on the island's northwest tip, are generally uncluttered. Visitors will find Corsica more tranquil, more economical and more family-friendly than many of France's other tourist destinations. From mountains that offer panoramic views, to rolling vineyards and some of the Mediterranean's most unspoilt beaches, this driving tour ambles its way across the island's loveliest country lanes.

KEY

🚗 Drive route

Below Skyline of Pigna on the Strada di l'Artigiani, *see p254*

ACTIVITIES

Feast on seafood at Erbalunga, one of the prettiest fishing villages on rugged Cap Corse

Stock up on the exceptional wines from the Patrimonio valley's vineyards

Spend a day dipping in and out of the Désert des Agriates' tropical waters

Take a walk in the hills, where Pigna's cobblestoned streets hide a warren of traditional artisan workshops

Visit Christopher Columbus' birthplace within Calvi's 15th-century citadel

Above Boats anchored at the harbour in the port town of Erbalunga, *see p252* **Below** Sleepy and ancient town of Algajola, *see p254*

PLAN YOUR DRIVE

Start/finish: Erbalunga to Calvi.

Number of days: 2–3, allowing between half a day and a day to explore the Désert des Agriates and the Plage de Saleccia.

Distance: 135 km (85 miles).

Road conditions: Generally good; some steep, narrow roads with tight turns, particularly along the Strada di l'Artigiani and in the Désert des Agriates (where there is no guard rail, lights or cat's-eyes). Traffic is heavier in August.

When to go: May and June, before the peak summer season, or in September, when prices drop.

Opening hours: The opening hours of churches and monuments vary but the main museums stay open all day. It is always best to check at the tourist office before visiting. Between November and Easter, most of the island shuts down entirely.

Main market days: Bastia: Tue–Sun; Calvi: Tue–Sun.

Shopping: Visit the towns along the Strada di l'Artigiani, each specializing in a variety of traditional crafts and local produce, from musical instruments and pottery to olive oil and honey.

Major festivals: Erbalunga: Procession de la Cerca, Jun; **Bastia:** Les Musicales de Bastia, late Sep; **Saint-Florent:** Porto Latino, Aug; **Calvi:** Jazz Festival, Jun.

DAY TRIP OPTIONS

Keen drivers can loop Cap Corse along the winding, coastal D80, while **souvenir seekers** should shop their way up to Calenzana on the Strada di l'Artigiani. For details, *see p255*.

WHERE TO STAY

ERBALUNGA

Castel Brando *expensive*
This hotel is a tastefully renovated mansion by the sea. Guestrooms are selectively furnished with antique beds and writing desks.
Erbalunga, 20222; 04 95 30 10 30; www.castelbrando.com

BASTIA

Hotel Central *moderate*
This tranquil hotel oozes romance. Lower floor double rooms feature antique tiles and period furniture.
3 rue Miot, 20200; 04 95 31 71 12; www.centralhotel.fr

SAINT-FLORENT

Dolce Notte *moderate–expensive*
Rooms all have a sea-facing balcony or terrace, and there is a private beach.
Plage lieu-dit Ospedale, Route de Bastia, 20217; 04 95 37 06 65; www.hotel-dolce-notte.com

Above View of the Ligurian Sea from the citadel in Saint-Florent **Below left** Village of Erbalunga **Below** Old port and the Église de St-Jean-Baptiste in Bastia

❶ Erbalunga
Haute-Corse, Corse; 20222

One of Corsica's most important ports for over 2,000 years, Erbalunga was strategically positioned between the alternately ruling republics of Pisa and Genoa. The latter's tower and lookout point can still be seen today on the headland. The village is home to the **Église St-Erasme**, where visitors can see crosses of the Cerca procession, in which hooded penitents participate in a candlelit procession through the village on Maundy Thursday and Good Friday. These days the sleepy fishing hamlet is the perfect spot to get acquainted with Corsican culture while snacking, sipping and generally unwinding. The harbour is lined with several seafood restaurants. Erbalunga also makes an ideal base for exploring the scenic Cap Corse peninsula.

🚗 *Head south to Bastia on the D80, which will lead directly to Place Saint-Nicolas. Park on the east side of the square, in the signposted car park.*

❷ Bastia
Haute-Corse, Corse; 20200

Bastia exudes a distinct urban air that contrasts with many of Corsica's resort towns. It was founded in 1378, when the Genoese governor established a hilltop citadel overlooking a small fishing port that was known then as Porto Cardo (now the *Vieux Port*). The ramparts were completed a century later. The **Place St-Nicolas** faces the wharf where ferries from the mainland and Italy arrive. The **Église de St-Jean-Baptiste**, with its remarkable Baroque façade and twin belltowers, is Corsica's largest church. There is plenty to do in Bastia: wander along the citadel's rampart walls, visit Place de l'Hôtel de Ville's morning produce market or book one of the port's quayside tables for dinner.

🚗 *Drive around Place Saint-Nicolas and take Avenue du Maréchal Sébastiani (D81) west, following signs to Saint-Florent. Park at the Parking de Saint-Florent in the port.*

> **The Vineyards of Corsica**
> The Patrimonio valley's chalky, clay-like soil is ideal for cultivating Corsican grapes, such as Vermentinu, used for white wines, and Niellucciu, pressed for rosés and reds. Stop at one of the local domains in order to sample and stock up. Medal-winning Domaine Orenga de Gaffory (*www.domaine-orengadegaffory.com*) is one of the region's finest.

❸ Saint-Florent
Haute-Corse, Corse; 20217

Nestled between the wine producing Patrimonio valley and the sandy white beaches of the Désert des Agriates, Saint-Florent is an animated port town. It has brightly coloured houses along the harbour and a lively promenade with boutiques, restaurants and cafés, open till late at night in summer. Stroll into the Old Town to discover a cluster of pastel buildings threaded with picturesque narrow streets and cobbled squares. For beautiful views over the Golfe de Saint-Florent, make the short hike up to the citadel just before sunset.

🚢 *Hop onto one of the frequent passenger ferries from Saint-Florent to Plage du Lodo. En route is the Genoese tower La Mortola on the left.*

❹ Désert des Agriates

Haute-Corse, Corse; 20246

A UNESCO World Heritage Site, the 160-sq-km (60-sq-mile) Désert des Agriates covers the eastern edge of the Balagne region. Its brutal sunshine and short, shrubby brushland bely the fact that in the 18th and 19th centuries, this zone was referred to as Corsica's breadbasket. Sadly, it proved to be one of the world's first lessons in the damages of over-farming. Slash-and-burn agriculture resulted in large-scale erosion and destroyed the area's natural biodiversity. The French government began slowly buying up the land in the 1970s and, in 1989, it was declared a nature reserve. It is illegal to camp, other than at designated grounds, or hike into the wild.

Above Serene Plage du Lodo in Désert des Agriates

A 90-minute walking tour

Disembark at the pier to the west of **Plage du Lodo's** ① shimmering white sands and bear left, then sharply right up the short, steep incline. Stick to the principal dirt path, which meanders between dry-stone *bergeries* (shepherds' huts). Inhale the aroma of *maquis*, the island's shrubby blend of aromatic plants, as the landscape opens onto beautiful vistas of jagged mountains to the south.

After walking for approximately 40 minutes, visitors will reach **U Paradisu** ② *(open May–Sep)* on the left. This basic campground hosts a freshwater fountain, a small shop, a bar selling cold drinks and sandwiches and a restaurant *(dinner by reservation only)*. Bear right past the handful of 4WD vehicles and head for the sea. A few steps will lead to the unspoilt turquoise shores of **Plage de Saleccia** ③ This sandy stretch was featured in the 1962 film *The Longest Day*, with John Wayne, Richard Burton and Sean Connery. Wander eastwards along the beach to pick out an exclusive patch of paradise.

Be sure to carry a copy of the ferry schedule, and allow enough time to retrace the route to Plage du Lodo to catch the ferry back to Saint-Florent. Note that there is no ferry service from Plage de Saleccia, hence the deserted nature of the beach. The more adventurous can take Le Sentier des Douaniers (the customs officers' path), east along the coast back to Plage du Lodo. More difficult but rewardingly pretty, this route will take around 75 minutes.

🚗 *From Saint-Florent's port, head west on the D81. Follow signs to Calvi-Île Rousse and turn right onto the N1197 just before Monetta. At Lozari, this road becomes the N197. Follow the road and park before Algajola town centre, at Aregno Plage, or near the train station.*

VISITING DÉSERT DES AGRIATES

Ferry Information
Le Popeye ferries drop passengers at pretty Plage du Lodo.
Place Centrale, Saint-Florent, 20217; 04 95 37 19 07; www.lepopeye.com

Parking
Parking de Saint-Florent is located in the town's port, just next to Le Popeye's ferry terminal.

EAT AND DRINK

ERBALUNGA

Le Pirate *expensive*
This restaurant serves specialities such as roast pigeon breasts on a Swiss chard gratin or John Dory on a bed of seared *foie gras*.
Place Marc Bardon, 20222; 04 95 33 24 20; www.restaurantlepirate.com; closed Mon, Tue, Jan, Feb

BASTIA

A Casserella *moderate*
Located in one of the side streets of the maze-like historic port of Bastia, this traditional restaurant offers authentic cuisine and friendly service.
6 rue Ste-Croix, 20600; 04 95 32 02 32; closed Sat lunch, Sun, Nov

SAINT-FLORENT

L'Arrière Cour *inexpensive*
The menu blends a Moroccan theme with classic French quiches, salads and roasts. Reservations are a must.
Saint-Florent, 20217; 04 95 35 33 62; closed Tue, Jan–Feb

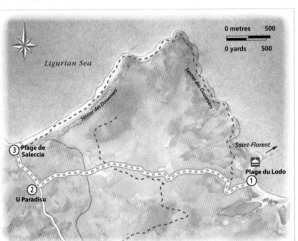

Eat and Drink: inexpensive, under €20; moderate, €20–€40; expensive, over €40

Right Cobblestoned street in Pigna on the Strada di l'Artigiani **Below left** View of Algajola from Pigna **Below right** Busy port and promenade of Calvi

WHERE TO STAY

ALGAJOLA

Camping de la Plage *inexpensive*
Tents and caravans sit under a 100-year-old wood at this family-friendly campground. The Arengo Plage is 50 m (165 ft) away, while Algajola centre is 5 minutes on foot. Bungalows and small studio cabins are also available.
N197, 20220; 04 95 60 71 76; www. campingbalagne.com; closed Oct–Apr

AROUND STRADA DI L'ARTIGIANI

Casa Musicale *inexpensive–moderate*
This is a colourful eagle's nest of a hotel. The seven guestrooms range from the fig tree-shaded Bassa to the family-sized Sulana. It also hosts Pigna's best restaurant.
Pigna, 20220; 04 95 61 77 31; www. casa-musicale.org; closed Jan–mid-Feb

CALVI

Clos des Amandiers
inexpensive–moderate
This is a scattered array of bungalows on Calvi's outskirts. Simply furnished, each features an outside terrace.
Route de Pietramaggiore, 20260; 04 95 65 08 32; www.clos-des-amandiers. com; closed Nov–Apr

The Manor *expensive*
One of Corsica's few hip hotels, the Manor consists of two exclusive guestrooms and one family suite.
Chemin Saint-Antoine, 20260; 04 95 62 72 42; www.manor-corsica.com

⑤ Algajola

Haute-Corse, Corse; 20220
The town of Algajola was founded by the Phoenicians. The Romans later made use of it as the base for their legions. Algajola then came into the hands of the Genoese who considered it to be a vital possession because of its central location within the region. The tiny town was destroyed by pirates in 1643. The citadel's structure was rebuilt by the Genoese by the end of the 17th century. Algajola is also home to the **Église Saint-Georges** which houses a 17th-century painting by the Italian artist Guernico. These days one of Algajola's main draws is its 2-km (1-mile) sandy beach, just east of the town centre. The bay is also a haven for activities such as windsurfing and snorkelling.

🚗 *Take the N197 back east to the right turn for Corbara, where the D313 leads to the D151, which loops past Corbara, Pigna and Aregno. At Cateri, turn right onto the D71, down to Lumio and the N197. This route is part of the Strada di l'Artigiani.*

⑥ Strada di l'Artigiani

Haute-Corse, Corse; 20256, 20214
Officially designated as the Strada di l'Artigiani in 1995, this "Artisans' Road" was established to preserve and encourage the creation of traditional Corsican crafts. It covers the most characteristic craftsmen's workshops as it weaves inland from

the island's northern coast, swooping from Occhiatana in the east to Calvi in the west. Pigna, at the route's centre, nurtured a successful artisan revival in the 1960s; today the town is filled with workshops producing musical instruments and sculptures. Nearby, pretty Corbara is particularly famed for its artistic sandstone pottery, original tableware and crockery. Lumio boasts cutlery makers, a small family-run production of essential oils and wineries producing *appellation d'origine controlée* red, white, rosé and muscat wines.

🚗 *Once back on the N197, follow the busy road west to Calvi's town centre. Park in the car park located at the base of the citadel.*

7 Calvi

Haute-Corse, Corse; 20260

Founded by the Romans in the 1st century AD, Calvi today is half military town and half holiday resort. The town is dominated by the massive Genoese citadel that sits on the rocky promontory overlooking the harbour below. Built during the 15th century, the citadel has huge bastions on all its four sides, three of which overlook the sea. Step into the **Cathédrale St-Jean-Baptiste** to admire **Christ des Miracles**, an ebony crucifix credited with banishing aggressive Turks from the city during a late 16th-century siege. The cathedral was almost destroyed in 1567 by a gunpowder explosion from the arsenal. Residents of the town claim Christopher Columbus was born here. There are even the remains of what is claimed to be his birthplace within the citadel.

Calvi is one of Corsica's most lively towns, teeming during the summer as ferries and yachts from mainland France pull in and out of its small harbour. The Quai Landry is the town's most renowned promenade and is lined with hotels, cafés and restaurants. Visitors can spend their time at one of the many outside tables, watching the boats anchoring or setting off. The 4.5-km (3-mile) long beach has fine white sand.

Below left Fifteenth-century citadel of Calvi overlooking the bay

EAT AND DRINK

ALGAJOLA

La Vieille Cave *moderate*
Subtle starters, including artichokes stuffed with *brocciu* cheese, give way to unfeasibly large mains: a whole seabass arrives in its own Le Creuset dish with a small vegetable plot of trimmings. The two evening set menus make for a well-priced meal.
9 Place l'Olmo, 20220; 04 95 60 70 09; closed Mon lunch, Jan–Mar

CALVI

E.A.T. *moderate*
Culinary cool and edible experimentation are the order of the day at Calvi's hippest restaurant. The portions of sushi, which come with spray-on soy sauce, and stone-baked scallop kebabs will satiate the biggest of appetites. There is also an exceptionally strong – and international in scope – wine list.
15 rue Clemenceau, 20260; 04 95 38 21 87; closed Wed, Feb, Nov

AROUND CALVI

Le Matahari *moderate*
A beach bar *par excellence*, Le Matahari is 10 km (6 miles) from Calvi, on the sunset side of the Golfe de Calvi. A clue to the cuisine is offered by the garland-wearing Buddha statue guarding the entrance. Try the Thai green curry, seafood tempura or Lebanese-style *meze* (tapas).
Plage de l'Arinella, Lumio, 20260; 04 95 60 78 47; www.lematahari.com; closed Mon dinner, Oct–Mar

DAY TRIP OPTIONS

Even at summer's peak, Corsican roads remain relatively traffic free. No matter where visitors choose to stay, it is always easy to get from Bastia to Calvi along the D81 or take the N197 west of the Désert des Agriates to quickly access either of these day trips.

Rolling hills and pretty towns
Rather than taking the D81 across the base of Cap Corse, keen drivers can opt for the shore-hugging D80 around the Cap. Drive northwards from busy Bastia **2**, through Erbalunga **1** to Macinaggio. Head westwards between rolling hills, with the shadow of scores of giant wind turbines the only modern touch in

this little-visited peninsula. Centuri is ideal for a plate of portside seafood, or stop and sunbathe on black sand beach below Nonza. Park up in Saint-Florent **3** and enjoy a sun-downer or take a walk around the picturesque narrow streets and cobbled squares.

Take the D80 from Bastia to Erbalunga and continue to Macinaggio. Turn west onto the D80, take a sharp right onto the D35 to Centuri, then the D35 and D80 to Nonza and then the D80 to Saint-Florent. From here take the D81 back to Bastia.

Calvi to Calenzana
They may be just 14 km (9 miles) apart, but Calvi **7** and Calenzana neatly encapsulate opposite

Corsican extremes. Clamber up to the citadel in Calvi for vast views over the Golfe de Calvi and the Old Town below. Walk along the port to see the day's catch then take the N197 south to the D151, the turn-off for Calenzana. Set well into the island's rugged interior, Calenzana is part of the Strada di l'Artigiani **6**. Shop for sandstone ceramics, or pick up local delicacies, like wild boar pâté with figs. Hikers can set off on the GR20, the 180-km (119-mile) trail that crosses Corsica from Calenzana to Conca on the island's east coast.

The D151, south of Calvi, loops through the hills, passing Calenzana and the Strada di l'Artigiani towns along the way.

Eat and Drink: inexpensive, under €20; moderate, €20–€40; expensive, over €40

General Index

Acknowledgments

Dorling Kindersley would like to thank the many people whose help and assistance contributed to the preparation of this book.

Contributors

Rosemary Bailey is the author of three travel memoirs about France and has written and edited numerous guidebooks, including the DK Eyewitness guide to France. Her most recent book, *Love and War in the Pyrenees*, won the British Guild of Travel Writers Award in 2008.

Fay Franklin is a professional travel editor and writer who spends a part of each year in northern France. She has co-authored five books on French cuisine.

Nick Inman is a full-time author, editor and photographer. He has written or contributed to over 50 travel guides, mainly on France and Spain.

Nick Rider has a Ph.D. in history and has written books on France, Spain and Mexico. He has also contributed to DK Eyewitness guides to France, Spain, Mexico, Great Britain and Poland.

Tristan Rutherford is a travel journalist and has written for *The Guardian* and the *Sunday Times Travel Magazine*. He also lectures in journalism at several universities.

Tamara Thiessen is a Sydney-Paris based writer and photographer. She has contributed to magazines and newspapers worldwide, as well as many travel guides.

Kathryn Tomasetti authors and edits guidebooks about France, Croatia, Turkey and her native northern Italy. Her photographs have appeared in numerous travel magazines and several DK publications.

Fact Checker Lyn Parry
Proofreader Swati Meherishi
Indexing Cyber Media Services Ltd.

Design and Editorial

Publisher Douglas Amrine
List Manager Vivien Antwi
Managing Art Editor Jane Ewart
Project Editor Michelle Crane
Project Designers Shahid Mahmood, Kate Leonard
Senior Cartographic Editor Casper Morris
Cartographer Stuart James
Managing Art Editor (Jackets) Karen Constanti
Senior Jacket Designer Tessa Bindloss
Jacket Designer Meredith Smith
Senior DTP Designer Jason Little
DTP Designers Jamie McNeill, Natasha Lu
Picture Research Ellen Root
Production Controller Linda Dare

Additional Design and Editorial

Claire Baranowski, Imogen Corke, Robert Harneis, Maite Lantaron, Hayley Maher, Nicola Malone, Catherine Skipper.

Special Assistance

Anne Dyson, Eric French, Catherine Gauthier, Robert Harneis, Anne-Marie Hautemanière, Sophie Lenormand, Pamela McNeill, Cristina Murroni, Lyn Parry, Xavier Ribas, Philip Smith.

Photography

Rosemary Bailey, Alex Havret, Nick Inman, Tamara Thiessen, Kathryn Tomasetti.

Additional Photography

Max Alexander, Andy Crawford, P. Enticknay, Philippe Giraud, John Heseltine, Roger Hilton, Paul Kenward, Jamie Marshall, Eric Meacher, Roger Moss, John Parker, Sallie Alane Reason, Kim Sayer, Tony Souter, Alan Williams.

Photography Permissions

Dorling Kindersley would like to thank the following for their assistance and kind permission to photograph at their establishments: Abbaye de Lessay, Cathédrale Notre-Dame d'Amiens, Cathédrale Saint-Tugdual (Tréguier), Château de Chambord, Cathédrale Nôtre-Dame-del'Assomption, La Maison d'Hotes, Le Hameau du Vin, Musee Des Vallees Cevenoles, Musee Somme 1916, Terre Vivante

Picture Credits

Key- t= top; c= centre; l= left; r= right; b= bottom.

Every effort has been made to trace the copyright holders, and we apologize in advance for any unintentional omissions. We would be pleased to insert the appropriate acknowledgments in any subsequent edition of this publication.

The publisher would like to thank the following individuals, companies, and picture libraries for their kind permission to reproduce their photographs:

4Corners Images: Taylor Richard 6cl; **Alamy Images**: John Eccles 21tl; Trevor Smith 12bl; SnowyWelsh 19br; Chris Young 21bl. **Château des Milandes**: 173br; **Corbis**: amanaimages/ Teruo Saegusa 230-31; **Culturalspaces**: Ephrussi de Rothschild Villa & Gardens 224cl, /C.Recoura 228br; Kérylos Greek Villa 229tc; **DK Images**: Christine Wildman Collection / Judith Miller 10tr; Courtesy of SNCM 10br; **Hostellerie de Levernois**: 22bl; **L'Assiette Champenoise**: 25br; **Musée du Désert**: 218tc; **Photolibrary**: Nigel Blythe 2-3; Jon Arnold Travel/ Doug Pearson 212-13; Jtb Photo 216tl; Juergen Richter 222-3; Robert Harding Travel/ Bruno Morandi 6br; Robert Harding Travel/ Lee Frost 10bl; **The Bridgeman Art Library**: Map of Lotharingia, from "Atlas sive cosmographicae meditationes de fabrica mundi et fabricati figura", published by Hondius in c.1632 (coloured engraving), Mercator, Gerard (1512-94) (after) / Biblioteca Universidad, Barcelona, Spain / © Paul Maeyaert 26-7.

All other images © Dorling Kindersley. For further information see: www.dkimages.com

Sheet map

4Corners Images: SIME/Olimpio Fantuz front.

Cover Picture Credits

Front: GETTY IMAGES: Shaun Egan.
Spine: GETTY IMAGES: Shaun Egan t.
Back: Dorling Kindersley: Alex Havret cr, cl; Tamara Thiessen c.

Phrase Book

IN AN EMERGENCY

Help!	Au secours!	oh sekoor
Stop!	Arrêtez!	aret-ay
Call a doctor!	Appelez un médecin!	apuh-lay uñ medsañ
Call an ambulance!	Appelez une ambulance!	apuh-lay oon oñboo-loñs
Call the police!	Appelez la police!	apuh-lay lah poh-lees
Call the fire department!	Appelez les pompiers!	apuh-lay leh poñ-peeyay
Where is the nearest telephone?	Où est le téléphone le plus proche?	oo ay luh tehlehfon luh ploo prosh
Where is the nearest hospital?	Où est l'hôpital le plus proche?	oo ay lopeetal luh ploo prosh

COMMUNICATION ESSENTIALS

Yes	Oui	wee
No	Non	noñ
Please	S'il vous plaît	seel voo play
Thank you	Merci	mer-see
Excuse me	Excusez-moi	exkoo-zay mwah
Hello	Bonjour	boñzhoor
Goodbye	Au revoir	oh ruh-vwar
Good night	Bonsoir	boñ-swar
Morning	Le matin	matañ
Afternoon	L'après-midi	l'apreh-meedee
Evening	Le soir	swar
Yesterday	Hier	eeyehr
Today	Aujourd'hui	oh-zhoor-dwee
Tomorrow	Demain	duhmañ
Here	Ici	ee-see
There	Là	lah
What?	Quel, quelle?	kel, kel
When?	Quand?	koñ
Why?	Pourquoi?	poor-kwah
Where?	Où?	oo

USEFUL PHRASES

How are you?	Comment allez-vous?	kom-moñ talay voo
Very well, thank you.	Très bien, merci.	treh byañ, mer-see
Pleased to meet you.	Enchanté de faire votre connaissance.	oñshoñ-tay duh fehr votr kon-ay-sans
See you soon.	À bientôt.	ah byañ-toh
That's fine	Voilà qui est parfait	vwalah kee ay parfay
Where is/are…?	Où est/sont…?	oo ay/soñ
How far is it to…?	Combien de kilomètres d'ici à…?	kom-byañ duh keelo-metr d'ee-see ah
Which way to…?	Quelle est la direction pour…?	kel ay lah deer-ek-syoñ poor
Do you speak English?	Parlez-vous anglais?	par-lay voo oñg-lay
I don't understand.	Je ne comprends pas.	zhuh nuh kom-proñ pah
Could you speak slowly please?	Pouvez-vous parler moins vite s'il vous plaît?	poo-vay voo par-lay mwañ veet seel voo play
I'm sorry.	Excusez-moi.	exkoo-zay mwah

USEFUL WORDS

big	grand	groñ
small	petit	puh-tee
hot	chaud	show
cold	froid	frwah
good	bon	boñ
bad	mauvais	moh-veh
enough	assez	assay
well	bien	byañ
open	ouvert	oo-ver
closed	fermé	fer-meh
left	gauche	gohsh
right	droit	drwah
straight ahead	tout droit	too drwah
near	près	preh
far	loin	lwañ
up	en haut	oñ oh
down	en bas	oñ bah
early	de bonne heure	duh bon urr
late	en retard	oñ ruh-tar
entrance	l'entrée	l'on-tray
exit	la sortie	sor-tee
toilet	les toilettes, les WC	twah-let, vay-see

free, unoccupied	libre	leebr
free, no charge	gratuit	grah-twee

MAKING A TELEPHONE CALL

I'd like to place a long-distance call.	Je voudrais faire un interurbain.	zhuh voo-dreh fehr uñ añter-oorbañ
I'd like to make a collect call.	Je voudrais faire une communication PCV.	zhuh voodreh fehr oon komoonikah-syoñ peh-seh-veh
I'll try again later.	Je rappelerai plus tard.	zhuh rapel-eray ploo tar
Can I leave a message?	Est-ce que je peux laisser un message?	es-keh zhuh puh leh-say uñ mehsazh
Hold on.	Ne quittez pas, s'il vous plaît.	nuh kee-tay pah seel voo play
Could you speak up a little please?	Pouvez-vous parler un peu plus fort?	poo-vay voo par-lay uñ puh ploo for
local call	la communication locale	komoonikah-syoñ low-kal

SHOPPING

How much does this cost?	C'est combien s'il vous plaît?	say kom-byañ seel voo play
I would like …	Je voudrais…	zhuh voo-dray
Do you have?	Est-ce que vous avez?	es-kuh voo zavay
I'm just looking.	Je regarde seulement.	zhuh ruhgar suhlmoñ
Do you take credit cards?	Est-ce que vous acceptez les cartes de crédit?	es-kuh voo zaksept-ay leh kart duh kreh-dee
Do you take traveller's cheques?	Est-ce que vous acceptez les chèques de voyage?	es-kuh voo zaksept-ay leh shek duh vwayazh
What time do you open?	À quelle heure vous êtes ouvert?	ah kel urr voo zet oo-ver
What time do you close?	À quelle heure vous êtes fermé?	ah kel urr voo zet fer-may
This one.	Celui-ci	suhl-wee-see
That one.	Celui-là	suhl-wee-lah
expensive	cher	shehr
cheap	pas cher, bon marché	pah shehr, boñ mar-shay
size, clothes	la taille	tye
size, shoes	la pointure	pwañ-tur
white	blanc	bloñ
black	noir	nwahr
red	rouge	roozh
yellow	jaune	zhohwn
green	vert	vehr
blue	bleu	bluh

TYPES OF SHOPS

antiques	le magasin d'antiquités	maga-zañ d'oñteekee-tay
shop	la boulangerie	booloñ-zhuree
bakery	la banque	boñk
bank		
book store	la librairie	lee-brehree
butcher	la boucherie	boo-shehree
cake shop	la pâtisserie	patee-sree
cheese shop	la fromagerie	fromazh-ree
chemist	la pharmacie	farmah-see
dairy	la crémerie	krem-ree
department store	le grand magasin	groñ maga-zañ
delicatessen	la charcuterie	sharkoot-ree
fish seller	la poissonnerie	pwasson-ree
gift shop	le magasin de cadeaux	maga-zañ duh kadoh
greengrocer	le marchand de légumes	mar-shoñ duh lay-goom
grocery	l'alimentation	alee-moñta-syoñ
hairdresser	le coiffeur	kwafuhr
market	le marché	marsh-ay
news-stand	le magasin de journaux	maga-zañ duh zhoor-no zhoor-no
post office	la poste, le bureau de poste, le PTT	pohst, booroh duh pohst, peh-teh-teh
shoe shop	le magasin de chaussures	maga-zañ duh show-soor
supermarket	le supermarché	soo pehr-marshay
tobacconist	le tabac	tabah
travel agent	l'agence de voyages	l'azhoñs duh vwayazh

SIGHTSEEING

abbey	l'abbaye	l'abay-ee
art gallery	la galerie d'art	galer-ree dart

bus station	la gare routière	gahr roo-tee-yehr
cathedral	la cathédrale	katay-dral
church	l'église	l'aygleez
garden	le jardin	zhar-dañ
library	la bibliothèque	beebleeo-tek
museum	le musée	moo-zay
tourist information office	les renseignements touristiques, le syndicat d'initiative	roñsayn-moñ too-rees-teek, sandee-ka d'eenee-syateev
town hall	l'hôtel de ville	l'ohtel duh veel
train station	la gare (SNCF)	gahr (es-en-say-ef)
private mansion	l'hôtel particulier	l'ohtel partikoo-lyay
closed for public holiday	fermeture jour férié	fehrmeh-tur zhoor fehree-ay

STAYING IN A HOTEL

Do you have a vacant room?	Est-ce que vous avez une chambre?	es-kuh voo-zavay oon shambr
double room, with double bed	la chambre à deux personnes, avec un grand lit	shambr ah duh pehr-son avek un groñ lee
twin room	la chambre à deux lits	shambr ah duh lee
single room	la chambre à une personne	shambr ah oon pehr-son
room with a bath, shower	la chambre avec salle de bains, une douche	shambr avek sal duh bañ, oon doosh
porter	le garçon	gar-soñ
key	la clef	klay
I have a reservation.	J'ai fait une réservation.	zhay fay oon rayzehrva-syoñ

EATING OUT

Have you got a table?	Avez-vous une table libre?	avay-voo oon tahbl leebr
I want to reserve a table.	Je voudrais réserver une table.	zhuh voo-dray rayzehr-vay oon tahbl
The check please.	L'addition s'il vous plaît.	l'adee-syoñ seel voo play
I am a vegetarian.	Je suis végétarien.	zhuh swee vezhay-tehryañ
Waitress/ waiter	Madame, Mademoiselle/ Monsieur	mah-dam, mah-demwahzel/ muh-syuh
menu	le menu, la carte	men-oo, kart
fixed-price menu	le menu à prix fixe	men-oo ah pree feeks
cover charge	le couvert	koo-vehr
wine list	la carte des vins	kart-deh vañ
glass	le verre	vehr
bottle	la bouteille	boo-tay
knife	le couteau	koo-toh
fork	la fourchette	for-shet
spoon	la cuillère	kwee-yehr
breakfast	le petit déjeuner	puh-tee deh-zhuh-nay
lunch	le déjeuner	deh-zhuh-nay
dinner	le dîner	dee-nay
main course	le plat principal	plah prañsee-pal
appetizer, first course	l'entrée, le hors d'oeuvre	l'oñ-tray, or-duhvr
dish of the day	le plat du jour	plah doo zhoor
wine bar	le bar à vin	bar ah vañ
café	le café	ka-fay
rare	saignant	say-noñ
medium	à point	ah pwañ
well-done	bien cuit	byañ kwee

MENU DECODER

l'agneau	l'anyoh	lamb
l'ail	l'eye	garlic
la banane	banan	banana
le beurre	burr	butter
la bière, bière	bee-yehr, bee-yehr	beer, draught
à la pression	ah lah pres-syoñ	beer
le bifteck, le steack	beef-tek, stek	steak
le boeuf	buhf	beef
bouilli	boo-yee	boiled
le café	kah-fay	coffee
le canard	kanar	duck
le chocolat	shoko-lah	chocolate
le citron	see-troñ	lemon
le citron pressé	see-troñ press-eh	fresh lemon juice
les crevettes	kruh-vet	prawns
les crustacés	kroos-ta-say	shellfish
cuit au four	kweet oh foor	baked

le dessert	deh-ser	dessert
l'eau minérale	l'oh meeney-ral	mineral water
les escargots	leh zes-kar-goh	snails
les frites	freet	chips
le fromage	from-azh	cheese
le fruit frais	frwee freh	fresh fruit
les fruits de mer	frwee duh mer	seafood
le gâteau	gah-toh	cake
la glace	glas	ice, ice cream
grillé	gree-yay	grilled
le homard	omahr	lobster
l'huile	l'weel	oil
le jambon	zhoñ-boñ	ham
le lait	leh	milk
les légumes	lay-goom	vegetables
la moutarde	moo-tard	mustard
l'oeuf	l'uf	egg
les oignons	leh zonyoñ	onions
les olives	leh zoleev	olives
l'orange	l'oroñzh	orange
l'orange pressée	l'oroñzh press-eh	fresh orange juice
le pain	pan	bread
le petit pain	puh-tee pañ	roll
poché	posh-ay	poached
le poisson	pwah-ssoñ	fish
le poivre	pwavr	pepper
la pomme	pom	apple
les pommes de terre	pom-duh tehr	potatoes
le porc	por	pork
le potage	poh-tazh	soup
le poulet	poo-lay	chicken
le riz	ree	rice
rôti	row-tee	roast
la sauce	sohs	sauce
la saucisse	sohsees	sausage, fresh
sec	sek	dry
le sel	sel	salt
la soupe	soop	soup
le sucre	sookr	sugar
le thé	tay	tea
le toast	toast	toast
la viande	vee-yand	meat
le vin blanc	vañ bloñ	white wine
le vin rouge	vañ roozh	red wine
le vinaigre	veenaygr	vinegar

NUMBERS

0	zéro	zeh-roh
1	un, une	uñ, oon
2	deux	duh
3	trois	trwah
4	quatre	katr
5	cinq	sañk
6	six	sees
7	sept	set
8	huit	weet
9	neuf	nerf
10	dix	dees
11	onze	oñz
12	douze	dooz
13	treize	trehz
14	quatorze	katorz
15	quinze	kañz
16	seize	sehz
17	dix-sept	dees-set
18	dix-huit	dees-weet
19	dix-neuf	dees-nerf
20	vingt	vañ
30	trente	tront
40	quarante	karoñt
50	cinquante	sañkoñt
60	soixante	swasoñt
70	soixante-dix	swasoñt-dees
80	quatre-vingts	katr-vañ
90	quatre-vingt-dix	katr-vañ-dees
100	cent	soñ
1,000	mille	meel

TIME

one minute	une minute	oon mee-noot
one hour	une heure	oon urr
half an hour	une demi-heure	oon duh-mee urr
Monday	lundi	luñ-dee
Tuesday	mardi	mar-dee
Wednesday	mercredi	mehrkruh-dee
Thursday	jeudi	zhuh-dee
Friday	vendredi	voñdruh-dee
Saturday	samedi	sam-dee
Sunday	dimanche	dee-moñshtourist

Driver's Phrase Book

SOME COMMON ROAD SIGNS

The majority of road signs in France follow international conventions, but you may see the following:

accotement non stabilisé	soft verge
arrêt interdit	no stopping
autoroute	motorway
autoroute à péage	toll motorway
autres directions	other directions
brouillard fréquent	risk of fog
carrefour dangereux	dangerous crossroads
centre ville	town centre
chaussée déformée	uneven road surface
chaussée glissante	slippery road surface
chute de pierres	falling rocks
déviation	diversion
douane	customs
école	school
embranchement d'autoroutes	motorway junction
entrée interdite	no entry
fin d'autoroute	end of motorway
passage à niveau	level crossing
passage interdit	no through road
passage protégé	priority road
péage	toll
piétons	pedestrians
poids lourds	heavy vehicles
premiers secours	first aid
prudence	caution
ralentir	slow down
riverains autorisés	residents only
route barrée	road closed
route départementale	secondary road
route nationale	main road
sens unique	one-way street
serrez à droite	keep to the right
stationnement à durée limitée	restricted parking
stationnement alterné	parking on alternate sides
stationnement interdit	no parking
toutes directions	all directions
travaux	roadworks
virage dangereux	dangerous bend
virages sur ... km	bends for ... km
voie pour véhicules lents	slow lane
zone piétonnière	pedestrian precinct

THINGS YOU WILL SEE

aire de repos	rest area
aire de service	service area
aire de stationnement	parking area
arrêtez votre moteur	turn off engine
eau	water
essence	petrol
gas-oil	diesel
horodateur	pay and display
huile	oil
lavage du pare-brise	windscreen washer
parcmètre	parking meter
parking	car park
parking à étages	multistorey car park
parking payant	paying car park
prenez un ticket	take a ticket

pression de l'air	air pressure
pression des pneus	tyre pressure
réparations	repairs
roulez au pas	drive at walking pace
sans plomb	unleaded
sortie	exit
station-service	petrol station

DIRECTIONS YOU MAY BE GIVEN

à droite	right
à gauche	left
au prochain carrefour	at the next crossroads
avancez	go forward
deuxième à gauche	second on the left
passez ...	go past ...
première à droite	first on the right
reculez	reverse
tournez à droite/gauche	turn right/left
tout droit	straight on

THINGS YOU WILL HEAR

Voulez-vous une voiture à transmission automatique ou à transmission manuelle ?
Would you like an automatic or a manual?

Puis-je voir votre permis de conduire ?
May I see your licence?

Puis-je voir votre passeport ?
May I see your passport?

USEFUL PHRASES

I'd like some petrol/oil/water
Je voudrais de l'essence/de l'huile/de l'eau
zhuh voo-dreh duh lessonss/duh lweel/duh l'oh

I'd like 35 litres of unleaded
Je voudrais trente-cinq litres de sans plomb
zhuh voo-dreh tront sañk leetr duh son plon

Do you do repairs?
Faites-vous les réparations?
fet voo leh rayparass-ion

Can you repair the clutch?
Pouvez-vous réparer l'embrayage?
poo-vay voo rayparay lonbrayaj

How long will it take?
Combien de temps est-ce que ça prendra?
kom-byañ duh ton es-keh sa prondra

Can you repair it today?
Pouvez-vous le réparer aujourd'hui?
poo-vay voo luh rayparay ohjoordwee

There is something wrong with the engine
Le moteur ne fonctionne pas bien
luh motur nuh fonkss-ion pa byañ

The engine is overheating
Le moteur chauffe
luh motur shohf

I need a new tyre
Je voudrais un pneu neuf
zhuh voo-dreh uñ p-nuh nuhf

Can you replace this?
Pouvez-vous remplacer ceci?
poo-vay voo ronplassay suhsee

The indicator is not working
Le clignotant ne fonctionne pas
luh kleen-yoton nuh fonkss-ion pa

Is there a car park near here?
Est-ce qu'il y a un parking dans les environs?
esskeel-ya uñ par-keeng don layz onveeron

Can I park here?
Est-ce que je peux me garer ici?
es-keh zhuh puh muh garray ee-see

I'd like to hire a car
Je voudrais louer une voiture
zhuh voo-dreh loo-ay oon vwahtoor

I'd like an automatic/a manual
J'aimerais une voiture à transmission automatique/manuelle
jemmereh oon vwahtoor ah tronsmeess-ion ohtomateek/manoo-el

How much is it for one day?
Ça coûte combien pour une journée?
sa koot kom-byañ poor oon joornay

Is there a mileage charge?
Est-ce qu'il y a des frais de kilométrage?
esskeel-ya day freh duh keelomaytraj

Can we hire a baby/child seat?
Pouvons-nous louer un siège pour bébé/enfant?
poovon noo looay uñ seeayj poor baybay/onfon

When do I have to return it?
Quand est-ce que je dois la ramener?
koñ es-keh zhuh dwah lah ramuhnay

Where is the nearest garage?
Pouvez-vous m'indiquer le garage le plus proche?
poo-vay voo mandeekay luh garraj luh ploo prosh

How do I get to …?
Comment va-t-on à …?
kom-moñt vat on ah

Is this the road to …?
Est-ce que c'est bien la route pour …?
es-keh seh byañ lah root poor

USEFUL WORDS

English	French	Pronunciation
automatic	**automatique**	*ohtomateek*
bonnet	**le capot**	*kapoh*
boot	**le coffre**	*koffr*
brakes	**les freins**	*fran*
car	**la voiture**	*vwahtoor*
car ferry	**le car ferry**	*kar fairree*
car park	**le parking**	*par-keeng*
clutch	**l'embrayage**	*onbrayaj*
crossroads	**le carrefour**	*karrfoor*
drive	**conduire**	*kondweer*
driving licence	**le permis de conduire**	*permee duh kondweer*
engine	**le moteur**	*motur*
exhaust	**le pot d'échappement**	*poh dayshappmon*
fanbelt	**la courroie du ventilateur**	*koo-rwah doo vonteelatur*
garage	**le garage**	*garraj*
gear	**la vitesse**	*veetess*
headlights	**les phares**	*far*
indicator	**le clignotant**	*kleen-yoton*
junction	**le croisement**	*krwahzmon*
(motorway entry)	**l'entrée**	*ontray*
(motorway exit)	**la sortie**	*sortee*
lorry	**le camion**	*kamion*
manual	**manuelle**	*manoo-el*
mirror	**le rétroviseur**	*raytroveezur*
motorcycle	**la moto**	*motoh*
motorway	**l'autoroute**	*ohto-root*
number plate	**la plaque d'imma-triculation**	*plak deematreekoo-lass-ion*
petrol	**l'essence**	*essonss*
rear lights	**les feux arrière**	*fuh arree-air*
road	**la route**	*root*
skid (verb)	**déraper**	*dayrappay*
spare parts	**des pièces de rechange**	*pee-ess duh ruhshonj*
spark plug	**la bougie**	*boojee*
speed	**la vitesse**	*veetess*
speed limit	**vitesse limitée**	*veetess leemeetay*
speedometer	**le compteur de vitesse**	*kontur duh veetess*
steering wheel	**le volant**	*volon*
traffic lights	**les feux**	*fuh*
trailer	**la remorque**	*ruhmork*
transmission	**la boîte de vitesses**	*bwat duh veetess*
tyre	**le pneu**	*p-nuh*
van	**la camionnette**	*kamionet*
vehicle registration documents	**la carte grise**	*kart greez*
wheel	**la roue**	*roo*
windscreen	**le pare-brise**	*par breez*
windscreen wiper	**un essuie-glace**	*esswee glass*

SPECIAL EDITIONS OF DK TRAVEL GUIDES

DK Travel Guides can be purchased in bulk quantities at discounted prices for use in promotions or as premiums.
We are also able to offer special editions and personalized jackets, corporate imprints, and excerpts from all of our books, tailored specifically to meet your own needs.

To find out more, please contact:
(in the United States) **SpecialSales@dk.com**
(in the UK) **travelspecialsales@uk.dk.com**
(in Canada) DK Special Sales at **general@tourmaline.ca**
(in Australia) **business.development@pearson.com.au**

Road Signs

SPEED LIMITS AND GENERAL DRIVING INDICATIONS

Give way

Compulsory stop

Your route has priority

Your route no longer has priority

You have priority at the next junction

Junction gives priority to traffic from the right

Give way to oncoming traffic

No overtaking

No left turn at the next junction

No access for vehicles over 3.5 m in height

Speed limit

End of speed limit

Speed limit for vehicles with trailers over 250 kg

Minimum speed limit

Residential area with special speed limit

WARNING SIGNS

Unspecified danger

Succession of bends

Risk of snow and ice or slippery road

Risk of strong crosswinds

Risk of rockfalls

Speed bumps

Road narrows

Road narrows on the left

Level crossing with barrier

Level crossing with no barrier

Steep descent

Wild animals

Children crossing or school

Pedestrian crossing

Road works